Praise for *Tab Hunter Confidential*

"This bio might be the best work of [Tab's] career. He takes readers on a gleeful romp dotted with cameos ranging from Clint Eastwood to Roddy McDowall. Perhaps in homage to the genre he's skewering, Hunter . . . has an excellent sense of tabloid TV rhythm." —*Entertainment Weekly*

"Hunter provides a mesmerizing account of his Candide-like journey through Hollywood. . . . [He] offers shrewd assessments of the studio moguls Jack Warner and Harry Cohn, as well as hilarious anecdotes about working with Natalie Wood, Rita Hayworth and Lana Turner."
—*The New York Times Book Review*

"[A] wry and unblinkered memoir. . . . With that golden hair and torso, the scrubbed skin and the jaw that could open cans, [Tab Hunter] was a whole Abercrombie & Fitch catalogue rolled into one package—except this package had a secret compartment." —*The Washington Post*

"There's enough juice in this book to satisfy the most hungry Hollywood fan." —*USA Today*

"A good read, gracious and wryly self-deprecating."
—*The Seattle Times*, "Critic's Top Picks"

"A page-turner. . . . Colorful." —*San Francisco Chronicle*

"A sensitively told, self-aware, well-written account of a life filled with rags-to-riches stories . . . [by] a first-rate memoirist."
—*St. Louis Post-Dispatch*

"His intelligent and spry, 'true to thyself' attitude presents a positive reflection on having to deal with the stigma and unacceptance of being just who you are, while at the same time being the hottest thing in Hollywood. . . . The book is a heartfelt and realistic account of his life until now." —*Buzz* magazine

"Surprisingly sincere and moving." —*The Philadelphia Inquirer*

"An honest look at this workaholic's life before and after the glory years."
—*The Boston Herald*

"His memoir is at all times intelligent and interesting."
—*The New York Observer*

"Few celebrity biographies chronicle tribulations, success, disappointments, and growth with such candor, charm, and lack of self-pity. The punchy, page-turning prose and terrific illustrations are worthy of the subject. It will make a great movie."
—*San Francisco Bay Area Reporter*

"*Tab Hunter Confidential* is the most cheerful portrait this journalist has ever encountered about what happens to a movie star when the spotlight clicks off."
—*National Post* (Toronto)

"Offers an emotionally engaging survivor's tale that would move film audiences."
—*The Book Standard*

"Celebrity biography mavens of the baby-boomer generation will especially welcome this memoir. . . . [Hunter's] private life was so well concealed that much of the information related in this heartfelt and candid autobiography will come as a surprise to his fans. . . . An engrossing tale of too much too soon, with a surprisingly happy ending."
—*Library Journal*

"A respectful and dignified autobiography."
—*The Atlanta Journal-Constitution*

"An entertaining read. . . . Hunter writes freely, yet discreetly, about his many affairs of the heart."
—*Booklist*

"The 1950s heartthrob has penned a brave, surprising and sad memoir about depression (his mother's), repression (his homosexuality) and redemption (a career revival and meeting his partner of 20-plus years). . . . This is an illuminating, emotionally charged and important piece of Hollywood's hidden history."
—*Publishers Weekly*

TAB HUNTER

Confidential

THE MAKING OF A MOVIE STAR

TAB HUNTER
with Eddie Muller

ALGONQUIN BOOKS OF CHAPEL HILL
2006

Published by
Algonquin Books of Chapel Hill
Post Office Box 2225
Chapel Hill, North Carolina 27515-2225

a division of
Workman Publishing
225 Varick Street
New York, New York 10014

First paperback edition, Algonquin Books of Chapel Hill, September 2006.
Originally published by Algonquin Books of Chapel Hill in 2005.
Printed in the United States of America.
Published simultaneously in Canada by Thomas Allen & Son Limited.
Design by Anne Winslow.

"Young Love," by Ric Cartey and Carole Joyner, © 1956 Sony/ATV Songs LLC. All rights administered by Sony/ATV Music Publishing, 8 Music Sq. West, Nashville, TN 37203.

Unless otherwise noted, all photographs are from the private collection of Tab Hunter.

Library of Congress Cataloging-in-Publication Data
Hunter, Tab, 1931–
    Tab Hunter confidential : the making of a movie star / by Tab Hunter,
with Eddie Muller.—1st ed.
        p. cm.
    ISBN-13: 978-1-56512-466-0; ISBN-10: 1-56512-466-9 (HC)
    1. Hunter, Tab, 1931– 2. Motion picture actors and actresses—United States—
Biography. I. Muller, Eddie. II. Title.
PN2287.H82A3 2005
791.4302'8'092—dc22
[B]   2005045335

ISBN-13: 978-1-56512-548-3; ISBN-10: 1-56512-548-7 (PB)

10 9 8 7 6 5 4 3 2 1
First Paperback Edition

TAB HUNTER
Confidential

INTRODUCTION

I HATE LABELS.

Coming from me, that's a strong statement. Anyone who knows me will tell you I'm a relentlessly positive person. I don't even like to use the word *hate*. Life's too precious to waste time dwelling on the negative things we all experience.

But labels are something I've unfortunately dealt with my whole life. I've had so many slapped on me you'd think I was a billboard, not a real person. Many of them were created by agents, producers, and public-relations types whose job was to turn me into a Movie Star—another label I've never been comfortable with, even after all these years.

I was only a teenager, and Harry Truman was still in the White House, when some Hollywood marketing genius tried to stick me with the title the Sigh Guy. Not long afterward, I became the even more ludicrous Swoon Bait. After that, take your pick: the All-American Boy or the Boy Next Door or Hollywood's Most Eligible Bachelor. Hell, even my name is a label, attached to me by a man who believed—correctly, I suppose, that Rocks and Rorys and Guys and Tabs cast a certain spell on the post–World War II American imagination.

It was all show business, all a game. After several years as a starving free-lancer, watching the decline of Hollywood's once-powerful studio system, I signed on as one of the last actors put under exclusive contract to a major studio. For five years I was owned—the property of Warner Bros. For the most part, I did as I was told, and reaped the kind of money and fame that millions of starry-eyed kids dream about. I performed opposite *real* stars, like Lana Turner, Gary Cooper, Linda Darnell, Robert Mitchum, and Sophia Loren. Only a few years earlier, I'd idolized them from my seat in the movie theater.

Then in the blink of an eye, my name—the new one, the one I never liked—was above the title on my own pictures, and I was Jack Warner's top money earner at the box office.

"Tab Hunter" truly was a Product of Hollywood. That's one label I'll concede is completely accurate. As anybody trying to sell a product in this society will agree—it's all about image. Whether it's toothpaste, automobiles, or movie stars, the strategy for success is to deliver the right image to captivate your intended audience. My bosses were convinced that I was equipped with the kind of wholesome, photogenic face and physique that would set young hearts racing. I was packaged for those girls, and kept the smile in place despite one ridiculous nickname after another.

Picture it, if you can: One day I'm a shy, withdrawn, insecure kid named Art Gelien who loves horses more than anything in the world. I wake up, and I'm a larger-than-life matinee idol renamed "Tab Hunter." When I go to the newsstand for the daily paper, my fresh-scrubbed face gleams from row after row of fan magazines, all trumpeting me as Hollywood's gift to American women.

Like any good workhorse, I didn't want to bite the hand that fed me. As foolish as those labels were, they afforded me a life I'd never have experienced otherwise. Sure, I'd fantasized about being in the pictures, like every movie-loving kid. But I hadn't done a damn thing to make it happen. Never did I crave the spotlight, unlike so many friends and colleagues I'd meet in the business. I happened to be in the right place at the right time. Not the counter of Schwab's drugstore. Better: mucking out a stable. That's when I was told I should be in pictures—as I was shoveling shit. Most appropriate.

My movie career was an accident that now seems both unlikely and inevitable. On the rare occasions I look back at it, I marvel at the bizarre, coincidental, unreal nature of it all.

Maybe that's why, even as I played the game, I reached a stage where image meant less to me than the reality of who I was. Once I decided to lead my *own* life, as an individual, not a packaged product—I was immediately tagged with other labels: "difficult" and "temperamental" and "immature." Payback for trying to escape the gilded box Hollywood had built for me.

In my professional life, I longed to be more than the Sigh Guy.

In my personal life, I was quite a different Boy Next Door than the one Mr. and Mrs. Middle America—and their fan-club daughter—imagined me to be.

In fact, plenty of those strange appellations that started popping up, like "immature" and "temperamental," were stuck on me by publicists from my own studio—a euphemistic way of dealing with the rumors that Warner Bros.' most popular male star was, in fact, a homosexual.

It was in 1955, as my popularity was starting to soar, that the magazine *Confidential* printed the first article intimating—in the smarmy, not-quite-libelous style that was its specialty—that I was gay. Some underworked bottom-feeder in the showbiz cesspool dredged up an ancient L.A. police report on the arrest of Arthur Gelien, and a crowd of others, for "lewd behavior" at what the magazine called a "gay pajama party."

Newer, nastier labels got glued to my beaming blond mug. Now when I dropped by the newsstand—an increasingly unpleasant experience—across from *Photoplay* and *Movie Life* and *Screenland,* up at Dad's eye level, were tabloids like *Confidential, Whisper,* and *Lowdown,* branding me "homo" and "queer."

I was twenty-four years old, an age when most of us are still trying to figure out who we are and what course our life will take. In 1950s America I was far from alone in struggling with the shame that was routinely associated with being "different." Meanwhile, though, I was starring in movies opposite America's latest sweetheart, Natalie Wood, and cutting a #1 hit record on my first trip to a recording studio.

I dealt with this surreal situation in a manner my mother had drilled into me since childhood. Stay quiet. Don't draw attention to yourself. Be discreet. And believe me, that's not easy when the world is throwing fame, fortune, and limitless opportunity at you with one hand while threatening to steal it all back with the other.

Professionally, the "keep quiet" strategy worked. Claims of some Hollywood historians that my career was ruined by allegations of homosexuality are absolutely untrue. That hit record I mentioned, "Young Love," topped the charts *after* half a dozen more smear articles soiled the presses—clear evidence that despite its self-righteous claims, *Confidential* magazine did not influence the taste and opinions of mainstream America.

I'll probably never be able to trust the press. It's something I've carried with me for decades. Although I long ago accepted my sexual orientation, I've never been comfortable discussing it. There are several reasons for that reticence. I'm a big believer in the right to privacy: my own, and that of the people who've been a part of my life. An increasing number of books and articles discussing "gay" Hollywood have appeared, but I've been an elusive interview subject.

I've denied certain stories—even ones that were true—because I was wary of the author's motives. You've heard the old adage "Once burned, twice shy." Well, having been burned *multiple* times, let's just say that my guarded nature has been well earned.

Believe it or not, the Boy Next Door is now seventy-four years old. Times have changed. Much of the prejudice I once feared, and the secrets I kept, are no longer considered shameful or career-threatening. That doesn't mean it's easy for me to speak freely about what really happened during my life in Hollywood, and beyond. Call me old-school on that score, for which I don't apologize. I'm neither ashamed nor embarrassed.

What I propose is a deal, with you, the reader. I'll write honestly and openly about the rumors, the innuendos—everything that people seem to crave in a "movie star" autobiography. In exchange, promise me you'll read the *whole* story. If I'm going to commit my life to the printed page, I don't want any skipping around, looking for only the juicy paragraphs. Trust me, you'll miss the *truly* significant moments that made me the person I am today: a happy, healthy survivor of the Hollywood roller coaster, grateful for every day I've gotten, and for every one I've got left.

Some may read these pages and recognize the Tab Hunter they thought they knew. More, I think, will be confounded by other revelations. Like the two times I came within a whisker of getting married. First to a gorgeous ingenue who barely spoke English, then to the widow of one of Hollywood's most famous studio bosses.

I don't suppose many will be surprised to learn that I pretty much abandoned the Catholic Church after a priest turned on me in my darkest hour, or that I was molested by the choirmaster of my parish when I was twelve. What may be of more interest is that I regained my spiritual bearings, to the point that I cherish my faith more than anything else in life.

My brother and I grew up mostly on our own, the fatherless, nomadic offspring of a strict, strong mother from the Old World, who worked like a dog to provide for herself and her children. I learned street smarts the hard way, on the boulevards and byways of Hollywood. It prepared me for what I'd encounter in the stable of Henry Willson, the notorious gay agent who wanted credit—and more—for "creating" me (as well as his other "boys": Rock Hudson, Rory Calhoun, Race Gentry, Guy Madison). I've experienced the tremendous thrill of being named the most popular male movie star in the world—even as I suffered the guilt and agony of committing my mother to an asylum for months of electroshock treatments.

Despair that comes from having your career nose-dive before you're thirty years old? I know all about it. But I also know the hilarity of having your career revived, twenty-five years later, thanks to a canny cinematic prankster and his cross-dressing star. My work with John Waters and Divine was a high point of my professional life, even though it led to another label being hung on me that I have no use for: Gay Icon.

These are some of the aspects of my life that I'll share in these pages. I figured it would be smarter to do the telling myself, on my terms, rather than have somebody else come along and twist the tale to suit their agenda. I had a one-dimensional image imposed on me once, a long time ago, and have no desire to relive the experience.

A good portion of my life has been spent diligently working on being true to myself—"listening to my inner," as my mother used to say—and trying to keep an open heart even when faced with thoughtless cruelty and the built-in perils of show business.

What I've realized as a result is that no one's story—not yours, not mine—can be, or should be, reduced to a mere epithet.

A full, rich, complicated life—like the one I'm about to relate to you—doesn't fit on a label.

PROLOGUE

THIS IS NO FAIRY TALE. It does, however, start out like one.

On a sunny Saturday morning in the spring of 1951, a nineteen-year-old boy who grew up in Southern California with a head full of movie-star dreams walked through the doorway of a soundstage at Samuel Goldwyn Studios in Hollywood and crossed over into a new life. A life of astounding make-believe. A life where you're rewarded with fortune and fame if you're good at pretending to be someone you're not.

The studio was a stucco fortress at the corner of Santa Monica Boulevard and Formosa. Across the street was the Formosa Café, a Chinese restaurant and working-hours watering hole for the most glamorous stars in the business. Like practically everybody else in Los Angeles, I'd passed Goldwyn Studios, and other industry compounds such as MGM, Paramount, and 20th Century Fox, and fantasized about being part of the magic that happened behind those walls. Dreamers like me arrived daily, by the busload.

That's why studios were guarded like Fort Knox—to keep the dreamers separate from the doers. No one slipped through the Magic Factory gates without an invitation. I hadn't mentioned my "big break" to any of my friends—I didn't want to be embarrassed if it all went up in smoke.

As I stepped into the inner sanctum, people swarmed around, steering me through makeup and wardrobe departments, preparing me for the camera. Everyone called me Tab, like we'd been colleagues for years.

Oh, right, I kept reminding myself—*they're talking to me.* In my mind I was still Arthur Gelien, or Art, to the few close friends I had.

All this fuss was for a screen test. If I measured up, I'd be cast as Michael "Chicken" Dugan, one of the male leads in *God's Little Island*. I'd gone over the script as devoutly as any priest studies his Bible. I'd practiced my lines endlessly during the week, until they crowded out everything else in my head.

Everything, that is, except my mother's constant, and contradictory, advice. "Don't worry," she had reassured me that morning, in her thick German accent. "You are going to get the part. See yourself doing it!" Mother was a big believer in the power of positive thinking. But she'd also spent years warning me and my brother against doing *anything* that might attract attention to ourselves. "Nothing for show, Arthur," she dictated. "Nothing for show."

Well, for better or worse, Mrs. Gelien's younger son was about to enter the show *business*.

The film's director, Stuart Heisler, was a grandfatherly veteran who'd been making pictures since the 1930s, supervising the likes of Gary Cooper, Alan Ladd, and Humphrey Bogart. He'd agreed to test me after an interview at his office earlier in the week. Stephanie Nordli, the screenwriter, was also there. I must have "looked the part," as they say, because her eyes lit up when I came in.

"That's the boy I want," she declared.

I tried not to blush too much when they asked me to take my shirt off. I overheard Heisler say, "If this kid can read his name off a piece of paper, we want him."

It was hard to believe that a veteran director would stake his reputation, maybe his career, on an "actor" whose most recent credits included Counter Boy at the Orange Julius stand on Hollywood Boulevard, and Soda Jerk at Wil Wright's ice cream parlor. As close as I'd come to working with a real actor? Serving two scoops of chocolate burnt almond to Gene Kelly.

Well, that's not entirely true. Strictly speaking, I'd made my film debut the previous year. Audiences would have seen the back of my head as I delivered one line, "Hi, Fred," had it not ended up on the cutting-room floor. That was the extent of my on-camera experience.

In a corner of the stage, a few potted palms were planted in piles of sand, surrounded by an elaborately painted backdrop left over from an earlier tropical extravaganza: our desert island. Up close, the magic of the movies didn't look so magical.

The mic probably picked up the sound of my empty stomach shuddering as, following Mr. Heisler's instructions, I ran through some action, then some simple lines.

Everyone was staring at me. Judging me. I felt naked. Especially after I was once again told to take my shirt off, leaving me only in tattered trousers.

At last, the moment of truth. The flesh-and-blood chemistry experiment. Mr. Heisler summoned the film's star from her dressing room. I don't recall breathing for several minutes, waiting for the most beautiful woman in Hollywood to glide in from the wings.

Not many people remember Linda Darnell. But in the 1940s, she was 20th Century Fox's most alluring star. Sensual brown eyes, stunning face, sultry voice, sexy figure. Staring up at movie screens as a young boy, I watched her mesmerize Tyrone Power in *Blood and Sand* and *The Mark of Zorro*. I may have been only a kid, but I knew it was Linda Darnell, unbilled, playing the Blessed Virgin in *The Song of Bernadette*. I'd recognize that gorgeous face anywhere.

Now here she was, in the flesh, wearing a costume of rags fashioned into a makeshift sarong. We're shipwrecked, you see, on "God's Little Island." Miss Darnell in stylish scraps, snugly covering her just so, and me in . . . next to nothing.

Stuart Heisler introduced us and we chatted briefly. Miss Darnell seemed unconcerned by the possibility she might end up costarring with a complete unknown. I tried gamely to act as if I belonged. It wasn't easy.

Flash back to Christmas, 1948, a bustling back room at Barker Brothers department store on Hollywood Boulevard. "Shipping Clerk" had just been added to my impressive professional résumé. I packaged orders from big-timers too busy to pick up their own holiday gifts. One frantic night, I lingered longingly over a gift addressed to . . . Linda Darnell.

"I'm going to deliver this one myself!" I crowed to a co-worker, full of teenage bluster. "Man, I'd love to get a good look at her!"

Two years later I was getting the best look possible.

See? I said this started out like a fairy tale.

"Okay, Tab—" the director called out. "Take her in your arms and kiss her!"

Take *Linda Darnell* in my arms? Kiss the Virgin Mary from *Song of Bernadette*? I started to tremble.

She sensed my discomfort. "Don't worry, honey," she whispered in a voice that could have softened stone. "Just relax. I'm good luck for newcomers."

With that, Miss Darnell initiated me into the art of on-screen kissing. Nervousness subsided. So did the stubborn notion that this was all an elaborate hoax, that without warning Tyrone Power would march in, shove me aside, and reclaim his rightful place in Linda Darnell's embrace.

Heisler shouted, "Cut!" Miss Darnell pinched me and softly purred, "Mmm, that was n-*i-i-i-i*-ce."

Evidently, the camera agreed. Two days later I was called back to the studio. Paul Guilfoyle, the casting director, gave me a big grin. "Better get yourself a passport," he said.

I was about to embark on quite a trip.

1

Male Kelm

ON JULY 11, 1931, IN New York City, twenty-one-year-old Gertrude Kelm gave birth to a second son. Her first, Walter, was born eleven months earlier, so small he could fit in a cigar box. To honor this additional blessing, the infant's father visited Bellevue Hospital bearing gifts — "gift," to be precise: a nickel candy bar tossed on his wife's bed. He left quickly, without suggesting a name for his squalling newborn. That's why it reads only "Male Kelm" on the official papers. Alone, Mother carried me home, wrapped in a blanket borrowed from a nurse.

Eventually, my mother named me Arthur, after a friend of her father's she greatly admired, the distinguished German actor Arthur Kronenberg.

Named for an actor. Maybe it *was* fate.

My mother was sixteen when she came to this country, arriving from Germany in 1927 with her parents and three siblings, aboard the United States Lines ship *George Washington*. Her father, John Gelien, known simply as Opa (the traditional German term of endearment for a grandfather), was a chef for the steamship company. Forever away at sea, Opa was like a phantom within his own family.

Gertrude, his eldest daughter, was an unconventional child. A tomboy, she never liked other girls and took no nonsense from anyone. She didn't get along with her siblings. Her brothers she branded the Spineless Wonder and Wishy-Washy. Sister Charlotte, nicknamed Lottie, was barely tolerated. Not that Gertrude was around any of them much. As soon as the Geliens arrived on these shores, she was put to work, doing housekeeping and odd jobs around Manhattan.

It was a lonely, loveless existence, made tougher by the botched tonsillectomy she'd suffered in Germany. The doctor damaged her vocal cords, leaving Gertrude with a horrible stutter. Ashamed, she communicated by means of a pad of paper she carried everywhere.

Although he was rarely around to offer any *Liebe,* Opa admired his daughter's fierce, independent spirit. Ida Gelien, however, displayed a different attitude toward the child. Gertrude's refusal to act in character—more like a "girl"—earned her mother's wrath. When Gertrude came home five minutes past curfew from her first date, her mother locked her outside overnight in the snow, to teach her a lesson.

Gertrude learned fast: she got the hell out.

I have no idea how or where my mother met Charles Kelm. It wasn't something she ever discussed. We weren't even sure what he did for a living. But he wasted little time in tying the knot with this stubborn and strong-willed working woman. She jumped at the chance for a new life.

MEMORIES OF MY New York childhood are sketchy but mostly miserable. I'm on a sled, being pulled along the sidewalk during a snowstorm. I tumble into the gutter, screaming and crying.

I remember a sobbing woman washing clothes in a sink by candlelight. I assume it's my mother. I can still see, too clearly, Charles Kelm beating a woman in a dank apartment. I *know* that was my mother. My brother and I, too young to do anything, could only plead for it to end.

When Opa learned how bad things were in our tenement walk-up, he orchestrated our escape. He bought new jackets, shirts, ties, and short pants for Walt and me, and we were shipped with our mother to the opposite end of the country—San Francisco, the Promised Land. Using his connections, Opa got mother a job as a shipboard stewardess with Matson Lines, for which he now worked. He even found an apartment and covered the first two months' rent. We reclaimed the family name, Gelien.

In a way, I owe everything to Opa. I can't imagine what life in New York would have been like if we'd stayed. More misery, for sure. Murder, maybe.

Almost immediately, the relationship Walt and I had with our mother started to mirror what she'd experienced with her father. We wouldn't see her for weeks at a time, as she went to sea to earn her salary. Imagine a single woman trying to raise two boys during the depths of the Depression. Imagine the emptiness she felt, able to see us only when her ship returned to port.

We never doubted our mother's love and devotion, but we saw more of our caretaker. We lived in a rented room in Mrs. Kelson's Divisadero Street apartment. Mother was away so much it made no sense to rent a place of our own. Always draped in a long fur-collared coat, cloche pulled down low on her head, Mrs. Kelson was a dour figure, like a ghostly image in a Depression-era photograph. I liked her gap-toothed smile, but we didn't see it often enough.

MOTHER GRADUALLY MASTERED her stutter and learned to speak normally. She never lost the husky Teutonic accent, though, which, combined with her Dietrich-like features and demeanor—perfect posture and a reserved elegance—gave her the appearance of a foreign agent in some spy serial. Her aloofness was accentuated by piercing pale blue eyes that could freeze you in your tracks.

Eager to better our station, she studied in her spare time to be a nurse, with a specialty in physical therapy. The bump in pay allowed her to enroll Walt and me in a private school. Nothing was more important to our mother than a good education: "What you learn," she declared, "no one can ever take away from you."

A Gelien family outing, 1937.
Mother takes Walt and me swimming
in San Francisco.

We'd almost get used to her prolonged absences, when some little thing would hit like a hammer. "Take this note home and have your mother sign it," a teacher told me one day. I almost burst out crying. Another time, Walt and I were horsing around outside when he tore his pants leg wide open. We exchanged frightened looks, anticipating the scolding we were in for—until we realized there'd be none. Mother wasn't due back for another three weeks.

Barely school-age, Walt and I had some adventures straight out of *Tom Sawyer*. We wandered near Fisherman's Wharf, where we got too adventurous and lost our shoes in the muddy shallows of Aquatic Park. Not wanting to trudge home barefoot after dark, we dug up a mess of worms, which we sold to a charitable fisherman. That's how we made carfare home. Naturally, it was one of the rare times Mother was ashore. We got a thorough lashing when we slogged in, shoeless.

Mother tried to make the most of our limited time together. Once, she took us to Pier 35 to watch the *Lurline* sail for Hawaii—cheap entertainment during hard times. I was seven years old and thrilled by the pomp and pageantry, the brass band and colorful streamers and billowing waves of confetti. We got as close as we could to the gangplank, where I stared at an adorable little girl with shiny blond curls and huge dimples, bundled up in a white fur coat—a doll come to life. Photographers swarmed around, flashbulbs popping like crazy. All this fuss over a kid my age—I couldn't believe it.

But then, I'd never seen a Shirley Temple movie. "She is a famous movie star," my mother explained. It was the first time I'd ever heard of such a thing. On the way home that day I'm sure I wondered how a kid like me could become a famous movie star.

IN THE CRAMPED ELEVATOR of a hotel on Mason Street, Mother introduced us to Harry Koster. He lived there when he wasn't at sea. Mr. Koster ran a ship's galley, just like my grandfather Opa. Maybe that's why Mother trusted him when they'd met aboard the *Monterey*, a Matson cruise ship.

Mr. Koster was a huge, dark-haired man with a Dutch accent, who reeked of tobacco. As the elevator rose, Mother dropped a bomb: "Harry and I have been married. You will treat him as your new father."

Walt and I reacted like miserable brats. We didn't get enough time with our mother to share any of it with another man, even one who vowed to provide for his new "family" so that Gertrude Gelien could remain home to raise her children properly. From Mother's perspective, it was a marriage of convenience. Tired of treading water, she saw Harry Koster as a life preserver. If Walt and I had been more mature, we'd have understood that she remarried for *our* sake, not hers.

Within months, we moved to Long Beach, where Mother's family had relocated. Opa had suggested his daughter and her family join them, with the expectation that they might become a close-knit clan, something they'd never been.

It didn't work out that way. Opa died not long after the move, and Gertrude Gelien remained distant from her mother and siblings. Her new husband didn't even bother to go south with us. His home was the *Monterey*, sailing back and forth to Australia, a round-trip, literally, to the ends of the earth. His paychecks, however, were faithfully routed to his wife.

When Harry did appear, Walt and I made his life hell. "You're not our father!" we'd taunt, dispensing sullen disrespect, nonstop. Unfairly so, because
Harry seemed to genuinely love our mother, and he treated her well.

But Mother didn't love him in kind. Not once did I see her show Harry any
kind of warmth, not even when they reunited after his long weeks at sea. Years
later, she would confide to me: "I have never been in love."

That reality was, I now believe, at the root of my mother's eventual crisis.

PROTECTION, MORE THAN AFFECTION, is what Mother offered to
Walt and me. Her stern demeanor may have masked a vulnerable, sensitive
heart, but the armor was virtually impenetrable. Her maternal devotion, overall, took the form of lessons, dispensed daily from the Gertrude Gelien Com-
pendium of Clichés:

"For every door that closes, two open."
"Always have a goal, and when you reach it—set another."
"Every experience in life is worth having—if you learn from it."
"Soap and water are cheap—never forget that."
"Good things happen to good people."
"Whatever you do, thank God every day."
"Constructive thinking brings good results."
"Things may not be good now, but they'll get better."

These platitudes were one reason why I never confided anything to my
mother: she wouldn't respond with a comforting hug or a reassuring smile, but
only with one of her patented bromides.

Harry Koster's salary couldn't keep us going indefinitely. Mother landed another job, this time as a nurse on the *Avalon*, which sailed overnight from the
mainland to Catalina Island. We moved to a tiny apartment on the island for the
summer of 1940 so we'd all be together when Mother finished her daily circuit.

Whenever Walt and I heard the whistle of a departing steamer, we'd race
to the end of the pier, dive off, and wave like crazy to the ferry passengers,
who'd throw coins into the water. We'd compete with other kids to scoop the
money from the shoals. That's how I became a good swimmer, diving deeper
and holding my breath longer than any of the other boys.

Walt and I would spend all day, every day, exploring the island and cap it off
at night hunkered over his bed, counting out what was left of our scavenged
loot: pennies, nickels, dimes, and sometimes—as rare as gold doubloons—
quarters!

Summer over, we moved back to Long Beach, where prewar life was idyllic. I couldn't have been happier. Our landlord lived in the house next door, and every morning he'd be out front by six, watering his garden. I'd jump out of bed, slip on shorts and a T-shirt, and run barefoot into the yard to help him dig in the dirt and tend the plants, something I still love.

We saw a lot of my aunt Lottie in those days—not to imply that Mother approved. You'd never believe they were sisters. Lottie always wore slacks, had a casual way about her, and brimmed with wisecracks and good humor. My mother disapproved of trousers on women, was very formal, and rarely appeared in public without gloves and a hat. Lottie's off-color jokes grated like nails on a chalkboard to Mother, who'd sniff, "Please, try to elevate your mind," whenever Lottie had us in stitches.

Lottie often took us to the Pike, Long Beach's grand harborside amusement park, where we'd spend hours in the arcades and on the rides: the Deep Sea Diving Bell, the Dodge 'Em Cars, the Laff-in-the-Dark Funhouse, the Crazy Maze, and the awesome Cyclone Racer. Sometimes Lottie'd get so wound up, laughing and carrying on, she'd pee her pants. Walt and I would have to stand around her on the bus ride home, hiding her big wet spot. Mother found no humor in our retelling of such stories. "There is nothing funny," she'd tsk, rueful that she was related to such a "low character."

ONE OF MOTHER'S fortune-cookie aphorisms was "I'd rather have one room in a good neighborhood than a mansion in a bad one." Maybe that's what led her to constantly uproot us. All things considered, it came as a shock when we abandoned Long Beach for a worse neighborhood in Los Angeles. Mother had gotten a wartime job with Lockheed Aircraft and needed to be nearer the factory.

Having so little, it was easy to start over. So we did. Repeatedly.

First, it was an apartment on 69th and Figueroa, a stucco-and-asphalt corner with little charm. At least it had Beverly Peck. She lived halfway down the block. Like us, no father in sight. She lived with her mom and a gigantic grandmother who had arms like wobbly ham hocks. I never saw Beverly's grandmother anywhere but parked on a kitchen stool, minding a perpetually bubbling pot. Every time I walked in, *every* time, she'd say, "You're too skinny. Here, eat this."

Our mother couldn't boil water. Walt and I spent a lot of time over at Beverly Peck's.

Beverly became Walt's girl, as much as an eleven-year-old can have a "girl." Once he lost interest, however, Beverly and I became inseparable. On my own, I'd never have been able to talk to her—I was painfully shy. But watching Walt, I learned. That's how it was for me, always coasting in Walt's wake. Without him, I might never have left the house.

Beverly and I would save dimes during the week, and on Saturday she'd gather them in a little handkerchief, tied tight. We'd hop a streetcar downtown to the Clifton Cafeteria, where Beverly's mother worked. *Free lunch!* The best thing about Clifton's was the Sherbet Mine—you stuck your arm into a frosty cave and pulled out a dish of lime or pineapple or rainbow sherbet.

Bellies full, Beverly and I would walk hand in hand to the downtown movie palaces. Our little stash of coins bought us entry to theaters like the Million Dollar and the Orpheum, where we spent the rest of the day watching the latest double features. I was ten years old. Those blissful Saturday afternoons with Beverly Peck—and *Robin Hood* and *Zorro* and *Captain Blood*—were what turned me into a lifelong movie lover.

Beverly wouldn't stay in my life very long. The Geliens were soon on the move again, this time to a nicer neighborhood, a better school.

That's what my nomadic childhood was like—never in one place long enough to develop "lasting childhood friendships." Not one. My mother's obsession—granting us a better upbringing than she'd had—produced a sorry side effect: it made us distant from people, just as she was. I later came to think of my mother as a self-sufficient survival machine. In her operating manual, it said in big capital letters: TO AVOID SERIOUS INJURY, NEVER GET CLOSE.

My childhood lessons came from the same manual: after Beverly Peck, I never got close to anyone, knowing I was only going to leave them behind in a few months.

2

Saddle Up

It came as a shock to learn we were Catholics.

Walt and I had no idea until Mother decided we'd get a better education, and more discipline, at St. John's Military Academy. Along with it came daily religious training, something that had never been part of our childhood. Mother explained that, technically, we'd already been initiated. A tenement neighbor in New York had shepherded us to the local parish to be baptized, but Mother had never said a word about it until she decided we belonged at St. John's.

Fearful she was raising a pair of strays, Mother ponied up extra money to actually board us—so we'd have more structure, a stronger foundation than what she, as a working mom, could provide. It was quite an adjustment for the two vagabond Geliens. We weren't used to a school without girls.

Behind the church there was a huge, creepy building, straight out of a Charles Addams cartoon. Walt and I lived in the third-floor dormitory. If you woke in the middle of the night, you'd catch a glimpse of Sister Aloysius, arms folded, gliding past in her billowing habit.

She made the hair on the back of your neck stand up.

I surprised everyone by taking to church like a duck takes to water. Going to Mass, especially when it was in Latin, was a high point of my day. There was such seriousness to it, such vital purpose, all cloaked in ancient, arcane ceremony—how could an impressionable kid not be enthralled?

I eagerly sent away to New York for my baptismal certificate so everything would be in order for my first Holy Communion and, later, my confirmation.

One of the first friends Walt made at St. John's was Mal Fink. We couldn't figure out what this Jewish kid was doing in a Catholic boarding school.

Turned out he was a day scholar, which meant he didn't board at the academy. He and his mom, Sylvia, lived a few blocks away, in a fourplex she owned. It was a much nicer neighborhood than ours, full of tree-lined streets.

Sylvia Fink and my mother, for some inexplicable reason, became best friends. No two people were less alike. Sylvia defined *blowsy*. Huge eyes, no chin, big bleached hairdo. She smoked like a refinery and swore like a sailor. "Please, Sylvia, please! Don't talk like that!" my mother would moan whenever Mrs. Fink cut loose with a torrent of cusswords.

Mrs. Fink owned a bar, so she took even less shit from people than my mother did. She kept a baseball bat behind the counter for "special" customers and loved to recount tales of the times she'd used it. Whenever my mother tried to read us the riot act regarding our "inappropriate behavior," Sylvia would clack her heels together, throw up her right hand, and shout, "Heil Hitler!"

Mother would burst into tears. "Oh, for Christ's sake, Gertie—get over it!" Sylvia would say in a voice that sounded like gargled gravel. No one else got away with calling my mother Gertie.

Despite their differences, my mother appreciated Sylvia for being an honest and truthful person. Sylvia told it straight, and my mother respected that. "I don't care what you do, Arthur," she always said, "so long as you never lie to me. And more important—never lie to yourself!"

Another of my mother's favorite lines was "If you make five good friends in life, you are very lucky." Ironic, since she had so few herself. Not even five. But during those war years, Sylvia Fink was as close to my mother as anyone.

A German and a Jew. Go figure.

Since it wasn't easy for me to make friends, I just trailed along after Walt. That's how I came to join St. John's Marching Band. Walt signed up, so I did, too. He played the bass drum; I chose the slide trombone. It was a struggle, and not only because I didn't do well with musical instruments or formations.

Another friend of my brother's, Wayne, took too much of a shine to me. He wanted to be my friend, in the worst way—physically. I sensed right off that it was wrong, that it was dirty.

I quit the band before the end of the semester.

THE WAR WAS A VAGUE backdrop to my childhood. I was only ten when Pearl Harbor was attacked, but I have vivid memories of searchlights roaming the night sky and the widespread fear of direct attacks on Los Angeles.

I knew my family had come from Germany and that we were fighting Germans in addition to the Japanese—but I never sensed in my mother any kind of discomfort. She was an *American* now.

We never saw Harry Koster once the war broke out. Matson converted its ships to military service, and Harry spent virtually all his time in the South Pacific, feeding GIs aboard the *Monterey.* Then one day, in 1942, word reached us that Harry was dead. I was convinced he'd been killed when his ship was sunk by a torpedo. In reality, he'd had a heart attack aboard ship.

I can't say we missed our stepfather, since he never seemed a part of our lives. But as I grew older, I felt horrible regret over Harry Koster. Still do, to this day. Regret that I'd never accepted him, that I never treated him with respect. He supported us and cared for us the best way he knew how, and he received virtually nothing in return. Like my true father, he was an enigma—but at least Harry was a heroic one.

If Mother was heartbroken, she kept it hidden. She soldiered on, like she'd always done. With the man in her life gone, our mother put even more pressure on herself to provide the best for us. But without Harry's regular paycheck, she couldn't afford to board us at St. John's any longer. We became day scholars and moved into a duplex on West 23rd Street with our mother.

THE CONSTANT IN MY early life was my brother. We were totally different. Walt was stronger, more adventurous, a natural athlete, eager for action. I was the loner, the dreamer, off in my own fantasy worlds. It was difficult for me to look people in the eye, let alone talk to them. Walt, by contrast, was outgoing, gregarious. He'd lead me to new places, get me to try new things, make me aware of a life outside the shell I'd built for myself.

Like all brothers, we got into it plenty of times. The bottle of ink, thrown in a rage, that splashed all over the walls. The BB Walt fired, leaving a permanent bump beneath my right eye. Once, we had a huge dustup, turning the entire apartment upside down. When Mother came in, she collapsed in a chair and started crying. "What am I going to do with you two!" she wailed.

Our neighbor, a real nosy type, yelled from next door: "Put 'em in Juvenile Hall!"

Mother leaped to the window, and to our defense: "If half the children in this country were as good as my two boys," she hollered in her thick accent, "there would be no need for such institutions!"

Walt and I howled, our battle forgotten.

Sometimes, though, we'd make an effort to be good, surprising Mother by having dinner ready when she dragged in, dead tired from work. Whatever awful thing we served up, Mother appreciated it. If there was a movie we wanted to see at the nearby Arlington Theatre, Walt and I would suggest we all go for a walk. As we passed the blazing marquee, we'd hoist Mother by the elbows and carry her to the box office, meanwhile fishing in her purse for the price of three admissions. I wanted to share my newfound love of movies. Mom's favorites starred Fredric March, Melvyn Douglas, Gary Cooper—"so solid, so sensible," she'd say. Nothing *showy*.

Eventually, it was watching Walt perform in a school play, *The Wedding Shoes,* that started me thinking that maybe I could act, too.

The greatest thing my brother ever did for me, however, was introduce me to horses. One weekend, on a lark, he took me to Du Brock's Riding Academy, at the corner of Riverside and Los Feliz. It was a ramshackle old stable, located behind a huge green fountain that shot a geyser of water high into the air.

I tried not to let on that I was scared to death as we rented a pair of nags and headed out on the bridle trails. I'd chosen a western saddle so at least I'd have a horn to grab onto if I started to fall.

Although I didn't like riding at first, soon Walt and I were starting every Saturday with a trip to Du Brock's. I even had a favorite horse, Star, a plain bay with a white star on his forehead.

On the trail one day, Walt yelled over to me, "If you want to gallop, just give him a kick. Harder . . . Harder!"

"I am kicking," I complained. Star wouldn't go faster than a slow trot.

"Keep kicking!"

That old rent horse finally broke into a canter. I grabbed tight to the horn and started laughing uproariously as I bounced all over the place.

"Sit down!" Walt whooped. "You're giving that poor horse a headache!"

Maybe so, but I was grinning ear-to-ear, probably the biggest smile I'd ever had on my face.

That was the day I fell in love—with horses.

Walt moved on to other interests, but Du Brock's became my home away

Mother, Walt (right), and me, Parade Day at St. John's Military Academy, 1943.

from home. Before this, I'd secretly save a week's worth of lunch money and bus fare to buy movie tickets. Now, I hoarded every penny so I could buy an extra half hour on horseback. Saturday mornings I was up and out by six, hitchhiking to the barn. Bud and Melba Du Brock, the owners, got to know the blond-haired Gelien kid on a first-name basis.

Soon I was spending all my Saturdays there, doing chores for the grooms, Slim and Tommy. I'd trade labor for riding time—mucking out stalls, cleaning tack, feeding horses, stacking hay bales, anything to be around those animals.

Smiling Joe became my best buddy, a cute buckskin with a dished face and a stripe down his back. I hated it whenever he was rented out to a paying customer. I thought of him as *my* horse, and I dreamed about making pots of money, buying Smiling Joe, and taking him away from the rent string to a little horse world of my own that I'd someday create.

First, I joined a regularly scheduled riding class, of which Richard Peterson and I were the only boys. He was a handsome guy, with a blazing smile, big dimples, a terrific personality—and he had his own horse! The girls were nuts for him. I was nuts with jealousy.

MY FIRST ENCOUNTER with a girl came soon after that. It was memorable, for all the wrong reasons.

Every day on the way home from St. John's I'd pass an apartment building on the corner where a hot little number named Lois lived. She was always on the front steps when I passed. Sitting there brazenly, legs spread wide, wearing a short dress and loose panties. Very loose. On a clear day you could see all the way to Catalina.

I couldn't help staring, and Lois didn't seem to mind. She just smiled. Then she rubbed herself. She was only about twelve but acted like she'd already been around the block a few times.

One afternoon I worked up the courage to stop and say a few words. It didn't take Lois long to coax me into following her around the block, down the alley, back by the garages. I nearly keeled over as she slowly pulled off her panties. With shaking hands I managed to undo my trousers, revealing my prepubescent penis. I pressed it against her privates.

Immediately, an image of Sister Aloysius leaped inside my head, beating my brain to a pulp. *Wrong! Wrong! Wrong!* The guilt overwhelmed my arousal, and I hastily stuffed myself back into my pants and sprinted home, where I sulked around, waiting for God to strike me dead.

When it came to sex, I was clueless. Mother was so tight lipped about it that Walt and I joked we were immaculate conceptions. "Show some respect!" Mother would shriek, but she'd never say anything to disabuse us of the notion, nor would she offer us any guidance on the facts of life. Saying the word *sex* in front of my mother, or even the word *men*, made her shudder with revulsion. Needless to say, the Lois debacle would go unmentioned.

Later that same night, a knock came at the door. It was the police.

They marched me down to Lois's apartment, where I was confronted by her mother. She'd been told that I dragged her daughter into the alley and pulled off her panties. Lois was still muttering about all the disgusting things I'd done to her.

Scared shitless, I stammered incoherently as my mind raced with consequences: the cops were going to lock me up forever; my mother was going to disown me; my brother's sterling reputation would be blackened beyond repair.

But nothing happened. All I can figure is that Lois protested a little too much, and the cops got wise to the fact that she was making it all up. Most of it, anyway. Maybe her mother was used to this routine.

The damage, however, was done. I was now afraid of women, in a way I had never been before.

TUITION AT ST. JOHN'S Military Academy became too heavy a burden, so Mother moved us next door, to St. Paul's Parochial School. A chain-link fence separated the two. St. Paul's had nicer nuns, plus girls. Good girls, in school sweaters and simple blue cotton uniforms, who kept their knees together.

The church itself, looming over the school yard, was majestic and inspiring. During recess, while other kids ran around blowing off steam, I often sneaked into the church to be by myself. It was so serene and secure in the cool immensity of the basilica. Just like when I'd ride Smiling Joe through the hills overlooking the valley, inside the church I sensed a reassuring connection to something greater than myself. At twelve, I couldn't articulate it, but I sure could feel it.

One day a baseball came crashing through one of the magnificent stained-glass windows, scaring the hell out of me. Running outside, I discovered the guilty one was Walt, who'd fouled a fly ball through St. Sebastian's face.

My brother went straight to the rectory and turned himself in. That summer, he worked like a dog at a variety of jobs, until by the fall he'd saved enough money to pay for the window's restoration. Walt was the most honorable and responsible person I knew. All that, and he was still just a kid.

My dismal experience with the St. John's Marching Band didn't deter me from enjoying music. Mother filled the house with it, especially on Saturday mornings, when she'd listen to the Metropolitan Opera on the radio. She encouraged me to sing, and I'd make like Dick Haymes around the house, especially in the shower. She pushed me to join St. Paul's choir, where my voice blended in with all those soprano boys and girls every Sunday morning at nine o'clock Mass.

Mr. Biggs was the choirmaster and organist. He'd written several popular hymns and was well respected throughout the diocese. Everyone put him on a pedestal, including me. I figured that when he played, they probably heard it in heaven. The sound from the organ's pipes rattled the rafters, and Mr. Biggs attacked the keys so ardently the choir loft shook like it was going to collapse.

One afternoon, Mr. Biggs asked me to stay after practice, to help put everything away. The other kids had been dismissed. I collected all the hymnals and followed him into a small storage room at the far end of the loft.

Suddenly his arms were around me and he started kissing and fondling me. He stank of stale cigars. Repulsed and humiliated, I squirmed out of his grasp and sprinted across the loft, down the twisting stairway, all the way home.

I never told anyone.

Mr. Biggs appreciated my silence. Maybe he just felt guilty and ashamed. Whatever the reason, he decided not long after the loft incident that I deserved a Sunday-morning solo. In Latin.

I practiced devoutly. Mr. Biggs's motives didn't matter to me—I'd been summoned to sing on God's behalf. As a good Catholic, I believed it was my duty to perform.

When the big day rolled around and my shining moment arrived, nothing came out of my mouth. Stage fright stole my voice. A timid girl in the rear of the choir, whom I'd never spoken to, but who obviously was *studying* me, immediately realized my predicament. She picked up my part without missing a beat. Once I joined in and had settled down, she faded out and let me finish on my own.

That's how I met Mary Lu Valpey.

She had straight auburn hair, thick glasses, a mouthful of braces, millions of freckles, and was built like a two-by-four. A two-by-four that blended completely into the woodwork. Unlike a lot of the girls at my school, she had no designs on Art Gelien. We got on famously.

Mary Lu lived around the corner from me, with parents she liked to get away from. Her mom, Lucille, carted around the weight of the world, and her father, Paul, was a cherub who turned into a holy terror when he hit the sauce. Mary Lu was an only child, and her folks were thrilled that we were pals. They approved of me because I was in the choir. I was "safe."

Mary Lu became my best riding buddy.

I taught her to horde her lunch money so she could buy extra riding time. Together, we'd hitchhike to Du Brock's, saving carfare to spend on the horses. She joined the kids' riding group. As long as a girl could share my love of horses, I was comfortable around her.

One day Richard Peterson's family suddenly moved. For once, somebody other than me had taken a powder! Since I was now the only male in the riding class, everybody at Du Brock's started referring to us as "Art and his harem."

I'd always found it easier to be around girls, but now, going through puberty, it got complicated. The "harem" jokes had a suggestive edge that made me uncomfortable. The attention girls paid to me became different—less chummy, more aggressive. It made me nervous and even more withdrawn. Girls must have found my bashfulness endearing, however, because they only came on stronger. I simply wanted to be left alone with my real friends, the horses.

Griffith Park's bridle trails followed the Los Angeles River, and you could ride the river bottom into the valley, right past the Warner Bros. Studio, all the way out to Republic Pictures. I'd gallop through Ace Hudkins's sprawling ranch, jumping Smiling Joe over fences and hedges, while another of my mother's endless clichés bounced through my head: "In life, one must have dreams—they give you a lift."

As I gazed over the picture factories, my mind swam with dreams—that one day I'd be a top rider in the world of show jumping.

Movies were great, but horses . . . horses were *real*!

At sundown, after the customers had left the stable, I'd still be hanging around, helping with feeding and bedding. Mother was now supplementing her Lockheed salary with a part-time night job, so, unsupervised in the evening,

I'd sneak over to the Riverside Rancho, the glittering nightclub across the road, to watch couples in their fancy western duds arrive for a night of dancing. Hiding outside, listening to Spade Cooley fiddling away, crooning his signature tune, "Shame, Shame on You," I couldn't wait to grow up and dive into the high life.

I had no idea what the "high life" was, but by then I was itching to find out.

The gang at Du Brock's Riding Academy, 1946. I'm on the end at the left; Mary Lu Valpey (before her big bust-out) is second from the right.

3

Bless Me, Father

WALT GOT INTO A HUGE FIGHT with Mother just before the start of summer, 1943. It began with something trivial but quickly escalated into all-out verbal war. My brother blurted out the most hurtful thing he could think of: "My *real* father is probably nothing like you make him out to be! I'll bet he left *you!*"

Mother fell deathly silent. Then she said, "I think you should find out for yourself." Without another word, she made plans to ship Walt east for the summer. We didn't even know that Charlie Kelm was still alive, and were even more surprised that Mother knew where to find him.

With my brother sent away, Lupe, Lenore, and Gustavo Feist, classmates at St. Paul's, became my new best buddies, the ones I ran around with. They came from a huge Catholic family. I especially looked forward to those summer days when Lupe invited me over to swim at her uncle's house. It was a fifteen-block walk to Gramercy Place, an enclave of gorgeous, exclusive homes. Lupe's uncle's home was surrounded by a high brick wall and wrought-iron gates. Vast, dark, and forbidding, it was the kind of place that forced you to talk in whispers.

Before being allowed in the pool, we had to rake leaves off the tennis court, a strenuous job that left us in a sweat. Once the court was leafless, the woman of the house, Lupe's aunt, would bring us into the kitchen for homemade lemonade. We never did see Lupe's uncle Ramon.

Once, Lupe sneaked me through the place for a quick tour. The master bedroom was cloaked with heavy curtains and stuffed with ornate religious artifacts. There was also a theater, complete with a stage and lights, for plays and musical performances.

She explained that her uncle Ramon Novarro had been a handsome silent-movie star, as popular in his day as Rudolph Valentino.

I'd never heard of either of them.

THE STUDIOS DID LOTS of business with Dubrock's, and photographers often came by to shoot layouts for movie magazines. I'd gawk from the sidelines as some beautiful young actress would stand on a mounting block, slip her leg over the saddle, and smile pretty for the camera.

I noticed a lot of these gals being escorted by the same guy, a charming Irish fellow who was a regular at Dubrock's and a pretty good rider as well. I hadn't met him, but I knew that Irish Lad was his preferred horse. I overheard someone say that he was an actor. One day, he showed up with actress Ann Blyth and a photographer in tow. In the middle of the photo session, the guy spotted me and walked over. I was grappling with a pitchfork of manure.

"Hi, kid. You must live here. You're here every time I show up. What's your name?"

"Art Gelien."

"How old are you, Art?"

I think I lied and said, "Fourteen." I was twelve.

"Ever thought about being in pictures? You got the look for it."

My face burned with embarrassment. And excitement. I was speechless.

"My name's Dick Clayton," the guy said, shaking my hand. "If you ever want to get into the movies, talk to me."

I figured this Dick Clayton character had to be crazy. How could I have known he'd end up being the most important person in my life?

WALT RETURNED FROM New York exactly one month after he'd been shipped off. I pestered him relentlessly: "What's he like? What's our dad really like? Tell me! Tell me!"

"Don't ask," was all Walt said.

He never mentioned our father again.

OUR STINT AT ST. PAUL'S ended in the ninth grade. Money was too tight for Mother to make the monthly tuition. She enrolled us in Mount Vernon Junior High, even though it killed her to send us to a public school.

Outside the Catholic cloisters, my education was radically different.

Day one at Mount Vernon was a rude awakening. I was surrounded in the

on my knees, praying for help, for some clarity to cut through my confusion. Why would I let a stranger touch me, a man no less?

I finally mustered the courage to go to confession, convinced that one of the parish priests would grant me forgiveness and, I hoped, absolution. After all, belief in divine forgiveness, we'd learned in the catechism, was the cornerstone of Catholic faith.

I entered the anonymous confines of the dark confessional, my heart pounding. Because of my acute claustrophobia, confession was already difficult for me. I thought I'd die as I haltingly explained to the priest what had happened. Saying the words was torture, but confessing was the only way I could go on living with myself.

I never finished. Through the latticework boomed the priest's voice, branding me the most despicable creature in the world. I was unfit to receive God's forgiveness, unfit to set foot in His house, unfit to live. On and on this "man of God" went, mercilessly, until I ran shaking from the confessional. Instead of offering sanctuary, the church I loved now felt hateful and oppressive.

I'd been taught to love God, to trust Him, to believe in His forgiveness. In minutes, this priest had undone everything.

For people like *me*, he raged, God had no love, only wrath.

Fortunately, my mother's advice—one of her blessed homilies—proved to be a salve for the priest's curses: "Every experience in life is worth having—if you learn from it."

I was determined to do just that.

What I was learning about firsthand, at fourteen, was God's greatest gift: free will. I was also learning, the hard way, the price you paid for using it.

4

At Sea

I LIED ABOUT MY AGE to join the Coast Guard in November 1946. Suddenly, finishing high school wasn't as important as getting out of Los Angeles. I convinced my mother I'd absorb a more valuable education aboard ship and in foreign ports of call—following in her footsteps—than I'd get staying cooped up in a classroom, fending off girls during recess.

The ink was barely dry on the enlistment papers when I was assigned to the U.S. Coast Guard cutter *Minnetonka,* nicknamed the Mighty Minnie. A steady diet of movies had me envisioning exotic locales ripe with intrigue, where I'd be Tyrone Power one day, Jon Hall the next. It didn't take long for my shipmates to give me my nickname: Hollywood.

How stupid was I—thinking we'd sail for Singapore or Shanghai? This was, after all, the *Coast* Guard. We charted course for a weather station in the Pacific called Bird Dog One, somewhere between the mainland and Hawaii. Our mission was to patrol a fifty-mile radius of saltwater for thirty consecutive days. Circling. No land in sight. Any adventure was limited to your dreams.

I'd stand watch, swab decks, chip paint. When the boredom got to be too much, I'd chip more paint.

Only once did the captain allow us to swim. *That* was an experience. Floating in the depthless sapphire sea, thousands of miles from civilization, nothing but a speck in the universe. Cleansing, in a way. A catharsis. Puny insecurities dissolved by an even more powerful feeling . . . insignificance. Not in a negative way, but in a spiritual way, the way religion was supposed to work, instilling a reassuring sense of your relative place in the immense order of things.

The church let me down on that score, but not Our Lady of the High Seas. Whether I was riding in the mountains or sailing on the ocean, nature gave me a sense of belonging, even when I was entirely alone, completely cut off from other people.

That's how I felt, high up on the ship's tower, standing watch as the Mighty Minnie plunged through giant swells on the way back to San Pedro. Surrounded by endless ocean, millions of stars overhead. Horribly homesick, but aching to get on with my new life, a life somewhere else. Anywhere else.

On liberty, the guys wanted me to go on bar crawls through San Pedro or on forays through the Pike. I didn't drink, hated cigarette smoke, couldn't stand the relentless babble about skirt chasing. Macho bullshit is something the Coast Guard served in steady rations.

My liberty typically began on Sepulveda Boulevard, with my thumb out. It was a straight shot, fifty-four miles, to the San Fernando Valley. A family in Northridge, whom I'd met at Dubrock's, kept a gorgeous little chestnut mare out there and let me ride for free. The only place I felt completely comfortable was on horseback.

Eventually, they let me enter the horse in competition at the Flintridge Riding Club in Pasadena, my first foray into "the big time." I made a fool of myself in the first Jumper Class. Forgot the course. Second class of the day, my horse had three refusals and we were eliminated. Last class, I had numerous faults for crossing my own line. I packed a lot of schooling into that one day.

After riding, I'd hitch over the hill to Hollywood Boulevard, to sneak into the latest movies. Had to stretch that hundred-dollar-a-month government check. Still tortured by what happened in the Arlington, I'd change my seat if some guy crept too close. Not that I'd leave—I've never left a movie half-watched. I love them too much for that.

I was quite the loner in those days. Kept to myself mostly, living in a little fantasy bubble. The only friend I had my age was a kid nicknamed Bicycle Tommy, who came from a well-off Beverly Hills family but seemed as lost and untethered as I was. We'd just wander the boulevard, where all levels of show business seemed to collide in a nonstop public spectacle.

There was an all-male hangout on the boulevard, a bar, the name of which I can't recall. It was intriguing, full of nattily dressed, sophisticated-looking men, and when the door opened, popular tunes of the day like "Nature Boy" and "I'm Looking Over a Four-Leaf Clover" leaked out. However, the cigarette haze and alcohol smell stunted my curiosity—bars weren't my style at all.

Sometimes curiosity would get the best of me, and I'd test the waters with other boys, intrigued and relieved to find kids my age who shared my "unspoken secret."

Coffee Dan's, on Hollywood near Highland, became a regular people-watching hangout. One of the locals I enjoyed watching was Del Cleveland. He had performed show tunes in New York supper clubs and loved to sit around spinning tales of his days back east, hobnobbing with the likes of George Gershwin, Cole Porter, and Rodgers and Hart. Now he was in the L.A. music scene and lived in an apartment across from Hollywood High. With no sexual strings attached, Del would let me sack out on his sofa when I was too bushed to hitch back to base. He played Cole Porter records endlessly—not exactly what my Coast Guard buddies were listening to in San Pedro saloons.

It was at Del's that I again crossed paths with Dick Clayton. Three years had passed since we first met. Now in his late twenties, Clayton was still trying to make it as an actor. His claim to fame, so far, was giving Jane Withers her first screen kiss.

I'd encountered Dick plenty of times at Du Brock's after our initial meeting, usually on weekends. When he came around, he made a lively impression—especially when he volunteered to teach some of the kids how to drive, letting us steer his fancy blue '41 Pontiac convertible around a secluded part of Griffith Park.

"I was impressed that you had a movie-star car," I told Clayton when we saw each other again.

"I was impressed that you had girls following you around everywhere," he replied.

Dick was disappointed I hadn't gotten serious about an acting career. He recalled when some of Du Brock's gang, myself included, went one night to see him in a picture called *A Very Young Lady.*

"You know, Art," he suddenly said, "your voice is bad. You need to work on your voice if you want to be an actor." I figured he was trying to prove that his belief in my acting potential was real, not just some line he was feeding me.

Dick had scored a spot in an Olson and Johnson comedy revue, *Pardon My French,* being produced on Broadway. "Art, if you get to New York anytime soon, be sure to look me up."

I was glad Dick Clayton accepted me as a friend. I hoped it wasn't because he was *after* something.

• • •

HITCHHIKING BECAME LESS of a carefree experience. I was looking for a lift back to San Pedro one night, exhausted after the Del Mar Horse Show, when a spiffy new Oldsmobile stopped for me. The driver was drunk, so I suggested he let me drive. It was late, the road was empty, and I was desperate to get back. Good thing he didn't ask to see a license, because I didn't have one. I'd been behind the wheel only a few times.

We hadn't gone a mile when the guy tried to undo my trousers. My driving was bad enough without having to fend off this creepy lush. Fortunately, he passed out before I needed to hit the brakes and make a run for it. Unfortunately, his snoring was insidious. Pretty soon, I was dozing off, too.

We smashed straight into the back of a flatbed truck. Not hard enough to kill anybody, just hard enough to crush the front end of that shiny new Oldsmobile.

Mr. Cop-a-Feel stirred but didn't wake up.

The trucker pulled over and ran back hollering. I hollered right back: "This drunk picked me up and was trying to put the make on me." Seeing his rig wasn't damaged, the trucker signaled for me to come along. In seconds, we were barreling through the night, leaving the randy Good Samaritan dead to the world in his freshly crumpled Olds.

I felt terrible about it later. For all I knew, maybe he *was* dead.

APPLICATIONS WERE BEING taken for yeoman's school, and I didn't hesitate. Two months after enlisting, I was headed east on the Union Pacific, bound for the Coast Guard Training Center in Groton, Connecticut. Quick study of a map showed that New York City was only a short train ride from Groton. I had stowed Dick's number with my gear, just in case.

Weekend liberty in Manhattan left Hollywood in the shade. I'd barge into Clayton's Greenwich Village apartment on Friday nights, sometimes with a couple of buddies in tow, and we'd set out to take New York by storm. I rode in Central Park, ice-skated at Rockefeller Center, tentatively explored some of the city's "special" bars. I was more relaxed in ones that catered exclusively to women. Spotting a pair of attractive girls in the corner, I asked one of them to dance. Her girlfriend looked me over and barked, "Beat it, square balls!"

Always learning, a little at a time—that's me.

Dick Clayton bought me a ticket to my first Broadway show, *Mrs. McThing,* starring the First Lady of the Broadway stage, Helen Hayes. The energy, the excitement, the glamour—it was intoxicating.

Dick saw the fire all this put in my eyes, and he loved stoking it. He talked to me for hours on end about acting. Before long he was inviting me to cocktail parties with his theater friends, a constant, bubbling current of talented, urbane men and witty, sexy women. Boot camp was a breeze compared to the sink-or-swim challenge of keeping your head above water in this crowd.

At one of these parties, I heard a familiar song. Eager to share my new-found musical knowledge, I said, "Hmm, that sounds like Cole Porter."

"Why, yes, dear," I was informed, "—he's right over there."

Cole Porter! Playing the piano and singing in someone's apartment. The genius behind all the wonderful songs Del Cleveland had introduced me to— right in front of me!

It was as if I'd gotten out of my seat in one of those Hollywood Boulevard theaters and walked right into the movie.

What was most impressive about show people, men and women, wasn't their sexual bias, but their elegance, sophistication, intelligence, and *style*. As if that wasn't enough, they were talented. They were *contributors*. I wasn't sure I fit in, but at only fifteen years of age, I did my damnedest to stay afloat.

Experiences like these might never come again, so I acted like a sponge, soaking up as much of this unexpected energy and diversity as I could. I'd never experienced anything like it before. Yeoman's school became something that filled the time between my Manhattan weekends.

Many of the men I met in the social ramble were gay, but they had nothing in common with Mr. Biggs or the Undertaker. Maybe that's why I didn't feel the same sort of shame when I woke up one morning in the swank Park Avenue apartment of an older gentleman. The details? Having a fantastic breakfast made by his cook while a February blizzard raged outside. Lounging in a Sulka robe, drinking fresh-squeezed orange juice, having French impressionism explained to me—the framed originals that lined the walls serving as examples.

It was like being handed the keys to a spectacular kingdom, one I'd never imagined. But even as a teenager, I knew I didn't want to pay the cost of living there. I wasn't cut out to be a well-kept "boy." The experience fascinated me, but it scared me, too. I immediately retreated back to where I felt safe, to what I thought I should be.

I MET RITA AT ROSELAND.

She was the finest-looking girl in the place, and I worked up the nerve to ask her to dance. Rita was a bit older, much more mature, and she made it easy for me. I'd talk a blue streak with any girl who put me at ease, and this blue streak lasted all night.

Rita didn't ride, or ice-skate, so the next time we met I took her to a fancy restaurant, trying to entertain her in the manner I'd been hosted uptown. That's what a boy did for a girl, right? Pretty soon we ran out of small talk. Poor Rita couldn't measure up to my other New York experiences, and I didn't want to sit there babbling on about the theater, and art, and all the fascinating people I was meeting. That would have been so . . . *showy.*

We stayed out late, strolling around . . . dancing . . . and that was all. The bloom was off the rose.

"I gotta get back to the base," I finally said.

I never saw her again.

WITH ONLY A FEW DAYS left to my stint at yeoman's school, one important thing remained to be done before I was sent back to the West Coast.

I was leaving a Times Square movie theater, alone, in the dead of winter, when I finally worked up the courage to track down my father. Before coming east, I'd bugged Walt endlessly till he finally caved in and coughed up the address. His refusal to talk about Father only made me more determined to find out things for myself. Walt and I had shared everything as kids; it was only right that we share this as well.

I ambled through a gentle snowfall to a run-down section of the Lower East Side. The streets were empty and silent except for the crunching of my footsteps. I thought I'd gotten lost—that block of dingy, dilapidated brownstones couldn't be where our father lived. I kept checking the paper on which I'd scrawled his address, like the numbers were going to magically change.

On liberty in Manhattan with Rita.

KELM was crudely written on one of the mailboxes. I hiked up a few flights of narrow stairs and down a dark hallway, searching for the apartment. Timidly, I knocked. Maybe I didn't really want to be heard. Minutes crept by. I'd already turned to leave when the dead bolts started clicking. The door opened a crack, and in the gap appeared an old woman's face, scowling.

"Is Charles Kelm here?" I asked.

She closed the door slightly but still peered out. I didn't know what to do. Finally, she said, "No."

"Well, would you tell him his son came by to say hello?"

"I will."

She slammed the door shut. I waited a long moment, shaking. If things had gone differently, it could have been my mother behind that door, trapped in that horrible building.

When I hit the street, the snow was cascading down. I jerked up my peacoat collar and started walking. No idea where, really. Just wandering, realizing that I was never going to meet my real father and that I no longer wanted to. Charles Kelm could stay locked in his lousy apartment, forever separated from his flesh and blood. *What was I hoping to discover by meeting him? What good was going to come of it?*

I roamed the frozen white streets for hours, wandering in such a daze that I missed the last train to Connecticut. It took me until dawn to hitchhike through a blizzard back to Groton. It was the worst experience of my young life. But by the time I got there, dead tired and only minutes from being declared AWOL, I recognized that the day's miserable experience had helped me come to an important realization: I truly was on my own.

5

Henry's Boys

IT ACTUALLY CAME AS A BLESSING when, in November 1947, the Coast Guard discovered I was underage and booted me out. I'd graduated from the training center as yeoman third class, but since returning to San Pedro I'd had nothing but desk jobs (thank God—no more "patrols" in the middle of nowhere!). I issued seaman's papers for a lardass petty officer who smoked a lousy pipe in his tiny little office all day. God, how I longed for liberty!

Dick Clayton had kept in touch with me, first from New York, and then after he returned to the coast. Despite his run on Broadway, Clayton had temporarily shelved his performing dreams and was working in the mail room at Famous Artists Agency. He caught the attention of the boss, Charlie Feldman, one of the most respected agents in the business. Feldman and his colleagues encouraged Dick to become a subagent. Clayton was a quick study and seemed to know everything that was happening around town—the ultimate advantage, I suppose, of doling out the mail at a major talent agency.

Dick encouraged me to pick up my education, so I enrolled in the Del Powers Professional School, just off Wilcox Avenue in Hollywood. The school was run by actress Mala Powers's mother and was crammed with kids who wanted to be in pictures. I went because classes only lasted till noon.

I graduated, pocketing a high school diploma, then drifted through a bunch of odd jobs, much as before. The only real difference this time was that I was supporting a new habit—figure skating. I practically lived at the Polar Palace, a rickety old wooden ice rink on Van Ness near Melrose. Forget about skating lessons—I had to scrape together the price of admission. That's where I met a whole new group of people, who became my extended family.

There was Bob Turk, who'd later become a choreographer for the *Ice Capades*; Bobby Specht, another *Ice Capades* star, with whom I kept up regular correspondence; Joyce Lockwood, with whom I skated pairs; Catherine Machado and Richard Dwyer, both of whom became stars on the ice. Then there was the extraordinary Ronnie Robertson, one of the finest skaters ever — who'd soon play a significant role in my life.

I still loved horses, but I'd soured on the prospect of making a living in that world. Horses were for rich people and therefore were out of my league.

Now, inspired by the era's popular ice shows, I dreamed of becoming a professional skater. Not that my passion for skating was entirely new. When I was little, I had kept a framed photograph of Sonja Henie beside my bed, and every night I'd finish my prayers with "And God bless Sonja Henie," and kiss her picture.

I loved the athleticism of skating, the rigorous training, practicing figures and diligently skating my way through levels of tests that ranked you in the nation's amateur standings. And I was good! I skated both singles and pairs.

A 1948 publicity photo of Arthur Gelien, competitive figure skater.

Joyce and I would win the California Junior Pair Figure Skating Championship in 1949, and the state's Senior Pair Championship the following year.

To support this new obsession, I worked at the Orange Julius stand across from Musso and Frank restaurant. I ushered at the Warner Bros. Theater on Hollywood Boulevard, making seventy-five cents an hour. That's where I saw *Cloak and Dagger,* with Gary Cooper and Lilli Palmer, about six million times. A young girl named Carol Burnett also worked there. We agreed that the manager was a nitwit, and we both quit after a few months.

Mother had moved back to San Francisco while I was in the Coast Guard. Walt and I were eager to be on our own, and after all those years of sacrifice—protecting us, providing for us—Mother must have felt ready for some time on *her* own, too. Walt and I rented a room in a big old Craftsman-style bungalow on Hobart Avenue. Our "landlord" was Terry Marsteller, an art student by day who sold tickets in the Torrance bus station by night. For someone not much older than me, Terry was an operator: he didn't own the building, but he rented a block of rooms and then sublet them at rates that afforded him a little extra off the top. An enterprising capitalist artist!

Dick Clayton kept hounding me about taking an acting career seriously, but I couldn't be bothered. I wanted to skate, not waste time in some stupid acting class.

Then one day Dick brokered the introduction that radically changed my life.

"There's this agent, Henry Willson, who can really help your career," Clayton told me. Willson, Dick explained, was more of a personal manager than an agent. He handled all aspects of a client's career: discovering them, pitching them to the studios, negotiating their contracts, counseling them—everything.

"Henry's specialty is finding new talent," Dick said. "And he represents the greatest-looking guys in town."

Willson, who came from a wealthy East Coast family, had been born in Lansdowne, Pennsylvania, but raised in New York. His father had been president of Columbia Records, and he'd made a fortune by figuring out how to put music on both sides of a platter. How Henry got into the film business, I don't know, but at a young age he moved west and established himself as the chief talent scout for producer David O. Selznick. He'd discovered future star Rhonda Fleming, among others, for Selznick. Some major actresses, such as Lana Turner, Jeanette MacDonald, and Ann Sothern, had Henry as their agent.

But Willson's real attention was focused on his list of male clients, specifically young, good-looking, all-American guys. Henry believed that young women craved a male equivalent of the pinup stars who'd boosted the troop's morale during the war. Acting skill was secondary to chiseled features and a fine physique. Guess I fit the profile, because Willson—at Dick's prompting—told me to come by his house for a look-see.

Dick accompanied me to the Bel Air spread, located on Stone Canyon Road. He was a nervous mother hen. "I have to warn you, Art—Henry doesn't have the most sterling reputation. People are always making jokes about Henry and his boys."

Whatever Henry Willson had to offer, it wasn't going to take me by surprise. "I've been around," I told Dick. "I can handle myself."

Henry was a bachelor, in his late thirties. He looked like a portly Vincente Minnelli: jowly, receding hairline, sleepy eyes. His "look" was surprisingly East Coast for Hollywood: conservatively tailored wool three-piece suits, monogrammed cuff links, expensive cologne, the whole bit. None of which disguised his homeliness. Henry didn't have a chin. His face sort of melted into the spread-collared shirts he fancied.

That night he took us to dinner at one of his regular nightspots, Scandia. It was a popular old-style restaurant on the Sunset Strip, a place with plenty of polished mahogany, swords and shields and battle armor promoting a Viking theme. Henry was a star there, and he relished the part: schmoozing with celebrities, beckoning the staff, granting an audience to publicists, taking urgent phone calls at his personal booth—generally holding court like the most important character in the place, if not the town. Despite all his showboating, Henry had enough natural charm and humor to not come off like a complete egomaniac.

When you dined in Henry's booth, no one questioned whether you were of legal age. So even though I hated alcohol, I gamely nursed a scotch and water. That's what I'd seen everybody drinking in New York, so clearly it was the cocktail of choice for sophisticates. Henry spun one Hollywood story after another until I started to feel like an insider. His personal triumphs were the focus of the discussion, of course. They explained why any bright-eyed newcomer should be thrilled to have Henry Willson as an agent.

Guy Madison, for example, was taking in a Lux Radio Theater show in 1944, on weekend leave from the Coast Guard, when Henry spotted him in the audience and arranged a screen test for Selznick's *Since You Went Away.* Now Madison was a big star, a household name, engaged to gorgeous Gail Russell, another of Henry's clients.

"Guy's real name is Robert Moseley," Henry revealed. "Can't get anywhere with a name like that. You like this hot redhead, Rhonda Fleming? You wouldn't know her if she was still Marilyn Louis. I changed it. Fleming sounds like *flaming,* plays up her hair."

"Ever heard of Francis Durgin?" Henry asked me.

"No, sir," I replied.

"Of course you haven't." Henry laughed. "Who'd go to the movies to see a guy named Francis? First thing I did was change his name. Rory Calhoun — *him* you know. That's somebody people will pay to see. Now my phone's ringing off the hook with producers who want him."

Throughout dinner I figured Henry was sizing me up as potential Guy or Rory material, staring at me over the rim of his whiskey glass. Typical behavior for talent scouts, I guessed. Henry had a way of staring *through* you, however, and when he gave me *that* look, there was no mistaking its meaning. The little nudges under the table, the lingering hand on my arm — merely extra hints for the uninitiated.

NOT TOO LONG after our initial meeting, Henry arranged to pick me up in his boat-size Chrysler. He was driving out to Burbank for an on-set visit to one of his other clients and thought I'd enjoy a firsthand look at how movies were made. If he was trying to impress me, it worked. Entering the gated kingdom of Warner Bros., being allowed on the soundstage to watch the filming — it was incredibly exciting.

The picture being shot was *Fighter Squadron,* and the director, Raoul Walsh, seemed to be acquainted with Henry. Walsh had been in Hollywood since the very beginning, first as an actor, then a director. He'd made some of Warners' most popular action pictures: *They Drive by Night; High Sierra; They Died with Their Boots On; Objective, Burma!* Walsh was Errol Flynn's favorite director. Not that I knew any of this at the time. To me, Walsh was just a salty old character with an eye patch, a director who commanded his set like a sergeant running herd on his troops.

Willson had convinced Walsh to cast one of his latest finds in a bit part, so he had come to the set to offer his boy moral support. It backfired, because when the cameras rolled, Henry's guy was incredibly nervous. He blew many takes, *dozens,* and things got so tense you could hear a pin drop on the soundstage. Walsh was patient, though, and never lost his composure. During a brief break between failed shots, Henry called his client over for a hasty introduction.

"Art, I want you to meet Rock Hudson. This is his first movie."

We shook hands and traded rushed greetings. I snickered to myself about his name: Rock. Henry obviously planned to mold this rangy, handsome guy into another Guy or Rory. I remember thinking, *Thank goodness I've already got a good, short, strong name: Art.*

We were on the Warners set for only about thirty minutes that afternoon, and no one who took the time to notice either of us kids—me all of seventeen, Rock in his early twenties—could ever have imagined what lay in store. There was certainly no hint that in a few short years Rock Hudson would go from bumbling bit player to being voted Most Popular Male Movie Star of the 1950s. Or that I'd return to this same soundstage to work with Raoul Walsh myself and for a while become Warner Bros.' biggest box-office attraction.

Not even Henry Willson would have tried to sell somebody on that fantasy.

I KNEW THE DREADED moment was coming. It was inevitable, yet when it arrived, I wasn't prepared.

It happened at Henry's office, a two-room suite in a nondescript building on Carol Drive, just off Sunset Boulevard, modest except for all the autographed photos of actors and actresses lining the walls. Dick Clayton was there for the meeting, too.

I'd decided to take the plunge and become a Henry Willson client. Dick assured me it was a smart move, and I'd come to trust Dick more than anyone. It didn't take much prodding for me to sign on the dotted line and become Henry's "property."

"Good decision," Willson said, beaming. "Now let's get down to business—the name's got to go."

Henry and Dick shot a bunch of horrible-sounding options back and forth. I kept my mouth shut, mortified. I'd always known that "Gelien" would never pass muster. Nobody had ever pronounced it right. (It's Ga-LEEN.) But what surprised me was they were discussing *first* names. Granted, I hated "Arthur"—only my mother got away with calling me that. But having grown up as Art, I never figured on being anyone *but* Art . . . ever.

"Maybe we can use my birth name," I ventured. Henry and Dick gaped in confusion. "Male Kelm," I said, thinking I was being funny.

They both did a double take, looked baffled, then ignored me. Clearly, I wouldn't be asked to participate in the process of choosing my own name.

Exasperated, Henry finally said, "C'mon, we've got to tab him something." He thought . . . for about two more seconds. "Hey, *that's* not bad," he announced. "Tab." He turned to me. "What do you like to do, *Tab*? Got any hobbies?"

I didn't know where Henry was going with this.

Dick was way ahead: "He loves horses. Rides hunters and jumpers."

"There we go," said Henry, flashing a satisfied smile. "Tab Hunter."

I hated it. Dick could see that from the glazed look on my face. As we left the office, he draped an arm around me and said, "A name is only as important as you make it." To this day, I have no idea what he meant.

I consoled myself by considering that I might have been named Tab Jumper.

The whole thing seemed unreal. I found it amazing that a big-shot agent like Henry Willson would add me to his client list. In 1948, I had far more interest in horses and skating than in being a movie actor. I didn't *long* for an acting career, not in the way I longed to be on the ice or at the stables.

But Henry convinced each of his clients that he'd conceived a master plan. The goal was to make them *all* motion-picture stars. Impossible, of course, but Henry had the essential quality any good agent requires: he made people believe. He convinced unsure talent they were going straight to the top; he made casting directors and producers believe he had the ideal lead for their production; and most important, he made everyone around him believe that Henry Willson was one of the most hard-charging, high-powered players in Hollywood.

Who was I to doubt the star-making savvy of Henry Willson? I was just a newcomer who'd blundered into the lair of a big-time operator.

Unfortunately, I displayed an immature, adolescent attitude toward any possible "career" as an actor. Part of me *knew* it was going to happen, that somehow I'd end up in pictures. But another part of me, the bigger part, couldn't be bothered preparing for that. Maybe I didn't want to be caught *trying* to make it come true.

Not that I minded rubbing elbows with the sophisticated Hollywood crowd. I started getting regular invitations to private parties and weekend getaways, sometimes because the hosts genuinely liked me, sometimes because they had other ideas. The industry chatter flew right over my head. I felt like window dressing most of the time, but I didn't let it bother me, as long as there was good food and interesting characters.

Before this type of lifestyle became "normal," Dick Clayton reined me in. He convinced my mother to move back to Los Angeles, "for the good of her son." Walt had enlisted in the navy, and soon he'd be married. Clayton felt that having my mother around would keep me "grounded." Mom got on famously with Dick, the only person in the world—other than Sylvia Fink—who ever got away with calling her Gertie.

Henry Willson found my mother and me an apartment in Burbank, at 137-A Cordova Street. It was so close to Warner Bros., we practically lived on the studio lot. Years later, when the studio expanded, our apartment *was* absorbed into the Warners compound.

But in 1948, despite being *that* close to the movie business, I was still a million miles away.

DICK CLAYTON WAS the only person who really believed in me, who constantly preached responsibility. He encouraged me to stick with my acting studies after I'd been disillusioned by brief classes at the Ben Bard School. The exercises seemed foolish—especially to somebody as shy and inhibited as me. It was much easier to direct my energy toward physical things than it was to practice the intellectual discipline and imagination that acting required.

I got irritated when Henry sent me on casting calls that interfered with my skating. I was ill at ease in the offices of casting directors, surrounded by dozens of other pretty boys, all desperately hoping *this* would be the interview that led to their big break. I'd deliberately stay on the ice until the last possible moment, then rush to interviews straight from practice, disheveled and stinking of sweat. No wonder I never got a callback.

Since I wasn't earning a nickel as an actor in 1948, I continued working an array of menial jobs. I packed ceiling-fan blades for the Torrington Manufacturing Company; pumped gas at a service station; cut up my hands working at a sheet-metal factory; briefly, I worked behind the soda fountain at the Rexall drugstore, Hollywood and Highland, where I'd previously hung out all night, reading movie magazines I couldn't afford to buy.

While making shakes there, I met my first bona fide movie star. It was the night of the big 1948 Christmas parade, and gawkers jammed the Hollywood Boulevard sidewalks. Once the parade passed, the place was swamped with customers, including Dick Clayton, who brought along Roddy McDowall. Roddy was only twenty, but he'd been in pictures his whole life, including classics like *How Green Was My Valley, Lassie Come Home,* and *My Friend Flicka.* We hit it off, gabbing and laughing—until the manager came over and said to me, "Can't you work any faster?"

"Not for a dollar an hour, I can't," I snapped. It was totally out of character for me. I was fired on the spot.

BY EARLY '49, I started to wonder if I was less a client than one of the "dates" on Henry Willson's dance card. No job offers were coming in, and I had no way of knowing just how hard Henry was working on my behalf. He'd take me out once every two weeks or so, part of keeping in touch with his stable of young colts. He had the same act with all his male clients, I'm sure—just never at the same time. The boys in Henry's stable may have shown up at the same casting calls, but never at the same dinner table with Henry. There was nothing fraternal about the way Henry ran his show. He kept us separated, making it easier to convince each of us that he was Henry's favorite.

His routine was to wine and dine you at Chasen's or Ciro's or the Mocambo, then come on to you. How things developed from there was up to whomever Henry was pursuing. If you put the brakes on, then Henry used his "out" line: "Come on, you know I was only joking," he'd say. If you took him seriously, he was prepared to follow through. If you were invited back to his place for drinks, it wasn't to admire the fabulous wall-to-wall carpeting in his den.

Well, maybe it was. In a way.

That's how Henry earned his less-than-sterling reputation as Hollywood's "lecherous gay Svengali." Personally, I don't label people, and I've never hung that tag on Henry. I wasn't comfortable with his sexual shenanigans, but I did play along—up to a point.

Henry had a magnetic personality, but it certainly wasn't strong enough to lure me onto the casting couch. I knew exactly where my line was drawn. Not everybody who wanted Henry to make them a star had such boundaries. And trust me, when it came to Henry Willson, plenty of young men were willing to play his game in exchange for a chance at "stardom."

Not all these guys were gay, either. Plenty of actors who want to make it in this business will conveniently shift their sexual orientation if they're ambitious—or desperate—enough to believe it'll get them ahead.

Basically, we're all whores—at some time, in some way. We eventually prostitute ourselves, one way or another, in hopes of winning what we want. In show business, especially, that's the name of the game. So the question is, how far are you willing to go?

Several months and many parried advances later, in the summer of 1949,

Henry got me my first movie job. The Paramount casting director didn't even conduct an interview, just signed me on. He must have owed Henry a favor—the same way Raoul Walsh probably paid back Henry by casting Rock Hudson in *Fighter Squadron*.

Within days I was on my way to Marysville, California, to shoot a picture called *The Lawless*. Gail Russell was the star. She'd just tied the knot with Guy Madison. The film costarred Macdonald Carey, who I used to see on occasion ushering Mass at the Church of the Good Shepherd, when my mother and I briefly lived in Beverly Hills. Carey was a good guy.

For my debut, I walked up Main Street with a bunch of other guys. Speaking part, two words: "Hi, Fred." For this I earned a coveted Screen Actors Guild card and five hundred dollars. Two hundred and fifty bucks a word! I wanted to get the check and wave it in that drugstore manager's face. Those two words made me as much money as I'd earn at Rexall in two months of eight-hour shifts.

When I got back to Los Angeles, I went directly to the California Bank on the corner of Wilshire and Beverly and opened an account. I ordered yellow checks with an American eagle in the corner. When the Paramount paychecks arrived—two of them!—they read "Pay to the order of Tab Hunter."

Suddenly my new name didn't grate on me nearly as much.

I'd officially boarded the gravy train.

Which immediately derailed. During the following months there were no more bit parts and precious few casting calls. I tried to convince myself it had nothing to do with rebuffing Henry's come-ons.

Broke again, I took a job at Wil Wright's ice cream parlor, an institution on the Strip. Everybody who's lived in Hollywood remembers the facade, decorated with a neon angel's face floating above the words IT'S HEAVENLY. Next door was La Rue, one of the town's toniest restaurants. For the next year I scooped pistachio and butter pecan, watching through the window as real actors tossed valets the keys to their Cadillacs.

WHEN I RETURNED to the big bungalow on Hobart Avenue on the evening of October 14, 1950, Terry Marsteller asked me if I wanted to go with him to a party. I'd end up having good reason to remember the date—although I'd just as soon forget it.

We drove to a house in Walnut Park, walked around to the back porch, and entered the noisy kitchen through a screen door. Right away, I could tell it was a gay party. Nothing but men. Some were drinking, some dancing; a few were standing with their arms around each other. Twenty guys, maybe more.

Now I'm not going to claim this scene took me by surprise. This wasn't the first gay shindig I'd been to. But to be honest, I found parties, gay or straight, pretty exasperating. Boorish, boozed-up behavior, too much cigarette smoke, bad music.

On the other hand, there was always something there that interested me—free food!

As I was looking through the refrigerator for something to eat, the cops came busting in. They made a big scene of shoving everybody around and barking a lot—just like movie cops who can't wait to spit out their one line of dialogue. "Faggot" figured heavily with these cops, as they herded us into several paddy wagons and hauled us down to the Firestone Park sheriff's station.

Under Section 647.5 of the state's penal code, we were all charged with being "idle, lewd or dissolute persons or associates of known thieves."

Imagine that—and I was barely *in* the movie business.

I was so naive. I had no grasp of the political climate at the time, no understanding of how conservative paranoia fueled the routine behavior of the police. Fifty years ago, being different in any way was practically the same thing as being a subversive. But in Manhattan, an assembly of gay men in an East Side apartment was considered the upper crust of theater culture. A group of gay guys hanging out at a house in Walnut Park, however, might as well have been a Communist cell meeting, as far as the LAPD was concerned.

From the sheriff's office we were carted to the county jail, where a couple of dozen of us stewed—dissolutely, no doubt—in the tank. Finally an attorney showed up, a guy by the name of Harry Weiss. Decked out in a broad-brimmed fedora and a trench coat, spouting off like a machine gun, he was a character straight out of central casting. But he was *connected.* We were out of jail in no time.

Later I learned that Weiss specialized in the discreet handling of such sticky situations: on-call to agents, producers, and studio bosses whenever "talent" got pinched by John Law. I've got no idea which one of us "lewd persons" had Weiss's number on hand, but it certainly wasn't me! I don't remember if he posted bail for everyone; I only know I had twenty cents in my pocket and no clue how I was getting out of that jam until Harry Weiss magically appeared.

Eventually a judge knocked the charges down to "disturbing the peace." I was fined fifty dollars, given a thirty-day sentence (suspended), and put on a year's probation. Terry and I vowed that we'd never mention the incident to anyone, and we figured that with a little luck, maybe the whole thing would be forgotten.

Wishful thinking was always my specialty.

6

That's the Boy I Want

IN THE GANGSTER PICTURE *White Heat,* Jimmy Cagney stuffs a weaselly henchman into the truck of a car. When the guy whines that he can't breathe, Cagney, laughing, shoots the trunk full of holes. Like the rest of America, I squirmed in my theater seat, guiltily thrilled by Cagney's wild portrayal of a homicidal maniac.

How could I have known that the perforated guy in the trunk, veteran character actor Paul Guilfoyle, was about to emerge as a crucial link in the fortunes of Art Gelien?

In addition to being a familiar mutt-faced thug in dozens of crime dramas, Guilfoyle was also a casting agent. He'd been hired by the director of an upcoming feature to find a fresh new face for the role of a young marine in a picture called *God's Little Island.*

As fate would have it, Paul Guilfoyle was also buddies with my guardian angel, Dick Clayton.

An interview was arranged with the film's director, Stuart Heisler. I went to his office straight from the Polar Palace, carrying my sweater and skates in a crumpled brown bag. Stephanie Nordli, the movie's screenwriter, was also there. Her eyes lit up when I walked in. She then uttered her prophetic line: "That's the boy I want."

Once I'd taken off my shirt, they led me to another office so the film's producer, David E. Rose, could look me over. To him, I didn't rate a word. "Hmmmm," was all he said.

But as I left, Miss Nordli handed me a script, told me to study it, and come back for a screen test on Saturday. If I measured up, I'd be cast as "Chicken" Dugan, the male lead in *God's Little Island,* opposite Linda Darnell, one of my favorite actresses and an established star. I was so unnerved I forgot my sweater and skates in Mr. Heisler's office.

The following Saturday I shot a screen test at Goldwyn Studios. By Monday, they'd decided to cast me. I barely had time to comprehend what was happening.

There'd be three months of filming on location in Jamaica, followed by another seven weeks of interiors and special effects shot in London. I'd have done all of it for free, but they were apparently going to *pay* me—$250 a week, a colossal salary compared to the going rate for scooping ice cream and mucking out stables.

When I told Mother the news, the first thing she said was, "You must have a suit in London. People will ask you out. You cannot wear Levi's. You are not going to a barn." I never dressed up. Jeans and T-shirts were all I ever wore. They were all I could afford.

I couldn't see myself in a suit—or paying for one. So Henry Willson fronted me the money for a sports jacket and trousers from Phelps-Terkel on Wilshire Boulevard's Miracle Mile. I was loaned the money, since paychecks were still weeks away. Trying on those new clothes was when the realization hit me.

My life was about to change, dramatically.

THE AIR IN JAMAICA held the inviting aroma of sweet-and-sour spareribs. At least that was my first impression as I bounded down the gangway at the Kingston Airport. Every place should smell like sweet-and-sour spareribs.

The crew was put up at the Tower Isle Hotel in Ocho Rios, on the island's north shore, right on the beach. The stars—myself included—stayed up the hill, overlooking the world, in the beautiful, understated Shaw Park Hotel.

Ocho Rios was a daydream: constant sunshine and perfect white-sand beaches; all the coconuts and fresh papaya you could eat; balmy nights sleeping under mosquito netting, in an elegantly spare hotel room; Mass every Sunday with the locals in a clapboard church at St. Ann's Bay.

I'd kissed off the church several years earlier, after that nasty experience in the confessional at St. Paul's. But now, halfway around the world, it felt entirely appropriate to get down on my knees and give thanks for my good fortune.

Six days a week, from sunup to sundown, we made a movie. While other kids my age worried about their grades and what they'd do after college, I was being paid to play in paradise. If this was how actors lived, I'd get used to it *very* easily.

Most of the cast and crew came from Britain. That added a polite, old-school style to the proceedings that was almost as foreign and beguiling as the Caribbean people, climate, and terrain. The movie, which by this time had been renamed *Saturday Island,* was a joint venture between United Artists and an English outfit, Coronado Productions.

The story was simple: Dedicated nurse (Linda Darnell) and brash, immature marine (me) are stranded on a South Seas island, sole survivors of a torpedoed supply ship. This is fine by him, not so thrilling for her. She gradually accepts the inevitable—romance and all—un-

With Linda Darnell in Saturday Island (Island of Desire *in the U.S.)—the kiss that launched my career.*

til an older Royal Air Force veteran crash-lands on the island and Linda nurses him back to health. The two men compete for her affection.

Donald Gray, who played the pilot, was a popular actor in England who'd lost an arm during the war. The producers were banking on British audiences turning out in droves to watch a proper English gent—a national hero, in fact—defeat a strapping young Yank in a battle for Linda Darnell.

Studio publicity would later claim our island saga was a landmark film due to its staging of "the most violent battle between two love-struck beasts ever filmed!" You've got to love PR. At the time, our only concern was making it look believable, especially my fight scene with the one-armed Mr. Gray and my love scenes with Linda.

The scene where she finally succumbs to my advances turned out to be particularly dangerous, for unexpected reasons. It took place on a raft in the lagoon. I was in the water, elbows on the raft, gazing up at her. In the middle of a take came shouts that a huge shark was within striking distance. *Cut!* I leaped on the raft with Linda. We resumed filming only after a guy with a sub-machine gun was hired to stand guard on the reef. Only he never took his eyes off Linda, which didn't relax my nerves any, or help my performance.

I never stopped fretting that I wasn't good enough. I was always seeking a telltale sign of approval from Stu Heisler, an easygoing director whose eyes always seemed to shine with a dewy glaze.

During another love scene with Linda, I caught a glimpse of Heisler beside the camera. Tears had welled up in those baby blues. Was he caught up in the emotion of the scene? Or was he wondering, *Why the hell did I ever hire this kid?*

Our fantasy island was hit by gusts of reality late in the production, when a hurricane slammed Jamaica. Fortunately for the filmmakers, the southern coast of the island, down around Kingston, took the brunt of it. But we got smacked pretty hard in Ocho Rios. Reporters were less interested in storm damage than in Linda Darnell. Amid a natural disaster, a film star was the eye of the storm. This was my first exposure to the media's bizarre fixation with celebrities.

Asked how she weathered the ordeal, Linda smiled and said, "With a prayer and a bottle of scotch." Sooner than I'd have dared imagine, I'd be longing for such ease in handling the press.

Linda *was* good luck for newcomers, as she'd claimed the day I met her. She was sweet and patient and helpful, befriending an inexperienced kid. My image of her as a movie queen, up on a pedestal, quickly evaporated. She treated me like a colleague.

She even threw a surprise party to celebrate my twentieth birthday. As we broke for lunch at the roaring river location, a cake appeared on cue, brought by the hotel at Linda's request. It was a simple gesture, but I was deeply touched.

Linda later presented me with a gorgeous leather-bound scrapbook, filled with stills and candid snapshots from the production. She inscribed it:

> For Tab,
> Hoping this is the beginning of a wonderful and satisfying new life for you . . . I'm sure it will be. You have everything it takes, darling, and everyone is pulling for you, including
> Your
> devoted
> Linda

From the Caribbean, it was on to England. The remainder of filming, interiors and special effects, took place in a quaint old studio at Walton-on-Thames, just outside London.

Big-city bustle wasn't Linda's style, so she stayed near the studio at a hotel called Great Fosters, which had been Henry VIII's hunting lodge. Bette Davis and Gary Merrill had recently spent their honeymoon there, Linda told me. She invited me out several times, but after two weeks she suddenly moved to London.

"I didn't mind climbing all those stairs," she explained, "and I didn't mind having to go down the hall every time I needed the bathroom—but when I bent over to clean the tub and burned my ass on those pipes, that was it! Enough of country life!"

Although Linda was a big star, she never took herself too seriously, which I could not say for our young pain-in-the-ass assistant director, who would endlessly yank open dressing-room doors and sourly shout, "You're wanted on the set!" He was particularly rude to stunt people and extras. Finally, I couldn't take it anymore.

"Stop your screaming," I told the little bugger. "From now on, you'll only *knock* on doors and politely *ask* people to come to the set."

He didn't like my reprimand one bit, especially coming from someone younger than him. But he did as told. And that was my first taste of "star power"—used wisely.

DURING THOSE WEEKS in England, I stayed in a flat at White House Regent's Park, lent to me by Terry Marsteller. That's right, the same Terry who'd rented me a room on Hobart Avenue in Los Angeles. The same Terry who'd been carted off to the clink with me that infamous October day, one year earlier. While I'd stayed in L.A., figure-skating and fantasizing about breaking into the movies, Terry had taken off for Paris to study art at the Académie Julian.

It was there that he encountered Charles Evelyn Baring, an heir to the Baring Brothers banking fortune, but one who much preferred life as a globe-trotting patron of the arts to time spent worrying over stodgy high finance. Terry had apparently become a worldly bon vivant since I'd last seen him. His flat was available because he and Mr. Baring were off on a world cruise together.

It was at Terry's place that I'd get my first inkling of how the publicity machine worked. I hadn't even finished making my first movie, but already fans were lining up in front of the building. They'd ask for an autograph or to have a picture taken with me. Sometimes they'd sneak snapshots of me coming and going. United Artists, it seemed, was staging a big buildup in advance of the movie's release.

One afternoon at the flat, I was ironing a shirt. The phone rang.

"If you're having trouble with that," said a sexy young voice, "I'll be glad to come up and help you with it."

"Who is this?" I asked.

"Look out the window."

On the street below, gathered around the red phone booth, was a gaggle of teenage girls, waving and giggling. They all had binoculars draped around their necks. I waved back. They went crazy.

I thought it was a practical joke.

Little did I know . . .

Memories of finishing *Saturday Island* pale, frankly, in comparison with experiences off the set. Terry had arranged for me to take a side trip to Paris after shooting wrapped, where I was escorted in style by his friend Suzanne Rateau. What a hostess! We dined on gourmet cuisine, sipped aperitifs on the Left Bank, painted at the Académie Julian, explored museums, and attended the unveiling of a new fashion collection. What did this stableboy know about Balenciaga! At twenty I was being exposed to a world—an unreal world, but a *possible* world—even more fantastic than what the movies could manufacture.

Guilt, of course, quickly set in. Here I was, living high on the hog, while back home my poor mother bided time in a tiny apartment, lonelier than ever with both sons gone.

Before returning to the States I roped Suzanne and her daughter, Francine, into helping me find the perfect gift for Mother. We settled on a gorgeous Dietrich-style hat, something my mother would *never* have bought for herself. I couldn't get out of the store before I'd added a tweed suit, playing to Mother's practical side. She obviously needed a camel-hair coat to go with it. And a charcoal gray skirt. Plus four cashmere sweaters, a pearl necklace, and a pair of earrings. To store them, I purchased a fabulous jewelry box. It played a little Schubert when you lifted the lid.

Okay, I went overboard. Nothing fuels a shopping spree like a little guilt.

I sailed back to the States, Cherbourg to New York, on the magnificent *Queen Elizabeth*. Crossing the North Atlantic was a rough and unforgettable ride. Monster storms tossed us around for days, and we fell a day and a half behind schedule, rare for the *Queen Elizabeth*. Most of the passengers stayed in their staterooms, but I loved every minute of it, roaming the deserted liner as if I owned it, marveling at how far I'd come, and how quickly.

I felt the thrill of a whole new life opening up before me. I'd left home as a kid and was returning as a movie star! It had been just a few short years since I was a miserable, confused fifteen-year-old, lying about my age to enlist in the Coast Guard. Now here I was, on the bow of what felt like my private yacht, plunging through the raging ocean, wondering how that lonely, insecure, shameful kid had managed to climb into the catbird seat, up on top of the world. It was heady, it was frightening, it felt like a dream.

What happens next? I kept asking myself.

7

Manufacturing a Movie Star

I WAS NOT PREPARED for what awaited when we docked in Elizabeth, New Jersey. (A dock strike in New York forced the detour to Jersey.) Photographers swarmed aboard the *Queen Elizabeth,* taking hundreds of shots of me. Fawning United Artists flunkies ushered me through customs, right to a waiting limousine. The ass kissing was beyond extreme. It was doubly embarrassing because these people were seasoned veterans, much older than I. They treated me better than they would a returning war hero.

"I can take a cab to the hotel," I protested. They wouldn't hear of it. It dawned on me, maybe for the first time, that I wasn't so much a person now as I was a valuable commodity.

Icing on the cake: UA's limo broke down midway through the Holland Tunnel. My claustrophobia kicked in. They should have let me take a cab.

Still recuperating the next morning, I was fed to the lions of the New York press. Publicity cards had been sent out featuring a shirtless photo of yours truly: EVER REACH FOR A STAR? the headline teased. Appropriately, I was scheduled to appear in the Carnival Room of the Sherry Netherland Hotel. The promo card invited one and all to "Bring Your Camera" for the unveiling of the fresh beefcake.

From the time I got out of bed until I crawled back to my hotel room after midnight, I did interviews and grinned for the cameras until my jaws ached. It was more exhausting than making the movie. In character, you get to be someone else, and that suited me fine. But here, on display, I couldn't separate myself from the attention. The promotion thing was about wearing the happy face—all the time. I shriveled under the constant glare.

I was right back in the school yard at Mount Vernon Junior High, hemmed in by the gawking girls. Then, I could run. Now, there was no place to hide.

At Sardi's, the legendary showbiz hangout, I sank into a booth, wary of the microphone in front of me. I was being interviewed, live, on the radio show *Luncheon at Sardi's*. Having pegged me for a dunce, the host, who'd clearly done her homework, steered the conversation in a direction intended to relax me.

"I understand you like to ride horses," she said.

"Oh, yes," I replied, perking up.

"Think you'll get a chance to do any riding before you head back to the coast?"

"I doubt it," I said, warming quickly to my favorite subject. Feeling my oats, so to speak, I bravely decided to ad-lib. "But if I had the time, I'd love to go foxhunting and ride out with the—"

I meant to say "Connecticut Hunt Club." My inexperienced lips, however, transposed things. Over the air went "The Honnecticut Cunt Club." My first big interview—a legendary blooper. Not exactly what United Artists had hoped for from their new matinee idol.

ANOTHER SURPRISE CAME when Henry Willson showed up at my hotel. He claimed he was there visiting his parents on Long Island and taking care of business in Manhattan.

"How'd you like to go to Bermuda?" he asked me out of the blue.

His invitation took me totally by surprise, which Henry could easily see.

"It'll only be a few days," he said, trying to sound casual and reassuring.

United Artists' publicists worked overtime to create a new star.

I agreed. At that age, when life throws you a seemingly golden opportunity, you don't search for the price tag.

We sailed on the *Queen of Bermuda,* one of the majestic British liners of the 1930s, which had served its country admirably in the war and been returned to pleasure cruising. The owner, Furness Bermuda Line, referred to it as a "Honeymoon Ship."

For Henry, it *was* a honeymoon of sorts. He was trying to strengthen our agent-client "marriage" by giving me a great big perk. Since I'd landed *Saturday Island* without his direct involvement, he wanted to restake his claim on Tab Hunter, just in case I was asking myself, *Who needs this guy?*

I'm sure Henry also planned on consummating the marriage in other ways during our trip.

Unfortunately—for him—Henry didn't take well to the ocean. While he recuperated in his stateroom, I promptly struck up a friendship with two vacationing sisters, schoolteachers, who were fortunately disembarking in Bermuda as well.

Henry had reserved rooms at the Princess Hotel, an enormous pink palace right on the water. From the moment we stepped off the ship, the girls and I were inseparable. We went to shops, we rented bikes, we did all the touristy things. Henry always tagged along on all these outings. He didn't have other business, or other friends.

The only place he wouldn't follow us was to the beach. Not his style. He'd wait for us on the hotel veranda, broiling in his buttoned-down attire, knocking back whiskey and sodas, watching me and my new friends cavorting in the surf.

Using the sisters as a shield, I kept Henry at bay during our brief time in Bermuda.

I was determined to reap the benefits of having Henry Willson as an agent, but I had no intention of getting caught up in his mingling of the personal and the professional. I was grateful to Henry and felt I owed him a lot.

But I didn't owe him *that.*

BACK IN HOLLYWOOD, the PR started spinning even faster. I was interviewed and photographed countless times for movie magazines. Thanks to that smooth-talking Irish charm of his, Dick Clayton was even able to pull my mother—against her will—into the act. We were photographed together in the tiny apartment we shared in Beverly Hills. That took some persuading. My mom was quoted as urging me to "watch for the right girl and settle down."

Most of the stories these magazines cranked out were fabricated pieces of fluff, but it seemed to be what people wanted to read, and I was told that it was a surefire way of getting "the powers that be" to take notice of up-and-coming talent.

Here's how one of those puff pieces concluded: "And with Tab Hunter's luck—or is it courage?—or is it faith?—there's no doubt he'll get what he wants, just exactly when he wants it."

I can assure you that I did *not* get what I wanted when *Saturday Island*—renamed *Island of Desire* for American audiences—was finally released in August 1952.

The first time I saw *Island of Desire* it made me sick. The second time wasn't quite so bad. The third time . . . I got sick again.

Critics, by and large, shared my reaction. Consider this rave from the *Hollywood Reporter*: "Tab Hunter, the Marine, is probably a good physical type for the part but is quite inadequate as an actor; his performance is wooden and his action is ungainly."

Wood was a recurring theme in the reviews. Another critic remarked that "This blonde pretty-boy has all the acting ability of a calcified tree stump."

At least *Los Angeles Examiner* reviewer Shirle Duggan spared me a hatchet job: "Tab Hunter should really set off a clambake among the teenage film fans. Not only is he a better than average actor, but he also has the physique and looks to make feminine hearts flutter."

Miss Duggan, I was convinced, had been bribed.

Ignoring the less-than-sterling reviews, moviegoers lined up for *Island of Desire*. Meanwhile, I spent a lot of my time standing in a different line—the unemployment line.

Despite being the subject of a publicity barrage, I couldn't get work. I'd burned through my United Artists salary and was flat broke—not an uncommon predicament for Hollywood performers. Many faces familiar from movie and television screens skulked through the office of the California Department of Employment, on McCadden Place, just off Santa Monica Boulevard. The place could have been mistaken for a casting office.

Photographers hung around outside to catch pictures of me leaving, clutching my fifty-five bucks. That money had to last until the next Wednesday morning, when I'd reclaim my place in line for a fresh state-issued handout. Heading to that ugly redbrick government building, I'd pass a newsstand where the latest issues of *Photoplay* and *Movie Life* detailed my whirlwind life as a new screen sensation.

The contrast between what was written and what I was really enduring couldn't have been more ironic. "United Artists has so much faith in this young blond 'Sigh Guy' that they have gone all out in their build-up of him," one glossy rag declared. "Three major studios have offered him contracts on the strength of preview reactions. They are that sure the public will go for him. To *Motion Picture and Television Magazine* he is 'The Squeal Appeal Fella.'"

Obviously, Tab Hunter was slated to be the next big thing. But the phone never rang with the next big offer. Or the last little one. Major studio contracts? What a crock. Once the *Island of Desire* reviews were in, it seemed unanimous: my big break had blown up in my face.

I'd lived like a prince during production of my first movie. I had no concern for the boring responsibilities of daily life. Everything had been taken care of. In no time flat, that luxury was finished. Bills piled up relentlessly. Even if the big call had come, chances were my phone would already have been disconnected.

The Squeal Appeal Fella wasn't much different from any other confused, insecure, disorganized, unemployed, twenty-one-year-old kid.

Henry, however, advised his latest sensation to remain patient. It was out of the question that his *Island of Desire* star would return to any of the menial jobs I'd had while awaiting my "breakthrough." And taking smaller movie roles wasn't an option, because Henry was holding out for the bigger parts. There were probably jobs being offered that Henry didn't bother to tell me about, since he considered them beneath the status of Hollywood's hottest new leading man.

8

Fame's Waiting Room

SUMMER 1952. I'm a rising "star" now—like the ones I'd ogled from behind the glass of Wil Wright's ice cream parlor, flipping car keys to a uniformed actor-in-training. Looming all over town are billboards for *Island of Desire*. The movie is doing solid business around the world. My face is plastered all over newspapers and magazines.

On my arm is the cutest little up-and-comer in Hollywood, Debbie Reynolds. We'd just exited a movie premiere where photographers climbed all over themselves taking pictures of us. Pulled from the crowd onto the red carpet, we chatted and laughed our way through several radio and television interviews.

It all happened just that fast.

Standing there with Debbie, a tape loop was running in the back of my mind, a nagging, skeptical voice, repeating, in a tone of utter disbelief:

You're living the life of a movie star.

Then I looked down. It was shocking how short the pants were on my rented tuxedo. And the little voice said, *Next time you get paid for making a movie—if there is a next time—get yourself a tux that fits.* I made lots of those promises to myself. They'd eventually get me in serious trouble.

As the throng exited, the parking lot's loudspeaker started blaring: "Bring up Mr. Peck's car! Bring up Mr. Wayne's car!" Fans craned their necks for a glimpse of the stars climbing into their glamorous rides.

Waiting curbside, I grimaced when I heard, "Bring up Tab Hunter's car!" All eyes turned our way as Debbie and I walked to my unpaid-for junk heap, a 1941 Ford coupe that smoked like Oscar Levant. It was squeezed between the town's two fattest Fleetwoods. I flashed the valet a bogus grin and handed him a scrap of paper on which I'd written:

IOU $1—PLEASE HOLD TILL I GET A JOB

On bad days, I blamed Henry Willson for my odd predicament—great promotion, no parts. After all, what had he really done for me? He hadn't gotten me my big chance in *Island of Desire*—that was Paul Guilfoyle's doing, and Paul was connected to Dick Clayton, not Henry Willson. Besides the minuscule bit in *The Lawless*, Henry hadn't delivered any film work in more than four years.

For the first two of those years, I was a terrible client. I didn't care whether I made it as an actor or not. But after *Island of Desire*, I became determined. I wanted the financial rewards that went with being a performer, of course, and I wanted the grand lifestyle as well. But I also wanted to act—or at least to prove I *could* act.

I wondered if I was being punished for not playing along on that little side trip to Bermuda, but I knew in my heart that it wasn't Henry's fault my career stalled after *Island of Desire*. There was a clearer, more crushing reason: I wasn't leading-man material. In my debut, I came off as awkward and imma-

Arthur and Mary Frances (Debbie Reynolds) getting used to signing their new names.

ture, with a voice so high it squeaked. Clayton had always told me it needed work, and Dick was right about most everything.

Even though no offers were coming in, Henry still treated me well. He paid for private voice lessons with coaches Marie Stoddard and Lester Luther.

He'd still do the wining-and-dining routine, even if it didn't pay off in my visiting his swanky boudoir. "Dates" with Henry were now strictly on the level: he'd orchestrate nightclub meetings with industry insiders like *Variety*'s Army Archerd or the *Hollywood Reporter*'s Mike Connolly. Once in a while he'd score an audience with the real heavy hitters, nationally syndicated tastemakers Louella Parsons and Hedda Hopper. Louella liked Henry; she got a kick out of his sense of humor.

So did my mother, which was odd because she had no use for Hollywood types. When *Island of Desire* was released, Henry took my family out on the town to celebrate. Walt got leave from the navy and brought along his bride, Pat. It was one of the rare times we were all together, and Henry made it a memorable occasion. A magnificent host, he spent money like it was going out of style, convincing everyone that my career was in the most capable of hands. My mother may have hated *Island of Desire,* but she thought Henry Willson was a real charmer and that he had nothing but her son's best interests at heart.

She, of course, knew nothing about his "secret" reputation.

To the industry in-crowd, however, I had clearly become one of "Henry's boys." They probably assumed there was something sexual between us. I didn't care. I marched along and did what I was told, because I figured that's how I'd get work.

CREDIT, OR BLAME, for imprinting the image of Tab Hunter in the public's consciousness can't go to Henry Willson. By all rights, it goes to the fan magazines. Henry was surprised—delighted, yet surprised—by the number of requests that poured into his office for stories and photo layouts on Tab Hunter. *Silver Screen, Filmland, Modern Screen, Screenland, Movie Play, Movie Life*—all of them called, plus dozens more. It was these magazines that concocted my celebrity, completely out of proportion to my actual on-screen status.

The capper came toward the end of 1952. Readers of *Photoplay* voted Tab Hunter the #1 New Male Star in the magazine's annual popularity poll.

In this case, it's entirely appropriate to refer to "Tab Hunter" as a separate being, since I felt no connection between myself and this two-dimensional icon for which the public was clamoring.

The *Photoplay* award was presented during a luncheon ceremony, handed to me by none other than Tyrone Power. In my book he was the most handsome actor ever in the movies. I paid more attention to him in *Blood and Sand* than to either Linda Darnell or Rita Hayworth! Shaking his hand, I recalled a day when I was maybe fourteen years old, hanging out on the beach in Santa Monica. Loafing in the sun, I glanced up to see Tyrone Power running by, hand in hand with Lana Turner. Talk about a California fantasy! Turned out I was catching rays right behind Darryl Zanuck's beachfront home.

Lots of kids probably dreamed of meeting a star like Tyrone Power, but how many have actually lived it? Incredible coincidences like these were a hallmark of my early days in the business—like the thing with Linda Darnell's Christmas gift, years before I'd make a movie with her. Or crossing paths with Lana Turner, with whom I'd soon costar. While endlessly watching *Cloak and Dagger* at the Warners Theater, how could I have known that I'd make movies with both its stars, Gary Cooper and Lilli Palmer?

Kismet seemed to be working on my behalf, but enough Catholic indoctrination was still ingrained in me to make me guiltily question why I deserved such good fortune, over all the other struggling kids who so badly craved recognition and acceptance.

Tyrone Power presenting Lori Nelson and me with Photoplay *magazine awards, 1952.*

Was it because of how I looked? It was the only possible explanation. It wasn't my talent. The realization embarrassed me and made me self-conscious—just like it had in high school.

Not that I didn't appreciate what was happening. Who in that situation wouldn't? But I couldn't help feeling like a fish out of water. Why did so many people want to see me in these absurdly fake situations? Tab Hunter tries on a sport coat! Tab Hunter goes on a picnic! Tab Hunter water-skis!

Then things turned more surreal. The *New York Daily News* named Tab Hunter its Heartthrob of the Year. Topping that, when 1952's year-end theater receipts were totaled up, exhibitors declared Tab Hunter the #5 box-office attraction in America.

My popularity was spurred by magazine editors who recognized, and tapped into, a completely new readership—teenage girls. In the past, Hollywood made movies primarily for adults. Kids never really had movie stars of their own age to moon over, unless you want to count Mickey Rooney and Judy Garland as teenage sex objects . . . which I don't.

When a young girl developed a crush, hell and high water couldn't sway her loyalty. Take my word for it. Apparently editors, and, more important, their advertisers, discovered there was a mint to be made force-feeding desirable young celebrity bachelors to starry-eyed girls across America. It was those shrewd businessmen—not me—who were cashing in on the boy-next-door appeal of this Tab Hunter character.

My growing popularity—primarily in print—didn't go unnoticed in the offices of Henry Willson.

At that time, the winter of '52, I was stuck in the stable's second tier. That's not meant to sound like sour grapes. Henry, after all, was a gambler. His life revolved around searching for whatever "next big thing" could keep him at the table, keep the chips rolling in. He probably felt I'd crapped out with *Island of Desire*, which by this time had come and gone. But he kept me in play, one of the many hands he was holding. It soon became clear, however, that Henry was placing almost all his chips—a huge personal stake—on Rock Hudson.

Almost all of Henry's energy went into promoting Rock. In the time since I'd finished *Island of Desire,* Henry had gotten Rock parts in ten movies, from bits to supporting roles to second leads. He'd gone from being under personal contract to Raoul Walsh, to inking a long-term deal with Universal International. Yet Rock still hadn't landed a leading role, like I had right out of the gate. Despite that, I started to feel that Rock's steady progress was preferable to the sudden leading-man status that had fallen on me like a ton of bricks.

Thanks to the magazines, Henry realized he needed to do *something* for me. At Dick Clayton's prompting, Henry took one last roll of the dice on Tab Hunter. The plan seemed absurd, even a little embarrassing, considering the reality of my situation. But this was Hollywood, remember, where you're obligated at all times to keep the smile in place and act as though you're turning down offers left and right when you're really dodging bill collectors.

What Henry Willson did was send out a barrage of telegrams to virtually every producer in Hollywood, boldly announcing . . .

TAB HUNTER IS NOW AVAILABLE!

9

"Don't Worry . . .
It'll Only Play Drive-Ins"

THANK GOD FOR EDWARD SMALL. He took Henry's bait.

Small had been making movies since 1927, the year my mother arrived in this country. He'd started his show-business career in New York as a talent agent. Once he became an independent producer, he prospered among the bigger boys by adopting a conservative strategy, maintaining a tight rein on budgets, and keeping a low profile himself. So low, I can't recall ever meeting the man—even though he was the savior of Tab Hunter's acting career.

Small offered Henry Willson a two-picture deal for my services. My short-comings as an actor obviously didn't overwhelm the impact of Tab Hunter features filling the movie magazines. Small figured he could risk $750 a week, which is what he paid me to be in *Gun Belt* and *The Steel Lady*.

Although the script was no great shakes, I was eager to make *Gun Belt* because it was a western. That meant horses. We filmed it outside Hollywood, at the Korrigan Ranch, backdrop for practically every low-budget oater ever made. John Ford could afford to shoot on location in Monument Valley; Eddie Small was stuck with the San Fernando.

From the start, I was determined to gain the stuntmen's respect by showing that I could handle horses. One early scene called for my character, Chip Ringo, to race up to a team of runaways, grab the lead horses, and bring them to a halt. I told the director, Ray Nazarro, that I could do it myself. A single shot, no cuts necessary.

Everybody wanted to see the new kid pull off this stunt—which I did. After Nazarro yelled, "Cut!" I was feeling pretty good about myself. Up sauntered an old guy with a face like ten miles of rough road: "Lemme tell you something, kid." He pulled me aside.

"We all know you can ride," he said, giving me a flinty gaze. "But you see that guy over there?" He nodded to a cowboy sitting on the sidelines, dressed in duds identical to mine.

"So can he. That's your ridin' double, and he's gotta eat, too. So why not let him do the shot? Then you tell the director to cover you with a closer angle. Everybody'll be happy that way . . . got it?"

He winked. I got the message, loud and clear. The movie business is bigger than one person.

That was my introduction to Jack Conner, stuntman extraordinaire. We ended up making many films together, and he and his wife, Kay, became two of my closest friends. Under Jack's rugged veneer was one of the keenest minds I'd ever encounter. "I didn't go to school to eat my lunch," he'd always say.

Taking the tip, I spent my time between takes studying salty old veterans like John Dehner and Jack Elam, who made acting seem effortless. Walleyed Elam, in particular, was a natural in front of the camera. I was surprised to learn that he'd backed into acting. He'd been Eddie Small's accountant!

The Steel Lady was a more interesting script than *Gun Belt*. A team of oil surveyors crash-land in the Sahara and uncover a buried German tank. There are stolen diamonds, feuds between the starving crew, and a running battle with Berber pirates (the Hollywood kind—with British accents).

Rod Cameron starred, but John Dehner and Richard Erdman stole the picture with juicy, hard-bitten character roles. I was the fresh-faced radio operator. The challenge was to appear convincing as I spewed all sorts of technical jargon I didn't really understand. Halfway through the story I get shot, and spend the rest of the film in a sweaty, near-death delirium.

When *Gun Belt* and *The Steel Lady* were eventually released, in the summer and fall of 1953, my billing was ten times the size of guys like Erdman, Elam, and Dehner, even though their performances carried those movies. The greenhorn got bigger play than the veterans. Eddie Small was getting maximum return on his modest investment. He recognized that "Tab Hunter" had become catnip to teenage girls, who normally would have steered clear of a couple of action movies aimed at a male audience.

Small understood this strange business, even if I, at the time, didn't. Back in the twenties, at the age of fifteen, he'd formed his first talent agency with the slogan: "Personality is a commodity."

• • •

MY "PERSONALITY" WAS pulling in about a thousand pieces of fan mail a week by the end of 1953. Despite my best efforts, plenty went unanswered. That's because I had to do it myself. I couldn't afford a service, like lots of successful actors used to handle their fan mail.

With the exception of the few weeks spent making those two features, I still had no work and no career. Half of my salary went to taxes, Screen Actors Guild dues, and Henry's commission. You'd think by age twenty-two I'd have matured enough to have gotten control of my finances. Not a chance.

The kind of hand-to-mouth existence I'd lived growing up teaches some people the value of saving a buck. Not me. I never *had* money, so I never learned to save it, except where horseback riding was concerned. I didn't have the slightest idea how to create a budget, let alone stick to it. For example . . .

I decided to boost my morale with a present to myself, something I'd always wanted. I bought my first horse. In honor of a friend, Maggie Stewart, who'd been arrested for drunk driving leaving a horse show, I named it Out on Bail. I was delighted . . . for a few months. I had to sell the horse when I couldn't afford the costs of boarding, shoeing, vet fees, and show expenses.

Did I learn a lesson? Quite the contrary. I bought a '53 flamingo-red Ford convertible, even though it put me deep in hock.

I was now on my own. My mother was by herself in the small Beverly Hills apartment we had shared. One morning I called her up and said, "Look out the window and tell me what you see."

"No one is outside, Arthur. Just an automobile, parked at the curb."

"I'll be right over—with the keys."

It was a brand-new beige 1953 Chevy. Nobody'd ever given her a gift like that before, and for once she couldn't conceal her excitement. Mom flipped.

So did Dick Clayton, only not in a good way. He saw what was happening, and time and again he'd lecture: "You may be on your way, but you're a freelance actor, you're not getting a weekly check. Another dry spell could hit. No pictures, no money. You've got to build a reserve to fall back on."

This sage advice went in one ear and emerged, unmolested, out the other. When I had money, I spent it—as fast as it came in. The world, after all, was trying to convince me I was a movie star. So I figured I'd better start acting like one.

I became a fixture in the Hollywood circuit, offering newspapers and magazines the perfect image of a rising star with the world by the tail. My picking and choosing from a Whitman's Sampler of gorgeous starlets was dutifully recorded, month by month, allowing teenage girls around the world to track my love life.

All a ruse, of course. Most of the young actresses I dated were, like me, gamely fostering the impression that they were "hot," even if they hadn't worked in months. I was linked to starlets such as Gloria Gordon, Pat Crowley, Betty Barker, and Terry Moore, as well as many others. Having ourselves described as "an item" or "deeply involved" was a small price to pay for access to lavish parties overflowing with delicacies otherwise unavailable to actors living on saltines, sardines, and soda pop.

These high-life snapshots fueled the fantasies of young girls, letting them dream that one day they might meet Tab Hunter, the same way Art Gelien met Tyrone Power and Linda Darnell, two of *his* adolescent fantasy figures.

There was an underlying pattern to this conspiracy of wishful thinking. Tab Hunter, and other young, handsome actors like him, were only useful as bachelors. America's nubile class needed to believe they actually had a chance! But what was the theme of virtually every story? *Marriage!* In order for lustful adolescent urges to have the culture's seal of approval, every feature story, every interview, had to conclude with the actor's wistful admission that, beneath the glitz and glamour, all he truly craved was a simple life of wedded bliss.

I learned quickly how the game worked, and coughed up the required answers. If I strayed off target, no problem—the writers simply made up what they needed, such as:

"Sure, I want to get married—but who knows when?"

"I know the perfect girl will eventually come along, and things will take their obvious course."

"Next to a successful career, there's nothing I want more than to be successfully married."

On occasion, a kernel of truth found its way out of the fluff:

"Sometimes I wonder why I'm unable to concentrate on just one girl for any length of time . . . It might be a matter of self-defense on my part: that I know I shouldn't get married at this time, and consequently, every time I get serious about a girl, subconsciously I start looking for someone else . . ."

OF ALL THE GIRLS I dated during the early days of my career, only two developed into genuine friendships.

Debbie Reynolds was the first movie actress I ever dated. We met in 1949, right before she made a big splash with the "Aba Daba Honeymoon" number from MGM's *Two Weeks with Love*. Mary Frances—that's how I always knew her—didn't put on any airs, which I appreciated. She lived with her family in a simple little house in Burbank. When she made some money, she had a pool built in the backyard; it took up the whole lot.

We saw a lot of each other during the early 1950s. Our favorite hangout was the New Follies Burlesque in downtown L.A. Debbie was a bawdy gal, with a delicious sense of humor, and we'd whoop and holler and have a fine old time. We were such regulars that over time we watched one stripper rise from chorus girl to star attraction.

Debbie was ambitious but suffered little anxiety about her career. While I constantly worried where the next job was coming from, she enjoyed the security of a long-term contract at MGM. The studio had mapped out a strategy, guiding her step-by-step, coaching her singing and dancing, arranging all her publicity, managing her steady progress in a way any freelancer would have envied.

I wasn't jealous, because I simply don't think that way. But I was certainly aware of the advantages Debbie had being part of the MGM "family." When she broke out as a star in 1952's *Singin' in the Rain*, it seemed preordained. I started hoping that I'd land a studio contract, like the one Henry had gotten Rock at Universal International. Maybe then I'd enjoy a little financial security.

My other "steady" during those days was Lori Nelson. She was from Santa Fe, and her childhood was a nonstop succession of beauty pageants and talent contests, culminating in her signing a seven-year contract with Universal in 1950, when she was seventeen years old.

She was the studio's wholesome all-American ingenue, in movies like *Ma and Pa Kettle at the Fair*, *Francis Goes to West Point*, and, appropriately enough, *The All-American*, where she played Tony Curtis's good-girl love interest (opposite Mamie Van Doren's bad girl).

Some actresses come at you like a Mack truck—me, me, me, me, me. Lori, by contrast, was a quiet, reserved girl. Under that glamorous facade was a homebody. We shared the feeling that our being in the movies was both accidental *and* inevitable. Lori even seemed a bit scared of show business, which made me empathize with her all the more.

Although Debbie and I still dated after she hit it big with *Singin' in the Rain*, it was Lori and I who became a hot item in the gossip columns, where writers worked up a lather about our supposed engagement.

A committed relationship with Lori, something deeper than the pal-around way I'd always dealt with women, did seem like a possibility. On the surface, we were completely compatible. More than once I thought about bringing her home, introducing her to my mother, and announcing, *Mom, meet the girl I'm going to marry.*

Of course, I never did introduce Lori Nelson to Gertrude Gelien.

Mother would have scoffed. She didn't like movie types and would have been disappointed if I'd gotten engaged to an actress. Anyway, that's what I told myself.

In truth, the disappointment would have been all Lori's.

If we'd followed the program, she would have been getting engaged to a very confused young man. I believed, wholeheartedly—still do—that a person's happiness depends on being true to themselves. It was a lesson my mother, and Dick Clayton, drilled into me. The dilemma, of course, was that being true to myself—and I'm talking sexually now—was impossible in 1953.

I didn't know who I was. More to the point, I hadn't admitted it to myself.

At the same time I was pondering marriage to Lori Nelson, I was involved in a relationship with one of the best young figure skaters in the world, Ronnie Robertson. The way teenage girls were infatuated with me, I was infatuated with Ronnie.

I first saw him skate at an amateur ice show in his hometown of Paramount, California. It was 1950, and this little redheaded teenager did a solo that knocked everyone for a loop. He was a cat on his feet, his spins were blurs, and he had style to spare. I was in awe.

During the next few years, I was Ronnie's biggest supporter, convinced he was destined to be the next Dick Button.

Ronnie's phenomenal gifts set him apart from everyone else. I could tell that he was putting up the same kinds of barriers against the world that I'd erected when I was a teenager. It made him seem cocky and aloof, like he had a chip on his shoulder. His attitude wasn't going to win any admirers in the skating world.

As my own career was starting to develop, I followed Ronnie's progress, determined to encourage and protect and support him. He had a burning desire to do things on the ice that had never been done before. He learned to block everything out of his mind that could deter him. I wanted that to rub off on me. Although his talent, desire, and athleticism were certainly appealing,

I was especially drawn to the vulnerability Ronnie worked so hard to hide. That's what I could *really* relate to.

Eventually, we had a physically intimate relationship. I hesitate to use the word *relationship* for two reasons: first, we didn't really see enough of each other to be in a "relationship"; second, it wasn't possible, in the early fifties, to even put a name on it—two young men, both in the public eye, in a *relationship?*

It was inconceivable. Even to us.

We shared something we wanted, it felt right, we allowed it to happen. Even if we *could* have talked about it, I doubt we would have.

If some people made snide comments behind our backs, it didn't even register on us. It didn't concern me what people, even Ronnie's family, might have been thinking. It's not like we had to *deny* anything—in 1953 homosexuality was pretty much denied by the culture at large. To most folks, Ronnie and I were good buddies, sharing the ice. Few people considered what else we were sharing. Those who did wouldn't have dreamed of making comments publicly. Such things simply weren't talked about.

Ronnie and I watch Muriel Reich perform a layback spin at Lake Placid. Ronnie's sweater, a gift from me, was decorated with school figures to remind him to practice.

Fear that we might be "found out" nagged me, certainly, especially as my career picked up steam and I had more to lose. My greater concern, however, was internal. *Be true to yourself.* The concept was essential, but it was a struggle to know exactly what it meant, to consider where it might lead, and to understand the consequences.

Did I owe it to Hollywood—which had given me an opportunity to live out a fantasy—to become a real-life version of the stereotype it was creating of me? Would I have to give everything back if I turned out to be someone else entirely? And who *was* that someone else? Hell if I knew.

All I was sure of was that being with Ronnie conveniently eliminated any chance of a commitment to Lori. Even if I hadn't been a public figure, I wouldn't have revealed my secret to her. I was still too young, too confused, and too guilty to accept what I *might* be.

I'd never expect any woman to accept less than 100 percent—which I couldn't give. Some people could live that double life, but I wasn't one of them.

I could ignore all these conflicts when I had work. For my next movie role, the casting director was a thirteen-year-old girl. Doesn't that make perfect sense?

Englishman Aubrey Wisberg, who'd written the original story for *The Steel Lady,* was producing an updated version of Robert Louis Stevenson's classic adventure tale, *Treasure Island.* While Wisberg was visiting associates in New York, a friend of his daughter's wouldn't quit bugging him about casting Tab Hunter—her dreamboat—in his next picture. All I can say to that young lady is, *Thanks for nothing.*

There are bad movies . . . then there's *Return to Treasure Island.*

For this abomination I reunited with director Ewald André (E. A.) Dupont, who'd managed to forge something credible from *The Steel Lady's* nonexistent budget. Dupont had been a highly respected silent-film director in his native Germany, creating masterpieces like *Variety, Moulin Rouge,* and *Picadilly.* Once he came to this country, and pictures started talking, the quality of his films deteriorated. By the time he encountered Tab Hunter, he'd become a contract director for Aubrey Wisberg.

Return to Treasure Island was Wisberg's lavish crack at an A picture. My costar was a charming and sexy English actress named Dawn Addams, whom Wisberg collared when MGM dropped her contract.

The first day of shooting was up the coast in Palos Verdes, on a barren, rocky stretch of beach. It was substituting for the Caribbean, where I was supposed to be shipwrecked. (Why was I always *stranded* in movies?) This certainly wasn't Jamaica. Not a palm tree or coconut in sight. In the script I've been marooned for quite a while, so whiskers were in order. The makeup guy hung the World's Phoniest Beard on me, then marched me to the boss for approval.

Dupont gave me a gimlet-eyed stare. That's all it took. In his heavy German accent, the veteran director declared, "Jesus Christ—this is the biggest piece of shit I've ever directed in my life." This, from the man whose two previous pictures were *Problem Girls* with Mara Corday and *The Neanderthal Man,* starring Beverly Garland.

Maybe he was right. *Return to Treasure Island* prompted Dawn Addams to immediately marry Prince Don Vittorio Massimo and move to Italy. It prompted Dupont to never make another movie. *His* decision or not, I don't know. For my part, whatever strides I'd made as an actor were lost in the stink of this fiasco. Even my mother weighed in with a brutally frank assessment: "You were lousy," she pronounced, bolting from the theater lobby.

Dick Clayton tried to cheer me up, saying: "Don't worry . . . it'll only play drive-ins."

MY CONFIDENCE TOOK another hit when I lost the one decent live television part I was offered. It was an out-and-out comedy. You can fake a lot of things as an actor; being funny isn't one of them. I was shown the door after only a few minutes of rehearsals.

Dawn Addams and I contemplate the fate of our careers while trapped in Return to Treasure Island. *(Photo © Metro-Goldwyn-Mayer Studio, Inc. All rights reserved. Courtesy of MGM CLIP & STILL.)*

What difference did popularity make? *I couldn't deliver!* I'd been blithely imagining, despite its fits and starts, that my career had only one direction—up. Being unceremoniously dumped should have devastated me. But part of me was relieved. Whether it was in front of cameras or an audience, the thought of performing *live,* without the safety of multiple takes, absolutely terrified me.

On top of that, I still had bad memories from the previous year, when I'd read for the coveted role of Turk Fisher in *Come Back, Little Sheba*. I was eager to take on more challenging parts, and this was one of the best for an actor my age. The bug had bitten me. I desperately wanted that part. Halfway through the reading, the director, Daniel Mann, stopped me cold. "You don't need to go on," he said.

Richard Jaeckel got Turk. The experience left me convinced that I'd never get beyond being a second-rate B actor, an assessment *Return to Treasure Island* seemed to cement. Casting directors clearly believed that complex characters were beyond me. I began to wonder if they weren't right.

Something dramatic needed to happen, literally, for me to overcome my incredible insecurity.

A PRODUCER NAMED Jim Terry was planning a revival of Thornton Wilder's *Our Town,* with the idea of staging a series of shows in different towns around California. He suggested to Dick Clayton that I'd be good for the part of George Gibbs. Granted, I wasn't Terry's first choice. With his eye on that growing crop of young ticket buyers, he'd gone after Robert Wagner, then Jeffrey Hunter. But 20th Century Fox, to which both actors were under contract, wouldn't let them loose.

I was thrilled to be asked. The pinup boy would be thrown into an American classic, alongside trained, disciplined *thespians*. Here was the chance to prove myself as a legitimate actor.

The infamous Mount Vernon Junior High production of *The Wedding Shoes* was, up to that point, my only onstage experience. In contrast, the part of George Gibbs's sweetheart, Emily, was offered to a respected stage actress practically born on the boards, Marilyn Erskine. She'd begun performing in her native New York at three and had worked consistently since. She'd just scored terrific reviews opposite Keefe Brasselle in *The Eddie Cantor Story*, was dating singing star Merv Griffin, and was on the verge of stardom.

Somewhere in her hectic schedule, Marilyn Erskine found time to watch *Island of Desire*.

"I won't do your play if *that* clumsy ox is in it!" she told the producer.

I wanted to wring her neck.

Fortunately, cooler heads prevailed. Jim Terry convinced Marilyn Erskine to at least watch me do a read-through. Luckily, my voice had dropped an octave since *Island*. Once I'd finished, Erskine said to Terry, "You're the producer. *You* want him. I'll just have to assume you know what you're doing."

Then she turned to me: "Buster, you need work. Let's get to it!"

During the three weeks that led up to *formal* rehearsals, Marilyn Erskine put me through her personalized version of actor's boot camp. Locked in her apartment, we went at the script all day, every day, sometimes till 4:00 a.m. We dissected the character's background, analyzed every nuance, visualized his behavior and how it could best be expressed.

Marilyn challenged, provoked, and inspired me. She got me to approach acting on a much deeper level than I ever had before.

Own Town premiered in Taft, a tiny town on a barren stretch of Highway 33 in California's central valley. It was Jim Terry's inspiration to open in a place akin to Grover's Corners, the small town depicted in Wilder's play. Taft had never seen anything like us. The town's lone auditorium was packed, probably for the first time since they'd crowned the homecoming queen. If I was going to fall on my face, at least it'd be in some out-of-the-way place and not splashed all over the trades the next day.

As butterflies swarmed in my stomach, Harriet Erskine, Marilyn's mom, presented me with an opening-night gift, a bottle of Aphrodisia cologne. Always one for superstition, I dabbed a little on for luck. Then word filtered backstage that lots of people had made the trip up from Hollywood, including a number of girls I'd been dating: Terry Moore, Debbie, Lori. They'd come to offer moral support to the Squeal Appeal Fella for what was, truly, his acting debut.

Suddenly I was onstage. When I glanced at Marilyn, I felt in her smile a secret dose of encouragement. My first line came out fine. From that moment on, my acting career began in earnest.

To understand why that night was special, I need to compare acting to ice-skating. You skate alone. Drop your shoulder too much on a landing, and you're flat on your ass. To avoid such embarrassment, a skater has only himself to rely on. I'd approached acting the same way—in isolation.

That night in Taft, performing with veterans like Edgar Buchanan and

WARE-HAZELTON ATTRACTION

LOBERO THEATRE

THURS. and FRI. NITES — NOV. 19 and 20 — 8:30 P. M.

FRIDAY MATINEE 3:00 P. M. — SEATS ON SALE AT LOBERO THEATRE
Nites: $4.20-3.60-3.00-2.40 Incl. Tax — Matinees: $3.00-2.40-1.80 Incl. Tax

AMERICAN THEATRE ARTS, INC.
PRESENTS

IN PERSON

EDGAR BUCHANAN   MARILYN ERSKINE   TAB HUNTER

in

THORNTON WILDER'S PLAY

'OUR TOWN'

CAST OF TWENTY

"One of the great plays of our day"

"One of the most important theatrical experiences of this generation."

ALMIRA SESSIONS

JAMES TERRY, Producer   CHARLES W. CHRISTENBERRY, Director

Almira Sessions, it dawned on me that acting *isn't* like skating. It requires the same level of concentration, but your imagination must kick in. You have to divorce yourself *from* yourself and become part of the ensemble. Slip-ups aren't fatal. Someone will be there, literally, to catch you if you stumble. That night I let go of the pressure I'd always been putting on myself to *perform*. I relaxed, and for the first time I was truly *in* character.

"Thornton Wilder might very well have had Tab Hunter in mind for the role of George Gibbs, so well did the young Hunter play it," wrote one critic.

Can an actor ask for more?

Honoring that magical opening night in Taft, I always applied a touch of cologne before any show—no matter how lousy it smelled—to recall the good luck I got from Harriet Erskine. As for her daughter . . .

Marilyn Erskine pointed me in the right direction. Without her, I'd never have been prepared for what was coming.

10

Battle Cry

ONE OF MY HORSE PALS, Danny Wills, invited me to move with him back to Bluemont, Virginia, to work on the horse farm he was going to buy. The adopted son of a wealthy Connecticut family, Danny had burned out on Hollywood after a two-year trial as an actor. He had only one film to his credit, a bit in 1952's *Sailor Beware*. By contrast, I was (supposedly) Mr. Popularity. But to Danny it was obvious that horses, not Hollywood, were our destiny. It was hard to argue, once bills outpaced the press clippings.

As December approached, I was hopelessly in debt and disgusted. "I can't keep up this farce," I groused to Dick Clayton. "There's no place for me in pictures. It's high time I quit kidding myself."

I was dining out one night with Marilyn Erskine and her beau, Merv Griffin.

"I'm reading a book that has the perfect part for you," Merv said, whetting my appetite.

Battle Cry was a current best seller by first-time novelist Leon Uris. It told the story—multiple stories, actually—of a battalion of marines, weary veterans and raw recruits, following them from boot camp through combat in the South Pacific. Uris had joined the Marine Corps after dropping out of high school, and the novel was a thinly veiled account of his own World War II experiences.

Having watched me perform opposite Marilyn in *Our Town,* Merv thought *Battle Cry*'s Danny Forrester, an all-American boy from Baltimore who gets a crash course in love and war, was tailor-made for Tab Hunter. When he noted that Warner Bros. had already snapped up the rights to the novel and had Uris working on the screenplay, my appetite *really* kicked in.

I badgered Henry Willson to get me a meeting at Warners. At the very least,

I rated a *test,* I argued. Henry noted that Warners was scrambling to cast the movie ASAP, so it wouldn't take long to learn if they were interested in me. *Battle Cry* quickly assumed symbolic stature as the make-or-break point in my career. If I got the part, I'd commit to Hollywood. If I didn't, then I'd head east with Danny and devote myself to the horses.

Based on my track record, I worried that a major studio might think the part beyond my reach. I prepared for the worst.

I'D HAVE BEEN A nervous wreck if it wasn't for the Happy Hut.

During this anxious period I lived in relative serenity at 255 North Barrington, in Brentwood. It was a fenced-off nursery with a guest cottage in the corner, a tranquil little hideaway tucked among a tangle of flora and fauna.

"Bless this house," my mother had said with a sigh the first time she visited the cozy nest. And we did, with a simple prayer of gratitude—something I've made a point of doing from then on, everyplace I lived. As usual, my mother's advice was sage, but this time it was dispensed in a strange, disconnected manner. She seemed distant, slightly spooky.

Over the previous months, her behavior had grown increasingly odd. She had always been high strung, working so hard to make ends meet, wanting so much for her two kids. She could be like an exposed nerve end. She also spent an awful lot of time alone, reading, thinking. She studied obsessively and would slam down forceful opinions, like bricks that built a protective wall around her. It cut her off from people, me included.

I wanted to be with her, wanted to help her—but it was so difficult. Sometimes she'd fly off the handle for no apparent reason or be seized by fits of laughing or crying. But she'd always managed to rein it in, get herself under control. Now she'd started to spontaneously pray, out loud. I passed it off as part of her eccentricity, or maybe menopause. What did I know?

If I hadn't been so self-absorbed with my erratic career and newfound friends and partners, maybe I'd have recognized the signs of an imminent crisis. Or maybe that's just the hindsight that comes with a guilty conscience.

Whatever the case, that day she visited the Happy Hut we both gave thanks for Watson Webb. He owned the estate that contained the cottage, and he let me stay there on the cuff. Watson lived around the corner, in the main house on Crescenda. Many evenings he'd have me over for a glass of sherry and a quiet dinner, prepared by his housekeeper, Bernice.

As usual, it was Dick Clayton who'd brokered the intro. Dick was pure genius at hooking you up with the person you needed, when you needed them most: a natural-born agent.

Watson Webb came from a prominent East Coast family. Two, in fact. His father, James Watson Webb Sr., was a descendant of Cornelius Vanderbilt, of the New York Central Railroad dynasty. His mother, Electra Havemeyer, was the daughter of Henry Osborne Havemeyer, who founded the American Sugar Refining Company. Watson was too much his own man to fit comfortably into his blue-blooded pigeonhole, so after graduating from Yale in 1938, he came to Hollywood to make his own mark.

After a few years as an apprentice film cutter, he was made chief of the film-editing department at 20th Century Fox. Watson cut dozens of features, including *State Fair, The Dark Corner, Cheaper by the Dozen, Kiss of Death, Broken Arrow, A Letter to Three Wives,* and his favorite, *The Razor's Edge.* He was great pals with that film's star, Tyrone Power. (Watson's hands appear on a commemorative postage stamp, issued in 2003, celebrating American film-making. It's from a photo taken while he was editing *The Razor's Edge.*)

One of five heirs to a vast family fortune, Watson Webb wasn't in show business for the money. He could have written a check to buy 20th Century Fox. In fact, he'd retired from Fox in 1952, after finishing his last picture, *With a Song in My Heart.* He dabbled in directing and even cast me in a television show later that year, *While We're Young,* with Claudette Colbert and Patrick Knowles.

Watson's full-time job was as a philanthropist and gentleman of leisure. He was conservative, straight-laced, and thoroughly refined: so old-school, you were never quite sure if he was gay or not. At least *I* wasn't. He kept his private life *private.* I learned a lot from him.

In addition to the Brentwood spread, he had a retreat at Lake Arrowhead. He'd bought Hilltop from Jules Stein, the legendary founder of the Music Corporation of America. It was an extraordinary, lavish retreat, at which Watson regularly hosted his many moviemaking pals, Cary Grant, Judy Garland, Rock Hudson, and Marilyn Monroe among them. Debbie Reynolds and I spent weekends there water-skiing. That's where I met Hollywood's other Hunter— Jeffrey—and his fabulous wife, Barbara Rush.

In my eyes, they were the ideal Hollywood couple, the model I'd need to emulate if I was ever to be perceived as "normal." I put Hank (his real name) and Barbara on a pedestal and told myself that if they ever fell off—well, there would be the proof that a perfect marriage was impossible in this business.

BY MID-DECEMBER, as I was seriously considering packing my bags for Bluemont, Virginia, Henry finally called: Solly Biano, top casting director at Warner Bros., wanted to meet me. I went in the next day for a once-over. Mr. Biano thought I had the kind of all-American appeal that was right for the role of Danny—they'd test me.

I went straight to a bookstore and bought a copy of *Battle Cry*, hitting up Dick for the $3.75 cover price. Business expense, I figured. Rushing home, I devoured all five-hundred-some pages, a miracle, considering my limited attention span in those days.

The character of Danny reminded me of Walt, an upright guy eager to serve his country. By this time, my brother had already been in the navy for five years. Since I'd emulated Walt all through childhood, it wouldn't be a stretch to base my performance on him. There was plenty of me in there, too: I could have signed "Danny Forrester" on my Coast Guard enlistment papers.

Overnight, I went from easy-come, easy-go to obsessive-compulsive. I worked up a twenty-page analysis of the character, like I'd done for George Gibbs in *Our Town*. My dog-eared copy of *Battle Cry* grew dense with crib notes. It was the first time I'd identified so strongly with a character, and I wanted that part more than any other I'd been offered.

I took it as a good omen that Raoul Walsh was directing *Battle Cry*—he was, after all, the first movie director I'd ever seen in action, back in '48, when Henry took me on the lot to meet Rock Hudson.

Walsh directed me in three tests before the Christmas holidays, all with different actresses. In the story, Danny leaves behind his hometown sweetheart, Kathy, when he heads for boot camp in San Diego. Once there, he has an affair with Elaine, a lonely—and sexy—military wife, married to a "dollar-a-year man," who manages the local USO canteen.

Phyllis Thaxter played Elaine in the first test. She was brilliant, and I figured she had the part sewn up. I also tested with Meg Myles, who had two big things going for her, encased in a 42D brassiere.

Walsh made his priorities clear in a memo he sent to Steve Trilling, Jack Warner's right-hand man: "Will leave it to you to get three heavy-breasted chickens for the roles of Kathy, Elaine, and Pat," he wrote. So maybe Meg had the inside track.

The third test was with Dorothy Malone, a down-to-earth Texan with a bombshell figure, a combination of Phyllis and Meg. We were completely at ease with each other and threw off genuine sparks.

Pat Crowley and Mona Freeman tested for Kathy, my teenage sweetheart. Lucy Marlow and Margaret O'Brien were also considered. Fifteen-year-old Susan Strasberg, daughter of Method-acting teacher Lee Strasberg, gave a strong audition but came across as too young.

Battle Cry was shaping up as the studio's most expensive production of 1954, which led to plenty of excitement, and anxiety, over the casting. Elia Kazan, a powerful theater director who'd successfully moved into movies, convinced the studio to send a crew east to test a New York actor named James Dean—a Kazan discovery—for the role of Danny.

Also up for the role was Paul Newman. He and Joanne Woodward, who were starring in the Broadway production of *Picnic*, tested under the watchful eye of production executive Bill Orr, Jack Warner's son-in-law. Orr was unimpressed: "[They] came in with a preconceived idea of what they wanted to do in the scene, which consisted of . . . rolling around the mattress and the floor, leaping to their feet, staging a boxing match, rolling her up in the blanket, and a few other sundry peccadilloes."

January was nerve-racking. Knowing that several of Henry's other "boys" were up for the role of Danny didn't help. It was the nature of the beast, I realized, but it still didn't sit right. I wanted my agent behind *me*, 100 percent. Henry, of course, was hedging. It wouldn't bother him if Tab Hunter didn't get the part—as long as it went to another Henry Willson client.

If you want loyalty, don't look for it in Hollywood.

Soon the studio began announcing the actors chosen for various parts. Van Heflin was cast. Aldo Ray was cast. James Whitmore was cast. Raymond Massey was cast. Eventually, the entire battalion was filled in—except for Danny Forrester. There were rumors that Dick Davalos was the front-runner. Still undecided, the head honchos called me in for yet another test. This time I filmed a scene with Aldo Ray and James Whitmore. I knew I did poorly, and left the studio certain that I'd ruined my best chance.

A week passed. The powers that be remained silent.

An advance crew was scheduled to begin location shooting in Puerto Rico the first week of February—two weeks away! Contracts had been signed with the Department of Defense, allowing Warner Bros. to use actual Marine maneuvers as part of the film. The military wasn't about to postpone its war games to accommodate a bunch of make-believe marines.

On February 1, 1954, Henry called me to his office. With precious little fanfare, he announced that I'd been picked to play Danny Forrester. The final test with Aldo and Jim Whitmore had cemented it, he said—proving I was the worst judge of my own work. I was handed a contract that made me a Warners employee for six months. At the end of that term, the studio had the option of giving me a long-term deal or cutting me loose. Popping out from all the legalese were the crucial numbers: $500 per week, payable every Wednesday, for twenty-six weeks.

"Don't take too long to look it over," Henry told me. "Sign it and let's go— you ship out in two weeks."

Hut, two, three, four—I was in the Marine Corps!

A PLANELOAD OF Hollywood soldiers stormed Vieques, Puerto Rico, on February 17, 1954. The island was twenty miles long, five miles wide, and had only three towns. The battalion lived in a tent city, nicknamed Camp Hollywood, where we shared cold showers and outdoor latrines. It teemed with scorpions, field mice, and billions of mosquitoes. Thankfully, the schedule called for only eighteen days of location work. *Battle Cry* was no *Island of Desire.*

One of the supporting actors, Bill Campbell, set the tone: "Look at it as if we're all away at summer camp," he recommended. I was so excited, the miserable conditions didn't bother me a bit. I was determined to do a great job and earn the respect I craved.

The Marine war games, which would climax our shooting schedule, included a massive amphibious landing, with five thousand troops hitting the beach. In the midst of it would be numerous camera crews, entrusted with seamlessly fitting the thespians into the staged combat.

Our troupe—stocked with wonderful young actors like Campbell, John Lupton, L. Q. Jones, Perry Lopez, Tommy Cook, Carleton Young, and Fess Parker—quickly established a camaraderie. We were determined to measure up in the estimation of Blood 'n' Guts Raoul and in the eyes of the real marines all around us. We even challenged them to touch football games on the beach. Aldo Ray, Perry Lopez, Carleton Young, and yours truly waxed the hell out of a four-man Marine squad in our first set-to. It got us some respect, not to mention agonized muscles. I hadn't played football since my days at St. John's Military Academy.

Aldo quickly emerged as the leader of the dogfaces. He formed an ad hoc drinking society called the FEOLOs, which stood for "Fuck Everybody or Lose Out." He'd captain evening forays into Isabel Segunda, a grungy little town at the tip of the island with a two-pronged economy: bars and whores. The FEOLOs spent many an hour at a saloon called La Bocachica, partying with the locals and downing vast amounts of rum and orange juice. We steered clear of the working girls, dancing instead with amateur senoritas, under the watchful, sometimes hostile gaze of their chaperones.

If you got thirsty again on the way back to Camp Hollywood, there was a USO officer's club. A bottle of Bacardi cost seventy-five cents. Friday nights, cocktails were only a dime.

I became the envy of all the marines once photos got passed around of me water-skiing at Hilltop with Debbie Reynolds. She was their ideal girl. Watson Webb, a dutiful letter writer, had sent the pictures in with one of his regular letters. I also received a few strange epistolary ramblings from my mother—nothing new. Her letters were always dense, handwritten diatribes: The World According to Gertrude Gelien.

I had a reputation as a letter writer myself and borrowed a typewriter from the production office to send notes to Mother, Dick, and Watson. "I was able

"Blood 'n' Guts" Raoul Walsh directs a tender moment with Mona Freeman and me in Battle Cry. (Photo © Warner Bros. Pictures, Inc. All rights reserved.)

to buy everybody a round of drinks for three dollars," I told him. "I felt like the Watson Webb of Vieques!" Coincidentally, I mentioned, our evening movie at camp that night was *Above and Beyond,* featuring Marilyn Erskine.

During the first week, we did more drinking than acting. I rationalized it as practice. In the novel, my character gets thoroughly shitfaced at the San Diego USO. I'd nail that, no problem, with all this offshore research. I hoped that scene had survived in the screenplay.

Frankly, I hoped there *was* a screenplay.

All we'd been given upon leaving Los Angeles were ten pages, mostly action stuff. After several scriptless days on location, Van Heflin blew his stack. I expected him to grab a radio, crank it up, and holler, *We need words, damn it! Words!*

Typically we'd get reveille at 6:00 a.m., arrive at the location at 7:30, and wait until 2:00 p.m. for the first take. There were no *scenes* to shoot, just endless marching and reaction shots, while the second unit was off capturing explosive battle footage during the actual war games. Many of the actors, with Walsh's blessing, came up with their own incidental dialogue.

Then the rains came, knocking us off schedule. At the rate we were going, we'd wrap by summer. Walsh finally cabled Warners, through the San Juan office, SEND SCRIPTS OR TELL THE BEST WRITER IN HOLLYWOOD TO GET HIS ASS DOWN HERE . . . FAST! Normally, nothing fazed the grizzled old pro, which made him, in the studio's eyes, the perfect director for a sprawling big-budget production.

He'd refer to some of the cast as "dogmeat" and rarely gave us more than the simplest directions, like "Shag ass up that hill," or "Okay, boys, put some sex in it!" His forte was action, not the subtleties of the actor's craft.

Finally, about a week in, forty pages of script arrived. Our ragtag band of misfits snapped into professional mode, bundled themselves in mosquito netting, and started studying. Once we were on track, Walsh and his production manager, Russ Saunders, kept things moving at a brisk pace.

Filming of the beach assault was brilliantly orchestrated. Everything went perfectly, which boosted the company's morale. Walsh memoed his bosses: IF THE REST OF THE PICTURE IS AS GOOD AS THIS, WE'LL HAVE OURSELVES A POT OF GELT.

When Walsh had the shots he needed, he announced he was "shipping actors back to their agents." Later, I'd see a memo from J. L. Warner's right-hand man, Steve Trilling: "Actors don't annoy me. They're just numbers—and some don't even rate numbers."

I'd have been angry if I hadn't seen Walsh's follow-up: "Van Heflin, James Whitmore, Aldo Ray and Tab Hunter are excellent in this film," he told the studio brass.

---
1 1

Breakdown

THE BOTTOM FELL OUT of my world when I returned home.

Not wanting to wear out my welcome at the Happy Hut, I decided to stay at Clayton's place on Norton Avenue until the studio paychecks started coming in. Then I'd find a place of my own. I hadn't been back more than a few hours when Dick revealed that he'd been getting some perplexing phone calls from my mother. He hadn't mentioned it in his letters, not wanting to upset me while I was so far from home.

We went straight to my mother's apartment. A different woman answered the door. She looked like Gertrude Gelien, sounded like her, but she wasn't anyone I knew. It was as if the gears in the woman's clockwork mind had been stripped. Out of her mouth poured religious rants, pious and pathetic.

Dick offered to put her up at his place so I could keep an eye on her. I was only twenty-two and hadn't experienced anything like this. I had no idea how to handle it.

Waking up the next morning in strange surroundings, my mother veered between long stretches of silent stupor and explosive outbursts. Gradually, the angry side won out. She became an unhinged fire-and-brimstone preacher. We tried to calm her, but she broke away, tearing at her clothes. Screaming, she ran half-naked onto Norton Avenue.

It was scary and confusing. Worse, it was heartbreaking.

Chasing her down, I held her in my arms and tried to comfort her. She went rigid as a statue, looked blankly in my face, and burst out laughing. Just as abruptly, she fell mute, as if some external force had taken possession of her. Losing all control, she started urinating right in the street, all down herself.

Then she collapsed.

Stunned, I carried her back to Dick's apartment. Everything about this woman—her strength, her decorum, her elegance, her wisdom, her discipline—had snapped, like her brain was a rubber band that had stretched past the breaking point.

We saw a slew of doctors in the days that followed. I was doubly anxious, as filming was scheduled to resume in a couple of days. Mother had shunned her parents and siblings, leaving me the only person on whom she could rely. Walt, stationed overseas, could only offer long-distance support. I didn't want to abandon her when filming resumed, but I didn't have a choice. I prayed for a simple explanation for her shattered mental state—and for some miraculous cure.

There were no second opinions among the specialists. It was unanimous: Gertrude Gelien needed to be committed to a mental hospital. Immediately.

On March 22, 1954, I was supposed to report for "duty" in San Diego. I blew off the call, telling the production manager I'd get there on my own as soon as possible.

The vanishing act outraged the studio, which was concerned about insurance liability, shooting delays, and so forth. Memos started flying: "Hunter refused to go with the company and insisted on driving his own car to the location . . . he claimed his mother was sick and he was taking her to a doctor and would proceed to San Diego from there."

The severity of the situation remained a secret. Dick advised me to soft-pedal it. "Mental illness" wouldn't play well in the press, especially after all those fan-magazine stories citing her influence on me. I was under enough pressure, Dick said, without callous reporters added to the mix.

As the *Battle Cry* team reassembled, I was driving into downtown Los Angeles, where a judge would decide if my mother should be remanded to the custody of the California state mental health system. I wanted to put her in a private sanatorium, but we couldn't possibly afford it.

The woman who'd sacrificed everything for me and my brother sat beside me, but she was as distant as if we were strangers on a bus. I stammered lame explanations about what was happening and why.

It was hopeless. There's nothing positive about putting someone—especially your *mother*—in an insane asylum. Particularly with no assurance she'd ever come out.

Somewhere on Olympic Boulevard I lost it. As I sat behind the wheel, I began bawling. For the tiniest moment, we seemed to connect as mother and

son. She reached over and gently touched my arm, quietly saying, "I know, I
know . . ."

She was only forty-three years old, for God's sake.

TWO DAYS LATER I caught up with the cast and crew in San Diego. I
was at a low point, and it helped to have people around, plus an all-consuming
job. It distracted me from thinking every minute about Mother being shipped
to the state hospital at Camarillo, the institution to which the judge had committed her. She'd been escorted away like someone headed to prison. Doctors
never provided straight answers. "You won't be able to see her for a while" was
all I heard whenever I called to inquire about her condition or tried to arrange
a visit.

When I returned from San Diego in April I found my own apartment,
something I could finally do now that I had some money. I was still not allowed to see my mother, however. I took a little one-bedroom in Westwood,
near UCLA. It was jinxed from the start. I tried cooking dinner there one
night for Ronnie Robertson and almost burned the place down. Okay, my
fault, not the apartment's. But I hated this place. I'd rented it while the UCLA
students were on a semester break, but had been too distracted by the chaos
in my life to realize it was surrounded by fraternity houses. Once classes resumed, all hell broke loose. I needed new digs, desperately.

During this time I saw a lot of Ronnie's family, who were very sympathetic
to my mother's plight. Although I always felt like an outsider, envious and ill
at ease around families, they were the only people I confided in, besides
Dick. I appreciated that the Robertsons didn't treat me like a "movie star." I
was simply Ronnie's friend. I don't know if they suspected us of being *more*
than that. The Robertsons were also Catholic, so we shared that bond as
well. They even gave me a set of rosary beads, to "help me through the rough
spots."

My major *Battle Cry* scenes came once shooting shifted to the Warner
Bros. soundstages. My initial impressions of Raoul Walsh's directing technique were confirmed while filming a scene in which Danny phones home.
The set fell completely silent as I guiltily talk to my fiancée while carrying on
an affair with a married woman. In addition to delivering my lines, I had to react to Mona Freeman, who wasn't actually there.

Walsh, rolling a cigarette, barked out: "Okay, now hang up the phone, sit back, and think about the old broad!" *Huh? Aren't we in the middle of a take? What "old broad"?* It completely shattered my concentration.

Later, it was explained that these occasional outbursts were a holdover from Walsh's silent-movie days, when it didn't matter if he howled directions as the camera was running.

Fortunately, there was no howling during my scenes with Dorothy Malone, who'd won the coveted part of Elaine. Over the course of several sequences, our mutual attraction flames up into an affair, "climaxing" back at her place, where we change into bathing suits for a midnight swim. I wear her husband's trunks—very suggestive stuff for the 1950s.

Working with Dorothy was so comfortable it resulted in the best acting I'd yet done on-camera. If I expected a pat on the back, however, it'd be a long wait. Unlike Stu Heisler, a director who reacted impulsively to a scene, Walsh remained aloof. If he got what he wanted, he simply moved on to the next shot. You could never tell if anything affected him emotionally.

When Walsh had Jack Warner view rushes of that scene, he played one of his customary practical jokes: as Dorothy and I run outside for our swim, he spliced in Hedy Lamarr's skinny-dipping scene from *Ecstasy*. Everybody roared.

I needed a good laugh. Incessant phone calls to Camarillo finally elicited the specifics of my mother's treatment: several times a week, electrodes were fastened to her skull and hundreds of volts of electricity were pumped into her head. This was supposed to realign the internal circuitry of her brain. How frying somebody's brain was supposed to fix it, I didn't understand. It seemed more like something out of a horror movie, not modern medicine. But what could I do, except go along with the "experts"?

I found myself a new home, the smallest furnished apartment in Hollywood, in the Franciscan Village on Sweetzer, around the corner from Dick's place. It was the size of a postage stamp, but the view was spectacular: across the road lived three former Miss Universe contestants, all angling for movie careers. They included Renata Hoy (who'd later marry my friend Brett Halsey), a cute little raven-haired Miss Something-or-other, and the pièce de résistance, Anita Ekberg—who five years later would become an international star in Fellini's *La Dolce Vita*. Singularly, in tandem, or as a trio, they routinely stopped traffic in the neighborhood.

Dick found me the place; he also found me business advisers. The management company Coulter and Gray—Carl Coulter and Bill Gray—was hired to handle my finances. Dick didn't trust me with money. He feared—rightly—that I'd fritter away my steady income.

"Tab, salt some money away and learn to invest it wisely," Dick would say, "or you'll end up like me—an agent!"

Clayton also brought his newest client, a New York transplant exactly my age, to the *Battle Cry* set. Dick had met the kid years earlier, on the set of the picture *Sailor Beware.* That was the first film James Dean had appeared in. Coincidentally, it would be the last picture Dick ever appeared in.

Jimmy visited my portable dressing room several times. We'd hang out on the steps, talking between shots. Unlike Henry, Dick fostered friendships among actors.

Jimmy was preparing to star in Warners' adaptation of the Steinbeck novel *East of Eden.* He asked lots of questions about my experiences in Hollywood—the place clearly made him nervous. We were the only male actors our age on the Warners lot under contract.

A few days before my work on *Battle Cry* wrapped up, Henry Willson got a call from one of the top directors in the business. William A. Wellman, flush with success from his last picture, *The High and the Mighty,* was scouting new faces for his next project. He'd seen *Battle Cry* footage and told Jack Warner he wanted me. With a couple of months left on my option, the Colonel was happy to get full value from his investment. Unlike the usual months-long hiatus between pictures, I barely drew a breath between *Battle Cry* and Wellman's *Track of the Cat.*

"Wild Bill" Wellman was a legend, both for the quality of his films—*Wings* won the first Best Picture Oscar—and his reputation as a "man's man," who'd lived a pre-Hollywood life as a World War I flying ace and later was a barnstorming stunt pilot. He was a wiry, irascible sort, who routinely tangled with studio bosses and more than once used his fists to get a point across on a set.

I was proud that he approved of me. I stuffed some clothes into a suitcase, along with guilt pangs about my mother, and flew to Mount Rainier, in Washington, for two weeks of location shooting in the Pacific Northwest.

Track of the Cat, based on a novel by Walter Van Tilburg Clark, is a snowbound-family drama centered around the hunt for a black panther that terrorizes the countryside. I was cast as Harold Bridges, the restless, untested kid brother of the movie's star, Robert Mitchum.

Now, if you want to talk about a "man's man"—start with Mitchum. He was the biggest star I'd ever worked with, which was a little intimidating when we tested. It worked to my advantage, however, as it mirrored the relationship between our characters. I got over my nervousness in a hurry; Mitchum was so easygoing, such a pleasure to be around.

Compared to someone like Van Heflin, who had extensive theatrical training and radiated an actor's aura, Mitchum approached work like a day laborer delivering a truckload of rocks to your backyard.

"What picture are we shooting today?" he'd crack on the drive to the location. Such coolness was actually made possible by a photographic memory—one glance at a script page, and Mitch had his lines down cold. He was the quickest study I'd ever seen.

That the audience would never see the *cat*, only its *track*, was just one example of Wellman's experimentation. He wanted to make a "black-and-white film in color." All attention should be on the actors' faces, he declared, particularly the color of their eyes. Wellman guaranteed this eccentric idea would result in a "beautiful, startling, and dramatic" impact. Practically, it meant designing the entire production with color drained from the sets, wardrobe, props, everything—except for a bright red mackinaw worn by Mitchum.

The location photography by Bill Clothier was spectacular, with Mitchum's winter coat floating like a flare among black trees and endless white snow. The late-spring weather was unpredictable, with magnificent sunshine suddenly consumed by cloudbursts, and rain turning the mountain snow to slush.

Things were just as tricky when we moved to Stage 22 on the Warners lot, where exterior scenes of the family's house and barn were re-created. It's a real challenge to act cold while dressed in full winter wardrobe on a broiling set, during a heat wave, as fake snowflakes stick to your sweating face.

Despite his obsession with visual innovations, Wellman maintained a human touch with actors. His blunt, no-nonsense manner was tempered by a sensitivity Raoul Walsh didn't have—or didn't choose to show. Wellman was terrific at setting the tone for a scene, like a conductor who knew all the notes and how they should be played: by far the best director I'd worked with.

Of all the cast members, I was closest to Beulah Bondi, who played my mother. Inevitable, I guess, considering what was happening in my life. In the months to come, I'd visit Beulah regularly in Whitley Heights, overlooking Hollywood, where she had a wonderful old Spanish-style house. I've always loved older people, and antique art, and Beulah's home was filled with religious artifacts and beautiful, old, elegant oak furniture. So tasteful and real, not the work of some uptight decorator. Understated, just like Beulah herself. When she spoke to you, you knew she was speaking from her soul.

Teresa Wright, I also liked a lot. My favorite song at the time was Kitty Kallen's hit "Little Things Mean a Lot." Teresa would catch me singing it between takes: "Stroke my hair as you pass my chair . . ."

"Oh, Tab—*please!*" Teresa would tease me. She listened to nothing but classical music in her dressing room. "'Stroke my hair as you pass my chair!' How ridiculous!" She'd roll her eyes. Teresa was fun.

Wellman got great work from all the actors. I pretty much stayed to the sidelines, trying to be as unobtrusive as possible. Reticence must have helped my characterization. When we wrapped, I told Wellman that I hoped we'd work together again.

"Likewise," he said, shaking hands. He was genuinely pleased with my performance.

That was the last I'd see of Wild Bill for a while. But we'd soon be back in each other's lives, in a big way. In a bizarre twist of fate, I'd land the leading role in the most important film of his life—and, in the process, end up being largely responsible for the end of his illustrious Hollywood career.

FROM THE STUDIO I drove straight to Camarillo. I didn't know what to expect, and the doctors did nothing to prepare me. My mother was in a private room, lying in bed. I stared at her from the doorway, stunned. Her head was shaved to facilitate the electroshock treatments. Her blank gaze finally settled on me. Those pale blue eyes were like laser beams, cutting through me. Neither of us could think of anything to say. As I bent down to kiss her forehead, she whispered:

"Why did you do this to me?"

Her words ripped me apart. I managed maybe thirty minutes alone with her, my love and respect and pity and anger all jumbled into a knot. The knot got larger on the drive back into Hollywood. I felt guilty, guilty, guilty. All those jobs she had to endure, those endless days and nights working to provide for me and Walt—that's what finally caught up with her and short-circuited her brain.

I swore to God that day—my mother would never work another day in her life. Ever. She'd never have to worry about another thing as long as she lived.

HENRY WILLSON LEFT my life that summer. After ten years with Charlie Feldman's Famous Artists Agency, he was ready to branch out on his own, as an independent agent. Universal was about to launch a big promotion for *Magnificent Obsession*, starring Henry's own magnificent obsession, Rock Hudson. After nurturing Rock's career, from extra to leading man, Henry clearly saw himself as the town's top star maker—one who no longer needed the safety net of a premier talent agency.

All along, Dick Clayton was my de facto agent, anyway. It was Dick, for example, who'd told Henry about an Italian director who wanted me for a period drama he was preparing. Henry dismissed the suggestion, didn't even take the name. To him, foreign films were a huge step down, the sign of a career in free fall. It'd be ten years before I learned that Luchino Visconti had wanted me for the lead role in *Senso*.

By this time, Clayton was ready to become a full-fledged agent at Famous Artists. For me, the decision was easy. Dick was my most loyal and dependable friend. I trusted him with my life, not only my career. When Henry went solo, I stayed at FAA, with Dick officially becoming my agent.

With both *Battle Cry* and *Track of the Cat* still taking shape in Warners' editing rooms, Henry had no way of knowing what was right around the corner. Neither did I. If he'd waited six months before hanging out his own shingle, Henry Willson would never have let me off his hook so easily.

Breakthrough

MY MOTHER WAS RELEASED from Camarillo in June 1954. Over the course of three months, she'd endured thirty-six electroshock-therapy treatments. Doctors pronounced her cured. I wasn't so sure, but I was certainly relieved. My mother could once again function as a relatively normal person.

I found her an apartment on Ocean Boulevard in Long Beach. She'd always liked being near the water, and the place brought back good memories of when we lived on Rose Avenue, in a pristine little board-and-batten duplex with fresh white paint and roses growing all over it.

Her new place was part of a four-apartment complex. Above her lived a single, middle-aged woman by the name of Bernice. She insisted we call her Bernie. She was a professor at UCLA and drove all the way from Long Beach to Westwood every day to teach class. That seemed weird to me. Maybe she preferred Long Beach to Santa Monica, or just liked long drives, twice a day.

From the moment Mother moved in, Bernie was her closest friend. They became inseparable. I was grateful, of course, because it took a load off me, at least psychically. Financially, I maintained responsibility for everything. I paid my mother's rent, all her expenses, even her tuition at Long Beach City College, where she enrolled in a full roster of classes. She loaded her car with textbooks and writing journals. No longer having to support herself, my mother indulged her obsession with researching and writing unfathomable essays on arcane subjects.

My mind was at ease. Especially with Bernie right upstairs, watching over my mother like a guard dog.

What I didn't realize was that she was watching *me* like a hawk. Or more accurately, a vulture.

THAT SUMMER, *Life* published a big feature called "The Stronger Sex," spotlighting Hollywood's next generation of leading men. Christened the Big Three heartthrobs for the bobby-soxer set were Tony Curtis, Robert Wagner, and Rock Hudson. They were shown clowning together, literally jockeying for position on the ladder to stardom.

On the following page was the next rank of contenders, in a footrace up a flight of stairs: Robert Francis, Cameron Mitchell, John Ericson, Steve Forrest—and Tab Hunter. My caption read: "Though he has appeared in only a couple of minor films, Hunter already has a wide adolescent following. His big chance will come with the release of *Battle Cry*. Boyish and blond, he hates screen name, likes to ride horses."

This kind of publicity, in a mainstream magazine with *Life*'s huge circulation, forced Warner Bros.' hand. My six-month option was about to expire. The studio brain trust, realizing my popularity with teenagers—and that I already had two films in the can—decided to up the ante: I was given a seven-year exclusive contract, something studios rarely offered anymore.

Some impressive tenants had been ensconced in my new home over the years: Bette Davis, Humphrey Bogart, James Cagney, Ann Sheridan, Errol Flynn, John Garfield, Edward G. Robinson—it was quite an elite household.

Equally thrilling was that after I survived twenty-three hand-to-mouth years, a contract meant guaranteed money. Unlike Jimmy Dean, who declined a long-term deal and limited his commitment to three pictures, I craved the safety and support of a major movie studio.

My mother had recovered, my best friend was now my agent, and I had starring roles in a pair of Warner Bros.' biggest upcoming films.

It was time to celebrate.

That meant ice-skating. The legendary skating master Gustave Lussi had agreed to take on Ronnie Robertson as his star pupil. Mr. Lussi had trained the incomparable Dick Button, guiding him to numerous national, world, and Olympic championships. With the Master as his mentor, Ronnie was going to soar to the top. What "extra" money wasn't being spent on my mother, I eagerly gave to Ronnie, to underwrite his training costs.

I got permission from the studio to travel to Lake Placid, New York. The site of the 1932 Olympic Games was the mecca for winter sports in America, and Mr. Lussi kept a home there. Ronnie and I drove cross-country together. I had a car fetish—I'll confess to it, but never apologize. When you're barreling into a bright future, holding the world by the tail, best to do it in a flashy red convertible.

We stayed at the Mirror Lake Inn. Lake Placid had an old-world charm and a small-town sensibility I'd never experienced. Summer storms hit often, loud enough to wake the dead. We made lots of new friends, including skater Evelyn Muller, who'd go on to become a world-class coach (as Evelyn Kramer). I trained diligently to get my "gold" in school figures. Ronnie's free-skating routines were already exceptional, and his spins were breathtaking. It was the compulsory figures that he needed to work on if Ronnie hoped to win a world championship.

We trained seven days a week. What little free time Ronnie and I had together was spent swimming or exploring. Evenings at the Mirror Lake Inn remained, of course, our private affair.

It seemed like heaven. Until the morning I noticed someone had run a skate blade down the side of my car, leaving a long, deep gash. Stan, the rink manager, had let me park my car in a special area, for safekeeping. Whoever vandalized it had gone out of their way to send a message. There were only two ways to read it: somebody was jealous either of my "movie star" status or of Ronnie and me being together.

Although I was royally pissed off, I did nothing. I also said nothing. That was my specialty—pushing the negative out of my mind. After all, I'd learned from the Queen of Denial herself, Gertrude Gelien.

As the summer session drew to a close, Warner Bros. beckoned. They needed me back at the studio right away. I was to costar in a picture with John Wayne and Lana Turner! Shot on location in Hawaii!

I zoomed west, leaving Ronnie to continue his training. I promised, come hell or high water, I'd make it to Vienna the following winter to witness his triumph in the World Figure Skating Championships.

I couldn't wait to read the script of *The Sea Chase* to see how I'd fit into a high-seas drama with two of the biggest stars in the business. Right off, something smelled fishy. The male lead was a German U-boat commander. John Wayne as a German? I flipped through the screenplay several times, searching for something more to my role than "Yes, sir," "No, sir," and "Aye, aye, sir." Nothing—not even a hint of character. If this was what I rated at my new "home," I regretted ever signing that big seven-year deal.

Dick, always patient and prudent, told me to bite my tongue. "Mark a little time," he counseled. "Go along with it. If they like you, you'll get better stuff in the future."

Warners made it hard to complain. We hit Honolulu in late September, greeted by hula dancers, orchid leis, and swaying palms. I kept looking for Dorothy Lamour. We skipped over to the Kona Coast, closer to the actual location, where a full orchestra serenaded our arrival. More hula girls, more leis, more, more, more of everything.

Once again, I was paid to live the lush life, sharing a beautiful little house on Black Sand Beach with Alan Hale Jr. and Dick Davalos, about a mile away from the Kona Inn, where most of the cast was bunked. Our place was where Lana Turner was originally booked, until the studio got nervous about prowlers on the unprotected grounds. I guess we three were expendable.

With no work the first two days, I slept on the beach, soaking in a brutal sunburn. Someone recommended vinegar as a salve; it worked, but for days I smelled like a tossed salad. I draped myself in a new aloha shirt and whiled away the hours futilely fishing native-style, with a simple bamboo pole.

Warners had purchased an old freighter, loaded it with movie gear, and sailed it into Kealakekua Bay, where it became our floating soundstage. It was a two-and-a-half-hour trip by boat every day to the actual location, which played havoc with the shooting schedule.

Aboard ship, I got my introduction to John Wayne. He'd already seen a rough cut of *Track of the Cat,* since his company, Wayne-Fellows, had produced it. (He and Wellman were pals; Duke was originally going to play Mitchum's role.)

"You have a nice quality when you act," Wayne said. "But I was like you at your age—had to learn to keep broader in certain scenes, not play down emotionally." I banked his generous advice. Wayne completely charmed me, claiming he should have gotten me under long-term contract before Warner Bros. did.

As a gesture of good luck, he gave me his navy jacket to wear on-camera.

The following day, Lana Turner arrived on the floating set. She broke the ice by hunkering down in the tight space with all the rank-and-file actors. She was *tiny,* but every inch the radiant movie star. I was tongue-tied, just like John Garfield when he first sees her in *The Postman Always Rings Twice,* wearing those little shorts and that white turban. I said the stupidest thing a twenty-three-year-old could say: "I've been a fan of yours since I was a kid." She shocked the hell out of me by reclining languorously across my lap, looking up at me with a teasing smile. I must have turned ten shades of red. I didn't know what to do with my hands.

Later, at a dinner party for some of the cast and crew at the Kona Inn, I got roped into dancing the hukilau. I won a coconut-frond hat. That must have been what gave me the courage to place a plumeria lei around Lana's neck. Her laugh was like champagne. She was sweet and funny and down-to-earth, and I couldn't wait to work with her.

Two days later I learned that my big scene with her was cut from the script. I was crushed. During the week, my frustration grew. "We need an actor over there by that rail," John Farrow, the director, would tell his assistant. "And set another one over by that hatch!" It was like the cast came from the prop department. The first week we did fifty minutes of montage shots, with no story. Farrow assured us the roles would "develop" as we went along.

It was so much lip service. Like the lip service he paid to his religion. John Farrow had years earlier made a showy conversion to Catholicism and was now a big muckety-muck in the Roman Catholic Church. But despite all his holier-than-thou piety—not to mention his marriage to actress Maureen O'Sullivan—he seemed like a garden-variety lecher. His only real interest

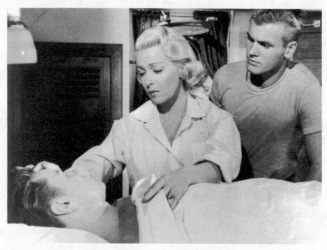

One of my few on-screen moments with Lana Turner in The Sea Chase. She attends to shark-bitten Dick Davalos. (Photo © Warner Bros. Pictures, Inc. All rights reserved.)

during production was his leading lady, on whom he doted lasciviously—until Lex Barker, Lana's husband at the time, arrived.

It may seem odd for me—considering my sexual orientation—to lambaste a prince of the Catholic Church. But I can't stand hypocrites, and that's how Farrow came off. Plus, he was just generally creepy, with beady eyes like a pair of piss holes in the snow. I couldn't work up any respect for him, professionally or personally.

Lana got a good laugh out of the single line of dialogue I had with her: "Thanks for doing my laundry." Still starstruck, I said, "Thanks for looing my daundry."

As the days dragged on, Wayne's charm wore thin. He was a consummate pro, which I admired, but his "leader of the pack" routine was overbearing. I'm not into macho bullshit. I didn't like football jocks when I was in school, and I didn't like them all grown up and transplanted to a movie set. Wayne clearly enjoyed quarterbacking his "team."

I began spending more time with Margaret and Betty, the local women who cleaned our house. We went to Mass together, where the Hawaiians raised the roof with their joyous hymns. They took me to a luau, where it rained and we danced barefoot in the mud. Amazingly, an *Ice Classics* show played in town, featuring a pal from the Polar Palace, Mae Edwards. I took Margaret and Betty to a performance. Mae got us front-row seats. It was a "tank show," with a little twenty-by-twenty-foot rink, under a single dangling light. Local kids eagerly touched and licked the ice. As she glided past us, Mae said under her breath: "Who can look sexy under a sixty-watt bulb?"

It was all great fun, for which I was grateful. But I quickly grew disillusioned and homesick.

Wayne suffered an ear infection skin-diving and was whisked away for treatment. Days later he was flown to a specialist in San Francisco. I wrote to Watson Webb: "They have nothing to shoot with Wayne gone . . . It makes you feel like you're accomplishing nothing. I've had it as far as this flick goes. You should thank God you're not even connected with a studio anymore."

News from the home front didn't improve my disposition. Walt and Pat, who'd been married for five years, with two children, had lost their new baby, Mary Claire, at birth. Walt was stationed overseas, and my heart broke thinking of Pat, how alone and miserable she must have felt. I prayed the rosary for her every night, with the beads Ronnie's folks had given me.

Then Dick wrote that Mother was acting odd again. Carl Coulter, my business manager, had noted that behind everyone's back she'd cashed a check made out to me. After all her preaching about honesty! She used the money to buy a television set and pocketed the rest. If she'd asked, I'd have given her whatever she needed. In the back of my mind, suspicions formed about Bernice and the influence she exerted on my mother.

Watson Webb wrote to me that Debbie Reynolds was getting engaged to singer Eddie Fisher. That would put an end to our dates—and it did. I also heard from Watson that Jeffrey Hunter and Barbara Rush were getting a divorce. I wrote back: "That does it—Hollywood marriages never work!" Maybe I was building up my alibi for staying a bachelor.

Wayne eventually returned, and shooting finally wrapped in early November. I celebrated my last night by throwing a party for Betty and Margaret, who'd set a valuable example when it came to living simply, kindly, and without care. Over the years, their friendship remained my fondest memory of *The Sea Chase*.

Well, that and Lana Turner, spread across my lap, toying with me.

I RETURNED HOME to more distressing news. First, Warners was under pressure to push back the release of *Battle Cry*, from February to as late as April or May. Those were the months enlistment was lowest, and the Marine Corps hoped the movie would inspire a wave of fresh recruits. Considering that the picture had already been six months in postproduction—an incredibly long time in those days—I wondered if *Battle Cry* would *ever* be released.

Even more disturbing was scuttlebutt that the Marines Corps had problems with the script—specifically the affair between Dorothy Malone and me. An internal studio memo said: "The Corps feels that Danny Forrester represents an idealistic type of boy . . . the type of youth they hope to appeal to. Showing him as an eighteen-year-old, humping a married woman twice his age, will have many detrimental aftermaths."

There already was anger in Washington about how the military was depicted in Columbia's big hit *From Here to Eternity*. Jack Warner had probably assured the Marines that any "humping" would be trimmed in *Battle Cry*'s book-to-script translation. If the affair was cut—there went the basis for my character. My "breakthrough" would litter a cutting-room floor, my career derailed by government intervention!

While I waited for a decision, another role was offered—one that, if it had

Arthur Gelien, aged seven, 1938.

With brother Walt, New York City, 1933.

Novelty photo of Mother, Walt, and me at the Long Beach Amusement Park, 1938.

Learning to drive at fourteen in Dick Clayton's Pontiac.

Stranded on the Island
of Desire *with Linda Darnell.*

On location, Shaw Park Hotel, Jamaica, 1951.

Vogue magazine,
1952, *People Are
Talking* column.

Preparing Swiz for a career before the camera.

*Doing the Hollywood circuit with constant
companion Debbie Reynolds, 1953.*

*A pair of Hollywood Hunters.
With Hank (Jeffrey Hunter)
at Hilltop, 1953.*

*Roddy McDowall and I pose for a fan magazine spread entitled
"Calling All Girls."*

Water-skiing at Watson Webb's Lake Arrowhead house.

Paying my dues, Gun Belt, *1953.*

Track of the Cat *with Robert Mitchum and Diana Lynn, 1954.*

Catching fire with Dorothy Malone in Battle Cry.

Showing off my brand-new 1955 T-bird.

Johnny Ray's opening night at Ciro's, 1954. Left to right: *Byron Palmer, Johnny Ray, Lori Nelson, me, and Gloria Gordon.*

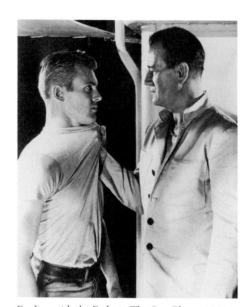

Dealing with the Duke in The Sea Chase, *1955.*

Beefcake on a board, Palm Springs Racquet Club, 1955.

Cuddling with Natalie on the frigid set of The Burning Hills, *1956.*

In Chicago, after Natalie successfully landed the plane.

America's Sweethearts, The Girl He Left Behind, *1956.*

DATE

Natalie Wood

Jan Chaney

Diane Varsi (Photo courtesy of Globe Photos.)

Lori Nelson (Photo courtesy of Globe Photos.)

Venetia Stevenson (Photo courtesy of Globe Photos.)

BAIT

Etchika Choureau

Dorothy Malone

Terry Moore
(Photo courtesy of Globe Photos.)

Debbie Reynolds

Recording "Young Love," with Randy Wood
and Dick Clayton, December 1956.

With Dick Clark on
American Bandstand.

In competition atop Indian Giver at the Monterey County Fair and Horse Show.

"Whatever Lola Wants,"
Gwen's showstopper from
Damn Yankees.

With Gwen Verdon and Bobby Fosse
during rehearsals of Damn Yankees.

Mother visiting the Damn Yankees set, 1958.

Tab-mania goes global, Gunman's Walk, *Tokyo, 1958.*

Stag jumps with Dick Button in Hans Brinker or the Silver Skates, *1958.*

With Sophia Loren in one of my personal
favorites, Sidney Lumet's That Kind of Woman.
(Photo courtesy of Paramount Pictures.)

They Came to Cordura, *Van Heflin, me, Gary Cooper, Nick Conte,*
Rita Hayworth. (Photo © Columbia Pictures Industries, Inc. All rights reserved.
Courtesy of Columbia Pictures.)

A career high point, Playhouse 90's "Portrait
of a Murderer" *with Geraldine Page, 1958.*

As the boy next door in the CBS special
Meet Me in St. Louis, 1959, *with Jane*
Powell, Ed Wynn, and Jeanne Crain.

Venetia Stevenson and I enjoy Ronnie's opening night performance in the Ice Capades. *(Photo courtesy of Globe Photos.)*

A pensive moment with Tony.

come to pass, would be considered some sort of camp classic today: I tested opposite Liberace for a role in *Sincerely Yours*.

What a concept—the most extravagantly effeminate man in Hollywood, teamed with the all-American boy. What's even more outrageous is that, in 1954, the majority of the public had no idea *either* of us was gay. While I stayed in the closet, Liberace escaped "exposure" by wildly overplaying his homosexuality, turning it into a nonthreatening caricature.

I was rejected for *Sincerely Yours*: too young. Thank goodness—it was another nothing role.

Track of the Cat came out that November. Wellman's experiment drew mixed reviews and did mediocre business. The trades, generous to an old veteran, heaped praise. The *Hollywood Reporter* declared it a "great motion picture" and an "artistic milestone." Bosley Crowther of the *New York Times*—the paper of record—called it "a heavy and clumsy travesty." My work didn't garner critical bouquets—but I didn't suffer any brickbats, either. I was pleased to have held my own with such an esteemed ensemble.

That winter, 1954, instead of acting, I hosted a Lux Video Theatre episode on television, did more silly interviews, posed for more photos, and was sent on press junkets. I accompanied Virginia Mayo on an East Coast tour for her latest, *The Silver Chalice,* which I wasn't even in. This was a studio strategy for garnering new actors some ink. The high point of the trip was Saranac Lake, New York, where Virginia and I tumbled off a train into a deep white blanket of snow and had a snowball fight. I was even able to sneak away for a while to visit Ronnie in nearby Lake Placid.

When I got back, Coulter and Gray called me on the carpet, steamed about my spending habits. They understood my need to cover Mother's expenses, for which they cut a monthly check. They were less thrilled about my contributions to Ronnie's training. They understood my need for every new car that caught my eye (it's a Hollywood thing). They tolerated my abundant gift giving to friends at Christmas. But they felt the line had to be drawn somewhere.

"Jeez, Tab," Carl Coulter said in his Kentucky drawl, "don't you think you oughta git ridda them horses?" I owned three at that point.

"Carl, I'd rather get rid of you first!" I snapped. He never complained about the horses again.

• • •

IN THE END, the humping stayed in *Battle Cry.*

After it was previewed for the Defense Department, Raoul Walsh received a letter of commendation: "This is the best Marine picture ever made. Your guys look like real fighting men, not Hollywood actors. In the last five or six Hollywood pictures, they've made the Marine Corps look ridiculous."

The Corps withdrew all objections to Danny Forrester's illicit affair. The top brass probably realized what Jack Warner had known all along: sex puts asses in the seats. If they wanted guys to enlist, bait 'em with Dorothy Malone in a tight red swimsuit.

But a weird thing happened. Leading up to the February premiere, the majority of *Battle Cry's* hype focused on its seventh-billed star. On January 18, Bill Hendricks, head of Warners' publicity department, received an interoffice memo from incredulous staffer Steve Brooks:

"Believe it or not, in the past three months, we have had 26 Tab Hunter interviews and/or major photographic fan magazine layouts. All of these are appearing and will be appearing with full *Battle Cry* credits."

Reporters swarmed around me like locusts, dissecting every bit of information from my pea brain, which they'd pound into grist for hungry Hunter followers.

Stories popped up everywhere: "Life with Tab" in *Movie Life,* "Tab's Plans for the Future" in *Movieland,* "A Day in the Life of Tab Hunter" for Pines Publications. Several were by the same writers, Peer Oppenheimer, Jerry Asher, and Dorothy O'Leary, including the choice titles "Why I Am Still a Bachelor" and "If You Were Tab's Wife." Drivel I'd been spewing out the past two months became, to the studio's surprise, the bedrock of *Battle Cry's* PR campaign.

Van Heflin and Aldo Ray were bigger stars, but the public was clearly clamoring for a new face. As they say in Hollywood, "Timing is everything."

The picture opened on February 2, 1955, to decent reviews. *Variety* said the film's "amatory" action, rather than its battle scenes, would make it a hit with "the younger masculine set and their dates." The *Hollywood Reporter* went overboard, calling it "a great women's picture" and noting that it had the "appeal of clean-muscled youthful bodies (of which those of Tab Hunter and Aldo Ray cause an audible amount of feminine swooning.)" Both papers predicted solid box-office business.

They underestimated. Ticket sales went through the roof. My fling with

Dorothy Malone, completely chaste by today's standards, proved irresistible to men and women, boys and girls. It became the film's focal point. Critics, by and large, bestowed the best reviews of my career, but it was the *public's* overwhelming response that shoved me front and center in the studio's biggest hit of the year.

Life picked up speed, careering like a car with no brakes—a brand-new '55 Thunderbird, in fact (black with red leather upholstery), which I bought as soon as it debuted at the local car show. Everything happened *so* fast. I hadn't yet celebrated my twenty-fourth birthday, but the media found endless fascination in my brief life, despite my spouting the same answers, over and over, in every interview. A service was hired to handle the avalanche of fan mail that poured in.

One particular item stood out from the rest—a telegram, sent from New York. It simply read:

Congratulations on your "Battle Cry" success.
Helm

Was it from my father, his surname accidentally misspelled by a Western Union operator? I've always wondered.

Keeping my promise to Ronnie, I flew to Europe to be with him for the World Figure Skating Championships in Vienna. The buzz was intense around the rink, as the blasé international judges couldn't help sneaking excited glances at Gus Lussi's new protégé. Ronnie was absolutely sensational in his freestyle program, and he knew it. He came flying off the ice, and he and I and Mr. Lussi shared a triumphant hug. Sadly, Ronnie's verve couldn't topple the conservative scoring system, which emphasized school figures over free skating. When the scores were totaled, Ronnie finished second to the reigning world champ, Hayes Alan Jenkins.

Not winning didn't faze Ronnie. He knew he'd done his best and was elated. We traveled around Europe with a group of American skaters for about two weeks, doing exhibitions in Italy and Switzerland. It was a marvelous time. Years later, Evelyn Kramer told me there were plenty of whispers behind our backs about me and Ronnie. She maintains that a well-connected person in the U.S. Figure Skating Association said, "Ronnie Robertson didn't have a chance at the Worlds as long as he was with Tab Hunter." To this day I have a hard time believing that antipathy existed. If it did, I'm sure it had more to do with my being a "movie star" than with me and Ronnie being an "item."

That was the last chance we had to spend time together. Life was about to take Ronnie and me in very different directions. He'd win a silver medal at the 1956 Olympics, then immediately turn professional, signing with the *Ice Capades*. His spins became legendary, earning him a place in *The Guiness Book of Records* and Ripley's *Believe It or Not!* He could clock eight revolutions per second on the ice, essentially spinning faster than an electric fan!

Returning to Hollywood, I discovered that I wasn't the only hot commodity at Warner Bros. A month after *Battle Cry* debuted, the studio released *East of Eden*. Critical reaction was excellent, and Jimmy Dean made a controversial leading man. To some, he was the new Brando, bringing brooding Method intensity to an even younger audience. But he had plenty of detractors as well, who said that his slouchy, mumbling style wasn't "acting" at all but only a pose, pandering to a growing audience of disgruntled, disaffected teens.

Teenagers were the fastest-growing segment of the movie audience. Kids still wanted to go out, while moms and dads were staying home to watch *I Love Lucy* and *Dragnet* and *Your Hit Parade*. The studios were trying to figure out how to court this new crowd.

Warner Bros. worked itself into a win-win situation. It had one twenty-four-year-old star with huge appeal for the "juvenile delinquent" set, and another one packaged as a wholesome alternative to it. I'm sure you can figure out which was which.

Dick Clayton set Jimmy up in a garage apartment on Sunset Plaza Drive. I was with Dick one night when he had to deliver contracts to Jimmy on the set of *Rebel Without a Cause*. Imagine my surprise when, years later, I'd see memos from Jack L. Warner indicating that Tab Hunter and Debbie Reynolds were his alternate choices for the leads in *Rebel*. The picture was shooting in the same spooky, abandoned mansion that had been Gloria Swanson's lair in *Sunset Boulevard*. Jimmy and I hung around outside while the crew prepped another setup. An enterprising studio publicity photographer saw us chatting and began snapping dozens of pictures—the polar opposites of America's youth culture, captured together.

I told Jimmy that I'd just signed a deal to buy a lot next to Dick's new place for six thousand dollars, and he playfully badgered me to sell it to him.

The assistant director called Jimmy to the set, but the camera guy wouldn't let up: "One more . . . one more . . . one more." Jimmy smirked and casually flipped the bird. Nobody in Hollywood then would have done something like that on-camera. Dick Clayton knew he had his hands full with Jimmy because he was so unconventional and unpredictable. But he believed in Jimmy and thought him well worth the "trouble."

On the set of Rebel, Jimmy slyly tells the photographer to get lost. (Photo © Warner Bros. Entertainment, Inc. All rights reserved.)

When *The Sea Chase* premiered in June, my billing was once again entirely out of proportion to my minuscule role. A head shot of me was slapped onto the original poster art. I was afraid the studio would get sued for false advertising. Warner Bros. then decided to make a big summer push for young audiences: it re-released *Battle Cry* and *East of Eden* as a double bill. By then, "James Dean" was above the title, and "Tab Hunter" had snatched top billing away from a cast of seasoned veterans. Jimmy, Natalie Wood, and I had officially become the studio's biggest stars, its Bogart, Davis, and Cagney for a younger generation.

Dick Clayton, figuring it was only a matter of time before reporters tracked down my mother, hatched a plan to short-circuit any embarrassing exposés about her treatment. He talked "Gertie" into posing with me for several photo spreads. Appealing to her literary bent, he even convinced her to pen an article—"That's My Boy!"—for *Movie Show* magazine. (It should be read with a German accent):

> People always ask: How does it feel to have a son who is a motion picture star? To me, my son, Tab Hunter, is a 'nobody,' I tell them, as often as I tell him, too. To me my son in just a person, a good, fine, admirable person whom any mother would be proud of in any walk of life. Being a motion picture star is his job, and while I appreciate his position and am grateful for his good fortune, I still do

not believe this should automatically merit a special cap of glory. The real rewards, so I believe, a man earns by the beat of his heart and the honesty of his soul.

She ended up by noting that, "Although my son Walter makes a wonderful husband and father, it's better that Tab isn't anxious to marry. He's still so young and so much is happening so fast. Marriage is a serious business, which Tab believes. Because he is good at sensing qualities, when the time comes for him to settle down, I know he will make the right choice. Some girl will be very, very lucky."

In truth, my mother had little interest in my career or my private life. Her dear pal Bernice, however, was paying very close attention to both, as I'd soon discover.

Success and Scandal

EVERYTHING WAS GOING so well that summer of '55 that I never imagined I'd end up firing Dick Clayton. In fact, I was more shocked than he was.

Martin Manulis was a producer for the prestigious CBS television show *Climax!* which presented original dramas each week. Dick told Marty I'd be perfect for an episode called "Fear Strikes Out," based on the current best seller by Jimmy Piersall, a baseball player who'd survived a nervous breakdown to become a star for the Boston Red Sox.

Dick convinced me this was the role I'd always wanted, the one that would break me out of the clean-cut, straight-arrow mold and show my salt as an actor. Dick was far more savvy about such things than Henry Willson. With a huge hit like *Battle Cry* under my belt, Henry would never have let me stoop to doing TV. But Dick believed the small screen offered fresh, exciting material that could easily translate to the movies. *Marty,* a huge hit that year, was adapted from a teleplay, he pointed out.

Dick Clayton had never steered me wrong, so I took the part. The producers didn't miss a trick, casting Mona Freeman, my *Battle Cry* sweetheart, as Piersall's gallant bride. Everything was set up for me to hit a home run. All I had to do was forget that *Climax!* was a *live* show.

Acting coach Joe Graham, who'd soon go to work for Warners full-time, worked with me intensively, helping me stretch my range. Jimmy Piersall was anything but the boy next door. This guy's psyche had a cellar, an attic, and lots of shadowy alcoves. I talked to him once, hoping to get some insights I could use. "My doctor looked just like Desi Arnaz" was all Piersall contributed during a long-distance phone call.

Fortunately, I didn't have far to go to find personal parallels: Piersall's mental illness stemmed from pathological fear of disappointing his overbearing father, a man who substituted stern platitudes for affection, much like my mother.

As I read further into the script, my jaw dropped. Piersall is playing for the Red Sox—his boyhood dream realized—when his mind simply snaps. He's committed to an insane asylum for months of electroshock therapy, which burns out his nervous disorder, along with chunks of his memory.

I wouldn't have to reach far for what I refer to as "associations."

Making movies, you always get another take. Doing theater, there's always another show the next night. In live TV—you get *one* shot. As the airdate approached, my nerves started jumping. I held it together until dress rehearsal. Only hours before we were to go on, the reality of the situation hit home. This wasn't some five-hundred-seat theater! The camera's eye would beam me into living rooms all over the nation, with millions of people watching . . . the panic came in waves.

I turned to Clayton: "You got me into this," I yelled. "I can't go through with it! It's all your fault—*you're fired!*"

Rehearsing with Mona Freeman for "Fear Strikes Out,"
my first major live television performance.
(Photo courtesy of Globe Photos.)

Being a former actor, Dick knew what was happening. He remained calm, hanging outside the dressing room, offering moral support. His last words to me, as I was ushered to the studio gallows: "You're good. Remember that."

Live TV is not for the fainthearted—or the unprepared. Once the host, William Lundigan, looked into the camera and said, "Tonight's show is about baseball star Jimmy Piersall and his fear of becoming . . . a mental case," there were no cuts, no redos, no excuses.

The public saw a different Tab Hunter that night. Intense, hyperactive, motormouthed, with a sweaty, psychotic edge to the wholesome image. I had to be scared, and scary, without overplaying.

Halfway through, I blew a major speech. It just slipped out of my mind, no way to reel it back. In a heartbeat, half a page of script mysteriously vanished. Rushing from one set to the next, I passed Marty Manulis and apologized profusely.

"Don't worry," he said, shoving me forward. "We're on to the next scene."

I regrouped during a short break while Bill Lundigan sold a Chrysler; in those days, even *commercials* were live! Thirty minutes later I was back in my dressing room, the show completed. I'd blown it. My inexcusable gaff was a devastating embarrassment. As I stewed, Clayton entered, chirping: "You did a really good job!" I threw him a deadly look.

Then Marty Manulis, director Herbert Swope, and a bunch of other crew members piled in, offering congratulations. Nobody mentioned the blown speech. They were too busy celebrating. Finally, Marty said, "You, me, and the writer know something was missing. But everybody else assumes that's how it was supposed to go. You were great!"

Sheepishly, I rehired Dick Clayton.

Overnight reviews of "Fear Strikes Out" were the best I'd ever gotten. Even the president of CBS sent a congratulatory telegram. Pretty soon I was telling everybody I knew at Warners that "Fear Strikes Out" would make a terrific movie. If anybody understood Jimmy Piersall and could play him on the big screen, it was me.

The studio turned a deaf ear. Not that I had reason to complain. It appeared in the trades that week that Tab Hunter had four films in development at Warner Bros.: *The Yanks Are Here, I'm Owen Harding, The Girl He Left Behind,* and *The Burning Hills.*

My time had come.

• • •

NEXT THING I KNEW, I was costarring with Marilyn Monroe. Not in a movie or a TV show, but on the cover of a magazine. And not just any magazine—this was the September 1955 issue of *Confidential,* the nation's most notorious scandal sheet.

"The Lowdown on That 'Disorderly Conduct' Charge Against Tab Hunter!" was the title of the article. It described, in the magazine's patented sneering style, "The night a cop moved in on that limp-wrist pajama party." Somebody had given—or more likely *sold—Confidential* the police paperwork from the bust Terry Marsteller and I got nabbed in with a bunch of other innocent partygoers five years earlier.

To quote directly from the purple prose used to recount the insidious event:

> It all started with a vice cop who was drifting in and out of Hollywood's queer bars on the afternoon of October 14th, looking and listening for tips on the newest notions of the limp-wristed lads.
>
> Pausing for a Scotch and water in one gay joint, the deputy struck up a conversation with a couple of lispers who happily prattled that they were set for a big binge that very evening, at 2501 Hope Street in Walnut Park, a suburb of Los Angeles. One drink led to another and the pair finally invited the snooper to come along. There was only one dashing requirement — bring pajamas.
>
> Since breaking up such queer romps was his business, the detective pretended to fall in with his barroom chums and arranged to accompany them. Between snorts, however, he called the Los Angeles sheriff's office for reinforcements.

Reinforcements? To handle a bunch of *lispers*? In hindsight, it's all ludicrous, especially classic *Confidential* lines like "He's come a long way since that night he rode off in the paddy wagon with a load of shrill nances." And for the record—there were no pajamas. Most galling to me personally was the magazine's insinuation that my love of horses was just phony PR intended to "accent the masculine."

Unfortunately, ludicrous as it was, there was nothing laughable about the article. It was as serious as a heart attack.

The studios had long since perfected a closed-loop system for protecting stars from bad publicity. Everything that appeared in the mainstream press—gossip items, magazine stories, interviews—was controlled by PR departments, which traded access for loyalty. The fortress walls started to crack in 1951 with a subscription-only paper called *Hollywood Life,* edited by a former publicist, Jimmy Tarantino. He made a cottage industry out of dishing dirt on Hollywood players, but his rag's circulation was limited to those in the business, sort of a slimy version of *Variety.*

The following year, *Confidential* hit the stands, with its provocative subtitle, "Tells the Facts and Names the Names." It cashed in on the wave of "exposé" journalism spawned by Washington hearings into Communist subversion and organized crime. Those televised spectacles created an appetite in the public for the "inside story." Especially when it was delivered in a smirking style that left readers feeling smug and in the know.

The publisher of *Confidential,* a slick Manhattan gadfly named Robert Harrison, had started as a purveyor of mail-order girlie magazines. After less-than-spectacular sales of *Confidential's* first few issues, Harrison realized that the private peccadilloes of movie stars far outsold "hard" exposés that took on corruption and con games in politics and business. Word around Hollywood was that Harrison had an army of informants feeding rumors to his editors. You couldn't trust anyone—not bartenders, not hairdressers, not high-priced hookers. Overnight, lots of jealous, disgruntled wannabes had a way of getting even.

It put a lewd spin on the politically charged paranoia that swept through Hollywood during the congressional witch hunt. The sexual escapades of celebrities were plastered all over its pages, but a special place was reserved for those suspected of being "queer": *Confidential* tarred "fairies" with the same acid-dipped brush it used to vilify "Commies."

By the time I debuted on its cover, *Confidential's* circulation topped four and a half million readers a month, inspiring a wave of imitators: *Whisper, Uncensored, Top Secret, Lowdown, On the QT, Hush-Hush, Exposed, Private Lives, Tip Off*—the list seemed endless. The floodgates were opened.

I'd all but forgotten about that ridiculous 1950 arrest. But it had taught me the importance of being circumspect. I'd seen how others in the business toed the line, and I followed their example. There was a gentleman's agreement in the Hollywood ranks, a "live and let live" attitude about homosexuality. In private and around other like-minded people, you didn't have to pretend. In public, however, you were always careful. Not that I behaved any differently, really—what you saw was what you got with me. I didn't suddenly change into someone else in private. The rule was, Act discreetly, and people would respect your right to privacy. I'd mastered it.

Then *Confidential* blew all that out of the water.

The irony wasn't lost on me. On one side of the newsstand there were dozens of innocent and naive movie magazines, pitching me as the perfect specimen of young American manhood, every girl's dream. Those magazines created Tab Hunter, virtually out of whole cloth.

Across from them, higher on the rack, up at Dad's eye level, nested the lurid new breed of tabloids, dedicated to gleefully making a buck by turning over every last rock in Eisenhower's buttoned-down America.

Those magazines were eager to destroy, in one fell swoop, all the good fortune that had come my way.

At the end of a long September, I received a phone call from somebody in the Warners PR department. I can't even remember who it was. All I recall thinking was that the *Confidential* fiasco had convinced the studio to renege on my seven-year deal. I was pretty paranoid and ready for anything—except what I heard.

I'd been nominated for the 1955 Audience Award for Most Promising New Male Personality, in a nationwide balloting of more than fifteen million movie fans. The contest was sponsored annually by the Council of Motion Picture Organizations. Insiders referred to the Audie as "Oscar's Sister." It was that big a deal. (Today, its equivalent would be the People's Choice Awards.)

Surely this would counteract any bad publicity—wouldn't it?

I called Dick Clayton to tell him the great news. He was virtually catatonic. "Dick, what's wrong?"

"Jimmy's dead," he muttered. "Oh, my God, Jimmy's dead. He crashed his car and he's dead." Dick could barely speak. All I could get out of him was that the accident happened up north, east of Paso Robles on Highway 466.

I was badly shaken—but Dick was devastated. Within days he'd suffer a bout of psychosomatic blindness, caused by trauma over Jimmy Dean's death. His sight would return, but frankly, I don't think he ever completely recovered from the shock, or the loss.

"Tab, we got another odd sorta call from your mother," Carl Coulter said over the phone. "We need y'all to come in and have a little talk about it."

At the Rodeo Drive office, Carl said my mother had demanded an increase in her monthly payment. "This is gettin' ridiculous," he said. "She doesn't have that many danged expenses. Where's the money goin'?"

"I guess I'd better find out."

I drove straight to Long Beach, hoping Bernice wouldn't be there. Financial matters certainly didn't need to be discussed in front of her. Of course, there she was, waiting. It smelled like a setup. I dreaded confrontations and was hesitant to bring up the reason for the visit: an "allowance" was an awkward thing for mother and son to discuss—especially when it's the son paying. Plus I knew my mother was bad with money. It's a trait I inherited.

When I finally broached the subject of expenses, Bernie leaped in—suddenly playing the part of prosecuting attorney.

"How dare you question your mother's needs!" she seethed. "After what she's been through! You should get down on your knees and give thanks—but instead you just shove her into this tiny apartment and go running off playing movie star!"

As "proof" of my status as a miserable son, Bernie listed my entire itinerary for the past year. Clearly, she'd put in overtime with the movie magazines.

"You should be ashamed!" she said, as though I'd committed a crime by earning the money I gave my mother. "Especially after all this woman has done for you!"

Whatever her motive, Bernie was clearly trying to turn my mother against me. It was a dramatic display. Exactly the kind of "show" that, in the old days, would have disgusted Gertrude Gelien. Now she just sat there silently, letting Bernice spew venom. My mother was mentally vulnerable and obviously didn't want to go against her only friend, her daily life-support system.

"Do you really need more money, Mother?" I asked, cutting Bernie off.

"If this is what she says," Mother replied. "These kinds of things I don't keep track of so closely anymore."

So Bernie's influence now extended to Mother's pocketbook as well. I knew that whenever they went out—movies, dinner, a show—my mother gladly paid. That was another trait I'd picked up from her. Maybe Bernice was getting spoiled by my mom's generosity. Or maybe they needed extra cash for the operation that would permanently join them at the hip.

"Mom, I'd give it to you if I had it. But there is no more. Every penny I make is already accounted for."

"Sports cars! Horses! While your mother lives like a pauper!" I got the sense that Bernie wasn't working the guilt angle entirely on her own. She and my mother had become a team, with Bernie the mouthpiece.

"Look—there is no more money," I protested.

That's when Bernie pulled me aside: "The stories in *those* magazines are very hurtful to your mother," she said, a threatening edge in her voice. "I'm sure you wouldn't want even worse ones coming out."

That stopped me cold.

"I know all about you and your ice-skater friend," she went on. "We're not stupid around here. If you know what's good for you, you should stop fooling around and start taking proper care of your mother."

I was shocked. My mother looked at me from across the room, wearing a blank expression that was impossible to read. I felt the walls closing in. This felt like extortion.

"Fuck you," I told Bernie, slamming the door behind me.

My mother knew Ronnie. She liked him. She'd seen him skate. She probably talked about him to Bernice. But she wouldn't have suspected we were anything more than pals. Bernie must have shown her the *Confidential* article. But Mother would only have turned up her nose and sniffed, *That's trash.* This shakedown had to be all Bernie's idea.

It had never occurred to me that Mother *knew* I wasn't straight. Whenever such thoughts *did* skulk into my mind, I'd kick them right out. *Always focus on the good, Arthur!*

Some people might call it denial. Back then, I preferred to call it positive thinking. By either name—it was one more trait I'd inherited from my mother.

As long as Bernie and my mother were friends—which would turn out to be years—I was never as close to my mother as I had been.

I ESCORTED NATALIE WOOD to the Audience Awards ceremony, held that November at the Beverly Hilton. The studio arranged our date. Warners executives were already strategizing in the wake of Jimmy's death. *Rebel Without a Cause* had opened to huge business, with teenagers everywhere packing theaters. Practical decisions had to be made to fill a void left by Dean's death. Having me escort Natalie was stage one of a larger plan.

Natalie accepted a posthumous award on Jimmy's behalf: the public had voted him Best Actor for *East of Eden.* He'd leapfrogged right over "promising." It was hard to believe that in barely over a year, Jimmy had starred in three major motion pictures. Harder to believe was that his entire career would be limited to those three movies. We were the same age; my life was just beginning. Losing Jimmy was a terrible way to gain perspective, to understand that your whole fluffed-up fantasy world can suddenly disappear.

Maybe that's what I was thinking when my name was announced, among a roster of nominees that included Jack Palance, Ernest Borgnine, Harry Belafonte, Jack Lemmon, Russ Tamblyn, George Nader, and Gig Young. None of it really registered until I looked at Natalie, who was laughing and pushing me out of my seat: "Get up there, silly—you won!"

What I remember of that valedictory moment was that the applause seemed very halfhearted, and I could hear sarcastic snickering in the crowd.

Rosalind Russell presented me the Audie trophy, and I offered a brief and sincere thank-you to the fans who'd voted. Backstage, photographers from press services worldwide jostled to get pictures of the winners. Warner Bros. made out like bandits, with winners in several major categories—Jimmy, me, and Peggy Lee, named Most Promising Female Personality for her role in *Pete Kelly's Blues*. Jennifer Jones was named Best Actress for 20th Century Fox's *Love Is a Many-Splendored Thing*. In the group shots, Jack Warner wedged himself front and center, a proud papa presiding over his stable of stars. It was a glorious moment. I'd truly arrived—even if some in attendance didn't want to believe it.

A photographer suddenly shouted: "Hey, Tab—smile pretty! This one's for the next cover of *Confidential!*"

Lots of laughter and popping flashbulbs—I threw up my hands in disgust and turned away. That joker may as well have spit in my face.

Jubilant Jack Warner steps into the spotlight as his studio dominates the Audience Awards, 1955. Peggy Lee and I bask in his glow.

Say what you will about Jack Warner, and Lord knows terrible things have been said, but I'll always remember him most for what he did next.

"C'mere, Tab," the Colonel crowed, throwing his arm around my neck and pulling me back into the winner's circle. "Remember this: today's headlines — tomorrow's toilet paper."

He was right. Warner's response was to simply let the whole nasty episode fade. *Confidential*'s purported four million monthly readers may have sounded like a lot, but Jack Warner knew it was a drop in the bucket compared with the number of people who read *Photoplay*, bought tickets to *Battle Cry*, and watched *Climax!*

He didn't panic, didn't issue retractions, didn't demand I start going on more "arranged" dates. Best of all — he didn't tell me how to live my life.

I'd heard tales of studio chiefs like Louis B. Mayer and Harry Cohn controlling the private lives of stars to avoid any hint of scandal that could harm their investment. Nothing like that ever happened to me at Warner Bros. The brass was happy to have me single, since it was an industry axiom that "Bachelors make better box office." Didn't matter to them whether I preferred women, men, or chimps — as long as I didn't flaunt it publicly. Beyond that, nobody cared. Certainly no one at the studio told me who I could, or could not, see — before *or* after *Confidential*.

It was only the on-screen Tab Hunter the studio cared about.

Several days after the Audience Awards show, the studio announced it was fast-tracking production of Louis L'Amour's western saga *The Burning Hills*, uniting "that boy from *Battle Cry*" with "that girl from *Rebel Without a Cause*."

The Ideal Couple

HUNTER AND WOOD.

Maybe it doesn't have quite the ring of "Tracy and Hepburn" or "Bogart and Bacall," but don't blame Warner Bros. for trying. In late 1955 the studio decided it could cash in at the box office by creating a "dream team" of its two hottest young properties: Natalie Wood and me. Unlike those sophisticated screen couples of the forties, Natalie and I projected a wholesome, ingenuous sex appeal for the 1950s' most sought-after ticket buyers: teenagers. Bill Hendricks, the studio's director of publicity, shifted his flacks into high gear, bent on convincing the world that Warner Bros. had a new William Powell–Myrna Loy combination for the underage set.

I'd first met Natalie in 1952, during a March of Dimes parade in Tujunga, outside Los Angeles. She was then a pigtailed fourteen-year-old who looked about ten, and already a veteran of more than a dozen films. Her real name was Natasha Gurdin, a Russian by way of Santa Rosa, California. She was precocious and adorable and everybody she met couldn't help falling for her. Four years later, she'd blossomed into a stunner, a gamine version of dark-eyed beauties like Elizabeth Taylor and Ava Gardner.

Natalie's mom, Maria Gurdin, was a classic stage mother whose every waking minute was dedicated to making her daughter a movie star. Natalie called her Mud—short for Muddah, her comical pronunciation of *mother*. Mrs. Gurdin was more of a force in Natalie's career than her actual agent—Henry Willson. (I learned later that Natalie was dead set on having Henry as her agent because he represented Robert Wagner, on whom Natalie had had a crush since she was a little girl.)

It was a well-guarded secret that Natalie's father, Nick, had been given a job as a studio carpenter as part of Natalie's deal with Warner Bros. Any influence he had on his daughter was buried by Mud. I never got the impression, however, that Mrs. Gurdin made Natalie do anything she didn't want to do.

Natalie craved stardom. It made her rambunctious and exciting. She always dressed for a performance, even when no cameras were around. One day she was a giggly high school freshman; the next she tried to come off as a worldly sophisticate. When I picked her up once for one of our studio dates, she was wearing huge false eyelashes. I told her, "You're so pretty, Nat—you don't need those things." She fluttered them a few times, then peeled them off. When I escorted her to the *Helen of Troy* premiere, she poured herself into a black gown, wore glittering drop earrings, and spoke in a low, sexy voice not even close to her own.

I'll always remember Nat in those first few months we got to know each other: she was like a newborn filly finding her legs—inquisitive, excitable, eager to discover new things. She tumbled a few times but easily shook off the scrapes. Her exuberance and vulnerability were *so* appealing.

As for any pain she might have been enduring behind the buoyant front, I was oblivious. Years later, I'd hear tales about her rebellious adolescence, her affairs with Dennis Hopper and *Rebel*'s forty-three-year-old director, Nicholas Ray, a traumatic rape at age fifteen, as well as other sordid accounts of wild behavior. That wasn't the Natalie I knew—although she was such a good actress, she could easily have camouflaged any inner demons.

AFTER MAKING *REBEL*, Natalie had starred in a suspenseful melodrama called *A Cry in the Night*. Eager to show her range, she portrayed a girl terrorized by a mentally disturbed kidnapper, played by swarthy veteran Raymond Burr. Natalie caused a bigger sensation offscreen, spending evenings out with her much older costar, on the town and at his home. She was taken with Burr's mature, urbane lifestyle, his love of high culture, gourmet meals, the whole bit. I'd met him a couple of times and was impressed myself. I'm sure Natalie saw him as a father figure.

I'd heard that Raymond Burr was gay, but I had no direct knowledge. Hell, it gets said about *every* unmarried man sooner or later. Some people suggested later that being publicly linked with Natalie gave Burr a good "cover." To me, that's so much stupid gossip. What I do know is that Warners frowned on them as an item. Whatever his feelings may have been toward Natalie, Burr was thirty-eight—Nat was only seventeen. Not exactly the optimum date for a budding starlet.

Tab Hunter was much more to the studio's liking, and its marketing advantage. For Warners, linking me with Natalie accomplished a three-in-one: it boosted us as the next big screen team, dispelled rumors about me, and hooked Natalie up with an "anti-Burr"—a young, wholesome straight arrow closer to her own age.

Kind of ironic, when you think about it.

In December 1955, Warners shipped Natalie and me to Zanesville, Ohio, to promote *The Court Martial of Billy Mitchell*—a film in which neither of us appeared. Our job: to convince kids to buy tickets to a military courtroom drama. What the studio had started with our initial Audience Awards date—making us into an item—kicked into high gear.

America was crazy for celebrity couples. Maybe the movies were trying to restore an image of domestic bliss after the upheaval of the Second World War. Whatever the reason, the public couldn't get enough of Debbie Reynolds and Eddie Fisher, Janet Leigh and Tony Curtis, Paul Newman and Joanne Woodward. Every studio had to have its "perfect pair." The magazines wanted Natalie and me to talk about each other as much as we talked about ourselves.

"Tab is the exact opposite of Jimmy [Dean]," Natalie obliged. "He's a card giver . . . Very sentimental . . . When he sees a gift that looks like you, he wants to buy it for you immediately—his business managers are trying to curb that habit."

She also offered this tidbit, pretty funny coming from a teenager: "We both talk a lot about the past."

Translation: *How did we go from kids to movie stars overnight?*

Privately, we laughed about our "romance," understanding it was all part of the publicity game. Our lives were totally different, and there was never anything serious between us—not like with me and Lori Nelson. We were just having fun, holding a tiger by the tail.

DURING THIS FABRICATED romance, Dick Clayton introduced me to Scott Marlowe. He'd just arrived in town from New York, where he'd been enrolled at the Actors Studio. He'd adopted Jimmy's hipster vibe and anti-Hollywood attitude. Not that it was "anti" enough to keep him from coming west to find a spot on the gravy train. And he wanted Clayton to help him find it. Dick had a reputation by this time as *the* agent for up-and-coming talent. He was as good as Henry Willson, without the smarm.

By now, I accepted the fact that there was something undeniable about the Actors Studio crowd. Producers and directors were more and more impressed by the Method's naturalism, and I knew I'd have to study and work harder just to hold my own. It wasn't only Brando, Clift, and Dean who made a mark. It was Paul Newman, Kim Stanley, Julie Harris, Geraldine Page, Eileen Heckart— a whole slew of actors were upping the ante when it came to dedication and acting craft. You couldn't help feeling their influence.

Clayton was all over me to keep improving. I took more acting lessons and began studying improvisational techniques in Rachel Rosenthal's classes, which I found challenging and fun. That's where I met Jan Chaney, a young dancer I thought had a very special quality. We started dating, not just because we were friends, but because I knew the publicity would be good for her career. Savvy showbiz veteran that I was (all of twenty-five), I knew how the game worked.

I also started spending more time with Scott Marlowe. I was impressed by his devotion to "real" acting. He was impressed by my success. He was a nice enough guy—but really strange, a poster boy for the Beat Generation: he only wore black, hated the sun, kept his drapes drawn, smoked constantly. I joked that he was more mole than human. A lot of it was a pose, part of the whole "troubled youth" trend. I laughed both *at* Scott and *with* him about his angst-ridden image. He couldn't pass a mirror without checking his hair. "If you're supposed to be so natural," I teased him, "stop checking your hair all the time!" Beneath the pose, Scott had a genuine vulnerability, sweetness, and sense of fun.

He and I ended up having a "little something."

It was dangerous, since the *Confidential* scandal was still fresh. But as Dick Clayton bluntly put it, "A stiff prick has no conscience." Terrible guilt and remorse usually followed—I am a Catholic, after all.

Finding out who I was, sexually, was one thing. *Admitting* it was something else entirely, since any evidence could have destroyed my livelihood (or so I thought). Accepting that I was wired differently was no cause for celebration, believe me. We all have our various urges and desires and shouldn't be made to feel ashamed of them. Being "proud" of your homosexuality, however, was a concept still years away. Not that I'd *ever* feel that way. To me, it's like saying you're "proud" to be hetero. Why do you need to wear a badge? You simply are what you are.

While trying to figure all this out for myself, I just wanted to be left alone. Instead, it seemed like the whole world was watching.

On the one hand, I had it easy: I was employed in one of the few industries where gay men were common. Everybody knew it took all kinds to make a movie. There was an acceptance within our business that didn't exist, I'm sure, for car dealers in Omaha or shoe salesmen in Little Rock who knew they were "different."

On the other hand, my career was based on my being the symbolic heterosexual ideal. In February 1956, United Fan Mail Service delivered to me sixty-two thousand valentines from young women all around the world.

Want to talk about *conflicted*? The pressures brought to bear on me, both external and internal, were overwhelming.

I could have benefited from a long talk with a sympathetic priest. But I was still distrustful after my initial confession on the subject. Other actors my age eagerly went through psychotherapy, Scott included, using it as a tool for digging deeper into their psyches to uncover the "real shit" they could use in their performances.

That wasn't for me. I didn't have a lot of time to "uncover" my inner self—my schedule was too full. When I wasn't in front of a camera, I got my therapy at the stables, digging up actual shit. That's what made me feel connected to reality and to something *bigger* than myself—like that ethereal feeling I'd had in the Coast Guard, floating alone in the middle of the Pacific Ocean.

All the babble about tunneling inward, burrowing into one's soul—how egotistical to always assume the answers are in your little brain! I've always felt closer to an "answer" when riding a good horse than I would be blabbing to the best shrink in the business.

So I kept my turmoil inside, like my mother did, and learned to separate my life into distinct halves: public life and private life. It left me painfully isolated, stranded between the casual homophobia of most "normal" people and the flagrantly gay Hollywood subculture—where I was even *less* comfortable and less accepted.

I never "acted" straight to get by. I wasn't "getting away" with something. I behaved the same way all the time. With me, what you saw is what you got—and what you didn't see was none of your business.

THE BURNING HILLS was an oater about a wayfaring cowpoke chased by cattle thieves who's rescued by a beautiful Mexican girl. Natalie couldn't ride, so I was happy to teach her. I took her out to Clyde Kennedy's training stables in Chatsworth, where I kept my horses. I'd just given myself permission to rent a fashionably chic new apartment off the Strip, 9080 Shoreham Drive—the designer-decorated digs of a young movie star. I loved the place but always felt that Clyde's barn was my real home.

Clyde was a terrific horseman, a bit rough around the edges, absolutely incorrigible around women. He had a line he'd use whenever girls trailed me around: "I'm Tab's brother—Cunt Hunter."

Clyde got issued a strict "hands off" order when it came to Natalie. I acted much more like her older brother than her boyfriend.

The Burning Hills reunited me with director Stuart Heisler, who'd survived my first film, *Island of Desire*, with his career intact. Plenty had changed in five years.

For starters, I was now a bankable "star," and the studio wouldn't tolerate any tampering with my boy-next-door image. When PR learned Heisler

wanted to grunge me up for authenticity's sake, Steve Trilling handed down a Clean Shaven Edict: TAB HUNTER IS TO GROW NO WHISKERS. Producer Richard Whorf memoed Trilling a promise: "We will just dirty him up and make him sweaty."

It looked like I packed an electric razor in my holster, not a six-shooter. So much for authenticity.

Natalie had her own problems in that regard. The poor thing had to apply a coat of bronze body makeup to darken her fair northern European complexion. Her Mexican accent was horrible—and she knew it. Not that a good accent would have helped dialogue like, "You dirty gringos! You make a rat's hole of this town—a scorpion's nest!"

They considered dubbing Natalie, and casting director Hoyt Bowers searched for a young Spanish-speaking actress to loop her lines. In the end, they elected to leave her alone. Warners was selling Natalie Wood, after all, and her growing legion of fans couldn't have cared less that her accent was miles north of the border. Veracity wasn't the issue. The charisma of the stars, force-fed through the studio's publicity machine, would carry the picture—or so they hoped.

Besides the pleasure of working with Natalie—who for a seventeen-year-old was completely professional and totally focused—there isn't much to recall about *The Burning Hills.*

At least it gave my horse, Swizzlestick, a job. I'd bought her from Dan Dailey's ex-wife, Liz. She'd been Green Jumper champion at the Del Mar Horse Show, and Clyde convinced me she'd be a good horse for me. Turned out to be a cranky old bitch, but you'd be, too, if you had a cyst on one of your ovaries. I eventually stopped showing her.

Warners, as a rule, didn't use mares in movies, but I stuck to my guns and demanded to ride Swiz. She even got paid—which ended Carl Coulter's complaints for good. She was a natural on-set: lights, cables, generators, all the stuff that could frighten a horse, didn't faze Swiz. She was a pro, and *The Burning Hills* was the start of a nice career for her.

We shot during February and March 1956, mostly at the old *Juarez* set in the hills of Calabasas, a few miles west of Burbank. The wardrobe department outfitted me with the boots Gary Cooper wore in *Springfield Rifle.* Talk about having big shoes to fill! Filming was uneventful save for a freak ice storm that shut us down one day; the temperature dropped to twenty-six degrees overnight. A slightly milder cold front moved in when my mother made a rare visit to the set.

It did little to alter her disdain for show business. The studio had beefed up my weekly salary to $750, which let me increase her monthly allowance. I convinced myself it was the right thing to do—and that it was unconnected to Bernice's thinly veiled threat. So it was especially galling when someone remarked, "You must be so proud of your son," and Mother would give her standard response: "Oh, yes, but Walter is the intelligent one."

Par for the course. A son can't win.

The only drama in *The Burning Hills* came in a couple of big fight scenes. At the Kern River, near Bakersfield, two stuntmen tumbled off a cliff into the raging current. For the close shots in the river, Skip Homeier and I had to wear wet suits beneath our costumes, with ropes tied around our waists to keep the rapids from carrying us away.

In another knock-down, drag-out brawl, Earl Holliman tried to kill me with a hay hook. We grappled around in a bear hug, the camera holding us in a tight shot. I finally wedge my gun in and shoot Earl point-blank in the gut. Before I could pull the trigger, however, Earl grunted, "Kiss me quick!" The whole crew broke into hysterics, even though we had to do the entire scene again.

I WAS DRIVING BACK to my apartment, over Laurel Canyon, having just finished my daily chores at the barn. It was one of those sunny winter days that makes everyone want to live in California. Instead of heading home, I decided to stop by the Chateau Marmont for a swim.

This famous re-creation of a castle in France's Loire Valley loomed over a legendary stretch of Sunset Boulevard, directly across from the Garden of Allah apartments, longtime homestead for many Hollywood stars, and only a stone's throw from Schwab's drugstore. The hotel cultivated a bohemian atmosphere and was a home away from home for many New York actors, whom you could spot by their pasty complexions. Despite its prominence, the cloistered Chateau provided plenty of privacy for its tenants, who could laze around the pool without being pestered by starstruck fans. A young movie actor could stop in for a quick dip, even if he wasn't registered.

As I toweled off, someone approached and formally introduced me to a new actor in town, Anthony Perkins.

Tony was tall and skinny, wearing a buttoned-down Brooks Brothers shirt and aviator-style reading glasses. He looked like a gawky New England prep school student who'd taken a wrong turn into this hipster's hideout.

He was living at the Chateau while he made *Friendly Persuasion,* an Allied

Artists picture with Gary Cooper and Dorothy McGuire, in which he played the son in a family of Quakers. Good casting: Tony had a naturally withdrawn quality, totally different from most performers, who were always *on*. By contrast, Tony was visibly uncomfortable and terribly shy. Since I'd never been attracted to aggressive people, men or women, I found his reticence appealing. Despite my door-opening looks, I usually felt insecure and awkward myself.

I sensed right off that Tony and I had a lot in common.

Once he relaxed, Tony invited me back to his room for lots more movie talk. He also regaled me with stories of his life back east, specifically how much he loved going out to the Cape, to a spot called Truro. He mentioned that his mother, Janet, and her friend, Michela, rented a beach house there every summer, south of Provincetown.

"Truro's one of my favorite places," Tony said enthusiastically. "I wouldn't miss the first week in July on the Cape for anything." I had no idea where Truro was, but it sounded fabulous.

My relationship with Tony began that day in the Chateau. We were drawn to each other because we were both ambitious young actors swimming in the Hollywood fishbowl, where the water is deep and murky and treacherous, especially if you've got a "secret."

We continued to see each other, off and on, over the next two years, as much as our workload permitted. Tony might have claimed he'd not skip Truro in July for anything, but the truth was that nothing came between Tony and his career. He was like Natalie in that way, but even more so. His father, Osgood Perkins, was a well-known stage and screen actor, who'd died when his son was only five years old. Tony felt an obligation to follow in his father's footsteps.

We shared the common bond of having grown up fatherless, but beyond that, our backgrounds couldn't have been more different. Tony had attended Florida's elite Rollins College, as well as Columbia University, and had established himself on Broadway as the college boy suspected of being gay in Robert Anderson's *Tea and Sympathy*. Also, his mother, unlike mine, actually appreciated acting as a profession.

I can't say I envied Tony, but I did tell him, repeatedly, how fortunate he was to have gotten training in live theater and television and to have worked with Broadway heavyweights like Kim Stanley and Elia Kazan. Much more than someone like Scott Marlowe, Tony had an intense, cerebral commitment to his craft. That's certainly part of what made him so interesting to me.

It was right at this time that movie magazines had started calling me a Product of Hollywood. Despite the success that brought, I admired Tony because he was a Product of New York.

WARNER BROS. ARRANGED for me to squire Natalie to the 1955 Academy Awards, held March 21, 1956, at the Pantages. We had to rush back to the studio from the *Burning Hills* location. Nat was a nervous wreck. She was more worried about how she was going to look than whether she might win the Best Supporting Actress Oscar for *Rebel Without a Cause*. As I passed the makeup and hair department, I peeked inside.

"What are we going to do about my hair?" Natalie was complaining to stylist Maggie Donovan.

"Cut it all off," I said. And I meant it. When I'd been in Europe with Ronnie, I'd been smitten by the sheared-off "waif" hairdos all the girls sported. Maggie loved it, too. She knew Nat had the perfect face for it.

The scissors flashed wildly. Sarita Monteil, the Spanish actress-singer, stopped dead in her tracks as she passed.

"Plumas locas," she exclaimed. "I like it, I like it."

From then on, Natalie referred to her new hairstyle as "crazy feathers."

Natalie was a sensation that night. In the electric blur, it barely registered on her that she didn't win the Oscar. Jo Van Fleet took home the award, for playing Jimmy's mother in *East of Eden*. The cameras, however, followed Natalie adoringly, as they always would. We went to the big victory party thrown by Harold Hecht and Burt Lancaster—their production of *Marty* won all the major awards, including Best Picture—and even there, Natalie stole the show, jitterbugging with me for hours. What a dancer! The cameramen couldn't get enough of us.

During the endless flow of industry people I greeted that night, one stopped me in my tracks—the drunk I'd left in his crumpled car, years before, after he tried to get in my pants. He was a high-powered agent! If he recognized me, he didn't let on, but I had no doubt it was the same guy.

After the buzz we created at the Oscars, and with *The Burning Hills* in the can, Natalie and I were photographed everywhere—eating at ritzy restaurants, attending gala premieres, lounging by her pool, riding in our Thunderbirds. Name the place—we were there.

The newsstands were chock-full of us: "At the Beach with Tab and Natalie!" "Tab and Natalie on Tour!" "Natalie Wood Talks about Tab!" "What

Every Girl Should Know about Tab Hunter!" Every minute Nat and I spent together was captured for promotion, feeding a seemingly insatiable public curiosity. And the great irony is that on many of these covers, there was Tony Perkins, right across from me, being sold as "swoon bait" to girls who preferred a slightly more intellectual heartthrob.

My public persona quickly assumed *multiple* layers of fantasy. When the press got tired of reporting on my relationship with Natalie, it started making up threats to our romance. One paper declared that I was about to be engaged to the daughter of an anonymous East Coast manufacturing tycoon. Another said I was "deeply in love" with Fox starlet Lili Gentle.

When Tony and I appeared together on popular game shows like *Juke Box Jury* and *Peter Potter's Platter Parade,* girls across America fell into love-struck spasms. If they knew the truth, it would have been like shattering the public's illusions about FDR . . . only this would have been more shocking than showing the president in his wheelchair. The culture needs to believe in its cherished icons. In some ways, they're the glue that holds everything together.

Around this time, the spring of 1956, my approach to doing interviews started to change. I resented being pushed and pulled whichever way the writers wanted. I wanted stories done in a way that didn't insult the reader's intelligence, or mine. *Movie Mirror* let me write my own article, titled, ironically enough, "Rumors Can Kill a Guy!"

Tony and me on the popular TV game show Juke Box Jury.

In this case, the rumors were that I'd gone "Hollywood," that I was immature and extravagant and, God forbid, "silly." It was impossible, of course, to directly confront the wave of innuendo that *Confidential* started. Instead, as sort of a catchall declaration, I started my article by quoting what I now realized was the best advice I'd ever gotten. It came from my first costar, Linda Darnell:

> Things happen fast in Hollywood and for as long as you're in the spotlight you remain a target for gossip and criticism and untruth. You have to forfeit all rights of privacy, but there are rich rewards that go hand in hand with the heartaches. No matter how hard you try you can't please everyone. So just hang on and do the best you can. The next five years will bring many changes and require constant adjustment. Don't complain—don't explain. Just concentrate on learning to live with yourself in peace—for that is the greatest goal of all.

No sooner had *The Burning Hills* wrapped than Warners immediately steered Natalie and me into our next film, *The Girl He Left Behind*. (We jokingly called it *The Girl with the Left Behind*.) I played a spoiled rich kid who learns his lesson after being drafted into the peacetime army. Natalie was my fiancée. The brilliant stage actress Jessie Royce Landis played my mother. David Butler was more of a traffic cop than a director, keeping us on time, under budget, and thoroughly uninspired. The most memorable thing about the film was the supporting cast, brimming with more fresh talent: James Garner, David Janssen, Alan King, Henry Jones, and Murray Hamilton—all destined for long careers.

Natalie was seven years younger than me, but she seemed to be growing up twice as fast. Her development between *The Burning Hills* and *The Girl He Left Behind* was incredible. She became freer with herself in the way she used her face and body. She was maturing as a woman and an actress, and while her mother drilled her to never bite the hand that fed her (*them,* more accurately), she privately groused about being stuck in such a tiny, lame role, unworthy of an Oscar nominee.

I thought Natalie would get a kick out of Scott Marlowe, since she was a devotee of the Actors Studio. Because Natalie soaked up experiences like a sponge, I figured Scott would be good for her. I orchestrated a meeting during filming. I'm no matchmaker—little did I know it would flare into a full-fledged affair. I knew Scott wouldn't mention our "little something" to Natalie.

I'll point out again that sexual orientation is rarely clear-cut in Hollywood. I don't know if Natalie knew Scott was bisexual or not. Nor do I know if Scott was "with" Natalie to get publicity (he did) and therefore score better roles (he didn't). At one point, the gossip columnists even announced that Scott and Natalie were engaged. It's even possible that Scott leaked the story himself. It wouldn't have been the first, or last, time that happened to Nat. In fact, she fed a counterattack to the press herself: "Attention all dates: If I read that I'm engaged to you, that will be the end of our dating."

Natalie's mother didn't like Scott at all. He was, unlike me, totally wrong for her daughter, imagewise. That ought to show you how superficial the whole "image making" business is.

Scott was indirectly responsible for the only argument Natalie and I ever had while making a film. Preparing for one of our scenes, I could sense her soul-searching, where previously she'd just *do it*. She was smitten with Scott and influenced by his approach to acting. I teased her, same way I did Scott, poking fun at all the seriousness. This was, after all, *The Girl with the Left Behind,* not *The Brothers Karamazov.* The ribbing must have stung, because Nat's next line—"I want to see some signs of your growing up!"—was blasted at me like a flamethrower.

I shouted back, "Thank you, Rod Steiger!"

Natalie ran off the set, furious.

A COUPLE OF MONTHS after we'd met, Tony rented a one-bedroom apartment on Horn Avenue, a few blocks away from me. He was at my place more often than he was home.

Tony didn't have many friends on the West Coast, certainly none outside the business. His confidants were dyed-in-the-wool New Yorkers like Helen Merrill, probably Tony's closest friend. She was a Manhattan-based photographer who shared her apartment with Tony when he was back east. She was very strong willed and looked like a younger Margaret Hamilton. She called me Hunty, in a German accent even thicker than my mother's. Helen had a very protective streak when it came to Tony, and he enjoyed the way she mothered him.

In fact, Tony loved being around older women and was at his most relaxed around them. He was devoted to the chic and elegant Dorothy Jeakins, the Oscar-winning costume designer he'd met making *Friendly Persuasion*. She already had two boys but treated Tony like her prodigal son. Half the time she acted like his mother; the other half, like his girlfriend. She had the style to pull it off without looking foolish.

My mother met Tony once or twice and was impressed by his "gentlemanly" manners and razor-sharp intelligence. He had a gift for inciting maternal instinct, particularly in mature women.

When I first met Tony, he didn't know how to drive—like a true New Yorker. He'd walk or hitchhike everywhere. My car mania must have rubbed off on him, because he learned pretty quickly. Before long, he'd buy a baby blue Thunderbird, the car of choice for young Hollywood. Mine was black, Lori's was yellow, Natalie's was pink . . . everybody had one.

Whenever we went out, Tony insisted on taking separate cars and arriving at different times—even if we were just going into Westwood to see a movie. It bugged me that, owing to the paranoia of the times, we couldn't show up in public together, as friends and colleagues, without arousing suspicion.

Tony felt safer in my inner circle, which included stalwarts Dick Clayton and Lori Nelson and newcomers Venetia Stevenson and Tuesday Weld, two new Clayton clients.

Tuesday was priceless. She was only fourteen but had been a model, stage actress, and breadwinner for her mother and sisters since her father's death in 1949, when she was six. A classic Tuesday story: Dick brought her to meet Danny Kaye, who was looking for a girl to play his youngest daughter in *The Five Pennies*. One look at Tuesday, and Danny said, "Dick, I think she's wonderful, but she's just too mature." Not missing a beat, Tuesday popped out her falsies and handed them over: "Daddy! How about now?" She got the part.

Venetia Stevenson, the daughter of director Robert Stevenson and actress Anna Lee, was labeled the Most Photogenic Girl in the World. I introduced her to the horse world, and we became close companions as a result. We'd meet almost every morning for coffee and a sweet roll at a little pastry shop on the Strip called Pupi's, then head out to Clyde Kennedy's to ride. (Clyde ended up marrying Venetia's sister, Caroline.)

Venetia was an essential part of my, and Tony's, social life—acting as a "beard" when we double-dated. Venetia was also under contract at Warners, and being a fashion plate, she took full advantage of the wardrobe department when we dated. She liked to joke that on many of our dates, she wore Natalie's outfits—"after I took all the padding out."

We all loved jazz, and we'd hit Sunset Strip clubs like the Crescendo or the Interlude, digging the sounds of Chet Baker, Dinah Washington, Jeri Southern, and Frances Faye. Sometimes Tony and I could go to these places on our own, but crowded hot spots like Ciro's and the Mocambo were out of the question unless we had girls on our arms. After dropping them off at home, Tony would usually stay over at my place.

My landlord, John Raven, enjoyed teasing people mercilessly. Whatever your shtick, John picked up on it instantly and would, from then on, relentlessly pick away at that idiosyncrasy. I'd gradually gotten used to him. Most people let John's barbs slide off, but they drove Tony crazy. He couldn't tolerate being mocked. Something John saw in Tony's fussy, uptight manner earned him the nickname Ma Perkins. Pretty soon Tony was peeking around corners and peering between drapes, checking to make sure Raven wasn't around before he'd enter or leave my place.

"Why won't that guy leave me alone?" Tony hissed. John was the only one who could get under Tony's skin like that.

On occasion, Tony would go with me to the barn or come to a show I was riding in, but he wasn't crazy about horses. Sometimes we'd head up to Watson Webb's place at Lake Arrowhead to water-ski. He wasn't the athletic type, however. His amusement came from using his quirky, brainy charm and extremely dry humor.

Beneath the boyishness, however, there was a lot of tension—not news to anyone who's seen Tony on-screen. The familiar body language wasn't an act. He slouched around with hands shoved deep in his pockets, and he jiggled his foot unconsciously—a nervous twitch. I figured he was just hyperanxious.

Postproduction of *Friendly Persuasion* took forever, but the advance word on Tony's performance was so strong he scored a seven-year deal with Paramount, which saw him as another contender in the James Dean replacement sweepstakes. His "arrival" made him a little arrogant, I felt.

Unlike me, Tony could be abrupt and condescending, even with the press. He'd arrive on the dot for interviews and immediately set his wristwatch in a conspicuous spot between himself and the reporter. Precisely one hour (or thirty-six thousand foot jiggles) later—even if it was in the middle of a question—Tony would scoop up the watch, flash his mischievous grin, and vanish.

His obsession with punctuality was a trial for somebody like me, who was cavalier about time. If I kept Tony waiting more than five minutes, he'd go ballistic. He was the first person to make me acutely conscious of time—mainly because I was so capricious about it. It was Tony who got me started keeping a calendar.

To relax, we shared an innocuous passion: Ping-Pong. We'd each reigned as table-tennis champs in our respective schools. Tony surprised me one Christmas with a deluxe portable table from Abercrombie and Fitch. We set it up on my apartment terrace and played marathon matches, all the while discussing our desires for our lives and careers. I probably drove Tony nuts, going on endlessly about how much I wanted Warners to buy *Fear Strikes Out* for me. What I desperately wanted was a big-screen role with more substance. Being famous meant nothing to me—I wanted to be taken seriously as an actor.

Tony sympathized with my frustration as Warners steadfastly ignored my pleas.

LIKE ME, TONY rarely dropped his guard to let other people get close. Actors are always dealing with people who have hidden agendas and want to become their new best friend. I could be as subtle as a Mack truck with phonies trying to get next to me. Tony was more deft at drawing the line without being mean. But sometimes he could string people along cruelly.

Braving an autumn chill to teach Tony to water-ski at Watson Webb's Lake Arrowhead retreat.

Gwen Davis was a young songwriter who was absolutely gaga over Tony. Their senses of humor meshed, and Gwen's crush grew into a romantic obsession.

A whole group of Tony's friends, including Venetia and me, went to see Gwen on her opening night at the Purple Onion. She tossed off a barbed comment regarding the public romance of Hollywood's hottest duo, calling them "Natalie Wood and Tab Wouldn't."

Unfortunately, for someone with such a sharp wit, Gwen was pretty naive. She had no idea, in those early months, that Tony was gay. I tried to cultivate a friendship with her, but she had no use for me. She was jealous of anyone else's closeness to Tony. Behind the scenes, I suspected she was being teased that Tony and I were the real item.

I can't say Tony led her on, exactly. It was always a tricky situation, when there was a mutual attraction with a woman. You didn't blurt out, *Don't bother, I'm gay.* In the 1950s, people didn't jump into bed right off, so it was possible to date for weeks, even months, without the question coming up. Back then, the average woman wouldn't have considered men like Tony or me gay—only proper and well mannered.

Venetia, however, knew the score, although I wasn't aware of it at the time. Once she and Tony became good friends, he'd unburden himself to her. "You never talked about it," she said to me much later. "But Tony would. He'd sleep over and tell me sad stories. He was totally crazy about you."

And I was crazy about Tony, but our careers pulled us every which way. We lived moment to moment, giving no thought to where our relationship might lead.

It came as a surprise when Venetia told me, "Everybody knew what was going on, and that you didn't want to talk about it. People respected your right to privacy." Apparently I wasn't as good as I thought at hiding my inner turmoil—Venetia said that being with me in those days was sometimes like walking on eggshells.

"At the stable once, I did something and you went berserk," she said. "Everybody treaded lightly around you. You could fly off the handle. I think you got that from your mother."

Going out with Tony in public got more problematic. Inevitably, we were recognized by fans. Tony started adopting disguises, typically a baseball cap and sunglasses. Practically a uniform for celebrities now, but back in the fifties it was so unusual I was afraid it would attract more attention, not less. The whole cloak-and-dagger thing got ridiculous, but I went along with it.

Eventually, I started to feel that Tony didn't want to be seen with me in public. He was afraid of getting the same kind of smear job *Confidential* had given me. His "people" were advising him about the problems that might result if we were linked, that it might foul up his Paramount deal. Tony was unhappy with the studio's plans for him, and he hated the staged publicity layouts and arranged dates (the studio's, not ours)—but he reluctantly did what he was told. His overriding focus was on building his movie career, and if he didn't always grasp the risks of scandal, I'm sure there were handlers at Paramount "educating" him.

One thing I can say with assurance about Tony is that he always knew exactly how to gain an advantage from any situation. He could charm the birds out of the trees when he wanted to, so long as it fit his agenda. Everything was on his terms, and you could see the gears in that brain of his, spinning a mile a minute.

I began to wonder how much of his sheepish appeal was genuine, and how much was manufactured, used to mask very calculated, methodical intentions.

1 5

Fever Pitch

TONY AND I SAW each other as much as we could in the spring of 1956, given that I was finishing *The Girl He Left Behind* and he was making *The Lonely Man,* his first starring role for Paramount. One night when he dropped by the apartment, during one of our epic table-tennis matches, Tony served one up with a devastating spin:

"Hey, guess what?" he said, that thin little smile creeping on his face. "Paramount just bought *Fear Strikes Out* for me."

Son of a bitch.

Tony knew how much that role meant to me. My constant ranting about it probably inspired him to use a little friendly persuasion of his own on the Paramount brass. I had suspected that he placed career ahead of friendship; now here was the proof. So much for loyalty among friends in the Hollywood fishbowl.

Our relationship didn't end after that, but it definitely changed. We still saw each other, but from then on we weren't nearly as close.

Production of *Fear Strikes Out* began in mid-July. By then, I'd swallowed the bitter pill and convinced myself that Paramount's purchase of the rights to Piersall's story was just a coincidence. Any animosity I felt should have been directed toward Warner Bros. for not snapping up the property when it had the chance. That wasn't Tony's fault. I may not have completely trusted him, but I didn't want lingering hard feelings to ruin our friendship.

To show my support and appease my own curiosity, I visited Tony on the Paramount lot.

That was a mistake.

There was already a lot of tension on the set, and my being there only made it worse. I couldn't tell whether Tony's anxiety was due to my looking over his shoulder or to his being so deeply "in character." There was, however, no way to misread the chilly reception I got from others.

Years later, in a couple of Anthony Perkins biographies, some members of the *Fear Strikes Out* cast and crew would claim that I repeatedly visited the set, causing Tony all sorts of grief. The implication was that, simply through my presence, I was confirming the "rumors" about Tony—about *us*.

That's utter bullshit. I went on the set once, got the cold shoulder, and never went back. Believe me, I didn't have time that summer to hang around watching my colleagues at work.

THAT AUGUST, NATALIE and I were flown to New York for the premiere of *The Burning Hills*. Manhattan was a nonstop swirl of radio, press, and television interviews. We must have been on every show, live or taped, that originated in the city. Cabbies would holler out the window: "Hey, Tabunter—howyadoin'?" Natalie and I were recognized everywhere we went, a new experience for both of us. She ate it up, but I found it very uncomfortable.

Warners put me up at the Gotham, and Natalie at the Essex House. Think of the rumors if we'd stayed in the same hotel! The riots!

Times Square was plastered with a huge twenty-four-sheet poster of me, bare chested, sprawled atop Natalie, looking for all the world like we were about to "do it." The floating caption blared: THAT SHY GUY FROM "BATTLE CRY" AND THE TEENAGE GIRL FROM "REBEL WITHOUT A CAUSE" BURN UP THE SCREEN!

They should have burned up the prints. Our first film together was no *Rebel Without a Cause*. Swiz, my mare, clearly gave the best performance. Actually, most reviews were more critical of the screenplay than of the cast—not that it stalled Irving Wallace's writing career.

Newsweek called it "a slight to all Western devotees" and noted that "Warner Bros., haunted by the memories of those profitable romantic couples of the '30s, is setting out to make the names of Natalie Wood and Tab Hunter as familiar as Loy and Powell, Rogers and Astaire, and MacDonald and Eddy. Fortunately, both are young enough to recover from their first joint excursion."

Some critics, however, thought the picture was foolproof. Kay Proctor of the *Los Angeles Examiner* wrote, "So popular are Tab and Natalie with both—

yes BOTH!—sexes of young theater-goers, I suspect they could appear in a broken down version of 'Pollyanna, The Glad Girl' and still make the box office rock 'n' roll!"

DURING REHEARSALS FOR our appearance on *The Perry Como Show,* Natalie suddenly confided, "Elvis has been calling me."

"Elvis! How long has this been going on?"

"He's called the hotel a couple of times," she said. Something in her voice made me suspect they'd already gone out.

"Are you actually interested in him?" I asked, incredulous.

I was one of the few young people in America immune to Elvis mania. I just couldn't figure what all the fuss was about. Knowing that, Nat enjoyed teasing me: "I'm in love," she sang. "I'm all shook up." She showed off a couple of Presley's patented pelvic thrusts for good measure.

"You really like him?" I whined. "For God's sake, he can have any woman he wants. Why can't he leave you alone?" Natalie just smiled like the Cheshire cat.

All right, I was jealous. Not because Natalie and I were supposed to be the item, but because I was so protective of her. Elvis was getting a reputation for cutting a swath through all the eligible young women in show business, and I didn't fancy Nat being one of his conquests. Call me corny, but I thought she should be dating somebody the caliber of Pat Boone or Ricky Nelson.

After the rehearsal, as we headed up Broadway to Natalie's hotel, my cross-examination continued. Noticing that the ES in the hotel's neon marquee had burned out, I said, "Let's hope Elvis doesn't get the wrong idea when he comes to visit you at the 'Sex House.'" Natalie belted me with the stuffed tiger she now carried everywhere—the gift from Nick Ray was a constant accessory to her pixie look, duly noted by girls nationwide.

Our TWA Constellation flight from New York to Chicago on August 28, 1956, provided one of my favorite memories of Natalie. We were invited into the cockpit, a standard perk for celebrities traveling first-class. It was a sparkling clear night, offering an amazing view of the diamond lights of America from twenty thousand feet up. While Nat enchanted the pilots, I went back to my seat and dozed off. When we touched down, I realized that Nat hadn't returned.

As the plane rolled toward the terminal, Natalie burst out of the cockpit. "I landed the plane!" she crowed, dancing down the aisle. She was as excited and endearing as a ten-year-old kid at Christmas.

Chased onto a warehouse fire escape, Howard Miller introduces Natalie and me to a sea of Chicago fans.

The Chicago leg of the promotional tour would be, in terms of my career, the most significant thing about making *The Burning Hills*. That's how I met Howard Miller, a disc jockey who was a star maker in midwestern music markets. He had a radio show that blanketed the Midwest, reaching 280 CBS affiliate stations. He could break a record wide open in the heartland, a fact that would soon be significant to my career.

After Howard had interviewed us on his show that morning, we did a whirlwind tour of the town, six different stops, with the press detailing our every glance, our every gesture. The afternoon culminated in a highly touted public appearance at the Chicago Theater, where Miller interviewed us onstage before a packed house. For this he paid us handsomely. Warners, of course, got half.

Even though more than one hundred police officers were assigned to crowd control, the event almost turned into a nightmare. As we left the theater through a rear fire door, we were spotted. Suddenly, hundreds of teenagers—most of whom didn't get into the show—swarmed the area. They came after us, swelling into a mob, breaking through the barricades. Natalie and I fled down an alley, chased by the wailing horde.

From out of nowhere, a door flew open and we were pulled into an abandoned warehouse. Through the walls, we could hear the mob chanting for us to come out. Natalie and I stared at each other, jaws hanging open. We'd never experienced anything *close* to this.

Howard Miller brilliantly transformed this chaos into show business. As soon as he had stationed photographers in strategic locations—covering the perfect angles—Natalie and I appeared on the second-story fire escape, overlooking an undulating sea of people that stretched for several city blocks. We felt like royalty, surveying our subjects from a rickety "palace" balcony. Finally, we descended to earth, after a battalion of Chicago cops had been assembled to escort us to a waiting limousine.

We laughed about it later over dinner at the famed Pump Room in the Ambassador East Hotel, but I was pretty shaken up. I had serious doubts about whether I was cut out for this kind of insane popularity.

The following day was more my speed. Miller took Natalie and me for a leisurely cruise on Lake Michigan, aboard his aptly named yacht, *Disc Jockey.* Natalie avidly took to this kind of high life, although she confessed to us that she didn't like being out on the lake, because she had a terrible fear of the water.

During the afternoon, Miller planted the seed that would bloom into a totally unexpected chapter of my life.

With Nat, clowning around on Howard Miller's yacht on Lake Michigan.

"Did you ever think of recording?" he asked.

"Nooo." I might even have laughed.

"You might want to give it a try sometime," he advised.

"Howard—I can't sing."

That fact didn't bother him in the least.

"Well, if you change your mind when you get back to L.A., I'd like to hook you up with Randy Wood. He's an old friend—owns Dot Records."

At the time, it was nothing more than idle conversation, the kind of thing I'd expect him to say. Shows how naive I was. When you put a hot commodity together with a whip-smart deal maker, there's no such thing as idle conversation.

The Burning Hills premiered in Hollywood the first week of September. Natalie sneaked off afterward for pizza with Elvis Presley at the Villa Capri. She then left on a much-needed two-week Hawaiian vacation, her mother in tow. The picture was a smash hit. To keep our publicity percolating, Bill Hendricks fed the movie magazines childish-sounding "love letters" Natalie and I were supposedly sending back and forth.

Warners then announced that Natalie and I were going to make three more movies together. This would have been fine—if the scripts weren't so lousy. Heading into my late twenties, I felt a little long in the tooth to be spouting dialogue like, "Gee, Dad, can I borrow the big car tonight?"

Okay, maybe that exact line wasn't in *Bombers B-52*, but I was hugely disappointed with the script for the next film Warners slated—a sappy romance wrapped in an air force recruiting promo. The planes had more dimension than the characters.

I turned it down flat. (As a result, Efrem Zimbalist Jr. got his first starring role.) This was Warners' first inkling that it had a "temperamental" star on its hands. The studio threatened to put me on suspension. Maybe I was getting a bit arrogant at that point, but only because I wanted a challenge, something that would test me as an actor and allow me to earn the respect of my colleagues.

The thing I deeply regret about nixing *Bombers B-52* was that I never got another chance to work with Natalie. Months earlier, it seemed like we'd be partners forever. As it turned out, we were the Dream Team for less than a year, with only two movies to show for all the hoopla.

• • •

Television, not the movies, gave me the chance to find myself, to offer more than an "image." Marty Manulis, who'd produced "Fear Strikes Out" for *Climax!* sent Dick a script called "Forbidden Area," a cold war thriller by a hot young writer named Rod Serling. It was to be the initial episode of a brand-new dramatic series, produced live at CBS's Television City complex, corner of Beverly and Fairfax.

Within days, I started rehearsals with costars Charlton Heston, Vincent Price, Victor Jory, Jackie Coogan, and Diana Lynn, with whom I'd worked in *Track of the Cat.*

The project excited me because, for the first time, I got to play the villain, a Communist "mole" trying to blow up a bunch of air force fighter planes. Heston was the good guy, a military investigator who exposes me as the culprit in the last act. Our director was a dynamic New Yorker with dozens of television credits already under his belt—John Frankenheimer. He was enthusiastic, resourceful, and inventive, a wonderful talent. Having worked with old-timers like Heisler, Dupont, Wellman, and Walsh, it was exciting to be directed by someone my own age. Only twenty-six, Frankenheimer would receive his second (of an eventual thirteen) Emmy nomination for his direction of "Forbidden Area."

The show aired on October 4, 1956—the first episode ever broadcast of the legendary series *Playhouse 90.* Wish I could say it was a blazing start to what would, eventually, be regarded as the finest anthology series in the Golden Age of Television. It wasn't. I got good notices for my change-of-pace performance, but critics were lukewarm to the show overall. It was the following week's installment, Serling's second contribution to *Playhouse 90*—"Requiem for a Heavyweight" — that scored the knockout.

Charlton Heston, Charles Bickford, and I rehearse "Forbidden Area," the first ever Playhouse 90 *production.*

That episode was a critical smash, swept the Emmys, and was made into a successful feature. It became so famous that people mistakenly remember it as the inaugural *Playhouse 90* show. For the sake of history—and my tiny place in it—I note that "Forbidden Area," not "Requiem for a Heavyweight," was the first *Playhouse 90* presentation.

ONLY ONE MONTH after *The Burning Hills* opened, Warner Bros. sent *The Girl He Left Behind* into wide release. America's teenagers were socked with a Tab and Natalie one-two combination.

And I took a few shots of my own. *New Yorker* critic John McLaren, reviewing *The Girl He Left Behind*, delivered this low blow: "Since Mr. Hunter discloses not one redeeming feature as an actor, the picture misses fire whenever he's around."

You can't ask for much less than that.

Oh, there were positive reviews as well, but those didn't stick with me. It was the nasty ones that got under my skin, especially the ones obsessed with mocking my "teen idol" status. The bad reviews didn't matter, however. *The Girl with the Left Behind* broke huge at the box office. "Tab Hunter" existed in some kind of infallible, impervious bubble. Critical brickbats couldn't dent my public appeal.

One day in Googie's, a popular hangout for Hollywood hopefuls, some two-bit wannabe, unaware that I was in a nearby booth, started mouthing off to his cronies: "Hunter's a freak! I don't care if he's big box office—he's strictly a no-talent pretty boy!"

I knew he wasn't talking about *Jeffrey* Hunter. Believe it or not, this kind of stuff hurt me terribly. Under the fame and notoriety that was being piled on, I was still an insecure kid, sensitive to the backlash that was mounting against me both in the press and in public.

The waitress, feeling sorry for me, took it upon herself to tell this clown, "You're just like all the rest of 'em—eaten up with envy."

Very nice of her. If only she could have served me a meaty role on a silver platter. That's what I really needed. Fortunately, one fell right in my lap.

FROM THE TIME William Wellman arrived in Hollywood in the late 1920s, he'd been carrying around with him the idea for a movie called *C'est la Guerre*. It was his pet project, one he'd written himself, inspired by his experiences in Europe during the First World War.

The lead character was based on Wellman's pal Thad Walker, a rebellious American boy who'd fled to Paris from the States after a brush with the law disgraced his affluent family. When the war broke out, Walker—like Wellman—wanted to prove his mettle by being accepted into the Lafayette Flying Corps. While in training, he fell in love with Renée, a local prostitute. Their covert romance led to a secret marriage. Thad convinced Renée to give up street life for a job as a conductress on the metro. After finally earning his wings, Walker was called to the front—and promptly shot down in an aerial dogfight. When Renée learned of his death, she committed suicide by jumping into the Seine, wearing the ID bracelet Walker had given her—the only physical evidence that remained of the link between the doomed lovers.

Now *that's* a story.

Wellman was a feisty sixty-year-old but suffered from advanced arthritis, among other ailments. He was determined to get this picture made, come hell or high water, before he was too infirm to direct anymore.

He was working with a studio that was at a crossroads. Other than its huge success with Natalie and me, Warner Bros. was hurting. It was confused about what kind of movies to make, during a period when new trends were shaking things up: competition from television, the influence of foreign films (both on filmmakers and viewers), the shift toward realism and naturalism, the cultural changes brought on by rock and roll—Warners wasn't too swift picking up on any of these. Studio executives could see the writing on the wall but had a lot of trouble translating it. It was a cautious and conservative company.

Jack Warner—like a number of studio bosses before him—didn't find much appeal in Wellman's dream project. Too depressing. Not to mention too "historical" for the young audience the studio was after. But—if Wellman could get Tab Hunter to play the ill-fated pilot! . . .

I jumped at the opportunity. Once more I'd be in the military, but this was taking *The Girl He Left Behind* to the glorious heights of romantic tragedy—exactly the kind of serious, prestigious project I was dying to make. Plus it reunited me with Wild Bill Wellman, my favorite among the film directors I'd worked with.

Jack Warner, always hedging his bets, decided he'd only give *C'est la Guerre* the green light if Wellman agreed to direct another film immediately afterward, sight unseen. To help the studio's cash flow, the Colonel required that Wellman forgo his usual salary in exchange for a percentage of the profits. In his prime, Wellman probably would have told Warner to stuff it. But in 1956, he agreed to the Colonel's conditions. Wild Bill must have sensed that his me-ter was running.

Or maybe, since he was a producer as well as a director, he'd scanned the trades, saw the booming grosses for *The Burning Hills* and *The Girl He Left Behind*, and figured making his "dream movie" with Tab Hunter might, in the end, lead to a handsome back-end payout.

With a bankable male star secured, Wellman could take a risk with his leading lady. For the sake of authenticity, he wanted a Frenchwoman for the part of Renée, someone who would make an intriguing contrast to the All-American Boy.

The studio consented. After I'd rejected *Bombers B-52*, there was no profit in the PR department continuing to promote a romance between me and Natalie. Instead, Bill Hendricks had his minions start preparing items about my hot-and-heavy romance with my latest costar—even though she hadn't yet set foot in the United States.

Out of the Blue

I FIRST LAID EYES on Etchika Choureau at a little art house in downtown Los Angeles, in a picture called *Fruits of Summer*. Wellman had told me to check it out if I wanted a sneak peek at my *C'est la Guerre* costar. The film was in French, but Etchika could have been speaking Chinese for all I cared. Her mix of coquettish sex appeal and childlike innocence captivated me; she was totally different from the blond and bouncy girls that were all the rage in America. In France, she'd become so popular, so fast, she'd already made twelve films since her debut in 1953.

Seeing her on-screen didn't prepare me for the night, several weeks later, when Jack Warner invited me to a small gathering at his home to celebrate the arrival of his latest "discovery." When I walked in and saw Etchika in the flesh, I was awestruck. She was adorable: porcelain skin with a delicate smattering of freckles, wavy flaxen hair, the bluest eyes I'd ever seen. She wasn't all dolled up, L.A.-style; her simple silk ensemble showed an understated elegance, like a Gallic Audrey Hepburn.

Her English was terrible. My French was worse. She laughed when I tried out my only two lines on her: "You are very beautiful. Give me a kiss." We spent the whole evening together on the sofa, staring at each other, oblivious to everyone.

The PR boys were going to have a field day—only this time it wasn't make-believe.

C'est la Guerre went into production in late October, at an airfield on the outskirts of Santa Maria, California, 150 miles north of Burbank. The studio had stocked it with dozens of antique aircraft, including Nieuports, Fokkers, and rare, authentic Blériots, which had to be borrowed from museums.

Right off the bat, Wellman realized that hiring me was a mixed blessing. Hordes of teenage girls descended on the location, routinely disrupting filming, using any tactic necessary to get a glimpse of Tab Hunter. But Wild Bill kept his legendary temper in check, since it was these nubile ticket buyers, and millions more like them, who'd be responsible for making his back-end deal profitable. It didn't pay to alienate them, as he'd eventually learn in a *big* way.

Wellman hired just about every French-speaking actor in Hollywood to surround his seven-member corps of expat American fliers. Fresh faces were picked to play the Yanks, including nineteen-year-old William Wellman Jr., portraying his father. It wasn't nepotism, since the PR department suggested the idea. I felt kind of sorry for Bill Jr., bearing up under constant tongue-lashings from his old man, who was determined to show no favoritism to his flesh and blood.

Keeping with the "sons of actors" gimmick, Joel McCrea's son, Jody, and Andy Devine's son, Dennis, were also cast. The corps was rounded out by three newcomers who'd make significant marks in the business: David Janssen, later to star in the long-running TV series *The Fugitive;* Tom Laugh-

A quiet moment with "Wild Bill" Wellman and Etchika Choureau on the set of Lafayette Escadrille. (Photo © Warner Bros. Pictures, Inc. All rights reserved.)

lin, who'd become famous as *Billy Jack;* and a quiet guy to whom nobody paid much attention: Clint Eastwood. Dick Clayton made one of the rare blunders of his career when he turned down Eastwood's request for representation. Clint has teased Dick ever since about "the one who got away."

Second time around with Wellman, I was totally different from the greenhorn who'd sneaked through *Track of the Cat.* Alongside Mitchum, I'd been the new kid on the block, quietly observing, minding my own business, soaking it all in. Two whirlwind years later, *I* was the veteran in the cast.

That's why I bristled when Wellman hired a drill instructor to teach us to march in formation. I didn't need more lessons. In *Battle Cry* and *The Girl with the Left Behind*, I'd marched my ass off enough for one lifetime. So when the "sergeant" hup-two-three-foured us past a line of dense shrubs, I fell out and made for the nearest café. Let the rookies count cadence for thirty minutes; I had more to learn from the morning paper and a hot cup of coffee.

A waitress who looked just like Olive Oyl was pouring me a refill when Hurricane Bill blew through the front doors. The customers couldn't have been more shocked if Dillinger had burst in, both guns blazing.

"What the fuck *are you doing!"* Wellman bellowed. No trace of arthritis this day. Wild Bill's throttle was wide open.

He got right in my face. *"If you think I'm gonna march for you, Hunter— you're fulla shit!"*

Lots more invective, which I won't repeat, was spewed. I could barely muster a stammer. Olive Oyl was so rattled she dropped a full pot of coffee.

"Listen you—get your lazy ass back out there and do your job!"

Cut to me, in formation: left, right, left, right, left—right back at St. John's Military Academy.

ALTHOUGH HE HAD incredible enthusiasm for this project, Wellman was frustrated by how the unpredictable wind conditions played hell with the fragile old aircraft. Day by day, you could see his epic vision being whittled away by cost concerns. There simply wasn't enough of a budget to open the piece up and do the action right. In the end, most of the aerial battles were lifted from an earlier Wellman film, *Men with Wings*. Cockpit shots of Ray Milland and Fred MacMurray would be removed, and close-ups of me and the other actors inserted.

After twenty days on location, Wellman was eager to get back to the studio, where he was more at home with the highly controlled, stage-bound style of filming. I was happy to return to Burbank as well—it's where all my scenes with Etchika would be shot.

Our first day back on the lot, Etchika came to my dressing room so we could run some lines. She spoke English as though it embarrassed her, and had to learn her dialogue phonetically. She coached me with my limited French. Since the language barrier was a big part of the story, perfect diction didn't matter. We used the rehearsals as an excuse to spend more time together.

Suddenly we heard Wellman outside, starting to fume. Gingerly, we poked our heads out.

"What the hell is *that*?" The director was shouting at a security guard and pointing at something new on the soundstage—a coffee-vending machine. "Where's our regular coffee guy?" asked Wild Bill, steaming. All activity came to a standstill.

"He's been let go, Mr. Wellman," the guard explained. "If you want coffee from now on, you're going to have to pay for it. New studio policy."

From the guard's little grin, I gathered he knew what was coming.

"New studio policy—*my ass*!" Wellman screamed. He ordered the massive soundstage doors opened. He grappled with the offending contraption himself, all the while issuing a stream of the foulest language imaginable. I didn't bother to translate for Etchika. Looking anything but geriatric, Wellman pushed the machine down the soundstage ramp and sent it on its way in the world. It hurtled to the street, crashed into some parked bicycles, bounced a couple of times, then blew apart, splattering coffee everywhere.

"My crew doesn't pay for a fucking cup of coffee!" Wellman roared. "And if Jack Warner doesn't like it, let that son of a bitch come down here and tell me to my face!"

Before the day was out, our regular coffee man was back on the set, brewing away. Wild Bill may have won that little battle, but, sadly, he wasn't going to win the war. When it came to minding nickels and dimes, nobody beat Jack Warner.

With cast and crew resettled in the studio, fortified with fresh caffeine, production picked up pace. So did my relationship with Etchika. Scratch that—so did my *romance* with Etchika.

I'd never before felt this way about a woman. Most of the girls I loved were "running buddies," like Debbie and Lori and Venetia. But Etchika had a mystery about her that drew me in. In her street clothes, little matador pants and bulky sweaters, she was the height of Continental style, radiating an intelligence and maturity far beyond her years. I've always been attracted to the *other*, and Etchika was marvelously different, from me and everyone else I knew.

Communicating with her was both completely natural and absurdly difficult. We'd go out a few times a week during filming, and our dates often mirrored scenes we'd shot during the day, where our declarations were delivered with a French-English dictionary in hand. Even with all the practice, her accent was barely decipherable. Not that words were important, or even necessary.

With Etchika, I had the same sort of deep connection—don't laugh—that I usually felt only with my horses. It went beyond the verbal, beyond the physical. It was a chemical energy, something I hadn't experienced with too many other humans.

Either that, or I was simply infatuated, like a schoolboy in the throes of his first crush.

"C'est tout à cause de vos yeux," I'd whisper in her ear, trying to impress her with a new bit of French I'd practiced. She'd giggle and look into my eyes, and I'd melt.

I felt completely at ease with her on my arm, even at swank parties like the one FAA's Charlie Feldman threw at his place, packed with industry players. Plenty of them—or at least the ones who read *Confidential*—probably thought the longing glances Etchika and I shared were so much PR hype. They weren't. Being with her was uncomplicated. There was no sense of pressure. It felt like how I imagined falling in love was supposed to feel.

DURING THIS OCTOBER–NOVEMBER romance, my thing with Tony was still going strong. *Fear Strikes Out* was in postproduction, and Tony was now making a western, *The Tin Star*, with Henry Fonda. We continued to see each other, privately, as much as our schedules allowed. At the time, he was dating Gary Cooper's eighteen-year-old daughter, Maria. Paramount flacks were trying to build their relationship into something, just as Warners had done with me and Natalie.

Friendly Persuasion, Tony's "breakthrough" picture—his *Battle Cry*—premiered at the Fox-Wilshire Theatre on October 30, two days after *The Girl He Left Behind* opened. It was a star-studded event: Gary Cooper, Henry Fonda, Gregory Peck, Audrey Hepburn, Mel Ferrer, Kim Novak, Doris Day, Eddie Fisher and Debbie Reynolds, Dorothy Malone, Natalie.

Those last three I'd dated often, but this wasn't a Warner Bros. premiere, so the studio couldn't have cared less who I escorted. I went stag, as did Tony.

If we had a lot in common ten months earlier, when we first met, by November 1956 we'd become virtual bookends. Tony was starting to get the same buildup in the media that I'd gotten, in an attempt to make him a matinee idol. Some of the articles carried such ironic titles as "Why Tony Perkins Is Girl Shy" and "Why Tony Won't Bring Girls Home to Mother."

He and I talked a lot about the weird ways of show business, which bothered Tony more than me. Arranged dates, like the one we went on with Jan Chaney and Norma Moore to the *Ice Follies,* never bothered me. Dating was just an accepted part of the Hollywood ramble for young actors. We never fretted about not being able to "be ourselves." There certainly was never any jealousy or acrimony when we'd end up dating the same girls. Why would there be? Tony probably felt that Etchika, whom I raved about, was just another girl on my showbiz dance card.

Going back and forth between Tony and Etchika made me horribly guilty. But then, I always felt guilty in a serious relationship. If it was with a man, I was sinning. If it was with a woman, I was lying. Now, the guilt was doubled.

I was one seriously conflicted young movie star.

ONE OF THE HIGHLIGHTS of shooting *C'est la Guerre,* for an auto aficianado like me, was the car that I steal at the start of the picture—not just any car, but a 1914 Stutz Bearcat road racer. Warners had one in its inventory: canary yellow, doorless, with wide running boards, colossal chrome headlamps, and a huge stick shift swooping up from the floorboards. A classic car specialist had to teach me how to drive it.

Tony and me "double-dating" with Jan Chaney and Norma Moore.
(Photo courtesy of Globe Photos.)

The car theft and near-fatal accident was to be the first scene in the movie. We shot it "day for night," using film tricks to simulate a night scene during the morning. When the assistant director called, "Lunch!" I couldn't resist "stealing" the Bearcat for a run around the lot. The place was jumping: Doris Day was on Stage 7, shooting the film version of the popular Broadway hit *The Pajama Game*; Susan Hayward and Kirk Douglas were wrapping *Top Secret Affair* on Stage 16; ageless Randolph Scott was making *Shootout at Medicine Bend*, with newcomers James Garner and Angie Dickinson; and *The Helen Morgan Story* was just getting rolling, with Ann Blyth and Paul Newman.

I piloted the Bearcat over to the set of *Untamed Youth*, which Lori Nelson was shooting with Mamie Van Doren (what was I saying about big, bouncy American girls?). I decided to squire Lori to lunch off the lot. The carhops' eyes nearly popped out when we motored into Bob's Big Boy for burgers.

No repercussions from that stunt. Maybe Wild Bill figured I was acting "in character."

Gossip columnists were, by this time, buzzing about Tab Hunter finally finding the girl he was going to marry. Army Archerd, Sheila Graham, Mike Connolly, and, of course, Hedda Hopper had Etchika's wedding dress all but picked out. Hedda was especially giddy to report on my impending nuptials, since she was the biggest Tony Perkins fan in town. She practically declared him her adopted son in print and was eager to publish anything that would bury those rumors about Tony's "secret friend."

Louella Parsons remarked that Etchika's name sounded like a sneeze, and she cattily suggested that Etchika was already in love with a French diplomat back home — the first time I'd heard anything about *that*. But . . . I knew better than to believe what you read in the papers.

Warner Bros., of course, was ecstatic about all the free publicity.

When Jack Warner saw rushes of my love scenes with Etchika, he quickly took out ads in the trades declaring that the name of the picture was being changed to *With You in My Arms*. He didn't ask Wellman's opinion. That was probably the point at which Wild Bill first felt his "dream project" slipping away. Leaving the title as *C'est la Guerre* not only would have appeased the director but also would have shown that Warner was hip to new trends, as French imports were starting to rack up significant grosses at the box office. But the boss was unwilling to give up his old-school approach to selling movies.

In truth, the Colonel wasn't the only one stuck in the past. So was Wellman. I gave him the best job I had in me, but the footage we were turning out

played like something from the director's silent days, with melodramatic romantic clinches, stagy fight scenes, and comedic pratfalls, all played at the
same pace before an almost defiantly static camera. It might as well have been
1928.

Maybe this was the director's subtle way of paying tribute to his early days
as a filmmaker. Maybe he didn't have the budget to do anything different.
Maybe, after seventy-four feature films, he was just plain tired.

I woke up in the small hotel room where Etchika was living. Her incredible eyes were looking right into me. Our passion was overwhelming. I
gathered her into my arms.

"Will you marry me?" I blurted out.

She smiled, unsure of what I'd said.

"Just say yes," I pleaded.

"Oui. Oui."

I clutched her to me.

"Cut!" Wellmam yelled. "Print it!"

It could have been that easy.

I was pondering my own improvised version of that scene when Etchika
and I celebrated her twenty-third birthday with a quiet dinner at Martoni's,
our favorite Hollywood restaurant. The photographers figured out where we'd
be, probably with help from the studio's PR flacks, which annoyed the hell out
of me. This time belonged to *us*, not Warner Bros. As we got deeper into the
production, the time we spent together seemed all the more precious and
fleeting.

"When we finish the film," Etchika said, "I return to Paris. To my family."

Propose, you idiot!

It felt like the press had already made the decision for me. There are lots
of people in this business, too many, who throw themselves into marriage with
a "let's live for today" attitude. They keep divorce lawyers in business. Maybe
because I'd been raised by a single mother, I idealized the concept of matri-
mony. To me, it really did mean *forever*. That word kept pounding in my head,
like a hammer. It was the Lori Nelson situation, all over again. I felt hemmed
in by all the *right* things marriage represented:

It was the normal thing to do.

It would end the rumors.

It would help my career.

It would also be a *lie,* and I could not go through my life lying every day to a person I loved. Yet if I could ever imagine myself married—Etchika was the one. What was holding me back?

Was I still too damn confused about who—or *what*—I was?

Was it because I knew I couldn't be faithful to her?

Was it simply that I was afraid she'd say no?—or, worse, yes?

The answer, of course, was all of the above.

I tried to enjoy Etchika's birthday as best I could, considering I spent the entire dinner with a marriage proposal stuck in my throat.

We wrapped production on *Whatever It Would End Up Being Called* under budget and eight days ahead of schedule, making Jack Warner a very happy man. All it meant to me was that there were only a few more days before Etchika returned to France.

She spent her last night in America at my apartment on Shoreham Drive. We were close enough by then that I could let my guard down and be completely intimate with her. We'd probably never see each other again. Maybe that's why I was bold enough to tell her I loved her. Knowing there was an airline ticket in her bag certainly made it easier.

I was safe from any genuine commitment.

Young Love

DOT RECORDS WAS HOUSED in modest second-story offices at Sunset and Vine, next door to Wallach's Music City, the biggest record store in Hollywood.

For a man who always wore a suit and tie, Randy Wood was the most down-home guy you'd ever want to meet. Most of the company's employees had followed him to Hollywood from Wood's hometown of Gallatin, Tennessee. That ought to tell you something about the man, right there. He was the leader of a close-knit clan, and his style was totally different from the way things were done over the hill at Warner Bros.

"Would you be interested in cutting a record for us, Tab?" Randy said to me, seconds after we'd shaken hands.

I repeated what I'd said to his friend Howard Miller, softening it a little: "Mr. Wood, I'm really not much of a singer."

"Do you have any experience?"

"Well, I was in the church choir and sang a little bit in school, but to be honest, Mr. Wood, I'm not really sure I'm good enough to cut a record."

He calmly explained that you didn't have to be a professional singer to make a good record. Randy Wood obviously knew the music business better than I did, but I remained skeptical. "I don't want to make a fool of myself," I told him. "If we record something and I don't like it—that's the end of it, okay?"

"Absolutely. But if we both agree it sounds good—then you're gonna let Dot release it. Okay?"

Sounded simple enough. We shook on it. No papers of any kind were signed, but I never doubted for a minute that Randy Wood would do right by me. You could just tell from the loyalty of his people, the camaraderie in those offices, that you were dealing with an honest, genuine, stand-up guy.

He'd started his modest music empire in 1947, in an appliance store, when he decided to carry rhythm-and-blues records not available in the Gallatin area. It quickly expanded into a thriving mail-order business. By 1950 the record side had gotten so big he started his own music label and began pressing his own sides. Pretty soon, Randy's Records was making a mark in regional R & B, gospel, and country-music markets. He renamed the label Dot.

Its first big hit was the 1952 release "Trying," recorded by the Hilltoppers, four kids from Western Kentucky University in Bowling Green. The song had gotten a big boost when the Hilltoppers performed it on *The Ed Sullivan Show,* an early example of how important television would be to making hit records.

Chief songwriter for the Hilltoppers was Billy Vaughn, who by 1955 had dropped out of the group to become Dot's musical director. He handled the arrangements and orchestrations for all of the label's top acts, including Johnny Maddox, the Fontane Sisters, Jim Lowe, and Gale Storm, the star of *My Little Margie,* one of TV's most popular shows. Her version of "I Hear You Knocking" went all the way to #2 on the pop charts.

I hadn't been at Dot twenty minutes before Randy took me down the hall to meet Billy Vaughn and producer Milt Rogers. They wanted me to hear a record by country singer Sonny James, which they'd decided might work for me. "Young Love" was already climbing the country charts. Back in those days, radio was completely segregated. If you wanted to listen to Tony Bennett or Jo Stafford or Peggy Lee, you tuned in to a "pop" station. "R & B" stations played black artists like Little Richard and Big Joe Turner. Hank Williams and Kitty Wells were heard exclusively on "country" radio.

I'd been in love with country music ever since I'd heard it on the jukebox at the Sip and Bite Café, back when we lived at 69th and Figueroa. Mother had set up an account there so Walt and I would have a hot meal while she was working nights. "San Antonio Rose" was one of the songs that was played over and over.

Great country or R & B songs were often "covered" by a pop singer to make the tune acceptable to a wider—and whiter—audience. Dot's biggest seller was Pat Boone, who became known as the King of Covers by "refining" rhythm-and-blues hits.

Anyway, Randy and Billy played the Sonny James record for me, then asked me to sing a few bars while Billy played along on the piano. I pretended I was home in the shower, since that's the only place I sang with confidence. The echo helped. I mustered my best shot.

"Set Saturday aside," Randy said. "We're gonna cut a record."

I was dumbfounded. But . . . I agreed. Hey, I'd tackled live television—I wasn't about to let my insecurities get the better of me again. At the very least I'd have something to give my mother for Christmas, since she was the one who always loved to hear me sing.

The recording date was Saturday, December 15, 1956. The place: Ryder Sound, on Santa Monica Boulevard, right across from my old haunt—the unemployment office. Dick Clayton went with me to lend moral support.

Randy had hired some singers to harmonize. *Some* singers—the Jordanaires, Elvis's backup group. Man, this was serious stuff. I was starting to feel the pressure.

While Billy Vaughn worked out the kinks in the arrangement with the session musicians, I rehearsed along with them, under the eye of producer Milt Rogers. Half an hour later, we were ready to give it a go. Randy was at the mixing console with the session engineer. Milt set me up in the glassed-in recording booth: "Relax and enjoy yourself," he said before joining Randy, Dick, and the engineer in the control booth.

To ease my jitters, I took off my shoes. Don't know why, but I felt much more comfortable singing in just my socks.

> *They say for every boy and girl*
> *There's just one love in this whole world*
> *And I know that I found mine,*
> *The heavenly touch of your embrace*
> *Tells me no one can take your place*
> *Ever in my heart*
> *Young love, first love*
> *Filled with true devotion*
> *Young love, our love*
> *We share with deep emotion.*

After a few takes, my nerves settled down. I concentrated on the song and tried not to listen to the sound of my own voice. I seemed to absorb confidence from being in the midst of a roomful of talented musicians, doing their thing with total professionalism, all of them acting like I belonged there.

We'd just finished the eleventh take when the engineer's voice crackled through the intercom: "That's the one." Randy called me into the control room to listen to the playback.

Hearing myself singing on state-of-the-art equipment was mind boggling. With all the tracks down and the sound sweetened—it wasn't half-bad. "It's gonna be a hit," Dick said. "Knew it when I heard the first eight bars," Randy Wood chimed in.

By now I was so jazzed I couldn't wait to jump back into the booth and record the flip side. I picked "Red Sails in the Sunset," a standard I'd always loved. Billy Vaughn, on the fly, threw together a fresh, terrific arrangement.

Once I was finished and out the door, Randy Wood went to work. Unbeknownst to me, the master was edited that afternoon and by nightfall a dub had been shipped to Howard Miller in Chicago. As soon as it was in his hands, he spun it for his vast midwestern audience. Meanwhile, vinyl pressings were made in Los Angeles, and by Monday morning 100,000 copies of "Young Love" were being shipped to distributors around the country.

Before the week was out, I was cruising along Sunset Boulevard when my voice wafted from the car radio. I almost piled into a palm tree. Swerving the T-Bird to the curb, I cranked up the volume, and sat there slack jawed, remembering what Randy Wood had said at our first meeting: "I can always tell a record's going to be a hit when I hear it on a car radio."

I'll be damned—"Young Love" sounded pretty good!

When I got home, the phone was ringing off the hook. Calls poured in from people all over the country. "Young Love" lightning was striking ten thousand places at once. Within days, a second pressing was ordered to keep up with demand.

Until that Christmas, I was an unlikely—you could even say unwilling—movie star, one who wanted, more than anything, to be a respected actor. Well, Santa surprised me. By New Year's Day I was also a "pop star."

I celebrated the way I always did: at 9:00 p.m. (midnight, New York time) I lifted a single glass of champagne to heaven, toasted my good fortune with a heartfelt, "Thank You," polished it off, and went to bed. I needed my sleep. That week I was going back into Ryder Sound to record a bunch more songs.

By January 5, Dot had shipped 400,000 copies of "Young Love." The week after that, it debuted on *Billboard*'s Hot 100 at #60. Another five days, and it had leaped to #15.

I kept waiting for the bubble to burst. It refused.

I DRAGGED CLAYTON with me to the Los Angeles convention center to scope out next year's models at the auto show. Having conquered new territory, I thought maybe I should reward myself with a late Christmas present. Dick probably thought he was chaperoning me as a preventive measure—he was seriously concerned that celebrity was going to my head.

As we entered the massive showroom, I stopped in my tracks. On a revolving platform, center stage, was the most gorgeous automobile I'd ever seen: a black 1957 Mercedes 220S convertible with red leather upholstery.

This was way before the Mercedes became the de rigueur (note Etchika's influence) Hollywood vehicle. It was still too soon after World War II for the largely Jewish, Cadillac-driving movie crowd to fall in love with a car made by Germans. But this machine clearly outclassed everything in the show, including the latest portholed Thunderbird.

I needed this glorious automobile. But I couldn't afford it. Ah, *what the hell*! Why not?

"Don't do it," Dick counseled.

"All right, all right," I said with a deep sigh.

The next day I went to the Mercedes dealership in Hollywood. I ordered a 220S, custom-made at the factory in Stuttgart, and scrawled out a check for the full amount: six thousand dollars.

I was riding the crest of a wave bigger than anything I'd ever imagined. Dot was scrambling to keep up with orders. "Red Sails" was also about to chart. The label was set to release another song I'd done, "Ninety-nine Ways," backed with "Don't Get Around Much Anymore."

Randy Wood called me up: "Tab, you've got to get back in the studio. We need to record an album!"

Euphoria can be so short lived.

When a Warner Bros. attorney heard "Young Love" on the radio, his first reaction was vastly different from mine. Dick Clayton immediately fielded an irate phone call in which he was informed, in the strongest possible terms, that Tab Hunter was under contract to Warner Bros. for *everything,* not only motion pictures. Jack Warner may have magnanimously declined to pass judgment on my personal life, but if there was a buck to be made—he *owned* me.

Dick felt bad for not foreseeing this predicament, but then—who would have? From the time I cut the record to its being on the air was less than *ten days!* Once the genie was out of the bottle, there was no way to get it back in.

Anyway, making a pop star out of its prized possession had never occurred to the Warners executives, since the studio didn't have a record division. In fact, Jack Warner seemed to have disdain not only for the rock-and-roll phenomenon sweeping the nation, but for the music business as a whole. I'm no businessman, granted, but it's interesting to note that in the mid-1950s, after he'd wrested control of Warner Bros. away from his brothers Harry and Abe, Jack Warner invested heavily in 3-D movies because he saw it as the wave of the future. He didn't think to spend a cent developing his own recording subsidiary, like MGM had done. Pretty shortsighted for the company that pioneered talking pictures.

"Young Love" helped change their perspective. By February 2, 1957, when the record reached #4 on *Billboard*'s pop chart, a deal had been cut. From then on, Dot had to pay Warner Bros. a hefty compensation for any Tab Hunter record in release. When the studio's lawyers found out I'd already cut enough songs for an LP, they barred Dot from releasing anything beyond singles that had already shipped.

Randy Wood was holding orders for 100,000 albums. He was sitting on a gold mine, but Warner Bros. had no intention of letting him, or me, profit from a singing voice *it* owned. At first I brushed it off, like I usually did. I'd been carried away by my enthusiasm and naïveté, resulting in a guileless breach of contract. Big deal. Then Randy Wood handed me my first "Young Love" royalty check. I don't recall the total, but I remember precisely the Internal Revenue Service's cut—$56,000. That was just the taxes!

I was making *way* more money as a pop singer than as a contract player at Warner Bros. That was a real eye-opener.

On February 16, 1957, I officially became one of the most popular singers in America when "Young Love" knocked Elvis Presley's "Too Much" from the top spot. Word got back to Randy Wood that Elvis was furious that his own backup singers had played a part in my recording success.

"Young Love" remained at #1 for the next five weeks and stayed on the pop charts for another twelve. Not only was it the best-selling record in stores, it was the most played selection on jukeboxes, the most requested of disc jockeys, the hottest-selling sheet music in the country, and it was #1 on the incredibly popular TV show *Your Hit Parade,* an American institution. Can't you just see Snooky Lanson (another Dot artist) crooning his version to Dorothy Collins?

At first, Jack Warner wanted to suspend me for having the gall to make money for anybody other than him. Money was always on his mind, but that winter he was particularly concerned about having spent more than $6 million on Billy Wilder's film biography of Charles Lindbergh, *The Spirit of St. Louis.* He hit on a unique way of exploiting me and, in the process, teaching me a lesson in humility.

His scheme even merited a mention in the February 18, 1957, issue of *Time:* "Warner Bros. . . . found with pained surprise that hardly anyone under 40 knew or cared anything about Charles A. Lindbergh . . . [so] the studio detailed Tab Hunter, 25 . . . to . . . give a from-the-heart sell to the Missile Age young who make up most of today's dwindling movie audience."

Receiving my gold record from Randy Wood at Dot Records.

When they told me I was being sent on a twenty-four-city promotional tour for, yet again, a movie I wasn't in, I wanted to suggest where they could stuff *The Spirit of St. Louis*. You have to admit, it was a shrewd idea: ship out Tab Hunter to get the nation excited about Charles Lindbergh.

For my part, I believed, for better or worse, that I owed something to my employer. Call me old-fashioned. By now, however, I had learned how to play this game. I agreed to the promotional tour on one condition: Warner Bros. would give me a pair of first-class, round-trip airline tickets to Europe—with open dates so I could use them anytime.

After the breakneck pace of the past two years, I needed a breather. I wanted to pick up my Mercedes at the factory in Stuttgart. Then I might scoot over to Paris to visit Etchika. I could zip down to Rome, where Tony was shooting a new picture at Cinecittà. I was a twenty-five-year-old movie star with the #1 hit record in the nation. I could do it all!

Before I headed out on the *Spirit* tour, Robert Balzer invited me to a small dinner gathering. Balzer was a true Hollywood eccentric, a Buddhist monk who owned a thriving "provisional" store for health-conscious celebrities in the Larchmont district. At that dinner party I met Gloria Swanson.

I couldn't get over how tiny she was. We spent most of the night on the sofa talking about my upcoming European trip ("Promise me you'll drive to Positano and stay at Le Sirenuse," she said) and her passion for proper nutrition. She recommended a place out in Glendale called Food for Life, which stocked nothing but organic produce. (Inspired, Venetia and I got into the three-day, juice-only routine, to cleanse our systems of poisons. As if three days would be enough. Fortunately, that's just as long as I could go without a cheeseburger, fries, and a chocolate shake.)

Every place I stopped on the *Spirit* tour, radio stations, theaters, colleges, high schools—the response was the same:

"Yeah, yeah, we know—he landed safely at Le Bourget. There was a fly in the cockpit that made the trip with him. Now tell us about 'Young Love.'" Warner Bros. was, in essence, paying me to make public appearances that drove sales of my record ever higher.

In my infinite wisdom, I decided Jack Warner needed to know, firsthand, about this groundswell of popular opinion. If he could hear directly from all these fans, maybe he'd lighten up and let Dot release my album. So . . . every-place I appeared, after extolling the virtues of that great American hero

Charles Lindbergh, I asked fans to drop a note to Mr. Jack L. Warner, c/o Warner Bros. Studio. I advised them to keep it short:

"Dear Mr. Warner: Why is Tab not being allowed to keep recording?" or "Dear Mr. Warner: Please let us buy Tab's album!"

This wasn't brinkmanship—hell, I didn't even know what that meant. I was absolutely sincere. If the public wanted to hear Tab Hunter sing, why couldn't they?

Near the end of the tour, in one of the endless hotels on the itinerary, I received a package from William Wellman. It was a script called *Darby's Rangers,* another war/romance melodrama. It was the movie Wellman was obliged to direct as part of his deal for being "allowed" to make *C'est la Guerre.* In a note, the director said he was putting the finishing touches on our last project, now called *Lafayette Escadrille,* and he wanted to reunite Etchika and me in his new picture.

The new script was, to put it mildly, underwhelming. I wanted the kind of roles Tony and Natalie were getting, not more of the same. Plus it was another war movie—at this rate I should have qualified for a veteran's pension. I called Clayton and told him to pass. He huddled with colleagues at Famous Artists to get second opinions on the wisdom of my decision. Next day, he called me back: "If you don't want to do it, don't do it."

Everybody, it seemed, was aware that I'd successfully branched off in a new direction—everybody except Warner Bros.

Before I hung up, I had a premonition. "Dick, make sure you pick up the Europe tickets *before* you tell them I'm not doing *Darby's Rangers.*" Dick was going with me to Europe. He deserved the perk even more than I did.

When I came off the exhausting three-week *Spirit* tour, I barely had time to unpack, then repack, for the big trip. Plus I was running scared—Wellman had left several urgent messages, demanding that I contact him.

Before I could hightail it out of the country, there were a couple of bits of business still hanging. Randy Wood wanted me to put the finishing touches on the album we'd recorded. After the session at Ryder Sound, I swung by Dot Records at Randy's request. He came out of his office, sidled up to me, and whispered, "How'd you like to meet Marlene Dietrich?"

"Huh? Where?"

"In my office. I just signed her."

In a heartbeat I went from big-shot star to starstruck kid. Even Randy Wood was awed in the presence of a *real* celebrity. Dietrich reposed in a chair, cross-legged, wearing a trench coat and matching broad-brimmed hat. While I babbled stupid small talk, she just sat there, radiating mysterious allure, every bit as gracious and gorgeous as I'd imagined. A photographer was summoned to snap our picture. Light-headed, I wasn't completely sure what was happening when Randy suddenly surprised me with a going-away present: a gold record. "Young Love" had by then sold more than two million copies.

The next day I had an audience with Hedda Hopper. Clayton figured it might be wise to offer a bon voyage interview to the town's biggest showbiz columnist, to assure the public that my "disappearance" was justified. She made a big deal out of the fact that I brought my own lunch, a couple of sandwiches I'd wrapped and stuffed in my pockets as I left home that morning.

Unlike the bogus gum flapping I'd done on the way up, I now spoke straight from the heart:

"I've been working so hard I haven't had a chance to do anything," I groused. "I've been working steadily for a year and a half. I had to turn down a picture in order to get away and I may be put on suspension . . . I finished an album last night; now I'm waiting for studio permission to release it. I have a new single ready for release, too, but I'll just have to wait until the studio decides when they want that to be."

"What does it mean to you in terms of money, having a hit?" she asked.

"My contract says four cents on each record, but I can't multiply. It isn't enough to complicate my tax returns because I'm not making that kind of money with my pictures. You know, there's a lot to be said for and against a studio contract."

"Contracts," she replied knowingly, "are awfully nice when you're on the way up."

For the first time, I really let loose: "I'm regarded as a child, not as a mature human being. I'm the product of Hollywood publicity, and publicity has exceeded output to

With Marlene Dietrich at Dot Records.

this point . . . I know how I feel inside and I haven't even scratched the surface."

She wanted to talk about my "romance" with Etchika and to learn if the European trip was just an excuse to see her again. I shied away, saying, "I'll pick up a car at the factory, and whichever way it steers, that's where I'll be going."

I picked up my laundry, made a stop at Coulter and Gray, then zipped home to finish packing. How long I'd be gone was anybody's guess. With no films scheduled, I could stay abroad for *months*. As I bolted out the door for the airport, the phone started ringing. My "inner" told me to ignore it, to keep going, straight into the idling taxi. Stupidly, guiltily, I picked it up.

Holy shit—it was Wild Bill Wellman.

"You lousy, dirty, no-good son of a bitch," he screamed. "How dare you turn down *Darby's Rangers*! If our paths ever cross again, so help me—" He slammed the phone down.

I panicked. Now Bill Wellman was out to get me! Frantically, I dialed up Charlie Feldman, boss of bosses at FAA, and told him what had happened.

"What'll I do? What'll I do?" I was practically hyperventilating.

"Fuck 'em, kid," Charlie said. "You've worked hard. Take a vacation. You deserve it."

1 8

Europa, Europa

WHEN WARNER BROS. FOUND out I'd turned Wellman down, I was suspended, effective immediately. Of course, the letter from the studio lawyers informing us of the suspension arrived in Dick Clayton's FAA office as we were taking off for Europe, on Warners' tab.

Being put on suspension meant that for an indefinite time, I wouldn't be allowed to work and I'd draw no salary. Obviously, this was a little worrisome for someone headed halfway around the world for an unspecified amount of time. When he learned of the suspension, Clayton told me not to fret; Jack Warner was always suspending Bette Davis for turning down pictures, and it hadn't hurt her career any.

Rock Hudson was on the same SAS flight to Europe. Eight years had passed since Henry Willson introduced us on the set of *Fighter Squadron*. Seemed like a long time, but it felt like the blink of an eye. That day in 1948, neither of us seemed like good bets for stardom.

But as we chatted en route to Copenhagen, on March 8, 1957, Roy Fitzgerald, aka Rock Hudson, was the most popular movie star in America. He'd become huge, thanks to a string of high-class soap operas created by director Douglas Sirk, including *Magnificent Obsession, Captain Lightfoot,* and *All That Heaven Allows*. He'd just been nominated for a Best Actor Oscar for *Giant*. Now he was headed to Italy to costar with Jennifer Jones in an adaptation of *A Farewell to Arms,* directed by John Huston. Henry Willson had certainly done right by his prized client.

He'd brokered a huge long-term deal for Rock at Universal, which was reportedly getting as much as $400,000 per picture to loan him out to other studios, investments that were a heavy risk and needed to be protected. Henry earned his commission, and more, when he purportedly bartered Rock out of *Confidential*'s clutches, brokering the burial of an exposé about Rock's private life that, in comparison, made my "pajama party" look like small potatoes.

For years after, rumors persisted that it was Henry Willson who had "given up" two of his former clients to *Confidential*—me and Rory Calhoun—trading information about our arrest records in exchange for Rock's immunity from any persecution. I don't know if it's true, but I wouldn't be surprised.

As for the facts: Rock had managed something I could never do—he got married. The same month I'd appeared on the cover of *Confidential*—September 1955—Rock had wed Henry Willson's secretary, Phyllis Gates. I'd met Phyllis several times before cutting Henry loose and had found her charming and intelligent. I'd certainly heard that Rock was gay, and I assumed Phyllis knew what she was getting into. Maybe they could work out some sort of arrangement that was, frankly, beyond my capabilities.

It wouldn't be long before their marriage fell apart—for precisely the reasons I elected to remain a bachelor. Lying about who you are doesn't make for a strong foundation in what's supposed to be a lifelong union. But Henry must have figured it was the price for keeping Rock rumor-free. A price Rock was willing, gladly or not, to pay.

Stuck on that plane for twenty hours, Rock and I could have had a long heart-to-heart about the different paths we had taken to keep our private lives from the public's prying eyes.

It didn't happen. My frantic schedule had left me exhausted, and all I wanted was to sack out. Universal had gotten Rock a sleeping berth, but he was too tall for it. He graciously offered it to me. Rock and Clayton stayed up all night, drinking cognac and gabbing, while I went to bed with my rosary beads and prayed the plane wouldn't crash on what seemed like an endless polar-route flight to Europe.

Rock flew on to Rome, while Dick and I disembarked in Copenhagen. We were squired on a whirlwind tour, including Elsinore Castle, by European representatives of Dot Records. Due to some tax situation, Denmark hadn't played American movies for several years, so I was surprised how often kids asked for an autograph. It was solely because of "Young Love," which meant the record was selling on its own merit, not because I was in the movies.

Back in the States, Randy Wood had somehow managed to smuggle out the latest record before Warners' attorneys dropped the Iron Curtain. "Ninety-nine Ways" would be my second Top Ten hit of 1957.

In Stuttgart, we got the grand tour of the Mercedes factory, culminating with the delivery of keys to my beautiful new convertible. A trio of dour Germans in dark suits escorted us to the autobahn entrance, then pulled us over to the side of the road. One produced a flask: "Prosit!" he toasted. Dick and I had a swig, *danke schön*ed and *auf Wiedersehen*ed, then zoomed onto the high-speed highway.

I could have piloted the 220S toward Paris and a reunion with Etchika. But I had to face the truth. I didn't want to get closer to Etchika. Sometimes when you're confused, you push away the people you shouldn't. You're either afraid of being hurt or of hurting them.

So we bypassed Paris and headed south toward Rome, and Tony.

Paramount had loaned him out to producer Dino de Laurentiis for a hefty $125,000. Remember, that's the amount paid to the studio, its "rental fee." Tony was only banking whatever weekly salary was stipulated in his contract. The numbers always looked better in movie magazines than they did in your bank passbook.

Tony was lodged in style, in a villa of his own off the Appia Antica, at the end of a long gravel drive that wound through vast fields of grazing sheep and olive trees. The place was an ancient ruin, crumbling and utterly charming. I loved it, the way I loved all the ravaged elegance of Italy. The relaxed aesthetic, seasoned by centuries, was literally a world apart from the tight-assed, small-minded rat race of Hollywood. (Later, when the trip was dutifully recounted for the movie magazines, no mention was made, of course, of my visiting Tony.

Movieland quoted me saying that I "arrived in Rome just at sunset and my well-known lucky star led me to an available Italian villa on the Appian Way.")

Tony had a driver ferry him to and from the villa every day—he'd come a long way from, only a year earlier, hitchhiking out Sunset Boulevard every morning to Allied Artists. He'd also been nominated for a Best Supporting Actor Oscar for *Friendly Persuasion,* and the studio was diligently promoting him as

Tony, and my new 220S, in Rome.

the next James Dean. Jo Van Fleet, who'd played Dean's mother in *East of Eden,* played Tony's mother in this one. Silvana Mangano, Mrs. de Laurentiis, was the female lead. The director of this Italian-French co-production was René Clément, who spoke not a word of English. Which was okay because Tony spoke fluent French. He was eager to make *The Sea Wall* because he longed to be accepted by the more cerebral European artists.

Our first night in Rome, Tony joined Dick and me for dinner at L'Escargot, where we got reacquainted in the warm atmosphere of a gravel patio strung with overhead lights. As enjoyable as the evening was, something wasn't right. A tension, beyond his typically high-strung anxiousness, clung to Tony.

I couldn't imagine that my being there was what rattled him. My arrival was no surprise; we'd talked on the phone at least a couple of times a week since he'd been abroad. But once I was there, Tony didn't want me around, probably out of fear that more rumors would hound him. As a colleague, I respected his concerns. As a friend, though, I felt slighted. But I wasn't going to let it ruin my hard-earned vacation. While Tony worked, Dick and I tooled around, doing all the touristy things. For two weeks the villa was our home base, but I didn't really see all that much of Tony.

In the meantime, Dick and I devoured Rome like two excited kids. We'd bivouacked in Palm Springs and done junkets to Vegas, but this was the first time we'd ever taken a long holiday together.

We visited endless museums and galleries and still barely scratched the surface. We went to St. Peter's, where thousands of believers jammed the square for a glimpse of Pope Pius XII as he was carried over the throng. "Viva Papa! Viva Papa!" the mass of humanity chanted. When he gave his blessing, His Holiness seemed to be looking directly at us. Although by this time he was a Christian Scientist, Dick had been raised Irish Catholic and was even an altar boy in his youth. Seeing the pope made tears stream down his face.

Clayton and I loved going to Mass. The majesty of the rituals, the immensity of Italy's spiritual devotion—it really worked on me, helping me overcome my estrangement from the Catholic faith. Even though my religion wanted to convince me that I was a rotten person and that God had no love for "my kind," I started looking past that part of the church's doctrine, choosing to believe I'd find spiritual stability by loving, not fearing, God.

As a movie star, you're always surrounded by temptation, and in your mid-twenties it's easy to give in, easy to assume that everything that comes your way is rightfully yours for the taking. And believe me, I was no choirboy. Reconciling with the church, even if it wasn't ready to reconcile with me, was a crucial reason that I never went completely off the deep end.

At the end of March, Dick flew to Ireland to spend a few days visiting relatives in County Cork. With the Italian leg of our journey coming to a close, Tony found some time for us. He and I toured the Amalfi Drive, wandered the ruins of Pompeii, enjoyed a side trip to Naples, and took a boating excursion to Capri. To cap it off, Tony joined Dick and me for a few days at Gloria Swanson's cherished Le Sirenuse, nestled in the spectacular cliffs of Positano, above the glittering Mediterranean.

I was ready to apply for Italian citizenship.

REALITY CAUGHT UP with us. Cables and phone calls were waiting at the hotel in Madrid. Maybe Jack Warner, buried under a mountain of irate notes from Tab-deprived teens, was calling to say he'd had a change of heart about not letting Dot release my album. Somehow, I doubted it. I ignored the cables and calls. Dick didn't. He had news for me—but I didn't want to listen.

Instead, it was lunch at Casa Botin, the oldest still-operating restaurant in the world. It's where Hemingway wrote *The Sun Also Rises.* Then we really splurged, dropping the astronomical sum of twenty-five dollars each on dinner at the world-renowned Jockey Club. We got front-row seats for the ballet, where we humiliated ourselves by applauding like mad over the performance of the great Antonio. Didn't realize it was customary for the swells up front to act jaded and applaud only grudgingly.

More cables were waiting at the hotel desk. Again Dick had important news, but I paid no attention. Instead I went riding with one of my heroes, Paco Goyoaga. Riding with Goyoaga was the equivalent of a kid from Nowhere, Nebraska, being hosted by his favorite star in the studio commissary.

How could Warner Bros. top that?

On to Paris, in April. I had a marvelous time reuniting with Suzanne Rateau, with whom I'd stayed after completing *Island of Desire.* I tried to contact Etchika, only to learn that she was vacationing in Morocco with her new beau.

At the Raphael Hotel, we ran into Ingrid Bergman, in Paris for a legitimate run of *Tea and Sympathy* in French. Minutes after we had met her, Bergman graciously invited Dick and me to be her guests at the theater that night. I must have been feeling my oats, because I said, "We'd love to—but only if you'll join us for drinks and dinner afterward."

Late supper at Horchers consisted of escargot and partridge, in the company of one of my all-time favorite actresses. "Am I glad we didn't stay at the George V," I whispered to Dick.

Ingrid Bergman could have taught me a few lessons about coping with scandal. She'd been run out of the United States for having an illegitimate child with director Roberto Rossellini in 1950, but five years later she was back on top in Hollywood, triumphant and unrepentant. I loved her for such strength of character as much as for her talent. Not that I would ever have broached the subject with her. The talk stayed small.

"I always stay at the Raphael," Bergman said. "I love the elegant rooms, the marble bathrooms."

"Mine's bigger than my apartment back home," I said, laughing.

She introduced us to her after-dinner drink of choice, Calvados. "Congratulations on your Academy Award," I toasted. Because of her commitment to the play, she couldn't attend the recent Hollywood ceremony at which she had been awarded the Best Actress Oscar for *Anastasia*. Frankly, more impressive than accepting the Oscar is having Cary Grant accept it for you.

The three of us stayed up talking and laughing half the night, an experience that remains one of the highlights of my life.

Returning to my hotel room, I found the phone loudly buzzing away. It could ring all night, for all I cared. Clayton, however, pushed right past me and snatched it up. I could tell right off, he'd set this up. Dick spoke solemnly, almost apologetically, to whoever was on the other end of the line. I started waving my arms around, mouthing, *I'm not here, I'm not here*! I didn't want the magic of this European escapade to end.

Clayton, wearing his fatherly face, not the brotherly one, covered the mouthpiece and turned to me. "Tab, you have to take this call."

I knew what it was all about, even though I'd tried to ignore it when Dick had told me, days earlier, the reason behind Warners' suddenly renewed interest in their suspended star.

While we were gallivanting around the Continent, a horde of teenage girls halfway around the world in Pasadena approached Bill Wellman in the theater parking lot after a sneak preview of *Lafayette Escadrille*.

"Are you the man who made this movie?" they asked.

Used to accolades, Wellman acknowledged that he was, indeed, the man responsible for the evening's heart-wrenching love story.

They started screaming at him: "You ought to be ashamed of yourself!" "Killing Tab Hunter—how dare you!"

Word got back to Jack Warner. He declared that the death and suicide of the two lovers—no matter how tragic, romantic, or *true*—was simply too dark for the *Ozzie and Harriet* generation. He ordered Wellman to shoot a new ending, one in which Etchika and I live happily ever after.

I had no desire to ever face Wild Bill Wellman again, not after the reaming-out he'd given me. My character was *dead,* damn it, and he'd *stay* dead! I couldn't believe Wellman would knuckle under to pressure from his nemesis, Jack Warner.

"I don't want to talk to them," I said to Dick. "Tell them I'm not going to do it."

Dick was growing weary of my holdout. He shoved the phone right in my face.

I could have killed him. But he was only doing his job. Dick hated it when there was dissension between a studio and a client; he wanted everything smoothed over. And he could spoon-feed a lion, that guy. I took the phone.

"Tab? It's Steve Trilling. I've been chasing you all over Europe. We need you back here. Gotta have a new ending for the picture." Trilling was the main guy I dealt with at Warners. I liked him and trusted him.

"I can't work for Wellman again," I explained. "He's still pissed about *Darby's Rangers.* He practically threatened me."

"Come back, Tab. There won't be any trouble. I promise."

"If Wellman so much as says one cross word to me—I'll walk off the set."

"We'll make sure that doesn't happen. We've got to get this picture finished."

I could feel myself caving. Saying no to Steve wasn't easy. I wanted to stand firm, I wanted to be contentious, I wanted to refuse to shoot a new ending unless Jack Warner agreed to release my album. If I had stuck to my guns, *Lafayette Escadrille* might have retained its original ending. Wellman might have been proud of the film he'd spent decades trying to get made.

"All right, all right," I finally said. "I'll come back."

C'est la vie, Paris. *Arrivederci,* Rome.

Welcome back, Hollywood.

The Deep Freeze

I married Etchika Choureau on May 24, 1957. We skipped the service and went straight to the rice throwing, since the church was only a facade, and the "guests" were in a hurry to get back to other acting jobs. Not that the event, however brief, wasn't costly—Warner Bros. had to rent the French street and church on the 20th Century Fox lot, since it didn't have one of its own.

The showdown with Wellman was straight out of *High Noon*. We'd managed to avoid each other up to the time I was called to the set. Wellman eyeballed me from a distance, like a flinty sheriff staring down his nemesis on the town's Main Street. We circled like wary gunfighters. Finally, his craggy face broke into a smile.

"God bless you, Buffalo Bill!" he said. He threw his arms around me and clasped me in a macho bear hug.

I could breathe again. When you got a "God bless you, Buffalo Bill!" from Wellman, that meant that everything was square between you. It was the infamously corny closing line from Wellman's 1944 movie biography of legendary western showman William Cody, played by Joel McCrea.

Wellman was putting up a game front; I'm sure this charade wounded his pride—having to knuckle under to the studio and kowtow to a popular young star. I just wanted to put this embarrassing situation behind us.

The press, of course, went crazy over the reunion of Etchika and me. I have to admit, the fantasy of it all was bizarre. For months, movie magazines had been splattering ink about us. One even went so far as to hire detectives (or so it claimed) to confirm or disprove that Etchika and I had been secretly married before her return to Europe the previous year. No matter what I said to the contrary, the press was intent on printing whatever it wanted.

For those two days in May, Etchika and I acted out the romantic fantasy everybody seemed to crave, a crazily fabricated dream of what *might* have been our story. We playacted for the cameras a blissful lover's reunion, falling into a passionate embrace on a faux French street. Thad Walker had survived his aerial dogfight in the skies over France! Renée wouldn't die in a lover's leap into the Seine! It was a miracle! Cut! Print!

Next scene, the bright-eyed newlyweds are showered with cheers and rice as they bound out the doors of a little rural chapel, all set for Happily Ever After.

Ah, the magic of the movies!

It was nice to see Etchika again, but our once-hot attraction was now only a flickering flame. Since that last night together, six months earlier, my life had changed dramatically. I was more self-possessed now, more sure of what I wanted, both personally and professionally. Etchika was a wonderful part of my life, but there was no chance for a relationship, with a man or a woman. The life of a movie star just didn't seem to allow for it.

We were all business those two frenetic days, trying to give Wellman something that would satisfy Jack Warner. At one time, I boasted to the press that this was the best role of my career: I got to run a gamut of emotions, going from callow youth to courageous soldier, from arrogant and reckless to vulnerable and passionate. Etchika thought the film would launch her Hollywood career. And Wellman, of course, anticipated a glorious swan song.

On June 7, Warners announced it was changing the title back to *With You in My Arms*. I can only imagine the decibel level of the argument in Mr. Warner's office between him and Wild Bill. Wellman, amazingly, seemed to win. On July 1 the title *Lafayette Escadrille* went back on the film. But nothing in this business is as it seems.

"That rotten bastard Jack Warner," Wellman ranted in an interview years later. "He gave my Greek tragedy a Pollyanna ending, then had the balls to call it *Lafayette Escadrille* when it didn't have a fucking thing to do with the Lafayette Escadrille. I told the dumb bastard it was the Lafayette Flying Corps. All the guys that were still alive thought I was nuts. I told Warner if I ever caught him alone, which in his case was damn near impossible, I'd put him in the hospital. I have never hated a man as much as I hate him. On top of it all — he wouldn't let me kill Tab Hunter . . . After that phony Hollywood ending and that crappy title change, I just threw in the sponge."

Indirectly, my popularity is what led to Wellman being forced to mutilate his own dream project.

But with all due respect to one of the great directors of the classic era, he wasn't entirely blameless—even where the title was concerned. If you see the movie, be aware that's Wellman himself narrating, speaking in reverent tones about the brave men of the "Lafayette Escadrille" who gave their lives for freedom. Compromise is as common in the moviemaking business as it is in politics.

The fate of Wellman's film was now inextricably linked to my fortunes as a singing star. The letter-writing campaign I'd instigated on the *Spirit* tour had worked beyond my wildest imagining. Warner's office had been swamped. But J. L. had no intention of being one-upped by some greenhorn pop star, especially one that he *owned*.

After demanding the new ending—ostensibly to capitalize on my popularity at its peak—Warners decided, in one of those serpentine twists of logic, to put *Lafayette Escadrille* on the shelf. Believe me, it wasn't *that* bad. I think the studio had two ideas: first, it would teach me a lesson about who was really in charge of my career, and second, they were stalling for time. To cash in on my popularity as a pop star, the studio decided to create Warner Bros. Records, with me as the first recording star on the new label. They wouldn't even have to sign me; I was already under contract.

By holding off on *Lafayette Escadrille,* they could buy time to get the record division up and running, so my initial WB album would coincide with the release of the film.

Those gears ground slowly, however. In the meantime, the Dot album sat in the company's warehouse, making no money for anyone.

That summer I languished in the Warner Bros. deep freeze. Word was out that I was "difficult." Part of the problem was that I'd been so naive and malleable up till then. The success of Brando, Dean, and Montgomery Clift—all of whom had been tagged "temperamental"—was evidence that studios aren't inherently opposed to "difficult" people. It's just that the powers that be like consistency. It makes their lives easier. They can put you in the slot they want, and you're supposed to stay there, performing your trick on demand. Warners would have preferred I stay wet behind the ears forever, grateful for whatever they decided to throw my way, whenever they wanted to throw it.

My falling-out with the studio proved to be a good thing for Edd Byrnes, a twenty-three-year-old New Yorker who got some parts Warners had originally slated for me. Mr. Warner took personal credit for signing Byrnes, and in all the PR that accompanied his promotion, the boss made sure to note that his latest discovery was "another Tab Hunter." Ironically, one of the bit parts that gained Edd good notices was as a teammate of Tony's in *Fear Strikes Out.*

Dick and I tried every angle we could think of to get work, but things got so dry I took a Gillette razor commercial that July. A good script came to us called *Cowboy,* a film Glenn Ford was making at Columbia. Dick asked Warners to loan me out for it, but they wouldn't budge, and Jack Lemmon got the part. Columbia seemed to like me more than my own studio, because it announced I'd be in its upcoming film *Beach Boy,* costarring Kim Novak. Never happened.

The magazines still dutifully recorded my every move, for which I was now especially grateful. Thanks to "Young Love," I now had entire *magazines* devoted exclusively to me, not just articles. It kept me from dropping off the public's radar screen.

I couldn't keep my frustration over the lack of work in check any longer. Plenty seeped into print, leading to headlines like the one in the October 1957 issue of *Motion Picture* (with Natalie on the cover):

> **They called him docile, amiable, agreeable.**
> **What they call him now is unprintable. Here's what turned**
> **Tab Hunter into Hollywood's wildest**
> **HELL-RAISER**

The slant of the story — fairly accurate, for once — was that I was fed up with my lot and was revolting against both my stereotyping and my indentured servitude to the studio. "The significance of the Hunter revolution is that Tab is leading a stampede of young Hollywood actors against the 'classification' system practiced by film studios for years."

An overstatement, to be sure. There was no stampede. I was completely on my own. By the middle of summer, I had to face the facts. A few years earlier, I'd have blithely tossed off the career and gone back to full-time work as a horse trainer. But life at the top rungs of the Hollywood ladder gets under your skin; it presents you with opportunities you'd never have otherwise, puts you in the orbit of the most talented, creative, and inspiring people you'll ever meet — not to mention some of the greediest, neediest, and most ruthless.

I wanted to work. I wanted to contribute. If I had to swallow my pride in order to keep going, so be it.

Dick urged me to write a personal note to Mr. Warner, an apology, a request for forgiveness. It was my message in a bottle, cast off from an isolated island in the middle of show-business purgatory.

Dick Clayton handled its delivery, through formal channels, acting as the peacemaking diplomat every step of the way. "Tab has matured—he's ready to behave," Dick told all the Colonel's men and eventually the Colonel himself. All I could do was cross my fingers and hope that my gesture wasn't too little, too late.

I was so lonely I needed a companion. The answer was a beautiful Weimaraner, whom I named Fritz. He was affectionate, if a bit disobedient, but having spent my whole life with horses, I knew I could train him. In late July, while I was playing at home with my new pal, a knock came at the door. In my perfect world, it would have been Jack Warner with a bouquet of roses. It was a process server with a subpoena.

Confidential magazine was back in my life.

I CERTAINLY WASN'T the only celebrity burned by that rag during the past two years. While I kept my profile low, enough celebrity "victims" had raised a stink to actually trigger government action. A Republican senator named Fred Kraft, with the support of Screen Actors Guild president George Murphy (soon to be a California senator himself), had held hearings on *Confidential*'s Hollywood racket earlier in the year. He joined forces with high-priced showbiz attorney Jerry Giesler, who'd already been retained by Robert Mitchum, Lizabeth Scott, and heiress Doris Duke to bring libel charges against the magazine.

Giesler wanted to take the whole campaign to Washington, to pass legislation that would wipe out the persecution of celebrities in print. The first step was to get the state's attorney general, Edmund G. Brown (on his way to the governorship), to okay a class-action suit against *Confidential*. George Murphy's job was to line up actors and actresses willing to testify to the lies that had been written about them.

In May, just after I'd returned from Europe, a grand jury was convened in Los Angeles in the hope of bringing indictments against *Confidential*; its publisher, Robert Harrison; Harrison's older sisters and business partners, Helen and Edith Harrison; his niece Marjorie Meade and her husband, Fred—the magazine's "Hollywood bureau"; and actor Bruce Cabot's socialite ex-wife, Francesca de Scaffa, who was purported to be the magazine's main source for scandalous stories.

The charges against these lovely folks were conspiracy to distribute obscene material, conspiracy to commit criminal libel, and—believe it or not—conspiracy to distribute material on abortion and male potency.

Arthur Crowley, the attorney hired to defend *Confidential*, went on the offensive: he attempted to serve subpoenas on more than a hundred celebrities who'd been the subject of *Confidential* articles, from Ava Gardner to Elvis Presley to Clark Gable to . . . Tab Hunter. Most of my colleagues decided that the first week of August 1957 was the perfect time to finally take that long-delayed Mexican vacation. Having just come back from my extensive, and expensive, European R & R, and with no money coming in, I was a sitting duck.

The defense strategy was brazenly simple. Crowley wanted to put stars on the stand and ask them, under oath, if what was printed about them wasn't true. *Confidential* claimed it spent a small fortune on fact checking, and Crowley declared he was ready to defend the magazine's journalistic integrity.

So if I was called to testify as to the truth of the "gay pajama party" story, I'd have to admit that it was indeed true, and the story would run in a million mainstream papers—ruining my career for sure.

What was so frustrating about *Confidential* (and its copycat competitors)

The original caption for this photo read: "Waiting off stage—Tab Hunter, one of the Hollywood stars placed on two-hour-call status for the libel-conspiracy trial of Confidential *and* Whisper *magazines, talks with Dep. Arne A. Knudsen while waiting for proceedings to start."*

was that while the articles may have had a grain of truth, the magazine felt entitled to rummage through the private affairs of public figures in the most smarmy, leering fashion. The average citizen would have screamed bloody murder if their laundry was aired in public this way—but because celebrities were perceived as "different," the law apparently allowed for entertainers to have their privacy violated.

On August 3, I was one of a handful of unfortunate "stars" brought in to testify as part of a media circus staged at the Los Angeles County Courthouse. I felt completely vulnerable in the midst of all these hyped-up crackpots; there was the palpable sense that the carnival could explode into actual mayhem any moment. While I sat there, an easy target for the press and whoever might freak out, Robert Harrison, the man behind the *Confidential* empire, was nowhere to be seen. In fact, he never set foot in Los Angeles, let alone the courtroom: New York had refused to extradite him, and he followed the proceedings from his Manhattan office. He asserted there was a conspiracy among the studios, that they had agreed to fund Brown's run for governor if he succeeded in bringing down *Confidential*.

One of the key witnesses for the prosecution was a man named Howard Rushmore, who had been *Confidential*'s managing editor until a fallout with Harrison. Rushmore had been a research director for Senator Joe McCarthy and was obsessed with exposing "subversives" in Hollywood. He reportedly quit *Confidential* when Harrison refused to run an unsubstantiated exposé on the secret love life of Eleanor Roosevelt. In court, Rushmore tried to hold himself above the lowbrow high jinks of his former employer. In fact, after he left *Confidential* he became the editor of rival *Uncensored,* where he recycled my 1950 arrest story into a longer piece about Henry Willson, called "Tab Hunter and the Man Who Made Him." (Rushmore's own life would end up *Confidential*-style fodder: he shot and killed his wife, and then himself, in a New York city taxi.)

Francesca de Scaffa, expected to be a star witness, fled to Mexico to dodge a subpoena and attempted suicide there during the trial. Another witness was found dead in the bathtub; one more died of a drug overdose. I couldn't believe that I was mixed up with this ilk, all because I went to a "gay" party in 1950.

What had initially been touted as the Trial of a Hundred Stars ended up focusing on only seven potentially "libelous" cases. Dorothy Dandridge took the stand to deny a story about her having a tryst with bandleader Hal Terry.

Maureen O'Hara turned out to be the crucial witness for the prosecution, contesting a *Confidential* report that she'd steamed up the back rows of Grauman's Chinese Theater, making out with a Latin Lothario. O'Hara was able to prove that she was out of the country on the date in question—and the pillars of the *Confidential* empire started to crumble. Leave it to a fiery Irish redhead to settle a score.

Although on "two-hour call status" for the duration of the trial, I was, fortunately, never called to testify. Thank God; He must have been watching out for me. Liberace, who wasn't called, either, announced to the press outside the courthouse that he was going to sue *Confidential* for $25 million (the magazine reported that he'd made a play for a young male press agent while on tour). It shows the tenor of the times: the court and the press were far more eager, and comfortable, delving into the alleged heterosexual indiscretions of O'Hara and Dandridge than they were dealing with Liberace and me. In 1957, the mainstream media couldn't even come up with adequate euphemisms for homosexuality—that's how taboo it still was.

The whole charade dragged on for six weeks, culminating in a fourteen-day jury deliberation, at the time the longest in the history of the California courts. After all that—no verdict. The jury was deadlocked, and the judge declared a mistrial. Both sides, of course, claimed victory. But since the attorney general had the pockets of the taxpayers to draw from, he immediately announced that he would seek a retrial. That prospect hit Harrison right in his wallet.

The attorney general, sensing the publisher was on the ropes, offered a deal, which Harrison accepted over the objections of his own counsel, who was spoiling to go back to court (and pad his bill). The state levied a fine of $10,000—nothing compared to the legal fees Harrison was racking up. The crucial point, however, was that Harrison had to agree, in print, that *Confidential* would back off celebrity scandalmongering, in favor of more publicly minded exposés focusing on consumer fraud, insurance scams, things like that. Later in the year, Harrison would settle out of court with Liberace, O'Hara, and Dandridge rather than face more legal fees defending the magazine from libel charges.

By the following year, *Confidential*'s circulation had nose-dived. The magazine was all but finished. The irony, of course, is that Harrison's brand of sensationalism was only getting started. Within a few years, it would become the blueprint for tabloid journalism in this country, and the sleazy baton would be passed on to the *National Enquirer*, its lurid clones, and eventually tabloid television.

ON AUGUST 19, right in the middle of the *Confidential* circus, Jack Warner and I officially buried that hatchet. That day he announced that Warner Bros. had bought the rights to *Damn Yankees,* currently the most popular musical playing on Broadway. It was his kiss-and-make-up gift to me for coming back into the fold.

The studio was about to release *The Pajama Game,* the filmed version of another hit Broadway show by director George Abbott and choreographer Bob Fosse, the team that created *Damn Yankees.* Warners' strategy for adapting Broadway shows was to basically buy the production intact—then insert a major movie star in the lead role. *The Pajama Game,* for example, featured the original Broadway cast, but for the movie version, its female lead, Janis Paige, was bumped in favor of Doris Day, then one of the hottest female stars in the business.

Jack Warner announced to the trades that *Damn Yankees* would feature the musical debut of Tab Hunter and that production would begin—with the rest of the original cast—as soon as the show closed its hugely successful Broadway run.

I'd just given an interview to *Liberty* magazine in which I said, "I rebel against playing the teen-aged baby-face 'boy next door' in my films. I'm twenty-six, and I'd rather play a murderer." So, of course, I land my biggest "boy next door" character to date, the role of naive baseball hero Joe Hardy.

If I learned anything from being put on suspension, it was to keep my mouth shut. Although I was anxious at the prospect of actually having to sing and dance in the company of true Broadway professionals, I knew *Damn Yankees* represented a major step up and a serious display of commitment by the studio.

Clearly, Jack Warner was hoping to cash in on my success as a pop star, and I took a measure of satisfaction in knowing that my outside deal with Dot, for all the strain it put on my dealings with Warner Bros., had eventually forced the studio into taking my career more seriously.

After the release of *The Burning Hills, The Girl He Left Behind,* and "Young Love," the public no doubt expected to be inundated with Tab Hunter. But by September 1957, no new movie had appeared, a void of almost ten months. It was pretty obvious to Tab Hunter's fans that something was wrong.

---
2 0

Don't Fence Me In

JACK L. WARNER was notorious for being a ruthless, cutthroat studio boss. His legend, however, was nothing compared to Harry Cohn's. When it came to crude, callous, stubborn, ornery sons of bitches, the boss of Columbia Pictures played second fiddle to no one. He may not have been the most powerful executive in Hollywood, but Harry Cohn knew how to act the part, and relished it. He wore the mantle of the Most Hated Man in Hollywood like a badge of honor. In early October 1957, I got my chance to experience the Cohn charm firsthand.

The studio wanted to borrow me for a western, *Gunman's Walk*. The script was suspenseful, loaded with psychological complexity, and best of all, I was up for the part of the heavy. It would completely change my image as an actor, taking me into uncharted territory. Plus Van Heflin had already been cast, and I was thrilled at the prospect of working with him again, this time as his costar, not just a supporting player.

Before the deal could be inked, however, I had to meet with King Cohn—or as writer Ben Hecht called him, White Fang. I was instructed to report to casting director Max Arno late one afternoon in the Columbia offices at the corner of Sunset and Gower. I'd met Arno years earlier, when I was making the rounds, newly minted as Tab Hunter. Back then, he'd been insufferable and insensitive. Now, jumping up to shake hands with a popular young actor and singing star, he couldn't have been a bigger ass kisser. Arno remembered our earlier meeting, I was certain, but I decided not to mention what a miserable SOB he'd been to an *unknown* actor.

Arno ushered me upstairs, then down a long hallway. I tried not to think of all the Harry Cohn horror stories Aldo Ray had told me when we were making

Battle Cry. Aldo was under contract to Columbia then, and his tales of Cohn's volcanic temper and his manic manipulation of his minions made my Warner Bros. war stories pale in comparison.

It wasn't a surprise that Harry Cohn badly wanted to cast Tab Hunter in a picture. Pulling performers away from other studios was one of the ways he'd transformed Columbia from a Poverty Row laughingstock into one of the most profitable studios in town.

In 1928, he put director Frank Capra under long-term contract, which proved to be his master stroke. Capra made some of the best films of the early 1930s, and it was the 1934 Columbia hit *It Happened One Night*—for which he'd gotten Clark Gable and Claudette Colbert on loan from MGM and Paramount, respectively—that changed the studio's fortunes forever. Nobody ever snickered at Harry Cohn again. Once Columbia was flying high, his brother, Jack Cohn, who'd gotten him started in the business at Universal, tried to wrangle the studio away from his little brother, leading to a rift that lasted until the day Jack Cohn died in 1956.

Harry Cohn was credited with creating Hollywood's Love Goddess, Rita Hayworth—and for driving her crazy with his incessant meddling in her private life. Legend has it that in the late 1930s Cohn brought Hayworth and another glamorous actress he was grooming, Betty Miller (renamed Joan Perry by Cohn), into his office and declared, "One of you I'm going to make a star; the other one I'm going to make my wife." Despite his obsession with controlling the lives of contract actresses such as Hayworth, Evelyn Keyes, and Kim Novak, Cohn and Joan Perry managed a solid marriage, with three children, including an adopted daughter.

By the 1940s Cohn had cemented his reputation as the meanest, crudest man in town, but by the 1950s he'd added *prestigious* and *profitable* to his résumé. While other studios struggled to find the magic formula for blockbusters, Columbia produced *From Here to Eternity* and *On the Waterfront* in back-to-back years, garnering an avalanche of Oscars. Cohn claimed to have only one secret to success: "I kiss the feet of talent."

We were about to find out if that extended to Tab Hunter.

Double doors led to a secretary's office. Arno presented me, then retreated downstairs. The secretary ushered me through yet another set of doors. I entered Cohn's lair and found myself gazing across the largest expanse of desk ever created. The Rams could have scrimmaged on top of it. Somewhere in the distance sat Harry Cohn, a barber hovering over him, trimming what little hair he had. Handshakes and such niceties were impossible at this range.

Cohn gave me the once-over. Didn't ask me to sit. By way of introduction, he said, "So . . . you're Tab Hunter."

"Yes, sir, I am."

"Robert Wagner wants to do this role," he said gruffly, like I was wasting his time.

I peered across the desk and said, "Well, then you should get Bob Wagner." I turned around and started back through the corridors of power.

"Wait a minute, wait a minute," Cohn yelled at my back. "What do you think of this script?"

"I love it," I announced. "It's the kind of part I've been waiting to play. It's the kind of part I wish Warners would *let* me play."

As his haircut segued into a manicure, we talked about the story, how it would be shot in Technicolor and CinemaScope on Arizona locations, the fact that I did my own riding, all sorts of specifics. Cohn raved about Frank Nugent's script, told me how much I'd love working with Phil Karlson, who'd been hired to direct. We both expressed unreserved admiration for Van Heflin. It was a spirited, inspiring talk. In no time flat, I'd decided that not only was Harry Cohn an incredibly hands-on executive who knew every detail about every movie he produced, but he was also much smarter and more sensitive than the legend would lead you to believe.

My recent "difficulties," with both Warner Bros. and *Confidential*, were never mentioned. Cohn's rabid bulldog act seemed to me a ruse, promoted to keep people on the defensive. That's how you become the "toughest man in Hollywood." Granted, I was with him less than thirty minutes, but I saw a sensitivity in Harry Cohn that wasn't part of his reputation.

Grooming complete, Cohn dismissed me. I wouldn't know for sure until Jack Warner approved the loan-out, but I felt certain that I had the part. Cohn never came around the desk to shake hands, never even rose from his chair. I optimistically took it as a sign we'd be seeing each other again. Instead, it turned out to be the only time I'd encounter the man.

What would Harry Cohn have thought, sizing me up that day, if he knew that in a few years his wife would be proposing marriage to me?

Frankly, if Harry Cohn could have seen into the future, he wouldn't have given a damn about me and his wife. In four months he'd be dead.

The following February Harry Cohn had one of the most well-attended funerals in Hollywood history, prompting comic Red Skelton to remark, "Give the people what they want and they'll show up every time."

IN HINDSIGHT, MAYBE I was drawn to *Gunman's Walk* because it was a story about unfinished business between fathers and sons, something I could relate to on a subconscious level.

It was a great script, I got to play a heavy for the first time, and it allowed me to work with my mare, Swizzlestick, and my friend and favorite stuntman, Jack Conner.

Jack was the one who set me straight about doing my own stunts on *Gun Belt,* and in the five years since, we'd become good friends. One of the perks of being a "star" was that I could request my own stunt double, and for westerns Jack was the only choice. He and his wife, Kay, lived in Glendale and were lifelong horse people. When not working in films, they taught young people, like Rita Hayworth's daughter, Yasmine, to ride. Kay was practically a second mother to many Hollywood children.

Like stuntmen in general, Jack was tough, funny, reliable, and without one ounce of bullshit. "Everything I got's for sale," he'd always say, "and the wife's for lease." When we had time off at the Arizona location, Jack and I would head straight to the racetrack. Not to gamble, but to look for horses that owners and trainers were hoping to unload. There was one horse I wanted badly, but the owner saw a celebrity coming and jacked the price up too high. Jack and I always had our eyes peeled for potential jumpers; we could turn them into show horses, Jack could turn them into movie stars, or he could move 'em down the road.

Speaking of movie stars . . . Swizzlestick was far more comfortable with the "star's" life than I was. She'd been shipped early to the location, south of Tucson, and as soon as I checked into the hotel I raced to the barn. I worry about my horses like they're my kids. There was Swiz, munching away on her alfalfa, relaxed as could be. Throw a stock saddle on her and put her in front of a camera, and she came into her own. She loved the attention, especially when she had a personal groom to dote on her.

For the spectacular stuff, Swiz had a double. Where I had Jack, she had Daisy, a chestnut mare with an ugly head who was a legend in the business. In *The Mark of Zorro,* Daisy was dyed black to match the star's horse and jumped over a covered wagon. In *The Unforgiven,* Burt Lancaster stepped into a doorway and shot an oncoming Indian—that was Jack, riding Daisy at full gallop. As he bit the dust, Daisy propelled herself all the way up onto the roof of the house.

One time at an open call for stunt horses, somebody called out, "Hey, Jack! Is that a falling horse?" With a subtle touch, Jack laid Daisy down right in the middle of Riverside Drive, stepped off, and drawled, "Ain't she a peach?" They got the job.

In *Gunman's Walk*, James Darren and I portray the sons of affluent rancher Lee Hackett, played by Van Heflin. Typically, I'd have been cast as the mild, pacifist brother, Davey. Instead, I played Ed Hackett, sort of an Aryan Youth on the American frontier. Ed has a compulsion to compete with his father, who's encouraged his boys to be old-fashioned macho cowboys long after the Wild West has settled into a more civilized place.

With James Darren and Van Heflin in Gunman's Walk.
(Photo © 1958, renewed 1986 Columbia Pictures Industries, Inc. All rights reserved. Courtesy of Columbia Pictures.)

Although I was clearly the villain, the character was far from one-dimensional. My approach was to play Ed like a tightly wound watch spring, a self-righteous young hothead who flares up when people don't accept that he's right about everything. Early on, there's a scene in which Ed, chasing a wild horse, runs another cowboy off a cliff. He shows no remorse, because the dead man was a "half-breed." This was going to be a whole new Tab Hunter up on the big screen.

The key to portraying this uptight psycho wasn't in the ferocious riding or the quick-draw gunslinging (which I practiced diligently), but in Ed's wardrobe. For once, looking crisp and starched in western gear suited the character, and I went one step further by snugly fastening the top button on my denim shirts, a touch Phil Karlson loved. I based it on an observation I'd always made about Tony: "Buttoned-down shirt, buttoned-down mind."

Karlson made his reputation as an action director, showing a particular flair for tough, gritty crime pictures. My impression of him, however, was very different. He handled action as well as, if not better than, Raoul Walsh, but his focus was always on characterization. He didn't go for the full-blown read-throughs that theater-trained directors loved, but Phil was always open and receptive to discussion with actors, on- or off-set, always on the lookout for the telltale bit of business that defined a character efficiently. He liked to discover things on the set, in costume, in the moment, and capture it while it was fresh.

Karlson quickly picked up on my worst habit as an actor: my tendency to try too hard, to give too much. He set a tone that brought my baseline down a notch, then shot scenes in such a way that Ed's pent-up fury was palpable without my having to push it too far. His easygoing manner and quiet confidence kept not just me, but the whole cast and crew, loose, comfortable, and completely engaged.

The intense one-on-one scenes with Van Heflin were my biggest thrill making *Gunman's Walk*. To me, Van was the ultimate actor. He completely disappeared into character, and everything he did was totally believable. I was surprised when he explained that his theatrical training was in the Delsarte system, a virtually forgotten discipline of gestures and movements created by the Parisian acting and singing teacher François Delsarte in the mid-nineteenth century. It involved a whole set of rules coordinating the voice with the body, very rigid and stylized, and it seemed miles away from the easy naturalism that was Heflin's stock-in-trade.

This proved to me there was no "right way" to build a performance. Every actor has his or her own way of getting from A to B and making it believable. For me, it always started with two things: imagination and concentration.

The climax of the picture, in which father and son square off in a final confrontation, was the most powerful and emotional scene I'd had to that point in my career. All his long-simmering anger released, Ed Hackett goads his father into a duel, and the old man, tears in his eyes, guns down his own flesh and blood.

Van had already figured how to play it for maximum effect. Wanting to make sure I was up to snuff, I asked him to take some extra rehearsal time with me. He was so committed to the play, to *everyone* being good, he'd have taken as long as I wanted to get it right. Believe me, not all actors are like that.

When *Gunman's Walk* premiered the following summer, it was one of the proudest moments of my career—seeing my name up there in wide-screen Technicolor, before the title, right alongside Van Heflin's. This time I felt like I'd earned the right to be there.

The critics—for once—agreed, granting me some of the most positive reviews yet. *Variety* said, "Tab Hunter comes to his fulfillment as an actor in one of the screen's most adult analyzations of what went into the making of a western gunman." Favorable comparisons were made to such huge hits as *High Noon* and *3:10 to Yuma,* and the picture was a solid earner at the box office. Over the years, *Gunman's Walk* has sadly fallen into obscurity, but it still stands up as one of the best, most tough-minded westerns of the 1950s and a high point on my acting résumé.

Another bonus from making the picture was waiting for me when we got back from the Arizona location. Jack Conner invited me over to his barn in Glendale. There was the colt we'd seen at the racetrack in Arizona, the one I desperately wanted to buy.

"How the hell'd you get that old guy to sell him to you?" I shouted.

Jack just winked, saddled him, and told me to mount up.

After some flat work and a few crossrails, we started building the jumps higher and higher. The horse was amazing. I had to buy him.

"Keep him here with me, and you can have him for what I paid, five hundred bucks," Jack said. "If you take him over to Clyde's [where I kept my other horses], I'll have to charge you a thousand."

I shelled out, and kept the skinny colt with Jack and Kay in Glendale. By the time I came back from New York two months later, they'd fattened him up. I was hauling him down the highway to his first show in Indio not long after that when I started singing, "Look down, look down that lonesome road."

That's how Lonesome Road got his show name. Same way Henry Willson had picked mine, out of thin air.

Renaissance

EVEN THOUGH 1957 CAME to a close with Tab Hunter missing from America's movie screens, I was once again officially "hot." Proof came in December with a sketch on Bob Hope's annual Christmas special that satirized Tab Hunter's immense popularity with teenagers, specifically girls. I'd also done dozens of television guest shots, including the highly rated *Dinah Shore Chevy Show,* in which Dinah coaxed me into singing live. Despite the hit records, performing live was still scary, and I have Dinah to thank for helping me overcome that obstacle. She wanted to do a duet and wouldn't let me off the hook. She could sweet-talk a beggar out of his last dime.

"If anything goes wrong," Dinah said, "I'll just signal the orchestra to play louder. Don't worry about it. We'll do fine." Dinah was the best.

If singing was daunting, how about singing and skating at the same time? I faced that challenge in February, when I appeared on the *Hallmark Hall of Fame* special *Hans Brinker or the Silver Skates.* It was a musical version of Mary Mapes Dodge's classic children's story about a poor Dutch family struggling to overcome all kinds of adversity. At twenty-seven, I was a little long in the tooth to be playing teenage Hans, but then there weren't too many actors around who

Duetting with Dinah, 1957. (Photo courtesy of Globe Photos.)

could sing and not embarrass themselves on the ice opposite the Olympic ice-skating champion Dick Button, who brought incredible pizzazz to the skating scenes. The pay was good for a one-shot show, but to be honest, I'd have paid for the chance to meet, let alone skate with, Dick Button, who was one of my real heroes.

Rehearsals began January 19 in New York, which gave director Sidney Lumet only three weeks to pull together an elaborately staged, fully choreo-graphed ninety-minute musical, with a huge cast in period costume. Lumet was another brilliant talent from the exciting wave of directors emerging from New York theater and television. He'd done lots of small-screen work since 1950, including several *Playhouse 90*s and *Studio One*s, and hundreds of episodes of *Danger*. He was now an Oscar nominee for *12 Angry Men*, his fea-ture debut, unanimously regarded as one of the best pictures of 1957.

Rehearsals of the nonskating scenes were held in a huge space above Ratner's Deli on Second Avenue. Lumet taped out the floor to the exact di-mensions of the sets we'd have in the studio. The diverse cast included in-triguing characters like Basil Rathbone and renowned Czech soprano Jarmila Novotna, who played my mother. My leading lady was "Pretty Perky" Peggy King, a regular on *The George Gobel Show,* who was best known for singing commercial jingles for Campbell's soup and Pepsi-Cola. The biggest charac-ter among us, no question, was vocal director and arranger Buster Davis, who coached us through all the great Hugh Martin songs. Buster was an outra-geously flamboyant queen, who always dragged himself to rehearsals laden with sheet music, which spilled everywhere. The kid who played Dick's little brother, Luke Halpin, was all over Buster, the way a cat is obsessed with the one person in the room who hates cats. He'd hang on Buster's pants leg, say-ing "Hi, Bus—I love you, Bus."

One morning I overheard Buster say to the kid, "Careful, sonny, you're play-ing with fire."

After a week and a half of the Ratner's rehearsals, the cast was shuttled daily to an absolutely frigid ice rink in Asbury Park, New Jersey, the only place in the area available for private skating practice. Buster was there every day, outrageous as could be, playing live piano accompaniment to our routines. Peggy King was game but couldn't skate a lick. I lifted her up and waltzed her around, her skates barely skimming the ice. Performing with Button, on the other hand, was perhaps the peak of my career on the ice, even if I was rusty.

That he could skate rings around me was a given; that he was a good actor was a real bonus!

Whenever I was in New York, my habit was to hit as many Broadway shows as possible. This time, of course, I was eager to see *Damn Yankees*. Like all the best musicals, it wrapped its extravagance around a strong, simple premise: a married, middle-aged baseball fan sells his soul to the Devil for a chance to lead his favorite team, the lowly Washington Senators, to the pennant. The portly businessman is reincarnated as Joe Hardy, a slugger with no past, who starts to pine for a return to his simple, domestic life. That's where Lola, the Devil's temptress, comes in. Her job is to keep the hook in Joe.

What a weird experience it was, watching that marvelous cast—especially Gwen Verdon as Lola and Ray Walston as Mr. Applegate (the Devil)—and realizing I'd pretty soon be in the middle of it, singing and dancing with a troupe that had been together for almost a thousand performances.

Stephen Douglass, who'd played Joe Hardy since the show premiered in 1955, had a set of pipes that wouldn't quit. No way I could sing like that. But I was confident that on-screen I'd be more believable. Surprisingly, I wasn't nervous about plunging into *Damn Yankees*. I was eager. Despite my typical two-steps-forward, one-step-back approach, by now I'd gained a lot of confidence as an actor.

Not enough, however, to waltz backstage and introduce myself to my future colleagues. On their turf, I felt like a trespasser.

That week I also witnessed Tony's return to the boards, in *Look Homeward, Angel*. He'd been eager to get back on Broadway, having been disappointed by his last two movies. *The Sea Wall*, like my *Lafayette Escadrille*, was in limbo: the studio had changed the title to *This Bitter Earth*, then *This Angry Age*, then stuck it on the shelf, unsure how to market it. (It wasn't released until the summer of 1958, on the bottom half of a double bill with something called *Screaming Mimi*.) His next picture, *Desire Under the Elms*, which was about to be released, had been a trial for Tony. Even though he liked his costar, Sophia Loren, he felt overshadowed and overwhelmed by her, leading to an awkward, unsatisfying performance. His intuition would be confirmed when the reviews came out.

Like me, Tony had also tried his hand at a singing career. He'd first recorded the title song to *Friendly Persuasion* and then, maybe inspired by "Young Love," released a record called "First Romance," written by his pal Gwen Davis.

(Gwen and I would also write a song together, "Don't Let It Get Around." It didn't.) Tony always joked that his tremulous voice could make any happy love song sound sad.

Tony had misgivings about how Paramount had used him, trying to mold him into something he was not. Like me, he'd started publicly venting his frustrations. Instead of complaining about Paramount, however, Tony picked on himself: "I'm not really suited to be a movie star," he told *McCall's*. "I have no confidence in myself. I'm not interested in money. I'm not good-looking. I have a hunch in my spine. I can't see worth a damn. I have a very small head. I haven't many opinions. I dislike nightclubs—the kinds of things that bring you easy publicity. I have no string of French girls. I'm not tough. I can't put on a show in public. I'm much too sensitive to be in Hollywood. I'm an ideal target."

I may have rubbed him the wrong way myself after watching an early version of *Look Homeward, Angel* during a short trip to New York the previous November to do some TV guest spots. Backstage, Tony asked what I thought of his performance, and I told him straight:

"You're afraid to give vent to what you're really feeling," I said. "You're only showing the side of yourself you want people to see."

It's what Jeff Corey, probably Hollywood's best acting teacher, had warned

At a Tony Perkins recording session, with Venetia Stevenson and Gwen Davis. (Photo courtesy of Globe Photos.)

me against as I prepared for *Gunman's Walk*. You're not there to be liked; you're there to portray a character. Some actors can't help watching themselves in the performance. That's the kiss of death. We talked a lot about the challenge of baring your inner self to make a character believable.

When I saw *Look Homeward, Angel* the second time, in late January, Tony had stripped away all the preconceived ideas and was mesmerizing. An actor has to find that zone of truth on his own. But it does help to have someone else looking *into* you, not letting you settle for the easy way out.

HAVING SAID THAT, it's hard to believe what happened next. Dick Clayton gave me the script for an upcoming episode of *Playhouse 90* called "Portrait of a Murderer." It concerned the real-life crimes of Donald Bashor, a seemingly normal, well-respected young man who'd recently been convicted of a series of grisly murders and then executed in the gas chamber. The script, based largely on Bashor's recorded jailhouse confessions and the recollections of his cell mate, was utterly compelling.

Eight months earlier, choking on the "good boy" bridle Warners had placed on me, I'd proclaimed to the movie mags: "I want to play a murderer!"

I immediately told Dick, "No way. Tell them I'm not interested." Always my first knee-jerk reaction to a challenge.

"Why the hell not?"

"Did you read it?"

"Of course! It's great! What a role!"

"But it's live. It's too intense. I can't do it."

I'd become so comfortable in the *Hans Brinker* ensemble, surrounded by wonderful supporting players, that it was easy for me to realize, once we were on the air, that the audience wasn't looking only at me, wasn't watching only me, wasn't judging only *me*. There was comfort and security in that.

"Portrait of a Murderer" was totally different: a small, claustrophobic drama in which I'd carry the load by myself for long stretches, without supporting players to hide behind.

"Turn it down, Dick. Don't want to do it. Tell 'em thanks but no thanks."

Next night I got a call from the man directing "Portrait of a Murderer," Arthur Penn. He'd just finished his first feature, *The Left-Handed Gun*, with Paul Newman. Penn was yet another bright, forceful, articulate New Yorker, like Frankenheimer and Lumet, who had the instincts of a fifty-year veteran, coupled with the enthusiasm of a kid. He wasn't going to let me off the hook, not without discussing it first. I made up all kinds of lame excuses, nitpicking my way through the script, debating everything. It was pretty pathetic.

In short time, Penn had steamrolled right over every reason I could think of for *not* doing his show. "We air February twenty-seventh," he said. "So let's get started as soon as you're back from New York." It's a confidence booster to have a director pursue you relentlessly for a part you think might be beyond your reach.

I attacked *Hans Brinker* on a wave of renewed confidence. It not only came off without a hitch but also scored a ratings bonanza, becoming the most watched show in the history of that Sunday-night staple, the *Hallmark Hall of Fame,* a distinction it would hold for the next fourteen years. Two days after it aired, I was back in Hollywood, preparing to play a character *very* different from Hans Brinker.

"It's a shame the judges can't kill the bad part and return the good part," Donald Bashor said just before he was executed. I delivered the line exactly as Bashor had, after studying a tape recording of his final statement before dying in the gas chamber. In a bizarre twist, this episode of *Playhouse 90* would be sponsored by the Southern California Gas Company.

We performed "Portrait of a Murderer" at CBS Television City in Los Angeles. I gleaned many insights on Bashor from his prison cell mate, who'd been hired as a consultant by the director. Penn's energy level, complete focus, and eagerness to work one-on-one and get to the guts of a piece proved that he was no traffic cop—he was a *real* director.

Costarring as Bashor's unsuspecting girlfriend was Geraldine Page, another of those fabulous "products of New York" I admired so much. She'd been a sensation on Broadway in Tennessee Williams's *Summer and Smoke* a few years earlier and was always taking on eccentric and challenging roles, whether it was on stage, screen, or television. While playing a murderer tied me in knots, I was amazed by the ease with which Geri could convey the most powerful emotions.

In one memorable scene, she returns from shopping to find police waiting. Her boyfriend's been arrested for murder, they tell her. In a daze, she restocks the groceries until gradually, inevitably, she comes apart at the seams, breaking down. In rehearsals it was breathtaking. Her choices were different and brilliant and always completely real. No matter how many run-throughs she did, there was no loss of emotion; it was as if she simply pushed a button and pulled everything from the bottom of the well. That was the level I aspired to.

Early every morning I picked up Geri at the Chateau Marmont and drove her to work. One day she admitted that she, like most true New Yorkers, couldn't drive. I explained, just like I had to Tony, that if you're going to work in Hollywood, you must drive a car. So, just as Dick Clayton had done with me years earlier, I sat Geri behind the wheel of my Mercedes, in the parking lot of the Pan Pacific Auditorium, and gave her driving lessons during lunch breaks.

We'd often go down the street to the Farmers Market. While feeding birds on the upstairs terrace, I started venting the pent-up frustration I felt about my career. (Geri was the kind of nonjudgmental person who invited such soul baring). On and on I went about no one taking me seriously. I may have been coming into my own as an actor, doing my best work yet, but the majority of critics still relished picking on me. They were determined to lock me in the "golden boy" box and never give me a scrap of respect.

Finally, Geri had enough of my whining. She clutched my arm and said, "Remember this, Tab—if people don't like you, that's their bad taste."

I've always cherished that moment. Geri's advice has helped me through the rough spots, and I always offer it to anyone insecure about being "judged," either as an artist or as a person. It's something we can apply in all our lives, whatever we do.

Reviews of "Portrait of a Murderer"—by television critics, remember, not movie critics—were my best, by far. The trade papers talked me up for an Emmy. It didn't happen, but I was proud that I'd helped create a memorable show.

MID-APRIL, I WAS summoned to Warner Bros. for a read-through of *Damn Yankees*. Entering a large conference room, I confronted the cast of the original Broadway show, with director George Abbott presiding. Odd that they'd need a read-through, considering these people had performed the show close to a thousand times.

Rumors had been sneaking around that Gwen Verdon—who some thought was too old and not pretty enough for the big screen—was going to be replaced by Marilyn Monroe or Mitzi Gaynor, even though Verdon had won a Tony Award for *Damn Yankees*. My sympathy for her was tempered somewhat by an item I'd seen in Walter Winchell's column: "Gwen Verdon is disappointed that Tab Hunter was selected to be her leading man in the movie version of *Damn Yankees* . . ."

That hurt. Critics dumping on me was bad enough, but getting it from a colleague—one I hadn't even worked with—was awful. I'd put the item out of my mind, my usual tactic for dealing with anything unpleasant. Maybe there *was* someone else who'd be right for the role of Lola, the Devil's right-hand woman. Nope. Nobody else could do "Whatever Lola Wants"—Verdon *owned* it.

I was just going to have to prove her wrong about me.

Cary Grant was petitioning hard to play Mr. Applegate, the Devil incarnate, the part Ray Walston—an unknown to movie audiences—had perfected on Broadway. Regardless of the casting rumors, I was the only new face in the room that day. This meeting, obviously, was all about the "new kid."

We started to read, and Abbott cut me off in mid-delivery: "You're emphasizing the wrong word," he said in a chastising tone. He gave me the "proper" line reading.

Several pages later, Abbott stopped me again. Another line reading. Annoying as hell, but I kept quiet and went along. The tension was getting thick. Third time he cut me off, it bugged the shit out of me. I tried to be respectful:

"Mr. Abbott?"

I'd caught on right away. Nobody called him George. Only "Mr. Abbott," though he'd have answered to "Your Holiness" just as well.

"Yes," he said, fixing me with a jaundiced gaze.

"From what I gather," I said, trying to keep my anger in check, "you'd like me to play the role the way Stephen Douglass did it on Broadway."

"Yes. Yes."

I thought it over for a second, then took the plunge: "I thought Stephen Douglass had a magnificent voice," I said, "but he was a real stick. Now, *if* I play this character, first of all he's got to be a human being."

Abbott looked like he'd been hit in the face with a pie, but he said nothing. The tension was now thick as a brick wall. Self-consciously, I finished the read-through, thanked everyone, and went home.

Wasn't in the door five minutes before Clayton called.

"You're fired from the picture," he said.

I was devastated.

What I didn't know was that I offended George Abbott for reasons beyond not being Stephen Douglass. Years later, I saw a memo the director had sent to Jack Warner, telling him that Tab Hunter was "too gay" to be believable as an all-American baseball hero. Abbott's choice, if he couldn't have Douglass, was Don Murray.

Clayton told me to stay calm—he'd smooth things over. Jack Warner was adamant that I star in *Damn Yankees,* but he decreed that I show Abbott some respect, since he was the co-writer of the play and the studio had paid a small fortune for the rights. Clayton called up my acting coach, Jeff Corey, and gave him the lowdown on what had happened. Jeff had a solution.

The next day, in his garage studio on Cheremoya Avenue, Corey grabbed my copy of *Damn Yankees* and started in on all my lines, having me imitate every one of his readings.

"What's going on?" I asked.

"Just shut up and do as you're told."

For hours, Jeff gave all sorts of interpretations and demanded I follow his lead to the letter. The point was for me to find an inner justification for delivering lines *his* way yet make it work for *me.* Corey allowed no compromise. I couldn't argue, couldn't say, *But that doesn't feel right. That's not how I'd say it.*

"Sometimes, there's no other way than how the director wants it," Jeff explained. "It doesn't matter what *you* think. Your job is to make it *work.* To make it comfortable and natural for yourself, even if it goes against your instincts."

It was a tough lesson, but a necessary one for a cocky young actor to learn.

2 2

Damn Yankees

IT WAS THE BEST of shoots, it was the worst of shoots.

With apologies to *A Tale of Two Cities,* that quote pretty much sums up my experience making *Damn Yankees.* It felt, on the one hand, like I was ready to break out as an all-around performer, but much of the time I was choking on George Abbott's short leash.

Within the first few days, we shot the scene in which Joe Hardy returns home to his wife, Meg, who doesn't realize the young baseball star renting a spare room is actually her missing husband. Shannon Bolin, the actress playing Meg, is trying to cope with her sadness by sprucing the place up with flowers. As she fussed with an arrangement, Shannon didn't notice one flower fall to the floor. I stepped over, picked it up, considered offering it to her, then decided to keep it for myself—a neat way to symbolize her husband's affection, which he can't express because of his Faustian deal with the Devil.

"Cut!" Abbott yelled.

Damn it. "Why did we cut?" I asked out loud. It had felt like one of those magical moments you long for.

"Didn't do it that way on Broadway," Abbott announced. He should have had that printed on a sandwich board, since it was his stock answer to every suggestion.

"I did it instinctively," I said. "I want to keep the flower because it reminds me of my wife. It's a nice moment."

Abbott vetoed the idea. We did it again, no doubt the way Stephen Douglass had done it a thousand times.

Could Abbott's obsession with keeping as much as he could of the Broadway show have been the result of a second director being needed to help him translate *Damn Yankees* to the screen? As had happened the previous year with *The Pajama Game*, Stanley Donen actually directed the film, with Abbott looming, making sure we didn't stray too far from the original. Stanley was good friends with the film's choreographer, Bob Fosse, from the days they'd worked together at MGM. He was brilliant with both actors and the camera, as he'd proved directing *Singin' in the Rain* a few years earlier. On a movie set, Stanley Donen's genius was George Abbott's security blanket.

As filming progressed, the initial tension I'd felt with the rest of the cast gradually evaporated. Following Gwen's lead, the entire cast took to calling me "Tabunter," in thick New Yawk accents. I suspect they took pity on me, having to bear up under Abbott's obsession with conformity. I'd have preferred more freedom in my interpretation of Joe Hardy, but all in all, I couldn't complain. Jeff Corey's guidance was invaluable when it came to maintaining my composure and staying focused on the job at hand.

That job was to be the "straight line" around which the more eccentric characters spin. In addition to Gwen and Ray, there were memorable moments provided by Rae Allen, Russ Brown, James Komack, and a young Jean Stapleton, already sketching the outlines of the character who would make her famous, *All in the Family*'s Edith Bunker.

Opening up the play led to other challenges — like actually playing baseball. Wrigley Field in downtown Los Angeles was redecorated to stand in for

*Hollywood meets Broadway — Stanley Donen and I discuss
Damn Yankees with Gwen Verdon and George Abbott.*

Washington's Griffith Stadium, with canvas backdrops hiding the palm trees. There was no place to hide on the diamond, however—so I diligently practiced my hitting and fielding, to seem believable as the Senators' answer to Mickey Mantle. In the movie, Joe Hardy knocks a homer virtually every time he swings. I managed it only once, and wouldn't you know . . . the cameras didn't catch it.

As for the challenge of singing and dancing . . . well, the dancing was far easier, thanks to the supremely talented Bob Fosse. Unlike set-in-his-ways George Abbott, Fosse could be intuitive and spontaneous, working within everyone's varying abilities to get the best possible result on-screen. He and Donen worked seamlessly together, like a two-headed director. Where Abbott saw things mostly from one perspective, Stanley and Bobby saw every detail, including camera moves, edits—everything. On top of all that, Bobby had his own moment in the spotlight, performing an incredible mambo duet with Gwen called "Who's Got the Pain?"

"Whatever Lola Wants," Gwen's famous seduction of Joe Hardy, was a cinch for me—all I had to do was react to her outrageously sexy routine. Not difficult. I just sat in the middle of her magic.

Far more challenging was the show's grandest number, "Two Lost Souls," Joe and Lola's falling-in-love duet, which starts quietly in a jazz-tinged netherworld and gradually builds into a full-blown, showstopping dance explosion. During rehearsals, I warned Bobby, "I'd love to dance, but I've got two left feet. I'm going to need a lot of help."

"Don't worry," Fosse said. "You're going to do fine."

He choreographed around me at times but knew exactly where, and for how long, I could hold my own with Gwen. For a few shining moments, she and I actually danced together! I confess: it was hard not to slip out of character for a split second—*Look, Ma! I'm dancing!*

Singing was *much* harder. Not because of my old stage-fright bugaboo—I'd sung the Oscar-nominated song "April Love" live on the Academy Awards that year—but for a more peculiar reason. Usually when shooting a musical, everyone lip-synchs the songs, which have been prerecorded. Well, as we went into production, a musician's strike gripped Hollywood. I wasn't allowed to prerecord my songs. An original *Damn Yankees* cast album already existed, so we all worked from that. This proved to be a nightmare for me—I had to sing to the disembodied voice of Stephen Douglass. The guy was haunting me! (It is, however, my voice in the finished film.)

When the twenty-eight-day shoot concluded, standard procedure would have been to return to the recording studio to cut final versions of all the songs, accompanied by a full orchestra. But the strike was still dragging on. We were forced to record our vocal tracks a cappella, without a single note of music. The film was then shipped to Rome, where an Italian orchestra recorded the music tracks, which were then married to the vocals back in Hollywood.

Not exactly the ideal conditions in which to make your big-screen musical debut, but by the time we wrapped, I honestly could say, despite my problems with George Abbott, that I loved being part of the *Damn Yankees* team.

As the premiere drew near, nerves rattled within the Warner Bros. marketing department. Some execs didn't want to use Gwen in the advertising: she wasn't enough of a conventional Hollywood beauty. But George Abbott demanded that they use the same art that appeared in the Broadway poster, highlighting Gwen and relegating her male costar to a postage-stamp photo in the corner.

The finished film proved irresistible, even to Bosley Crowther of the *New York Times*. He was one of those snooty movie critics who'd never found anything redeeming in a Tab Hunter picture. I'd given up reading his reviews. Someone had to force the *Times* into my hands when the film opened in Manhattan in September 1958.

> Tab Hunter . . . he has the clean, naive look of a lad breaking into the big leagues and into the magical company of a first-rate star. He is really appealing with Miss Verdon in the boogie-woogie ballet, "Two Lost Souls," which is . . . the dandiest dance number in the film.

Okay, he wasn't touting me for an Oscar, but coming from a man who'd specialized in belittling me in print . . . it was vindication. Crowther wound up his review declaring, "If you can't get to the World Series, get to see *Damn Yankees*. It's some show."

TONY PERKINS AND I had now both done baseball movies. We'd both recorded pop tunes. We'd dated the same girls. Maybe it was inevitable that we'd share a costar.

Sophia Loren was just about the hottest actress in the world. Take that any way you want. She'd hit Hollywood like a force of nature in 1955, following in the (usually bare) footsteps of other earthy Italian actresses like Silvana Mangano, Anna Magnani, and Gina Lollobrigida. But Loren had something extra propelling her into a multipicture deal at Paramount. She had Carlo Ponti, a powerful producer, partner of Dino de Laurentiis, who signed her to an exclusive contract after spotting her in a beauty pageant when she was fifteen. Ponti became her personal manager, the de facto executive producer of all her movies, and her husband. In Italy, however, the authorities didn't recognize their 1957 Mexican marriage because under Italian law Ponti had never divorced his previous wife.

Unlike my *Confidential* problems, Sophia's "scandalous" relationship with Ponti *helped* her career, etching in the public's imagination an image of a woman so spellbinding, so abundantly sensual, that any respectable, red-blooded man would sacrifice everything for her.

Not coincidentally, that's the plot of *That Kind of Woman,* a project Ponti chose especially for his wife. The screenplay, which came to me during the shooting of *Damn Yankees,* was wonderfully simple: On a train to New York during World War II, a naive soldier meets an exotic mystery woman and falls in love. Turns out she is the property of the Man, a wealthy munitions magnate. After an overnight encounter in a sleeper car, the woman bids the kid farewell at Penn Station. The love-struck GI proves relentless, however, and, with his buddy in tow, pursues the woman all over New York, battling the Man for her heart.

Any doubts I had about "enlisting" again were eliminated when I learned Ponti had picked Sidney Lumet to direct the film. I was thrilled that Sidney wanted me for the part. Clearly, he wanted to play up the "opposites attract" theme, contrasting the innocent, square-jawed blond farmboy with the sultry, curvaceous, experienced woman of the world.

Warner Bros. agreed to my loan-out, but first I had to be approved by Loren and Ponti. I met them at the Paramount offices. Sophia was even more charismatic and beautiful in person. Hard to believe she was twenty-four, three years *younger* than me. Ponti was short, balding, and twice his wife's age—physically, an utter mismatch. I wondered if he'd picked this script because it mirrored his relationship with Loren—a rich, powerful middle-aged businessman covets a woman who is lusted after by every man she meets.

I was ecstatic when Dick Clayton told me I'd gotten the part. Filming began in June, only days after I'd wrapped *Damn Yankees.* As part of his agreement to direct, Sidney had requested that the movie's original setting be switched from Texas to New York—his town—which he was inspired to capture in a fresh way, through the lens of Oscar-winning cameraman Boris Kaufman. The screenwriter, Walter Bernstein, was a New York pal of Lumet's who hadn't written a script in ten years, after having been blacklisted by the studios when his name came up in anti-Communist hearings in the late 1940s. Lumet figured that Ponti, being a Hollywood outsider, wouldn't care one way or the other about a writer's political leanings.

Sophia and Carlo arrived in New York from Europe, where she'd accepted the Best Actress prize at the Venice Film Festival for her performance in *Black Orchid*. She grabbed the award, gushed her thanks, and rushed to an idling jet, chartered by Paramount, that whisked her and Ponti out of Italy. The triumphant homecoming had to be brief, since they were at risk of being arrested on bigamy charges.

Upon my arrival in Manhattan, I checked in with Tony. "What do you think about working with Sophia?" he asked. By then I'd seen *Desire Under the Elms* and had to agree with the general consensus: next to Sophia, he came off weakly. Loren was a powerful presence, and with Ponti pulling strings, she could devour the screen, leaving everyone else stranded in the margins.

"Under all that fire and sex, she's like a kitten," I told him. I always look for the vulnerable side in people. That's how my character, Red, pierces the protective armor of the kept woman, Kay, and that's how I was going to deal with Sophia as well. Go right past the image, to the real person beneath.

Sidney assembled a marvelous cast: George Sanders, Keenan Wynn, Jack Warden, and Barbara Nichols. Shirley MacLaine was originally cast in Barbara's role, as Kay's loyal girlfriend, but Ponti dropped her at the last minute, fearing she'd upstage his wife. Beatrice Arthur also had a small bit in a bar scene with Jack Warden and me. Bea could do more with one line than most actresses could with a whole script.

I felt right at home, rehearsing again above Ratner's Deli. I loved how dedicated Sidney was to rehearsals. His thoroughness really paid off when we started shooting, because we were whisked all over New York, the city becoming as much the star of the show as Sophia.

We shot everywhere, from 125th Street in Harlem to Irish bars on Third Avenue, from the Brooklyn Bridge to Staten Island, from Sutton Place to Little Italy, from Fifth Avenue to Grand Central Station. It was during a scene at Grand Central that I relearned a vital lesson.

I'd done several takes that left Sidney cold. He wanted more than I was giving. "Tab, you're playing it safe," he told me. "If you want to play it safe, stay in bed all day long. That's the safest place to be—but it's also the dullest."

He'd caught me slacking off. Doubly embarrassing, considering that I'd called Tony's commitment into question months earlier, after seeing him in *Look Homeward, Angel.* Being caught like that left a huge impression, and to this day I've never forgotten Sidney's admonishment. It's essential advice for any actor.

That was one hot summer in Manhattan. Sophia would invite me into her air-conditioned limo between takes, where we'd crank up the local rock-and-roll station on the radio. She loved American pop music. Bobby Darin's "Splish Splash" was zooming up the charts, and we'd sing it together all the time. It became "our" song.

One afternoon on location, Sophia suddenly blurted out, "I'm upstaging you, Tab. I'm upstaging you."

I didn't know exactly what to make of this. Was it an apology or a warning? She went on for several minutes until I finally said, "Look, Sophia, sooner or later they're going to get tired of seeing your face filling the screen. It'll be like a refreshing breeze to catch a glimpse of someone else."

Sophia had an incredible sense of humor and a magnetic personality that drew everyone to her. Her on-screen persona was very misleading. She was no more a man-devouring tigress than I was the naive boy next door. She was a talented and guileless woman, and everyone she worked with should be thankful to have known her. She was, at least until 1981, my favorite leading lady.

It would be nice to report that *That Kind of Woman* was a smash hit, but that wasn't the case. There are lots of reasons why otherwise-good films fail at the box office, but bad timing and misleading marketing probably top the list. Paramount had cast me in the hope I'd attract a younger audience, which normally didn't go for European films or stars. It also packaged the movie as a romantic comedy, which Ponti seemed to feel would be more palatable to U.S. audiences, especially in the wake of Loren's success with her last picture, a comedy with Cary Grant called *Houseboat.* Sidney, however, had focused on the darker corners of the story, an approach reflected in the look of the film, best described as "neorealism comes to New York."

The reviews were mixed, many of them uneasy with the way the film veered between light comedy and dark drama. Paramount, which had made a huge investment in Sophia, premiered *That Kind of Woman* at the 5,868-seat Roxy Theatre in New York. That's a ton of expectation for a small "art" film. To pump things up, the studio even hired singers to open the shows. It was no use.

The picture flopped so badly it was pulled after three weeks, scaring off even the smaller art-house exhibitors who should have been the ones booking *That Kind of Woman* in the first place.

For my part, I got the usual critical treatment: good reviews called me "surprisingly effective" or "above par." Negative ones delighted in suggesting how unsuitable I was for a sexual powerhouse like Loren: "It's like watching a speedboat race a tricycle" and stuff like that. These lazy reviewers, it seemed to me, were more interested in having fun with our contrived public images, rather than actually critiquing the movie.

Not that long ago, I was shown a Sophia Loren biography in which the author noted that "with Tab Hunter as her costar, Sophia had to struggle to make it seem believable that she could ever seriously fall for him, let alone desire him for a husband."

It went on . . .

"The tall and naturally blond Hunter had sensational looks, but slight acting ability."

And on . . .

"Tab Hunter's homosexuality was no shock to Sophia, but it was apparently one reason why their love scenes lacked fire."

Sidney Lumet was quoted: "If you put [Sophia] in the arms of someone who's not responsive to women, or even worse, someone who can barely pretend that he is, then there's going to be problems."

I was shocked, especially by Sidney's comment. When I read these things, my first reaction was *Fuck 'em! Why did they hire me if they thought I wasn't right opposite Sophia?* Sidney had specifically asked for me, Paramount was all for it, and Sophia and her husband approved. But somehow, when it came time, years later, to unearth explanations for the film's failure, I was a convenient whipping boy. We all worked hard on the picture and gave the best we had. If it had been a winner at the box office—trust me—nobody would have been questioning whether I belonged in Sophia Loren's arms.

Regardless of what was said later, or if they even said it, I loved Sophia and consider Sidney Lumet one of the finest directors I've ever worked with. *That Kind of Woman* is a gem, still my favorite of all the films I've made.

Who Does He Remind You Of?

ALL I WANTED WAS to keep making movies, keep improving my craft. The last three pictures were my best yet. I was finally on the road I wanted to travel as an actor.

It didn't even faze me when *Lafayette Escadrille* crashed faster than a strafed Fokker. Originally, Warner Bros.' strategy was to release it to coincide with my "debut" as the first artist on the studio's new record label. But God created the universe faster than Jack Warner could assemble a music division, and by the time Warner Bros. Records finally started pressing and issuing vinyl, Bill Wellman's film had taken on the unhappy aroma of spoiled turkey.

Darby's Rangers, made months after *Lafayette Escadrille,* actually made it to theaters first. By the time *Lafayette* came out, Etchika had permanently returned to France, foiling any further publicity based on our "romance."

America's teenagers couldn't have cared less about a World War I story, even if it starred one of their idols. Which made it all the more aggravating that the studio altered the original ending to protect the tender sensibilities of those kids.

As soon as I returned from shooting *That Kind of Woman,* I signed a deal with Warner Bros. Records and began recording new songs. The boss, Jim Conkling, was in his early forties but had already gone into retirement after working at Columbia and Capitol. Jack Warner threw a pile of money at him to return to the trenches and get his new operation up and running.

Our sessions had the best musicians in town. We recorded at Ryder Sound, where I felt comfortable. Warners A and R man George Avakian and producer Don Ralke were absolutely great . . . but the magic wasn't there. What had been conjured at Dot Records couldn't be recaptured. Dot was run by a family of music makers; Warners was full of businessmen. At Dot I felt totally se-cure, even though I (infamously) didn't have more than a handshake agree-ment with Randy Wood. By contrast, my deal with Warner Bros. Records stipulated:

> You grant to us exclusively and perpetually all now or hereafter ex-isting rights of every kind and character whatsoever, whether such rights are now known, recognized or contemplated, and the com-plete unconditional, unencumbered title throughout the world in and to: your performance hereunder; and all results and proceeds thereof; and all masters, phonograph records, sound recordings and mechanical and other reproductions of such performances and any and all [blah, blah, blah]

To cop a jazzman's term, it was a totally different *vibe*.

My first single on the WB label was "Jealous Heart," which got decent air-play but never climbed higher than #62 on the charts. The following year, "(I'll Be with You in) Apple Blossom Time" made the Top 40, but that was as good as it was going to get on the WB label.

BILL ORR, JACK WARNER'S son-in-law, summoned me to his office one afternoon. He and another recently hired executive, Hugh Benson, had been put in charge of the studio's growing TV division. They were in pre-production on an hour-long detective series, a television first. It was called *77 Sunset Strip*, and they leaned on me to accept the lead role.

It never occurred to me to consider the economics. Now that Warners had a music division, TV programs would become the primary method of selling records—a possible explanation for *You're My Girl: Romantic Reflections by Jack Webb*, one of the label's earliest releases. The *Dragnet* star made me sound like Caruso. Warners wanted Tab Hunter to be a triple threat: movies, mu-sic, and television—all blanketed under the original terms of the seven-year contract I'd signed back in 1954.

I wanted no part of a TV series. The small screen had given me my best op-portunities, but those were guest-starring roles on quality live shows. I'd de-velop as an actor by stretching my range, not locking myself into the same character, week in and week out.

I turned them down flat.

Orr and Benson figured fresh air might uncloud my head, so they ushered me on a stroll around the lot. My thinking wasn't going to get any clearer: I only wanted to make feature films.

Orr pointed out a young blond actor chatting nearby.

"Who does that guy remind you of?" he asked.

"I don't know," I replied. "You tell me."

"Doesn't he look an awful lot like a young Tab Hunter?"

"We're thinking of signing him to a contract," Benson chimed in. "His name's Troy Donahue."

With a name like that, I didn't have to guess who his agent was. And Orr and Benson didn't need to spell out anything further.

I started pointing out people passing by. "See her?" I asked. "Who does *she* remind you of? *Nobody*? That's because she's one of a kind. The sooner you realize there's only one of me, and one of you, and one of him and one of her—the better off we'll all be."

They weren't going to intimidate me. Of course, they weren't going to listen, either. All I could do was stand up for myself and let the chips fall where they may.

77 Sunset Strip became a huge hit for ABC. Efrem Zimbalist Jr. played the part I passed on, just like he'd taken over *Bombers B-52* when I turned that down. Edd Byrnes, who'd gotten his break at Warners when I'd skipped *Darby's Rangers*, became a teen idol in his own right, playing Kookie. Just like the marketing geniuses calculated, the show's soundtrack album became the biggest seller in the WB catalog, peaking at #3 nationally. A smash single, "Kookie, Kookie (Lend Me Your Comb)," was a duet between Byrnes and Connie Stevens.

Orr and Benson immediately went to the well again, casting Connie as Cricket in *Hawaiian Eye*, a virtual replica of *77 Sunset Strip* costarring Robert Conrad and Anthony Eisley. The following year, Warners pumped out yet another clone, *Surfside Six*—starring Troy Donahue. He'd signed with Warner Bros. after a couple of years at Universal, where he'd developed his own teen cult, just like me. His first movie for Warners was *A Summer Place*—a film that, to this day, people think of as one of *my* biggest hits.

The moral of all this, I suppose, is that Orr and Benson were absolutely right—products of Hollywood *are* interchangeable and, ultimately, replaceable.

What applies in "the business," however, has nothing whatsoever to do with

the real world, where people are people, not disposable widgets in an entertainment machine. What the studio wanted from me and what I wanted for
myself were very different things. It was never my goal to be a "teen idol," and
at twenty-seven years of age, I had no desire to remain one.

Not Troy Donahue.   *Not Tab Hunter.*

THAT OCTOBER, AS 77 *Sunset Strip* premiered on television, I was on
location in Utah, making a *movie.* A movie with bona fide *movie* stars: Gary
Cooper, Rita Hayworth, Richard "Nick" Conte, and once more, Van Heflin.
And guess what?

I was in the military once again.

They Came to Cordura was a prestige production, made by Columbia Pictures, my home away from home. Aside from *Damn Yankees,* I hadn't made a
picture at "my" studio in a couple of years. Warners was perfectly happy to pay
my base salary, then rake in the gravy by loaning me to other studios at a much
higher fee.

This was to be Columbia's big-ticket title for the 1959 Christmas season.
The picture was being helmed by Robert Rossen, an Oscar-winning writer,
producer, and director, and was based on a best seller by Glendon Swarthout
that revolved around the U.S. Army's abortive 1916 "punitive expedition" into
Mexico. Pancho Villa's revolutionaries had earlier strayed into Columbus,
New Mexico, killing several civilians and soldiers. For eleven months, an army
detachment futilely chased the *villistas* south of the border, trying to take Villa

into custody. Sounds like an epic, but it was a small-scale character study, exploring themes of courage and cowardice by focusing on six Medal of Honor candidates, cut off from civilization, who reveal their true selves when stretched to the limits of their endurance.

The strong story wasn't my sole reason for making the film. I'd seen Gary Cooper's *Cloak and Dagger* more than a hundred times when I'd ushered at the old Warner Bros. Theater on Hollywood Boulevard. My mother loved him. Tony Perkins, who played Cooper's son in *Friendly Persuasion,* was fond of him. Like me, Cooper was by and large "untrained," a horseman with virtually no experience before his acting debut in the 1920s. In a business growing thicker by the day with all kinds of "schools" and "methods," Coop's legend was based entirely on unaffected simplicity.

As for Rita Hayworth . . . well, she was *it.* The Love Goddess. I'd fallen for her as a kid, as early as *Blood and Sand*—did one movie ever have three more beautiful people than Tyrone Power, Linda Darnell, and Rita Hayworth? Like every red-blooded American male, I fondly recalled that famous full-page *Life* photo of Rita kneeling on satin sheets in her negligee, probably the most-masturbated-to image of all time.

Throw in the chance to work again with Van Heflin—hell, I was thrilled to be in the mix, on equal footing, with such savvy veterans.

On top of all that, Jack Conner was our stunt coordinator, which on this picture was a huge responsibility. Jack worked closely with Robert Rossen to re-create the battle of Ojos Azules, the last mounted cavalry charge in U.S. Army history. With explosions everywhere, hundreds of horses and riders going every which way, it looked like utter confusion. But Jack worked the whole thing out, trained everybody, and responded to every demand for increasingly complicated stunts with his standard line: "Piece o' cake."

When it was time to roll film, there was Jack, hoisting the Stars and Stripes in the middle of it all, his trusty mare Daisy going full out into the line of enemy fire. Suddenly, Daisy tripped and went ass over teakettle. Jack hit the ground hard, and dozens of horses galloped over him. Rossen immediately yelled, "*Cut!*" Everybody raced to Jack, crumpled and motionless in the dirt.

"Jack! Are you all right?" I hollered. He looked like a goner.

Terrifying seconds passed. Then slowly Jack pushed himself up, staggering to his feet. He brushed off, rubbed his sore bones, and quietly said, "Yeah, but that would have killed an ordinary man."

They don't make 'em like Jack anymore. He could do anything and make it look easy.

One night, following dinner at the Filthy Fist (actually the Big Hand, the lone eatery in St. George, Utah, aptly renamed by cast and crew), Coop asked, "How 'bout a little poker?" The invitation was extended only to the "big guns": Rita, Van, Nick—and me.

One slight problem: "I don't know how to play," I told Coop.

A fist dug into my back. "'Course he'll play," said Jack Conner, right behind me. Figuring me for an easy mark, Coop let Jack sit with me to make sure the dummy didn't slow the game. "Don't worry," Jack whispered as the cards were dealt, "we're gonna sack 'em out."

I ended up the big winner that night, and I split the take with Jack. He'd wanted in on the game because his wife, Kay, was having a baby any minute. With all their extracurricular horse businesses, they needed all the money they could get.

Rita really enjoyed herself that night, laughing it up with the rest of us. It was good to see because generally she was all business on the set, distant and reserved, even a little sad. She seemed smothered by the watchful gaze of her new husband, producer James Hill, who came with her on location. Some nights they had screaming fights that were horrible to hear. To me, Rita was still *Gilda,* and *The Lady from Shanghai* and *Cover Girl*—she deserved adoration, not arguments. You wanted to put your arms around her and tell her it was going to be all right. She drank, but only in the evenings, and it never showed in her work.

Coop brought his family on location, too. Veronica "Rocky" Cooper was something else—a full-fledged New York socialite. Her stepfather, Paul Shields, had been a governor of the New York Stock Exchange, and her uncle, Cedric Gibbons, the head decorator at MGM. Rocky was a expert rifleman, deep-sea diver, and equestrian.

Frankly, Rocky frightened me. She was so . . . airtight. I found myself agreeing with everything she said, then later kicking myself: *What was I thinking? I don't believe that at all!* Only when I finally locked horns with her over some insignificant thing did her intimidation evaporate. From then on, she was much warmer.

The Coopers' daughter, Maria, was also around the set in St. George. I'd met her previously, through Tony. They'd dated off and on when she was still a teenager. By twenty-one, she was an accomplished artist and biochemistry major with movie-star looks, more worldly and sophisticated than most full-fledged adults. Her folks were proud, and protective.

Maria and I eventually did go out several times, which sent the scandal rags into an uproar. The gist of their mumbo jumbo was that Coop was sold on me as marriage material for Maria because I was good with horses, but Rocky didn't find me cultivated enough. Maria was an exceptional person, a good Catholic, and her family *was* Hollywood royalty. For more than a few moments, I found myself wishing that for once the scandal magazines might have had their story straight.

Hunting was Coop's passion, and one day on the set he mentioned it was the final day of pheasant season. Long about 3:30 p.m., he stood up, yawning, making a show of stretching his tired, aching body.

"Okay, that's a wrap!" the assistant director abruptly hollered. *That* was star power.

On the way back to the hotel, Coop said slyly: "I wonder why we wrapped so early today."

I had to laugh. "That AD saw you packing it in," I told him. Coop just smiled.

Several hours later a "tired and aching" Coop strode into the Filthy Fist with a freshly bagged pheasant, which he proudly presented to the chef. The

Coop calls it a day on Cordura. (Photo courtesy of Globe Photos.)

cook unfortunately deep fried the damn thing till it was as tough as a truck tire.

There was one other unlikely thing Coop and I had in common: we weren't allowed to die on-screen. In the novel, Coop's character, Major Thorn, is killed by his mutinous band of "heroes," who don't realize that he's led them to salvation, finding the way to Cordura. Fat chance of that. When screenwriter Ivan Moffat had suggested to producer William Goetz, a close friend of Coop's, that the star wear thick glasses, like the character in the book, Goetz pointed to a painting on his office wall:

"That's an original Picasso," he said, "and I intend to keep it. And that's why Gary Cooper doesn't wear glasses in my movie."

Moffat didn't even bother to *ask* about keeping the original ending.

The movies, of course, aren't anything like real life. None of us knew that this would be Coop's next-to-last film. He had lung cancer, not diagnosed until the following year. It made his performance, in essence a grueling near-death march, all the more heroic. He'd die two years later, a week after his sixtieth birthday.

In hindsight, making *They Came to Cordura* felt like the end of an era. Although they lived longer than Coop, Rita and Van didn't have many movies left in them, either. Starring roles for them were few and far between after this. Robert Rossen only lived another six years. Old Hollywood, which I cherished, was on the way out, and I'd rarely have the chance to work with people of this caliber again. I'm glad I had the opportunity, and if I had a hundred more chances to choose between 77 *Sunset Strip* and *They Came to Cordura,* I'd go with Coop, Rita, and Van every time.

Not that I always knew, or did, what was best for me. Throughout filming, Bob Rossen kept telling me about a terrific book, still in galley form, for which he'd already purchased the film rights. Rossen had great enthusiasm and kept trying to convince me that "Fast" Eddie Felson, a cocky pool shark, would be a great role for me.

"Bob—enough," I finally said. "I hate shooting pool. I'm no good at it."

That ended that. Two years later, when I saw *The Hustler,* I realized what a fool I'd been.

2 4

The Price of Freedom

IF YOU WANT TO BE your own man, sooner or later you have to bite the hand that feeds you. I bit it on January 24, 1959, after five years at the Warner Bros. trough.

The studio was still hung up on putting me in a television series, stuffing my future into the small screen. It wasn't that nothing less than a movie screen could contain my ego, believe me. As far as actors go, I barely had an ego. The problem was that Warners offered nothing but knockoffs of 77 *Sunset Strip*. My last two pictures were both challenging A-list dramas, with major costars, made for other studios. Life outside the Burbank compound seemed to offer so much more of what I was after.

Two- and three-picture deals with a studio had become, for many actors, far preferable to long-term contracts. The old-style seven-year deal was fantastic for a promising performer just starting out, but it was a straitjacket once you'd "made it." Freelancing was the way to go.

So I asked to be released from my contract. Jack Warner flatly refused. If I wanted out, he said, I'd have to buy my way out.

The asking price was $100,000.

My God, that's a fortune, I thought. *I'll never be able to pay it back.* Today, it'd be the equivalent of a couple of million dollars.

But I agreed to the cost of the buyout. That's how badly I wanted off the leash. Not to mention, I hated Warners getting between $75,000 to $150,000 each time it loaned me for a feature, while I never saw more than the weekly $3,000 stipulated in my contract.

Under the terms of the "Cancellation of Contract and Mutual Release," Warner Bros. would garnish 25 percent of everything I earned until the $100,000 debt was squared.

Obviously, this was a decision based on principle. As a business deal, it stank. But I was finally free. Free to take control of my career and make my own decisions.

One of the first decisions I made was to go very far away. An Australian impresario arranged a whirlwind concert tour of the continent, featuring three hot American acts: the Everly Brothers, Sal Mineo, and me. "You've got to do this tour," Dick advised. "For only two weeks, the money is unbelievable."

Not only did I want to pay down my debt to Warners—fast—but I had my mother's expenses, my agent's fees, horses, taxes . . . I hated being in the hole. When I got $20,000 for appearing in a television version of *Meet Me in St. Louis* that April, I signed the entire check over to Warner Bros., to whittle down the balance owed as fast as possible.

FLYING, AS YOU'VE realized by now, isn't my favorite mode of travel. Maybe that's what made the old anxieties kick in. Somewhere over the South Pacific I said to Dick, "I can't sing in public. In front of all those people? What'll I do?"

"Don't worry about it," Dick said. "If you feel a little nervous or forget a lyric, just raise your hand and wave at the audience. They'll scream so loud you could be saying anything. You could be singing in Chinese."

It was daunting to share the bill with Don and Phil Everly. At the time, they were the biggest thing on the radio: "Bye Bye Love," "Wake Up Little Suzie," and "All I Have to Do Is Dream" were all huge hits, crossing over between pop, country, and rhythm-and-blues stations. In their twenties, Don and Phil had become protégés of country music legend Chet Atkins, who put a little Bo Diddley beat under their gorgeous harmonies at a time when country music was in danger of getting drowned out by rock and roll. It was a whole new sound, produced at the small independent Cadence label in Nashville, an outfit very much like Dot Records.

Sal Mineo had a Top Ten hit with "Start Movin'," and the follow-up, "Lasting Love," also sold well. All made possible by his Oscar nomination as Jimmy Dean's adoring sidekick in *Rebel Without a Cause*. The downside was that Sal—like all the rest of us packaged for the teen crowd—struggled against typecasting. He was doomed to be the swarthy but sensitive juvenile delinquent who needed a girl's love to rescue him from becoming the Switchblade Kid. That's the nickname publicists hung on him.

Sal had just finished a picture called *A Private's Affair*, a lightweight military comedy in which he played a singing soldier. His costars were Jessie Royce Landis and Jim Backus, who were in *my* lightweight military comedy, *The Girl He Left Behind*. His film was directed by Raoul Walsh, with whom I'd done *Battle Cry*. We had more than that in common, though.

Sal was also starting to get tagged with "gay" gossip. He was already building his wall, trying to protect himself from the rumors. He would bravely deconstruct the wall later on, coming out publicly well before it was fashionable.

The tour was frantic. As soon as we landed Down Under, we were swept into a nonstop swirl of radio, newspaper, and television interviews. No time for sleep.

It was an old-fashioned revue-style show, each act doing a few numbers, then performing together at the end. The Everlys and I sang Don Gibson's big hit, "Oh Lonesome Me," which we all loved. The shows were actually the most relaxing part of the itinerary.

Hanging out with the Everlys was fun. Don and Phil were *always* making music. Even when we were just loafing in the hotel or flying city-to-city, they were coming up with new material. I contributed a lyric to a new song they were working on, "And Then She Kissed Me." The Everlys reinspired my love of country music, so much so that I'd talk Warners into letting me do nothing but country tunes for my second album, *R.F.D.* (rural free delivery, for you city folk).

The Everlys would, in fact, soon save Warner Bros. Records. The label was

On tour in Australia with the Everly Brothers and Sal Mineo.

failing and hadn't produced any best-selling singles. The company would drop my contract the following year. But only days before Jack Warner was set to pull the plug, Jim Conkling convinced him to sign the Everly Brothers, who by that time had fallen out with Cadence over royalty issues. Conkling must have slipped something in the Colonel's cigar, because Warner approved a ten-year, $1,000,000 contract for the brothers. Turned out to be one of the smartest things he ever did. "Cathy's Clown," the Everlys' first record on Warners, went straight to #1 on the pop and R & B charts, and *It's Everly Time!* was the company's biggest album since the *77 Sunset Strip* soundtrack. Don and Phil bailed out Warner Bros. Records just as it was going under, building the ground floor on which a gigantic music conglomerate would grow.

While on the Australia trip, Dick and I had soul-searching discussions about my career. It took a leap of faith to give up the weekly salary—faith that I was a good actor and that producers would recognize it. But as a freelancer, I learned that with more opportunity came more chances for disappointment. The meaty parts I'd had in *That Kind of Woman* and *They Came to Cordura* weren't easy to find, especially after those two films underperformed at the box office. In 1959 I worked steadily: a *Conflict* TV drama with Jo Van Fleet, *Meet Me in St. Louis* for *Hallmark Hall of Fame* (top-billed, incredibly, over Jane Powell, Walter Pidgeon, Jeanne Crain, Myrna Loy, and Ed Wynn!), numerous guest shots on *The Perry Como Show, The Steve Allen Show, The Pat Boone Show,* as well as a *Summer on Ice* special that briefly reunited me with Ronnie Robertson, now a star with the *Ice Capades.* I treated most of it like mere bill paying. It wasn't *acting.*

Clayton knew something was in the air. He tried, in his delicate way, to lead me, like a horse to water, to the inevitable conclusion: the movie business was changing, gradually but dramatically. There were fewer jobs because fewer movies were being made. Even superstars like Cary Grant were working picture-to-picture. As the studio system collapsed, competition for worthwhile parts become a free-for-all. If I expected to keep costarring with legends like Lana Turner and Gary Cooper, I was in for a rude awakening. The fantastic— which I mean literally, as in *fantasy*—part of my career was ending. If I didn't want to be remembered as a flash in the pan, I needed to find some meat-and-potatoes acting jobs.

Flying home from Australia, I had every reason to consider my "legacy." Our plane dropped two of its four engines at 2:00 a.m. over the most shark-infested waters in the world. This was only a month after the infamous plane crash that killed Buddy Holly, Ritchie Valens, and the Big Bopper, so we all held our collective breath, wondering if there'd be fresh headlines about another bunch of singing celebrities (and director Fred Zinnemann, who was also on that flight) perishing in the South Pacific.

We survived an emergency landing in Fiji in the dead of night.

IT WAS ALWAYS my intention to build a house in the Hollywood Hills, next to Dick Clayton's. But Coulter and Gray convinced me that what I really needed was flat acreage so I could keep my horses on the property and save on stable fees. I found a place out in Glendale, across the wash from my pals Jack and Kay Conner. It was almost an acre, secluded, even though the side of the property abutted a row of apartment buildings with which I shared a driveway. The house itself wasn't much more than a shack, but I used the time between jobs to knock out walls, remodel, and put in a gorgeous Japanese garden. Fritz, my Weimaraner, loved to help out digging in the yard, a habit I desperately needed to break him of before the landscaping was complete.

Little did I know how much a little doggy discipline was going to cost me.

With my thirtieth birthday right around the corner, I sensed that the whirlwind was over, that I needed a more stable situation, in terms of my lifestyle and finances. My love of Asian antiques and objets d'art (a taste I'd picked up from my mother, who was always fascinated with the Orient) led me to start an importing business, Tab Hunter's Far East, a retail shop in the heart of Beverly Hills. My partners were Eddie Stevens, a real-estate tycoon, and Billy Widner, a purser for Pan Am who conveniently arranged our buying and shipping while in the Orient.

This was as close to "settling down" as I'd ever come. I put a lot of time and effort into creating a home and a business, which led to one of the worst decisions I'd ever make—passing up an offer to replace Paul Newman in the Broadway run of Tennessee Williams's *Sweet Bird of Youth*. It was a chance to work with Geri Page again and to be directed by Elia Kazan, inarguably the best theater director in the business.

I passed, mainly because I wanted to remain available for the role I *really* coveted—Tony in the film version of *West Side Story*. I interviewed for the part and held out hope that the combination of my recent dramatic work and the popularity of *Damn Yankees* would convince director Robert Wise to cast me. Knowing that Natalie had already been chosen for Maria boosted my confidence. Who could pass up a reunion of America's Sweethearts in the biggest musical of the year?

When Richard Beymer, a virtual unknown, was picked to play Tony, it really hit home how much had changed, and how fast. If *West Side Story* had been produced in 1956, Natalie Wood and Tab Hunter would have been cast in a heartbeat. The public would have demanded it. But by 1960, Tab Hunter— the guy who'd been plastered across all those magazines, the epitome of all-American wholesomeness—seemed like a throwback to some bygone era.

The Sigh Guy definitely needed a new plan.

Walter Brennan, of all people, changed my mind about a television series. At a cocktail reception before the Academy Awards that year, I heard the great character actor—then starring in the TV series *The Real McCoys*—say, "My two years in television have done more for my career than the forty years I've been in motion pictures."

Maybe I just needed to hear it from someone outside my little circle of confidants. Dick, of course, had been nudging me to do TV, but it wasn't his style to hammer away at me. He let me discover what I wanted on my own. He presented me a script for a proposed series called *Bachelor at Large,* about a Malibu Beach cartoonist whose romantic entanglements end up as grist for his comic strips. Why do *this* and not a series for Warner Bros.? Owning 50 percent, and changing the name to *The Tab Hunter Show,* certainly helped me get over a lot of my skepticism.

Dick and I formed Shunto Productions, and NBC funded the pilot, which was shot at MGM in Culver City, where Jeannine Herrin and I, fifteen years earlier, had staked out actor Tom Drake and seen Elizabeth Taylor being driven through the gates. Now, one of the greatest of all movie factories was reduced to renting out studio space for television shows.

When the pilot of *The Tab Hunter Show* was previewed for potential advertisers, Lorillard and Westclox jumped aboard as exclusive sponsors, pitching Newport cigarettes and Timex watches. Later, Chrysler signed up, giving me a 1960 Imperial as a perk. Perfect for somebody with an ascot and a cigarette holder, but my fancy-car phase was behind me. The Mercedes had been traded in for a pickup by 1960. By then I was only interested in something that could pull a horse trailer.

Bachelor at Large had been written by Stanley Shapiro, a New Yorker who'd penned a pair of hit big-screen comedies for Blake Edwards, *The Perfect Furlough* and *Operation Petticoat.* He'd also shared an Oscar for co-writing the screenplay of the Doris Day–Rock Hudson smash *Pillow Talk.* When our series was picked up, with Stanley signed on as the producer, writer, and director, we'd caught lightning in a bottle.

Richard Erdman, an old pal from *The Steel Lady,* played my loyal sidekick, a wealthy skinflint who can't believe my luck with the ladies. Erdman has a marvelous way with dialogue, in addition to being naturally funny. Jerome Cowan, one of those fabulous faces from a million old movies (he was Bogart's partner in *The Maltese Falcon*) played my cranky boss. They were both great, but the show's biggest selling point was its roster of gorgeous guest stars: Elizabeth Montgomery, Nita Talbot, Pat Crowley, Gena Rowlands, Luciana Paluzzi, Ruta Lee, Suzanne Pleshette—those are only some of the knockouts who streamed through my playboy beach-house set.

As a producer, I was also able to cast some of my personal favorites as well: Lori Nelson, Tuesday Weld, Jan Chaney, and my Hollywood discovery, Vicki Trickett. I'd met Vicki at a horse show and was bowled over by how beautiful she was. All the guys were on the make for her. "You're getting nowhere," I told them. "*I've* got the line that'll work." I walked right up to her and said: "How'd you like to be in the movies?" Clayton took her on as a client and got her a contract at Columbia, but Vicki and show business didn't take to each other.

Unfortunately, Stanley Shapiro directed only our pilot episode. Feature films beckoned, and Stanley answered, going on to become a writer-producer of such terrific movies as *Lover Come Back* (Rock and Doris again), *That Touch of Mink* (Doris and Cary Grant), and *Bedtime Story*. Minus Stanley, we were treading water in no time.

Norman Tokar was brought in to patch the leaks, but the scripts resisted repair. Not that we didn't try. Maybe we tried too hard. The hours were incredibly long, with revisions always arriving at the last minute, indicated on blue, pink, yellow, and green pages—everything but black on white. We constantly struggled to make deadlines. When Norman burned out, a director named Phil Rapp was brought in. I can still hear him barking out his lone theory of comedy: "Fast is funny, but faster is funnier!"

It was filmed entirely in the studio, no audience. Comedy needs a crowd. Our laughs were canned: waves of guffaws, mild titters, wild chuckling—all delivered, later, at the push of a button, all utterly fake. As if this wasn't enough of a hill to climb, NBC's fall schedule had us slated for Sunday night . . . opposite the last half of *The Ed Sullivan Show,* the most popular variety program in television history.

But you know what? Even if we'd created the funniest sitcom of all time, it still would have bombed, largely because of a couple of teenage girls who lived behind my new house in Glendale.

2 5

Menace to Society

WE WERE BLOCKING a scene on our set at MGM when one of the production assistants called out, "Tab—phone call for you."

Dick Clayton, who was always around in his capacity as one of the producers of *The Tab Hunter Show,* cut right in: "I'll deal with it."

That's one of the things I loved about Dick. He saw it as his job to keep my life uncluttered so I could concentrate on the work. He was much more than just an agent.

"What was the call about?" I asked when we broke for lunch.

"Nothing to worry about," Dick assured me. "Just some silly questions about something in your neighborhood. I took care of it."

When I got to the set the next morning, July 10, the daily paper declared otherwise:

COPS TAB TAB HUNTER
FOR WHIPPING HIS DOG

What the fuck was this? Glendale police were investigating complaints that I beat my dog, Fritz, regularly and relentlessly. I was quoted in the article, responding to the charges: "I love the dog, but will give him away if it will solve anything." It even said I'd promised not to strike Fritz again.

Fuming, I called Dick at his office. "Did you see this bullshit in the paper? What the hell is this all about!"

"Calm down, Tab. When the police called—"

"*Police*? When did the police call?"

"Yesterday. You were working. I pretended to be you. I gave 'em those quotes. It's best to just get this over with. With the new show coming up, you don't need any bad publicity."

"You're kidding! I can't believe you'd do that!"

"Tab, maybe it'd be best if you just got rid of that dog."

I slammed down the phone. I was in shock. If I were still with Warner Bros. none of this would have happened. The publicity department would have swept this nonsense under the rug before it ever got into the papers. But I didn't have Bill Hendricks and the PR department calling the shots anymore. I realized Dick meant well, but his little bit of playacting with the police was a huge miscalculation. It put a serious rift in our relationship.

I was about to learn the pitfalls of being a star without a studio.

When news of the "dog beating" hit the wire services, it spread like wild-fire. Within days I was barraged by a whole new kind of "fan" letter:

> I wrote you once wishing you luck. Well, cancel it.

> I hope I run into you sometime. When I'm driving and you're walking.

> I always felt that with a little rehearsal you could be a good actor. Now I feel that with a little rehearsing you could be a human being.

> Dear Dog Beater,
> You are the lowest thing on the face of the earth, and if I had any say in the matter you'd be six feet under it. I hope they give you the death penalty.

There's no reasoning with animal lovers. I know, because I *am* one. I had the same chance of defending myself as the guy who's asked, "So, when did you stop beating your wife?"

Any hope that the incident would be dismissed as a bad joke ended two weeks later, when a cop showed up at my door and served a summons: the people of the state of California were taking me to court on a criminal charge of cruelty to animals.

The media swarmed, having a field day with the comedic possibilities they saw in my predicament. Need I point out that the following articles, and many more like them, appeared when it was only *alleged* that I had beaten my dog.

"We don't want to *hound* you," read a tongue-in-cheek editorial in the

Baltimore Sun, "but your career has become a little *dog-eared* by now anyway, and with this unseemly incident it will probably go down the drain altogether—which is where it belonged in the first place."

The cheap shots piled up. Tab Hunter's new job was to provide a diversion for otherwise-bored hack newspaper staffers: "Why is it that if you despise dogs so much you have taken, as your professional name, a name which is obviously far more doggish than Fritz, namely, Tab?" Such wit.

It wasn't just the print media, either. Disc jockeys all over the country played records with yelping-dog sound effects, joking that "Tab Hunter must be around here somewhere."

Louella Parsons even weighed in, advising me—publicly—that this shameful incident "could be damaging to your career."

How the hell did all this happen?

I'll tell you exactly.

There was an alley off Allen Avenue that I had to turn into to get to my property. It was protected by a chain-link fence. When some of the people in the apartment buildings on Riverside Drive learned that a movie star had moved in behind them, they found a variety of convenient reasons to be hanging around when I'd come home. I was fair game when I got out of the car to open the fence. These "accidental" meetings were cordial at first, but then the neighborly routine got out of hand. Teenage girls started lying in wait. Then their fathers and mothers. Next came the invitations to dinner.

I commuted all the way across Los Angeles—Glendale to Culver City and back—every day. After work I'd usually swing by the shop in Beverly Hills to see how things were going. By the time I got home, all I wanted was to relax, have dinner, and study the next day's shooting script. I guess my polite rejections of the neighbors' dinner invitations finally got a little too brusque. I'm certain that's what triggered the retaliation.

After the newspaper articles appeared, one of the girls next door was interviewed at length by—you guessed it—*Confidential:* "The first time I saw Tab Hunter beat his dog, he was whipping him with a doubled up chain and yelling at him, 'No digging.' Then he gave him a big kick in the midsection and yanked him by the collar to tie him up."

The "witnesses" relished their moment in the spotlight. One guy told the press that he'd confronted me directly—absolutely untrue—and threatened to "knock my block off" if I didn't leave Fritz alone. "I hope we can put an end to this barbarian's cruelty to animals forever," he was quoted as saying.

The debut of *The Tab Hunter Show* was only months away, and all the prepublicity focused on Fritz. Dick was livid: "I told you, you should have gotten rid of that dog." Everywhere I'd go, people would smart-ass me, asking, "Hey, Tab—how's your dog?"

"A lot better off than most people," became my stock answer.

THE PLEASURE OF HIS COMPANY was shot on location in San Francisco, which gave me a chance to briefly escape the three-ring circus that engulfed the "sanctuary" I'd tried to create in Glendale. The Paramount production was a lightweight affair about a divorced bon vivant whose return home for his daughter's wedding causes an uproar. I played a young rancher groom, who ends up competing with the bride's father for her affection.

My role was fourth-billed, but I leaped at the offer for reasons beyond the nice paycheck (of which Warners, of course, would be getting 25 percent). After everything I'd been through in recent years, including intimate exposure to the often-unpleasant inner workings of the industry, I remained, underneath it all, a dyed-in-the-wool movie fan. I'd have accepted tenth billing for the chance to work with a legend like Fred Astaire.

Fred was the epitome of grace, sophistication, style, and professionalism, both on and off the screen. He owned racehorses, so we bonded over that, boring everyone else stiff. Astaire and Coop were the two male costars I most admired, not only as actors but as people.

I'll never forget one little moment on the set, after director George Seaton had said, "Cut!" Fred turned to me and in the humblest voice asked, "Was that all right?" I broke into a huge smile at the absurdity of it: Fred Astaire asking *me* if he was doing okay in front of the camera.

Astaire's ex-wife was played by Lilli Palmer. I wish I could report that Lilli lived up to the glowing image I had of her when I was a movie usher (the *Cloak and Dagger* connection again). She gave a nice performance but was very aloof during filming, particularly to me. I got the impression she didn't like me. Not that I dwelled on it. After all . . .

I was marrying Debbie Reynolds! I finally got to play opposite my old pal, the first actress I ever dated in Hollywood. Debbie played Fred's daughter— my bride—and we had a ball spending time together again.

San Francisco was as much a star of the film as any of the performers, and Seaton made great use of its photogenic locations. We shot at Grace Cathedral, the Spreckels Mansion, Nob Hill, Golden Gate Park—it was a Technicolor travelogue of one of the world's great cities. After work, Fred, Debbie, and I would often walk down the steep hill from the Mark Hopkins for a fabulous dinner in Chinatown.

Making this movie with colleagues I respected and enjoyed was an escape from my dismal current circumstances. The respite was only temporary. In real life, the dog-beating trial started in mid-October, a month after my series premiered on NBC. The buildup to the trial offered plenty of opportunity for the press to refan the flames of negative publicity that had burned me earlier that summer. The heat prompted *TV Guide* to scrap a cover story it had done on the making of *The Tab Hunter Show*. During the first few weeks the show was on the air, Lorillard got sacks of mail chastising the company for sponsoring an animal-hating madman. These outraged citizens were placated with a generous "makeup" gift—a carton of Newport cigarettes.

Hordes of press and public swarmed as the trial got under way. Judge Charles R. Dyer, sensing the Glendale Courthouse was in jeopardy of being turned into the local zoo, set a stern tone right at the outset: "Despite the unusual nature of this case," he declared in his opening remarks, "I will permit no theatrics in this courtroom."

Good luck.

The first witness called by prosecutor William Dickerson was one of my complaining neighbors, a guy named Elmer Ludlow. He got things off to a fast start by drawling, "Sir, I've never seen anything like it in my life."

"Would you describe it for the court, please?"

"Yes, sir. I often have observed Fritz—that's Mr. Hunter's dog—in the backyard with Mr. Hunter. The dog always seemed to shrink back when Mr. Hunter came out. He seemed to be afraid of—"

"Objection!" shouted Henry Melby, my defense counsel. "The witness is forming a conclusion."

"Sustained."

"Exactly what did you see Mr. Hunter *do* to the dog?" asked the prosecutor.

"Well," said Elmer Ludlow, "he beat him savagely until the dog could scarcely stand it."

"And how could you tell that the dog was in agony?"

"His cries, sir. They were horrible. Long-drawn-out wails of pain."

"Could you be more specific?"

Elmer Ludlow threw his head back and cut loose with a yodeling wail that sounded like Slim Whitman with a sore throat. The gallery—and the jury—erupted in laughter. Judge Dyer went heavy on the gavel. "I'll tolerate no more such outbursts!" Ludlow's imitation of Fritz, however, was allowed into the record. I've always wondered how the court reporter took it down.

The parade of prosecution witnesses went on for days, a procession of outrage orchestrated by the pudgy, prissy prosecuting attorney, who spewed his arguments with very sibilant s's. In short, an uptight fag. Somebody should have coached him: if you're going to grandstand, get a costume that fits. His Brooks Brothers suits were one size too small; they made him look like an Oscar Mayer wiener.

Among the atrocities I was alleged to have committed was bribery. A female witness claimed to have received an ominous midnight phone call.

"Do you recall exactly what was said to you?" Dickerson asked her.

"I was told that I'd be given two thousand dollars if I kept my mouth shut."

"Did you recognize the voice?"

"No. It was a gruff male voice, though."

"Did you decline the offer?"

"Yes, sir. I told him he was out of his mind."

With that, Dickerson shamelessly played to the jury. "And would you please tell the court *why* you refused this ugly bribe? Wasn't it because, as you said to me earlier, the treatment this dog was getting was so awful that for no amount of money would you refuse to testify?"

"Partly."

The DA seemed surprised by this sudden improvisation: "What do you mean?" he asked, turning to his witness.

"Well, frankly," the woman answered, "two thousand wasn't enough. My husband has always said he'd give me a million if I'd keep my mouth shut."

Hilarity ensued. Even sour Judge Dyer laughed at that one. I should have hired this woman on the spot to write for *The Tab Hunter Show*.

The DA trotted out all kinds of dates: *Hunter beat Fritz for so many minutes on such and such date*—which backfired when I produced diaries proving I was out of town during many of the "beatings."

The final witness for the prosecution was the Chain Girl—so dubbed by the press, which predicted that she'd be the one to pound the nails in my coffin. In interviews, she'd made my backyard sound like Buchenwald.

This little sweetie was one of the Allen Avenue fence dwellers. Having been spurned by her teen idol, she was now proving that "hell hath no fury like a woman scorned" applies even in puberty. She described in graphic detail the

savage barrage of blows I viciously rained on my "doggie." Like Ludlow, she was encouraged to imitate Fritz's plaintive wails and wounded yelps. Finally, she described how I'd kicked Fritz so hard he took flight.

"He actually left the ground?" asked Dickerson, feigning shock.

"He flew right through the air," Chain Girl stated flatly.

The prosecution rested. Get the leg irons ready.

Defense counsel immediately pounced, calling as an expert witness a veterinarian with several decades of experience.

"Is it possible that Mr. Hunter could have kicked a ninety-pound animal into the air?"

"Under certain conditions," said the vet.

"And what would those conditions be?" Melby asked.

"If Mr. Hunter were a horse."

My favorite moment came a short time later, when Dickerson dramatically began rapping himself across the back of his hand with a doubled-up chain. He approached the witness stand: "If I beat my dog like this for ten or fifteen minutes," he asked the vet, "would it cause cuts and abrasions and bruises?"

"I'll tell you at the end of ten minutes," the vet replied.

Two other veterinarians testified to Fritz's perfect health. One of them said, "I've never seen a happier, healthier dog in my life." To rebut the idiotic contention that Fritz was scared of me, the owner of the Happy Glen Dog Training School—where I boarded Fritz when I went on the road—testified that my dog got sulky and ill whenever I *wasn't* around—that's how bonded Fritz and I had become.

Then I took the stand, explaining that I'd reprimanded Fritz on numerous occasions, slapping his paws with a "play strap" in an attempt to break him of his obsessive digging habit. I'd learned the technique from my show's dog trainer during the filming of an episode called, ironically enough, "Love Me, Love My Dog." Even my gardener, Mr. Tani, was brought in to verify that Fritz was an incorrigible excavator. "Dig, dig, dig—all time dig!" he declared in his clipped Japanese accent.

This madness went on for eleven days, breaking the Glendale Municipal Court's endurance record. DA Dickerson's summation lasted *two and a half hours*. Maybe he thought it was an audition for *Inherit the Wind*.

"It is true, perhaps, that Mr. Hunter was disciplining his dog," he bellowed. "However—are we to ignore that fact that bloodcurdling cries reverberated around the neighborhood for eight minutes at a time? . . . I submit that this behavior indicates a criminal design on the part of the defendant—criminal or insane, I'm not sure which . . . The defendant cannot fluff this off because he is a celebrity!"

"The defendant wouldn't be here if he *wasn't* a celebrity," Melby countered in his summation. He characterized the prosecution's witnesses as incredible. "Frankly," he concluded, "I think they lied."

The jury was out three hours. Verdict: *not* guilty.

"The longest previous trial in this court was nine days, for an abortion," Judge Dyer said in his closing statement. "This abortion lasted eleven. And I am glad to be rid of it."

I heaved a huge sigh of relief for the cameras and later posed for countless pictures with Fritz licking my face. There was much snickering in the newspaper accounts about the makeup of the jury: eleven women and one man. *Life* ran a multipage spread featuring pictures of Fritz and me cavorting in the backyard. It prompted this letter to the editor, which seemed to sum up the whole ridiculous affair:

> Sirs:
>   When my little cocker—Ruggles—is disobedient I say to him, "If you don't mind I'll send you to Tab Hunter!" You should see him toe the mark.
>
>   Mrs. Frank Gasparro
>   Havertown, Pa.

I blew out of Glendale as fast as humanly possible. I sold the house to a contractor who turned it into a big apartment complex. He sold me a place he owned in Beverly Hills. Given my druthers I'd rather not live in a celebrity-filled enclave, but someplace simple and unpretentious, filled with "regular" folks. Unfortunately, my recent experience rubbing shoulders with "regular folks" had convinced me otherwise.

Thankfully, there were still some true-blue types in my life. Randy Wood was one of the most loyal guys I've ever known. By now, Dot Records was a huge company, and Randy decided—despite all the negative press I'd been getting—to bring me back into the studio to rerecord, with a more "hip" sound, the infamous album he'd never been able to release in 1957.

The next time my name appeared on the music charts, it would be in connection with another #1 hit. I'd heard an unreleased live recording of Ray

Charles singing "I Can't Stop Loving You," and I decided to do my own rendi-
tion. When ABC-Paramount learned that Dot was planning to put it out as a
single, Ray Charles was whisked into the studio to cut his official version of
the song, which was rushed onto the market ahead of mine. They didn't want
anyone thinking that Ray was covering a Tab Hunter song. So it was weird to
see the songs listed jointly in *Cash Box* magazine as being by "Ray Charles &
Tab Hunter." Ray's version sold *all* the copies.

Right about this time, Dick found me a great role: the lead in a big-screen
version of Melville's *Billy Budd,* to be directed by Peter Ustinov. He'd set up
a base of operations at the Beverly Hills Hotel and invited me over for a meeting. His wife answered the door.

"All wrong," she announced, and slammed the door in my face.

THE ONLY DRAWBACK to my new house on Liebe Drive was that it
didn't have a pool, a luxury both Fritz and I had gotten used to. So as part of
the all-around remodeling of the place, I put one in. The morning the plaster-
ing was completed, I was paid a visit by Stephen Potter, set designer for *The
Tab Hunter Show.* While I fixed breakfast, Stephen let Fritz out, then started
horsing around with him on the patio. Next thing I knew, he'd backed right
into the freshly plastered pool, turning it into a one-man Grauman's Chinese
Theater, with hand- and footprints everywhere. Stephen was all right, thank
goodness, but he'd broken three fingers in the fall.

When some of Potter's "friends" heard that the infamous Fritz was involved,
they smelled money. I was hit with my next lawsuit, which claimed that Fritz
pushed Potter into the pool—resulting in physical and mental injuries worth
$75,000 in damages.

Dick Clayton said, "I told you to get rid of that dog."

Fuck that—I'd just as soon keep Fritz and cut loose everybody else.

I couldn't even stem the tide of bad publicity with the kind of movie-
magazine puff pieces that used to be a staple for me. By this time I'd been replaced in all those staged *Photoplay* and *Movie Life* layouts by Troy Donahue.
Actresses I'd been linked with at Warners were now shown at premieres with
Troy, at the beach with Troy, nightclubbing with Troy. Bill Orr's threat had
come true—Troy Donahue had become the new Tab Hunter.

In truth, the hot new "movie stars" were in the White House: just-elected
John Kennedy, his gorgeous socialite wife, their whole royal family. The public craved the lowdown on celebrities as much as ever, but Camelot had

mixed movies and reality to the point where manufactured movie stars just weren't good enough anymore. Jackie Kennedy was now gracing the cover of *Photoplay*.

Then came February 15, 1961. Along with the rest of the world, I was devastated by the news that the entire U.S. figure-skating team had died in a plane crash in Brussels, on their way to the world championships in Czechoslovakia. I knew many of the skaters on Sabena Flight 548, including Maribel Vinson Owen, one of the greatest American-born figure skaters ever. Maribel had been one of my skating coaches. Her two teenage daughters, "Little" Maribel and Laurence, seemed destined for greatness of their own. In fact, Laurence was on the cover of that week's *Sports Illustrated,* leading the youngest-ever U.S. team into a bright future. News of their tragic demise — in a plane crash, no less — hit me like Jimmy Dean's death, only eighteen times harder.

The world, once a seemingly limitless source of good fortune, was turning very cold and cruel.

BILLY WIDNER, EDDIE STEVENS, and I decided to sell Tab Hunter's Far East. It had been a fun hobby for the couple of years it lasted, but you can only sell so many Imari plates to Katharine Hepburn. Fritz even left his mark at the store, jumping out of my truck and pissing on the leg of an elegant Beverly Hills matron feeding the parking meter. Another lawsuit?

The shop had done well, but we were living on borrowed time. We'd hired a shopkeeper who was the sister of a big agent at Famous Artists — he wanted her to have something to occupy her time during the day. What she occupied, routinely, was a bottle. She'd get progressively more snockered as the day went on, until she was worthless by closing time. I regularly stopped by on the way home to make sure she hadn't passed out with the front door wide open. Eddie and Billy said, "We gotta get rid of her," but I couldn't bring myself to complain to Mr. Muckety-Muck, let alone fire her. I thought it might ruin my already-dwindling chances at more movie work. We tried to catch her drinking on the job but could never locate the liquor evidence. It was only after we'd sold the place, taken inventory, and cleaned up the store for the new owners, that we found her vodka stash in the toilet's water tank.

Unfortunately, selling the shop didn't end any problems — it only opened a new can of worms:

SEEK TAB HUNTER
IN SMUGGLE QUIZ

blared the headlines. MOVIE COLONY SHOPS RAIDED, said another. MILLIONS OF DOLLARS IN RED CHINA ART OBJECTS NABBED followed. Then, in rapid succession: TAB HUNTER SOUGHT IN SMUGGLING, and TAB HUNTER DENIES ROLE IN SMUGGLING.

As part of the general cold war crackdown, the Treasury Department had agents sniffing out illegal trades with Red China, which was commercially off-limits. Apparently some "contraband" turned up in inventory, well after we'd sold our interest in the place. But while sifting through the invoices, manifests, and letters of credit, the T-men came across a well-known name.

"These items were brought in by Tab Hunter," declared E. E. Minskoff, chief of the Treasury's foreign assets control enforcement division. "We have no import license on file for Mr. Hunter. I'd very much like to talk to him," said Minskoff, who, in addition to knowing all the ins and outs of international trade, clearly knew how to get his name and picture in the newspaper.

I called the Treasury Department immediately to volunteer my complete cooperation. I offered to provide our import license and told them that neither Billy nor I had done any buying in China. It could all have been handled on the phone, but I understood by now that no one would be satisfied until the celebrity was brought to heel for the amusement of the press and the public.

Two days later, Treasury agents, including Mr. Minskoff, were posing with a certain exasperated, unkempt movie actor in the middle of what some wire-service stories claimed was "millions" of dollars of Communist contraband. More BS: the whole lot of confiscated artifacts was worth several thousand dollars. The press loves to exaggerate.

The story broke internationally. I'd done absolutely nothing wrong—no charges were filed, no arrests were made—but the smell of guilt wafted from every insinuating paragraph. Photographs of me were displayed in embarrassing proximity to the word *smuggle*.

By contrast, you had to use a magnifying glass to find the tiny TAB HUNTER CLEARED OF ALL WRONGDOING squibs that ran in *some* papers a few weeks later, buried in with the obituaries.

LET'S RECAP. Since splitting with Warner Bros. almost three years earlier, I'd made a nice little romantic comedy with Fred Astaire and Debbie

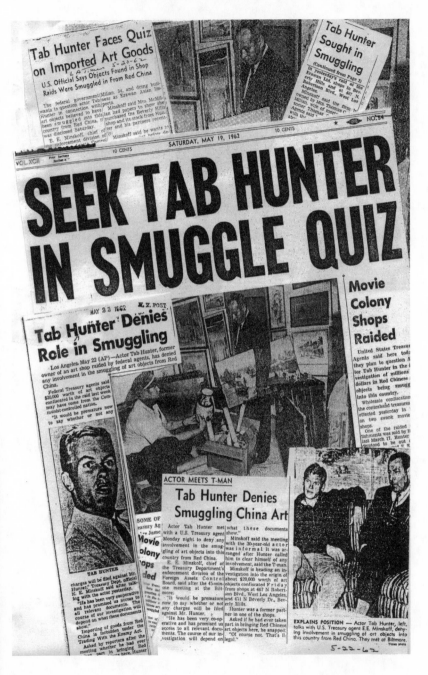

Tab Hunter Faces Quiz on Imported Art Goods

U.S. Official Says Objects Found in Shop Raids Were Smuggled in From Red China

The federal government wants to question actor Tab Hunter in connection with art objects believed to have been smuggled into this country from Red China, it was disclosed Saturday.

E. E. Minskoff, chief of the enforcement division of...

Milan, 34, and doing business as Erawan Asian Imports.

Minskoff said Mrs. McMillan had papers to show she had purchased the Beverly Hills shop and the stock from Hunter and his partners some time before the...

Minskoff said he wants to...

Tab Hunter Sought in Smuggling

(Continued from Page 1)

Erawan Ltd. shop in Beverly Hills and at 467 N. Robertson Blvd., West Los Angeles.

Minskoff said the firm belonged to Mrs. Thomas C. Milian, wife of motion picture actor Thomas C. Milian...

Agents said...

SATURDAY, MAY 19, 1962   10 CENTS

10 CENTS   VOL. XCII

SEEK TAB HUNTER IN SMUGGLE QUIZ

Movie Colony Shops Raided

United States Treasury Agents said here today they plan to question Actor Tab Hunter in the investigation of millions of dollars in Red Chinese art objects being smuggled into this country.

Wholesale confiscation of the contraband treasures effected yesterday in raids on two swank movie colony shops.

One of the raided establishments was sold by its last March 17. Hunter understood to be out of...

Tab Hunter Denies Role in Smuggling

Los Angeles, May 22 (AP)—Actor Tab Hunter, former owner of an art shop raided by federal agents, has denied any involvement in the smuggling of art objects from Red China.

Federal Treasury agents said $20,000 worth of art objects confiscated in the raid last week may have come from the Communist-controlled nation.

"It would be premature now to say whether or not any...

TAB HUNTER

...charges will be filed against Mr. Hunter," Treasury Dept. official E. E. Minskoff said after talking with the actor yesterday.

"He has been very cooperative and has promised us access to all relevant documents. The course of our investigation will depend on what these documents show."

Importing of goods from Red China is forbidden under the Trading With the Enemy Act.

Asked by reporters after the meeting whether he had ever part in bringing Red... ...here, Hunter

ACTOR MEETS T-MAN

Tab Hunter Denies Smuggling China Art

Actor Tab Hunter met with a U.S. Treasury agent Monday night to deny any involvement in the smuggling of art objects into this country from Red China.

E. E. Minskoff, chief of the Treasury Department's enforcement division of the Foreign Assets Control Board, said after the 45-minute meeting at the Biltmore.

"It would be premature now to say whether or not any charges will be filed against Mr. Hunter.

"He has been very cooperative and has promised us access to all relevant documents. The course of our investigation will depend on what these documents show."

Minskoff said the meeting with the 30-year-old actor was informal. It was arranged after Hunter called him to clear himself of any involvement, said the T-man.

Minskoff is heading an investigation into the origin of about $20,000 worth of art objects confiscated Friday from shops at 467 N. Robertson Blvd., West Los Angeles, and 451 N Beverly Dr., Beverly Hills.

Hunter was a former partner in one of the shops.

Asked if he had ever taken part in bringing Red Chinese art objects here, he snapped:

"Of course not. That's illegal."

EXPLAINS POSITION — Actor Tab Hunter, left, talks with U.S. Treasury agent E.E. Minskoff, denying involvement in smuggling of art objects into this country from Red China. They met at Biltmore.

Times photo

5-22-62

Reynolds and toured with the Everly Brothers. That about covered the good news.

On the flip side of the ledger: I still owed Jack Warner tens of thousands of dollars, I'd made a flop television series that was cancelled, my relationship with my agent and best friend was strained, I'd lost my recording contract, and I'd been publicly accused of being a dog-beating maniac and an anti-American art smuggler. On top of everything else, Fritz killed Mr. Kitzel, an adorable stray cat I'd taken in. Finally, I broke down and took Dick Clayton's advice: I gave away my beloved Weimaraner.

On my twentieth birthday, Linda Darnell had thrown me a surprise party, welcoming me to the movie business with sincere best wishes for a long and successful career. Ten years later, I was sick of Hollywood, sick of the media, and sick of people in general. I'd lost all faith in just about everything.

Tab Hunter's sweet ride was officially over.

Searching for Open Doors

ROSSANA PODESTÀ DRAPED herself against a date palm in the desert oasis. In her diaphanous gown, she oozed sex appeal. I tossed the loose end of the burnoose over my shoulder, adjusted my sword, and descended on her. She rose slightly, inviting my kiss.

A million flies swarmed into our hair, our eyes, our mouths. They were all over everything, everywhere.

"Cut!" screamed director Antonio Margheriti, in Italian, his native tongue."

We were on location in Egypt, shooting a sword-and-sandal spectacular for the Italian company Titanus Studios. Margheriti stormed around, spewing lots of vowels, gesturing wildly at the mostly Egyptian crew.

"What's he saying?" I asked Rossana as we battled the insect invasion. Rossana, of course, spoke English. Six years earlier, at twenty-one, she'd won an international casting search to fill the title role in *Helen of Troy,* Warners' 1956 mythological extravaganza. The American experiment failed, and Rossana was now back home earning a living. After this, she'd make *Virgins of Nuremberg.*

"Antonio is asking how to say *shit* in Arabic," Rossana explained, spitting flies.

At times like this, I doubted the wisdom of putting everything I owned in storage, turning my horses out at a friend's farm in Northern California, and accepting the lead role in *La Freccia d'Oro,* aka *The Golden Arrow.* Like Rossana, I was entering the career phase in which you're no longer looking for the keys to the kingdom—you settle for an open door. Most of the films I'd made at the end of the 1950s had just come out in Europe; the name Tab Hunter still had marquee value across the Atlantic. So Dick Clayton set me up with the Kaufman and Lerner agency, a Rome-based representative of Famous Artists.

Thomas Milian, a friend who'd struggled for years as an actor in New York, was doing fabulously well making pictures in Italy. "Over here I'm a star," he'd written to me, noting that he was now officially "Tomas." He encouraged me to give the Italians a try. I'd loved Italy when I vacationed there, so I figured— why not get paid to go back?

Not being able to speak Italian wasn't a drawback. The script of *La Freccia d'Oro*—my copy was the only one in English—featured page after page of truly horrendous dialogue. I played a bandit named Hassan who learns he's actually the son of the sultan. To earn my rightful place in the royal family, I must retrieve a magic amulet. All I could think of was Tony Curtis in *The Prince Who Was a Thief*: "Yonda lies da castle of my fadda." I spent every night in my hotel, rewriting my lines so I'd at least have fun delivering them. I camped it up shamelessly. Not that it mattered—all my dialogue was eventually dubbed by a stiff-as-a-board Italian baritone with no sense of humor. I ended up sounding like Rossano Brazzi.

Disappointment over being stuck in a stinker was eased considerably by weekly infusions of cash, delivered personally by the production manager. I'd sign a voucher and he'd hand over a bundle of lire, some of the old notes as big as place mats. On top of that, Kaufman and Lerner had gotten me a nice stipend for weekly living expenses. A simple, old-fashioned way of doing business, which I appreciated.

This wasn't a fly-by-night production. Titanus Studios spared no expense. Wardrobe fittings alone took two weeks, with every costume made to order. The Italians kept leisurely production schedules. It gave me plenty of time to sightsee, in both Rome and Egypt. It did, however, make it harder to save my lire, which I needed to stockpile if I was ever to get out of hock to Jack Warner.

Bugs notwithstanding, *La Freccia d'Oro* was a fun shoot. How could I not love racing a purebred Arab across the desert, hamming it up like Errol Flynn? Unfortunately, horseback riding wasn't my sole mode of transportation in this film. The other was a flying carpet. But *La Freccia d'Oro* was no *Thief of Baghdad*.

Considering what he had to work with, Antonio Margheriti wasn't a bad director. He worshipped American movies and didn't seem to care how lousy the material was, as long as he could follow in the boots of his boyhood idols.

Sporting a ten-gallon cowboy hat and a five-gallon belly, he'd ride up on his horse, rein in, and say: "Very John Wayne, no?"

That was about the extent of his English. We tried to make script improvements, through an interpreter, but at a certain point I just gave in and accepted that there was no pony under the pile of shit. *La Freccia d'Oro's* overextended budget ended up sinking Titanus, at least temporarily. Margheriti, however, landed on his feet—renamed Tony Dawson. While "Tomas" Milian became an honorary Italian, Antonio Margheriti became the American he'd always wanted to be. It was like a cinematic cultural-exchange program. Under his new Hollywood name, Margheriti would grind out four decades' worth of profitable dreck like *Devil of the Desert against the Son of Hercules, Mr. Superinvisible,* and *Cannibal Apocalypse.* "Tony" would have a long, successful career knocking off popular films of every genre.

RETURNING TO ROME was a case of going from the ridiculous to the sublime.

"Luchino Visconti wants to meet you," Tomas told me. "He wants us to come to dinner at his villa."

Tomas had just completed a starring role for the great director in *Boccaccio '70,* an anthology of short films by some of Italy's greatest directors: Visconti, Vittorio de Sica, Federico Fellini. I was a huge Visconti fan. Roddy McDowall and I had seen *Rocco and His Brothers* at the Sutton Theater in New York when it first came out, and I'd gone back to relive it five consecutive nights, stunned every time by Alain Delon's brilliance and Annie Girardot's incredible death scene. I enjoyed *Rocco* more than anything since *The Black Swan,* which I saw when I was eleven. I couldn't believe that the maker of this wonderful movie wanted to meet *me.*

Arriving at his magnificent villa on Via Salaria, we were greeted by a white-gloved manservant flanked by a pair of huge, slobbering Great Danes. The entryway featured enormous Renato Guttuso paintings, which puffed me up a little bit. On my earlier trip to Italy, I'd purchased a Guttuso from a dealer in Rome. I'd later learn that Guttuso and Visconti had grown up close friends. There were few people, I'd learn, that Visconti *didn't* know.

The man was an intriguing contradiction. Born into an affluent, aristocratic family—his full title being Count Don Luchino Visconti Di Modrone—he became a full-fledged Marxist after lending his palazzo to the Communist resistance during World War II. He survived being imprisoned by the Gestapo and went on to create neorealist films that attacked Fascism and championed the working poor. Yet he lived like royalty.

We were ushered into a fabulous living room filled with art, antiques, and piped-in classical music. Visconti was holding court. Annie Girardot and Renato Salvatori, the costar who'd killed her in *Rocco,* were sunk into an enormous sofa, engulfed in down pillows. Marina Cicogna, who was either a marchesa or a contessa, sipped champagne with her companion, who was definitely an investment banker. The conversation flowed from French to Italian to German. Three young butlers in immaculate white uniforms attended to the guests.

"I didn't know Communists could live like this," I quietly cracked to Tomas.

Visconti welcomed Tomas with a big hug. He was like an elegant panther, supremely relaxed in his own skin, a commanding presence with a rich, mellow voice. Looking at me he said, "So, finally we meet . . . Welcome." I wasn't sure what that "finally" was about.

We dined at a great table set with pounds of silver and gigantic candelabras dripping wax over everything. Butlers hovered discreetly. I'd never seen anything so decadent—and I loved every minute of it.

Visconti's gatherings were legendary for the eclectic mix of guests. Not only movie players, but people from the stage, opera, politics, fashion—the man's interests and passions were boundless.

One of those passions was horses. Even as he cultivated youthful interests in music and theater—he was friends with both Puccini and Toscanini— Visconti's real job was breeding racehorses. It seemed to be his calling until he moved to Paris and became friends with Coco Chanel, who introduced him to director Jean Renoir. That's when cinema became Visconti's *ossessione.* After the war, he smoothly alternated between directing films, theater, and opera, becoming accomplished, and established, at each. Maria Callas credited him with teaching her how to act.

He also earned a reputation for favoring "beautiful" leading men. I couldn't help wondering if this was why the Sigh Guy rated an invitation to the villa. Luchino's preferences were well known but never discussed. To be flagrant was to be gauche, something no elegant nobleman could abide. The Italian press, unlike its American kin, paid little attention to Visconti's sexual orientation. His public politics earned the ink, not his private affairs.

Whatever his motives for wanting to meet me, I was surprised, and delighted, when during dinner Luchino revealed that he'd tried to contact me years earlier, through Famous Artists Agency. He was looking for a fresh young Hollywood actor for his lush 1954 costume melodrama, *Senso,* and thought I might have been right for the callow Austrian officer with whom Alida Valli falls in love. But when Henry Willson didn't respond, Farley Granger—a much more experienced actor—got the part.

I'd heard lines like this before, but Luchino was serious.

"We are going to make a film together—soon," he told me. It was like getting a benediction from the pope. In Hollywood, I'd have passed it off as predictable show-business party patter. Luchino wasn't like that. You felt you were in the presence of a man who made a difference, and you took everything he said as gospel truth.

MY NEXT PICTURE, regrettably, was a far cry from Visconti's realm. While he prepared a masterpiece, *The Leopard,* I signed on for *Operation Bikini.* The producers, Samuel Z. Arkoff and James H. Nicholson, were the brains behind American International Pictures, a low-rent studio catering exclusively to the teen market. Going back to Hollywood put an early end to my European excursion, but it also meant I'd finally be able to pay off my debt to Jack Warner.

Despite the title, the suggestive ads featuring the producer's buxom girlfriend in a skimpy swimsuit, and Frankie Avalon as one of the costars, *Operation Bikini* was *not* a beach-party movie. Oh, no. It was yet another war movie, and I was once again in military uniform—a demolitions expert in the South Pacific in 1943, escorted by a submarine crew to Bikini Island for the top secret test that will change the course not only of the war but of history. My Polynesian love interest, who helps me fight off the Japanese, was played by Eva Six, a bountiful blond Hungarian starlet in a black wig who sounded like Zsa Zsa Gabor. Frankie sings about going home, surrounded by warheads.

Only AIP would have the chutzpah to advertise a story about the development of the atomic bomb with the tagline

**TEMPTATION IN PARADISE . . . NEITHER HELL
NOR HIGH HEELS COULD STOP THEM!**

Train Wreck

YOU'RE LUCKY IF YOU get a second chance in this business. In the fall of 1963 I got to rectify the mistake I'd made by not taking over for Paul Newman in *Sweet Bird of Youth*. Tennessee Williams rewrote *The Milk Train Doesn't Stop Here Anymore*, one of the few Broadway failures he'd ever endured, and a stellar team of talent was quickly assembled to resurrect the show in its new form.

Strange life, isn't it? Making *Operation Bikini* one day, the next delivering a soliloquy on the verities of human existence written by America's greatest living playwright. You can't say my life didn't have its share of intriguing twists and turns.

Milk Train seemed like a surefire proposition even though its previous incarnation, staged earlier that year, lasted only two months. A New York newspaper strike had stifled any hope for its success. The revival was spearheaded by the indomitable showman David Merrick, who'd become a Broadway institution since he'd mounted his first show in 1954. He wanted to prove he was as adept with high art as he was with his stock-in-trade, musicals. He hired British director Tony Richardson, who'd scored a popular and critical success with the movie *Tom Jones* and had New York reviewers raving about his staging of John Osborne's *Luther* and the still-running Bertolt Brecht drama *The Resistible Rise of Arturo Ui*.

I wasn't Richardson's first choice for the role of Christopher Flanders. Tony Perkins was. Tony suggested me to Richardson after a scheduling conflict prevented him from playing the part. This gesture meant the world to me and healed any lingering resentment I had from the *Fear Strikes Out* incident. I'd always envied Tony's theatrical background and training, and for him to endorse me to the hottest director of the day was wonderful validation. I only wish I'd known all this at the time so I could have thanked him—but in a very classy move, neither Richardson or Perkins ever let on that I wasn't the first choice. It would be many years before I learned the truth, too many to be able to thank my old friend.

David Merrick wasn't sold on me. But Richardson used the old quid pro quo negotiating technique to ensure my place in his cast. You see, Richardson was dead set against the legendary Tallulah Bankhead playing the leading role of Flora Goforth. He'd heard about the living hell she could put directors through. He told Merrick and Williams he'd accept Bankhead only if they'd accept Tab Hunter. They insisted on Tallulah. Merrick believed her Broadway return had ticket-selling potential, though at a ramshackle sixty she was well past her prime. Williams told everyone he had revamped the play specifically for her.

The character of Flora Goforth was another of Tennessee's powerful, needy, provocative grandes dames, staring death in the face and preparing for her inevitable demise, this time on the sun-bleached shores of Italy's Divina Costiera, attended by a secretary, a nurse, and a young male companion. It was Tallulah to a T. Williams and Merrick hoped they'd stage a fitting finale to Bankhead's legendary, if erratic, career.

Tallulah presided over a get-acquainted dinner party in her East 57th Street apartment prior to the start of rehearsals. She received us in the drawing room, sitting cross-legged in a pair of luxurious gray silk pajamas, a frail version of her formerly fabulous self. I was too young, of course, to know of . her earlier stage work, when she lit up Broadway as the star of *The Little Foxes* and *The Skin of Our Teeth,* performances that left even Bette Davis starstruck.

My everlasting image of Tallulah Bankhead was from Hitchcock's *Lifeboat*: lounging in a full-length mink, not a hair out of place, as oil-soaked men dragged themselves aboard after their ship is torpedoed. When she tried to catch a fish by dangling her diamond bracelet in the ocean, she created an unforgettable movie moment.

Somewhere along the way, Tallulah became more celebrated for her notorious self than for her gifts as an actress. "Say anything about me, dahling, as long as it isn't boring," she was famously quoted. Her sharp wit, and willingness to embrace scandal rather than shrink from it, went a long way toward making her an icon. She encouraged, rather than denied, all the tales that swirled around her of bisexuality, promiscuity, casual nudity, drug use—yet she still rated an audience with FDR at the White House. A gay man flaunting her kind of cavalier lifestyle would have been deported or maybe drawn and quartered.

That night in her apartment I didn't see a legend; I saw a little old lady with dreadful burns on her hands, the painful result of her regularly dosing off while chain-smoking. One burn on her wrist was so deep a patch of chiffon had to be wrapped around it onstage so patrons in the front rows wouldn't be distracted.

Once we'd all assembled, Bankhead hollered in her gravelly voice: "Cunty!"

A massive black woman ambled from the kitchen with a tray of hors d'oeuvres. Cunty muttered a few private words to Tallulah, pulling raspy laughter from her employer. You could feel emphysema sucking the life out of her. It didn't bode well for a long run. The housekeeper excused herself, but Bankhead called her back with a snarl. With theatrical flourish, she pulled the woman's face down to hers and planted a huge wet kiss on her lips.

"I love you, daaahhling," Bankhead drawled. She wanted us all to know that the notorious Tallulah, the woman who'd say and do *anything,* still had gas in her tank.

Six of us had come to discuss the play: Tallulah, Tony Richardson, me, actress Marian Seldes, Merrick's production manager, Neil Hartley, and a late-arriving Tennessee Williams. Well, *seven* of us, once you included Dolores, Bankhead's mouthy little white poodle, who had the run of the place—and the most to say. All night long, Tony seemed dangerously close to hurling Dolores out the window, insulted by the dog's constant yapping interruptions and Tallulah's obstinate refusal to shut her up.

Tony gamely tried to explain his plan for interpreting the material, but Tallulah didn't feel the need to discuss themes or symbols or motivation. "Everything in this goddamn play he copied from me," she declared, glowering at Tennessee, who only chuckled in response, wiping cigarette ash from his shirtfront.

At one point, his British reserve finally having evaporated, Richardson snapped at Tallulah: "Fuck you!"

And this was only day one. Tallulah's campaign, intentional or not, to drive her director crazy—to drive all of us crazy—was officially under way. Tony Richardson probably went to bed every night after that dreaming of Katharine Hepburn, his first choice for the part of Mrs. Goforth. She'd declined, to care for ailing Spencer Tracy.

I approached rehearsals with equal parts enthusiasm and apprehension. I loved the play. Christopher Flanders was perhaps the best role I'd ever had or might ever have, and I took it *very* seriously. So did Richardson. When I'd first read for him, it was obvious he wasn't sure about the wisdom of casting a former "matinee idol." But something clicked between us. I grew a beach-comber's beard and worked diligently with Jeff Corey, digging deeper into this character, into myself, than I'd ever done before. Tony and I were in a conspiracy, determined to surprise the critics, to make my unexpected casting seem inspired, not misguided.

Many people, critics included, saw Christopher simply as "the gigolo." But in Tennessee's vision, he was the Angel of Death, a former disciple of the Devil who now served God by helping souls make their crossing to the other side. His observations contained some of the most meaningful dialogue I'd ever delivered.

"Everybody has a sense of reality of some kind or another, some sense of things being real in his particular world. And when one person's sense of reality seems too disturbingly different from another person's sense of reality—he's avoided! Not welcome! . . . You see, people hang labels, tags of false identification, on the people that disturb their own sense of reality too much, like the bells that used to be hung on the necks of lepers."

I could relate, having spent my whole life hiding my own sense of reality and being unable to escape the labels that made me feel like a leper. The play had powerful spiritual undercurrents as well, where I felt Tennessee was bravely tapping into his desire to relate to God on a deeper, transcendent level.

My commitment to the play and its themes led me to confront Tony over a crucial bit of direction. After Mrs. Goforth dies, Christopher stands at the edge of the proscenium, holding Mrs. Goforth's rings in his palm. Tony wanted me to ponder the rings, then pocket them before exiting. This "theft" of Flora's rings, to me, made Christopher seem like a garden-variety hustler. I wanted to drop the rings into the orchestra pit, symbolizing the ultimate worthlessness of material possessions. We did it Tony's way, but not before I declared his staging a cop-out. For me to even argue the point shows how deeply affected I was by this part, by this play.

Despite the inspiration I absorbed from Tennessee's words, there was no getting around the fact that this was Tallulah's show. Every day she'd totter in late to rehearsal, station herself at a table center stage, and spend an hour caking on stage makeup as though this ritual was the most vital part of our preparation. She'd leave a mountain of greasy tissues around her, then scout around for the assistant wearing the cleanest clothes. "Come over here, darling!" she'd command. They came every time, and every time she'd wipe her greasy hands on their fresh shirt.

Marian Seldes, one of the finest, most generous actresses I've ever worked with, was routinely dragged off to the ladies' room to run lines for Tallulah while she sat on the toilet. Marian catered to Tallulah's every whim—exactly as her character, Blackie, does in the play. Marian's patience was endless, even touching, considering how difficult Tallulah could be. She tried so hard to hold us all together, while Tallulah's insecurities threatened to blow us all apart.

Tony would suggest character notes to her at great length, and Tallulah would merely gaze back through those drooping eyelids and say: "Loud or soft—how do you want it?" Slowly but surely, she was grinding the director down. She incessantly interrupted the rest of the cast during rehearsal. Our first day off-book—always a difficult time—Tallulah kept running her mouth during one of my long, critical passages. I couldn't take it anymore.

"Why the *fuck* don't you shut up!" I screamed.

"You are the rudest man I've met since Marlon Brando," she announced, faking indignation.

"Thanks for putting me in such good company," I snapped.

Ruth Ford, as the Witch of Capri, was the only one in the cast capable of lighting a fire under Tallulah. She was a stage and screen veteran, married to Warner Bros. character actor Zachary Scott. Early in the play, she and Tallulah had a dinner scene that required complex staging and timing, with the Stage Assistants serving various courses at a comic pace. The two women would stop at nothing to upstage each other, including kicking their chairs off their marks to subtly gain more audience attention, causing problems for Bobby Dean Hooks and Konrad Matthaei, who played the Stage Assistants, responsible for setting the chairs and wrangling the actresses. Despite their nightly handshake and the shared vow of "Fifty-fifty" that always preceded

With Fritz, 1961. (Photo courtesy of Globe Photos.)

The proprietor displays his wares—Tab Hunter's Far East, Beverly Hills, 1960.

A trio of teen idols—Fabian, me, and Pat Boone, at yet another Hollywood function, 1959.
(Photo courtesy of Globe Photos.)

"Summer on Ice" TV special, with Tony Randall and Rosemary Clooney.
(Photo courtesy of Globe Photos.)

Publicity photo, circa 1960.

Publicity photo, 1961.

THE TAB HUNTER SHOW

With Nancy Walker.

With Elizabeth Montgomery.

With Joanna Barnes.

With Gena Rowlands.

Publicity photo, 1961.
(Photo courtesy of Globe Photos.)

The Pleasure of His
Company, *1961—
Fred Astaire, Lilli Palmer,
Debbie Reynolds, me, and
Gary Merrill.*

*Trying to keep my career
aloft in* La Freccia d'Oro,
an Italian-Egyptian production.

"The Merchant of Menace," Vincent Price
in War Gods of the Deep, *1965.*

Swimming with Flipper in Florida.

"Function-ing" with a teenage Tuesday Weld.
(Photo by David Sutton courtesy M.P. & T.V. Photo Archives.)

My Hollywood "discovery," Vicki Trickett.

Attending the Lawrence of Arabia *premiere with Joan Cohn, the start of a long relationship.*
(Photo courtesy of Globe Photos.)

Opening night of Milk Train, *with producer David Merrick and costar Tallulah Bankhead. The smiles were short-lived.*

Waimea Bay, Hawaii, shooting Ride the Wild Surf, *1964.*

Jet-setting in Europe on board Jack Kleiser's yacht, the San Luis . . .

. . . and soaking up the Riviera sun with Rudy.

Spaghetti Westerns were the rage in the late 1960s. Durango, *renamed* Shotgun *for U.S. release, was a misfire.*

About to be hanged in John Huston's The Life and Times of Judge Roy Bean.

Happy in competition, 1972.

Joan visits her newly acquired show jumper Happy, aka Collector's Item, at El Capitan Ranch, Santa Barbara.

At the Piedmont Hunt in Virginia, with Dody Vehr.

With Betty Meade at her farm in White Post, Virginia.

Relaxing at home in Dana Point with Rat, Whipper, and Dana.

"WITH SPECIAL GUEST STAR"

The 1970s was a decade of television appearances

Portrait of a Centerfold
*with Kim Basinger, who
exuded star quality from
the beginning.*

*With Sandra Dee
on* Police Woman.

Hawaii Five-O *with Jack Lord
and Samantha Eggar.*

Making a McMillan and Wife *episode
with Rock Hudson.*

Circus of the Stars *with Brooke
Shields and Steve Ford.*

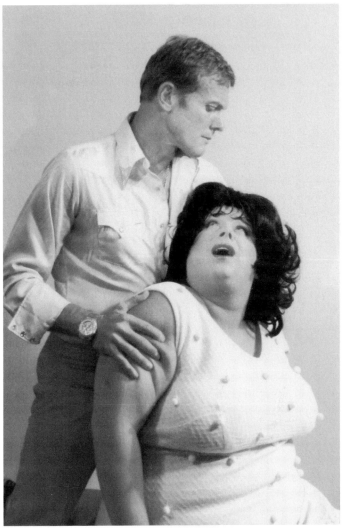

Striking a classic Hollywood pose with one of my favorite "leading ladies,"
Divine, in John Waters's Polyester.

Grease 2: Connie Stevens and I share a musical moment. (Photo courtesy of Paramount Pictures.)

Surrounded by the "ladies" of Chili Verde—Divine, Gina Gallego, Nedra Volz, and Lainie Kazan in Lust in the Dust.

Jim Katz, Allan Glaser, and I attend the Lust in the Dust *premiere, 1985.*

The photo I took of Tony at Shoreham Drive, 1958.

Trent Dolan, Dick Clayton, and me at Trader Vic's, Beverly Hills, 1999.

Toasting the new year and a new century with my mother in Santa Barbara, 2000.

Scouting locations with Allan for The Road Rise Up *in Hollywood . . . Ireland.*

their scene 3 entrance, Tallulah and Ruth never stopped trying to upstage each other.

One week before we were to open on Broadway, I gave the actresses a joint Christmas gift: a gorgeously wrapped box with a card inscribed, "All right girls—fifty/fifty." Inside was a pair of handcuffs. They showed me matching smiles, neither containing the slightest trace of good humor.

I gave Tallulah an additional gift: asbestos gloves. She didn't laugh, and I didn't care. I hadn't found it all that funny, either, when she blurted to some reporter during a rehearsal, "Tab *must* be gay—he hasn't gone down on me!"

The outrageousness, calculated as it was, wasn't what bothered me. What pissed me off was Tallulah's complete lack of professionalism, her inability to see beyond herself, beyond her reputation. She was dissipating an incredible God-given talent, especially when she'd decide to turn anything—*anything*—into high camp.

The most unforgettable moment of the *Milk Train* saga came during rehearsals in the tiny Lunt-Fontanne Theatre off Times Square. We were running the first scene of the second act: "We don't all live in the same world, you

Delivering Tennessee's message. Was anyone listening?
With Tallulah Bankhead in The Milk Train Doesn't
Stop Here Anymore, *Broadway, 1964.*

know, Mrs. Goforth," I was saying. "Oh, we all see the same things—sea, sun, sky, human faces and inhuman faces, but one person's sense of reality can be another person's sense of—well, of madness! Chaos!"

Tallulah and I both heard a low wailing offstage. It sounded like Ruth, in some kind of pain. It persisted and became a distraction. Just then, Tennessee rushed down the aisle, flushed and disheveled, cradling his Boston terrier and a silver flask from which he took copious swigs.

"The president's been killed!" he blurted out.

We all fell speechless, stunned in a profoundly incomprehensible way. Rising from her chair, Tallulah yelled: "So that's what that bitch has been wailing about!" She then threw herself down at the foot of the stage and began crying hysterically. Seconds later, Ruth Ford was kneeling beside her, also convulsing in tears. Even in their grief, they had to outdo each other.

Tony Richardson suddenly seemed very much a foreigner, wondering about his place in our national calamity. He called a ten-minute break. Everyone went through the side door and up the street to watch the news crawl along Times Square's electronic billboard. People were in a daze, as if the entire city had suffered a concussion.

Then it was back to the boards: "Madness! Chaos!"

So there's my answer to the most asked question of the twentieth century: Where were you when Kennedy was killed? It was a cultural benchmark, all right. The starting gun for a far less innocent chapter in American history. At thirty-two, I was still a young man, but one who more and more feared he was in danger of being an icon of the era that Kennedy's death wiped out. In many ways, November 22, 1963, felt like the day the 1950s officially ended and the rough ride of the 1960s truly began.

THE MILK TRAIN *Doesn't Stop Here Anymore* was scheduled to open at the Brooks Atkinson Theatre on January 1, 1964. In the wake of the president's murder, and his murderer's murder, everyone was staying home, waiting to see who'd be killed next on live TV. Nothing like this had ever happened before. Ticket sales weren't brisk.

Tony Richardson escaped back to his native England, his contract having stipulated liberty over the Christmas holidays to visit his wife, Vanessa Redgrave, and their daughter, Natasha. Tony wouldn't make it back in time for opening night, the lucky dog.

We'd done previews out of town, in Wilmington and Baltimore. The press had started circling early, smelling trouble in Tallulah's wobbly performances. Physically, she simply wasn't up to the daily rigors of a stage play. Despite her being such an extravagant pain in the ass, I actually felt sorry for her.

David Merrick considered canceling the show. Tennessee begged him not to. He harbored the fantastic delusion that Tallulah, fortified by constant B_{12} injections and the heat of the Broadway footlights, was going to find within her the performance of a lifetime come opening night. He went around telling everyone that Tallulah was perfect in the role, that she was going to stage a comeback to surpass Laurette Taylor's triumph in the 1945 premiere of *The Glass Menagerie*.

We all wanted so badly to believe. Even great playwrights, who should know better. Even suddenly aging actors, craving the defining part that will prove they're so much deeper than their pretty-boy image.

We opened New Year's Day, 1964, and closed three nights later.

The show, in one way, was a very fitting finale to Tallulah's Broadway career. All the work Tony Richardson and his cast and crew put into bringing out the play's deeper meaning—from Ned Rorem's incidental music to Rouben Ter-Arutunian's fantastic costumes and scenic design—was completely buried under Tallulah's offhanded trademark campiness. The moment she sniffed that first precious reaction to one of her patented mannerisms, she was un-stoppable, shamelessly playing to the crowd.

Half the seats in Brooks Atkinson were empty. Judging by the whoops and hollers, the other half were filled with screaming queens. Bankhead's devoted following had come to pay raucous tribute. To them, the play was nothing more than an excuse to wallow in their idol's patented shtick. No wonder Tallulah was so disconnected during rehearsals: she knew from the start the rest of us were going to end up as nothing more than props in her one-woman show.

Toward the end of act 3, Christopher sits at the feet of Mrs. Goforth and concludes an explanation about her passage to the afterlife by saying, "Don't you see?" He looks up into Flora's haughty face. The heavily lidded eyes looking back showed complete indifference. Disdain.

"No . . . you don't see," I said. It was a personalized reading, meant especially for Tallulah.

She arched an eyebrow and got her laughs.

Then I turned to the audience, which had spent the night guffawing up-roariously at every twist of Tallulah's wrist, every dangle of her foot.

"I guess none of you see," I ad-libbed. The theater fell deathly silent. I went on with what the playwright had to say.

The two-month ordeal would have been a complete disappointment, a personal and professional disaster, were it not for the telegram I received when the show was still in previews.

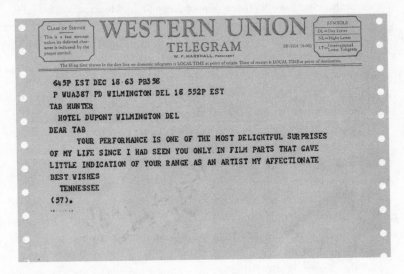

WESTERN UNION
TELEGRAM

CLASS OF SERVICE
This is a fast message
unless its deferred character is indicated by the
proper symbol.

SYMBOLS
DL = Day Letter
NL = Night Letter
LT = International Letter Telegram

W. P. MARSHALL, PRESIDENT

The filing time shown in the date line on domestic telegrams is LOCAL TIME at point of origin. Time of receipt is LOCAL TIME at point of destination.

```
645P EST DEC 18 63 PB358
P WUA387 PD WILMINGTON DEL 18 552P EST
TAB HUNTER
    HOTEL DUPONT WILMINGTON DEL
DEAR TAB
        YOUR PERFORMANCE IS ONE OF THE MOST DELIGHTFUL SURPRISES
OF MY LIFE SINCE I HAD SEEN YOU ONLY IN FILM PARTS THAT GAVE
LITTLE INDICATION OF YOUR RANGE AS AN ARTIST MY AFFECTIONATE
BEST WISHES
    TENNESSEE
(57).
```

2 8

Ride the Wild Surf

REACHING SO HIGH with *Milk Train* left me in a vulnerable spot. Down the rabbit hole I went, spinning through the showbiz chutes and landing pretty much back where I started. Columbia's *Ride the Wild Surf*, which I was lucky to get only weeks after my Broadway debut fizzled, was cut from the same cloth as the movies I'd done with Natalie in the midfifties. Only this time it was: "Dad, can I have the big surfboard tonight?"

If you have to slide backward, and land hard, it might as well be on a white sand beach in Waimea Bay, Oahu. That's where location work was done for a movie that, to my surprise, would become a touchstone for American surf culture, helping spread the Pacific Coast phenomenon to the rest of the world. The craze actually began a few years earlier, in 1959, with a fifteen-year-old Malibu girl named Kathy Kohner, whose Austrian father, Frederick, was a longtime Hollywood screenwriter. He helped his daughter turn her love of surfing and summertime into a novel—*Gidget*—which launched a movie and television franchise. My *Gunman's Walk* costar James Darren hit it big as Gidget's boyfriend, Moondoggie, in a couple of the Sandra Dee *Gidget* movies.

Beach movies of the early 1960s offered the same kind of fantasy that Busby Berkeley musicals did during the Great Depression: an escape, especially for kids, from the disturbing issues of the day—the Vietnam War, civil rights unrest, lingering pain over the president's assassination. Sunshine, sea spray, and the infectious sounds of the Beach Boys, Jan and Dean, and Dick Dale and the Deltones proved an irresistible alternative. At least until Bob Dylan and Jimi Hendrix and *Easy Rider* kicked sand on the luau.

From the start of shooting, I was a misfit. Literally. At the decrepit age of thirty-two, I was the oldest guy in the cast. I'd slipped to third billing, behind twenty-year-old Fabian and nineteen-year-old Shelley Fabares. He was the hot new teen idol; she was big with kids, thanks to four years on the tube playing the perky daughter Mary on *The Donna Reed Show.* Also in the cast was Jim Mitchum, the twenty-two-year-old spitting image of his father, Robert. Wasn't it just a few months earlier that I was costarring with his dad? Or had it been *ten years* already? Time was catching up with me.

Once again, as with my character in *Battle Cry,* I drew on my brother, Walt, for inspiration. Odd to realize that what I did in front of a camera, Walt did in real life. Like playing soldier so profitably over the years, while Walt actually supported a wife and seven kids on a modest navy salary. While I was kicking around Hollywood after being booted out of the Coast Guard, Walt's adventurous spirit took him to Honolulu, where he worked the night desk at the Ala Moana Hotel and spent every day at the beach. My brother was one of the first haole surfer dudes of Hawaii, mastering the original wooden long boards before fiberglass was even heard of.

Back in 1948 he'd sent Mother and me a newspaper clipping from the Honolulu paper, celebrating the conversion of Matson's *Lurline* from a troop transport back to a passenger liner. The article described how the legendary ship sailed around Diamond Head amid a fanfare of spurting fireboats, pleasure craft, and "one lonely surf rider bucking the waves." Walt had circled the line— and a little speck in the photo—and scrawled, "That's me!" on the clipping.

When he returned to Northern California later that year, Walt enlisted in the navy and met Patricia Dicker. They were married before Walt turned twenty, and Pat started having kids like clockwork. Walt more than made up for my choosing not to extend the Gelien legacy.

Except for a year spent in Norfolk, as part of his hospital corpsman training, Walt and family spent the 1950s stationed in the San Francisco Bay Area. In late '64, however, they'd be assigned to duty in Hawaii, where Walt got to surf the big waves again, waiting on orders to ship out for Vietnam.

By all rights, it was Walt Gelien who should have played the part of Ralph "Steamer" Lane, not me.

Ride the Wild Surf may not have had dialogue by Tennessee Williams, but it was work and I was glad to have it. Some of my callow colleagues, however, had yet to learn how fleeting it all can be. Making a film about the hang-loose, carefree surfing life was an excuse for some of them to waste time and money clowning around, intentionally screwing up takes.

"Wait a minute!" I finally hollered, fed up. "Are we or are we not professionals? For every one of us idiots lucky enough to be here, there are hundreds of others who can do the job just as well, if not better—so let's cut the crap and get serious."

The crew applauded. I was now officially the Old Fart on the set.

It's amazing to think that anybody was taken in by this pasted-together version of surfer culture. Maybe audiences were hypnotized by the sight of those Waimea waves. Not that any of the actors actually rode them. All we did was sprint into the water and paddle out. Fabian, Peter Brown, and I wore trunks to match a trio of genuine surfers in footage already shot. Pete and I dyed our hair to complete the illusion. That's why my hair looks darker than normal, while Pete's is bleached blond— a rare case of the stars doubling for the stunt men!

Close-ups of us "shooting the curl" were done back on the Columbia lot. We were positioned in front of a rear projection screen, in little Radio Flyer wagons, while assistants nudged us around and doused us with buckets of water. The result wasn't exactly state-of-the-art movie magic.

Don Taylor, director of this waterlogged epic, was a former actor, best remembered for the movie *The Naked City,* where he played an eager, fresh-faced New York cop opposite wizened old Barry Fitzgerald. *Ride the Wild Surf* was his first feature assignment, after ten years of directing everything on television from *Alfred Hitchcock Presents* to *Dennis the Menace* to *Dr. Kildare.*

Catching a wave, Hollywood-style. With Fabian and Peter Brown on a Columbia soundstage for Ride the Wild Surf.

Halfway through the schedule, Taylor's mother died unexpectedly and he went back to the mainland to be with his family. To stay on schedule, Columbia shipped in a replacement director for the week—Phil Karlson, whom I hadn't seen since *Gunman's Walk*.

His first night on the North Shore, we had dinner at a local hangout near Sunset Beach. "I don't have any idea what the hell's going on here," Phil admitted.

I convinced him to juggle the shooting schedule so he could direct one of my few remaining scenes, the one in which I assure my future mother-in-law that I'm an upstanding citizen, not a beach bum. It was the only halfway decent scene I had. Karlson was a true pro, and I was happy to work with him again, however briefly.

Ride the Wild Surf was a big hit. Jan and Dean's title song hung in the Top Ten for months. The most uncanny thing about the movie, for me personally, is how it dropped me into the cultural Mixmaster with beach movies, surf music, California Dreaming, and the whole Endless Summer fantasy. People who didn't actually live through the 1950s hear the name Tab Hunter and still say, "Oh, yeah—he did all those beach movies."

I did *one*—and it's not all that hot. How strange it should remain such a vivid little piece of America's consciousness.

THE NIGHT WE GOT reacquainted at Sunset Beach, Phil Karlson told me how much he missed Harry Cohn. He'd screened a rough cut of *Gunman's Walk* for the Columbia boss in early 1958, and Cohn had wept at the finish. He called Karlson a great director, one of his favorites, and declared that from then on he'd get only the best scripts the studio had to offer.

"He died a couple of weeks later," Phil said. "And I've never made another picture for Columbia."

For some reason, I thought better of mentioning that for the past two years I'd been dating Harry Cohn's widow, Joan.

IT BEGAN AS ONE of those across-the-room things, at a cocktail party hosted by Ernie Kovacs and Edie Adams. "Wow, who is that?" I may have blurted out, because I remember someone turned to me and said, "That's Joan Cohn, Harry Cohn's widow."

Older women have always intrigued me, especially when they're elegant and sophisticated and intelligent: the way they drink a cocktail, the way they smoke a cigarette. Joan Cohn had clearly been to finishing school. She knew the proper way to dress, the proper way to move, the proper way to handle things . . . with style.

We struck up a conversation. I immediately got the impression that she was a girl playing a game. The worldly airs didn't fool me. And she seemed to approve of the rough edges I never bothered to smooth down in polite society. There was a teacher-pupil byplay in our banter, which was perhaps appropriate, considering the twenty-year age difference. Not that I noticed. I never paid attention to that stuff. If someone intrigued me, I'd go right in for the close-up, ignoring the long master shot that everybody else was seeing.

She was surprised that I knew the proper way to eat caviar, biting off the tip of a hard-cooked egg and spooning on a bit of beluga. "Merle Oberon taught me," I said, smiling. Joan and I took to each other immediately, in a teasing, flirtatious way.

I began receiving regular invitations to dinner parties at 1000 North Crescent Drive, the Beverly Hills estate Joan had shared for years with her husband.

One of our earliest dates was the black-tie premiere of *Lawrence of Arabia*, a double date with Cliff Robertson and Dina Merrill. I'd been out at the barn and barely had time to shower and change into evening clothes before zooming over Coldwater Canyon Drive to Joan's. As was always the case, Joan received her guests in the loggia, which had a fabulous vaulted ceiling with a mural of hand-painted birds. Champagne and caviar awaited her guests' arrival.

Columbia provided a limo to take us to the theater. A respectful gesture, considering that it'd been five years since the boss's death. Joan remained the largest stockholder in Screen Gems, Columbia's television subsidiary, and she still dipped her hand into the studio's business on occasion, if only to make sure no one forgot who built the empire from the ground up. She lived like Hollywood royalty, but without King Cohn, Joan was a queen without a country. She had no real role to play in the business, beyond hosting fabulous parties for what remained of the "old guard."

Jean Louis, Columbia's renowned costume designer, and Luis Estevez were Joan's personal designers and close friends. For the *Lawrence* premiere, Joan wore a chic gown beneath a full-length white mink. Draped around her neck was a diamond necklace set with Ural Mountain emeralds the size of quarters. She kept fingering the stones during the limo ride down Sunset. In the midst of the four-way chitchat, Joan eyed me and said: "I know what you're thinking, Tab." She fondled an emerald. "You're thinking, *How many horses could I buy with one of these?*"

"No," I replied. "Actually I was thinking . . . how gauche."

She wasn't sure how to respond. My refusal to kiss up to Joan—like a lot of her acolytes did—became, I believe, the linchpin of our friendship.

We didn't get back to Joan's that night until the wee hours, following a post-screening party that was almost as epic as the film. Both starving, we went into the kitchen, Joan still decked out in Jean Louis and jewels. We fixed scrambled eggs, bacon, toast, and coffee. When the sun came up, we were still gabbing. It was a special night, and the start of a long, unusual relationship. Sitting in her kitchen, not an ounce of pretense between us, I saw an entirely different side of Joan, a side few people knew existed and fewer still ever got to see.

It was Betty Miller with whom I greeted the dawn. It was Betty Miller, the straight-shooting girl from Tampa hidden deep inside the meticulously constructed Joan Cohn, with whom I was becoming infatuated.

Just like Harry Cohn had fallen for her, years earlier.

He'd first seen Betty on the dance floor of the Central Park Casino, waltzing in the arms of another man. It was 1935, and she was a twenty-one-year-old model. Harry Cohn was forty-four and playing out a loveless marriage with his wife, Rose. He decided to make Betty Miller a movie star, but after renaming her Joan Perry, he saw more promise in her as a wife. He divorced Rose in the summer of 1941, after eighteen years of marriage, and tied the knot with Joan three days later in the ballroom of the St. Regis Hotel in New York.

Joan was loyal and dutiful throughout the marriage, an old-school type who believed that a woman's job was to "please a man." Harry Cohn's pleasure was to have the most elegant and refined wife of any studio head, to step him up in class—vitally important to a man all of Hollywood had branded vulgar and uncouth. Joan accomplished the mission. It was a bonus when she got pregnant—but devastating when she lost the baby, Jobella, less than two hours after giving birth. Eventually, though, the Cohns would have two sons, John Perry and Harry Jr., and an adopted daughter, Katherine.

Harry Cohn's death left Joan in limbo. An unbelievably opulent limbo, but limbo nonetheless. She had everything money could buy, but she seemed lost at the core, as though her own identity had gotten misplaced between being a trophy wife and a mother.

When I'd accompany Joan through her social ramble, plenty of people saw an aging, affluent beauty clinging to her youth by keeping a handsome younger man on her arm. I'm sure we seemed like a pair of Hollywood-manufactured characters: the idle-rich doyenne and her hanger-on gigolo. Our relationship was a through-the-looking-glass reflection of Flora Goforth and Christopher Flanders in *The Milk Train Doesn't Stop Here Anymore*. But as with the play: How deeply are you willing to look? Only at the surface, at the stereotypes? Or beneath, where you find real people—Betty Miller and Art Gelien— enjoying a genuine friendship in spite of the public "masks" they'd adopted and the whispered insinuations they had to endure.

And . . . just to complicate matters . . . there was already a handsome lead- ing man on Joan's *other* arm.

Laurence Harvey had adopted a mask, too. He was born Laruschka Mischa Skikne in Lithuania in 1928 but grew up in South Africa and later England, where he refined his social skills and trained at the Royal Academy of Dra- matic Arts. In his twenties, he'd lived in England with actress Hermione Baddeley, a woman twice his age. She'd coincidentally played Flora Goforth in the first aborted Broadway run of *The Milk Train Doesn't Stop Here Any- more*. Weird life-imitates-art analogies apparently didn't apply solely to me. In 1957, Harvey married actress Margaret Leighton, but they were divorced— coincidentally?—right around the time he met Joan.

Larry first came to Joan's attention—as he did for a lot of smitten women— playing a sexy heel in 1959's *Room at the Top*. He was quickly ushered to Hollywood from England to star in pictures like *The Alamo* and *Butterfield* 8. A screen version of Tennessee Williams's *Summer and Smoke* followed, co- starring my pal Geraldine Page. About the time I started seeing Joan regularly, Larry was getting great reviews as the brainwashed soldier-assassin in John Frankenheimer's *The Manchurian Candidate*.

He and Joan were already a regular thing. She'd invited him into her inner circle and he quickly settled in, a fixture at her side, dashing and quick wit- ted. Some of Joan's confidants labeled Larry a user, or worse, based on his track record with older women and the ease with which he accepted Joan's considerable largesse: an electric blue Rolls-Royce, endless trinkets, eventu- ally a palatial home of his own in Beverly Hills. "Pleasing a man," after all, is how Joan fulfilled her self-image.

I don't want to think that Joan was using me to ignite a little jealousy in Larry, to make sure he stayed attentive to her. I wouldn't put it past her, but it certainly wasn't the main reason she liked having me around. She'd try to bestow the same kind of generosity on me that she did on Larry, but I was a tougher sell. I hated receiving gifts. Joan was surrounded by people looking for a handout. What she needed—and what she got in me—was a loyal companion who asked for nothing.

I'm not putting the knock on Larry. He was good for Joan. She loved having one or the other of us around, sometimes both. She didn't care at all what people might say behind her back, or to her face, regarding the sexual orientation of her boyfriends.

Larry was, if not homosexual, at least bisexual. His mentor, James Woolf, obsessed over him the same way Henry Willson obsessed over Rock Hudson. Woolf had produced *Room at the Top,* and gossip persisted that their relationship went beyond the professional. Defusing such rumors was pretty easy for Larry, especially in this country, where Americans always told themselves, *He's not gay—he's just British.*

Joan would dismiss disparaging commentary about her choice in men by saying things like, "He won't be gay when I get through with him," or, when wit failed her, "What fucking business is it of yours?"

How could such a glittery triangle escape the watchful eyes of the scandal sheets? Well, obviously, it couldn't. In April 1964 I was once again a *Confidential* cover boy. *Wait . . . wasn't that rag dead? Hadn't that 1957 trial killed it?* Yet there I was, depicted in a graphic ménage à trois with Joan and Larry. FUN'S FUN, the headline blared—BUT WHEN IT COMES TO LOVING, WHO GETS THE GIRL? The story surpassed even that rag's typically low standards for absurd prose.

> We hesitate to spread such evil gossip, but the fact of the matter is that the Two Boy Princes and the Maid Joan have become a very jolly threesome at the cinema kingdom of Camelot . . . The smart spots and the beat joints jump joyously when the Royal Entourage appears as so often happens . . .
>
> "Egad, what is Hollywood coming to that a Maid should thus be bracketed in parenthesis?"

I don't enjoy reviving these smarmy excerpts, but in hindsight they *are* fascinating for what they could, and could not, openly reveal. Only between the lines could allusions be made to the most unusual aspect of our supposed triangle.

"From a celluloid land of sugar and spice, it turned into a fairyland where gay Princes reveled and cavorted," the article insinuated, before once again dusting off my ages-old "pajama party" arrest. Larry wasn't openly alleged to be gay, but the portrait painted of him as a social-climbing cad was even less flattering.

Over time, Joan and Larry's relationship became volatile. There was a lot of possessiveness involved and, I sensed, duplicity. I tried to stay out of it, bouncing all over the map in my search for work while maintaining my friendship with Joan. If she wanted people to think she'd somehow "turned" me, if that made her feel like more of a woman—it didn't bother me. I didn't care anymore about what people thought. I loved Joan but didn't feel the need to qualify, or consummate, our relationship.

After a night on the town and our ritual kitchen-table conversation, I'd say to her, "Sweetheart, I've got to run. Got to get up in the morning and work the horses." I'd go back to my new place on Riverside Drive and check the animals in the stable. Still in my formal wear, I'd shovel a little shit. Sometimes I'd bring out a last glass of wine and lie down in the stall with Louise, my thoroughbred hunter. We'd share little sips before I'd brush off the straw and turn in for the night.

Trivia and Tragedy

LUCHINO VISCONTI PROVED true to his word. In the spring of 1964 he summoned me to Rome to shoot screen tests for his next film, *Vaghe Stelle dell'Orsa*. It was a mystery about an Italian girl who returns to her childhood home in Tuscany with an American husband, only to be haunted by dark secrets from her childhood. Claudia Cardinale and I were cast as the married couple, with Jean Sorel playing the brother who shared her guilt. We were a hot trio. The trial footage was only a formality, Luchino explained, to help him visualize how he'd use us once filming began.

Thanks to his concern for character and his attention to detail, merely shooting tests with Luchino was more fulfilling than making entire features with other directors. I was elated to be included in his vision. But during preproduction, the trapdoor opened. The film's financial backers were interested in furthering the career of another actor, Michael Craig, and they insisted Visconti cast him as Cardinale's husband. Luchino stood up for me as best he could, but when artists knock heads with the money boys, the money boys usually get what they want. And these boys didn't want Tab Hunter.

It was a crushing blow.

Instead of a Visconti film on my résumé, I added another American International winner, *War Gods of the Deep*, which I grudgingly accepted once I learned I was exiled from *Vahge Stelle dell'Orsa*. It was like being tossed a soggy sandwich after having been invited to the nine-course banquet. The only consolation was that *War Gods* was made in England, and I'd costar with Vincent Price.

I'd first met Vinnie in Jamaica, where he and his bride, Mary, had honeymooned while I was there making *Island of Desire*. Back then he was an in-demand supporting actor, specializing in urbane Continental oddballs. He was so good at it, you'd never suspect he was from Missouri. By 1964, Vinnie was officially the Merchant of Menace, thanks to a franchise of low-budget horror films based on Edgar Allan Poe stories, mostly made for AIP by a resourceful producer-director named Roger Corman.

Vinnie had no problem with being typecast. Success allowed him to indulge his passion for art. He was quite the collector, with a side business buying art for Sears Roebuck. Obviously, there wasn't any pretension in the guy. I loved joining him on excursions to local antique shops, where he'd make tasteful purchases of simple oils, watercolors, and prints.

Evelyn Baring, Terry Marsteller's longtime companion, invited me to stay at his posh flat at Bryanston Court during the production. He was a perfect host—Edmund Gwenn would have played him on-screen—delightedly sharing stories nightly with his guest over a postsupper scotch.

Every morning at dawn a chauffeur called for me, then picked up Vinnie, delivering us to Pinewood Studios. End of the day, we'd be driven back to London. Not to pull a "star trip," but my contract stipulated my *own* car and driver. The production manager, a cool British cookie in tweeds, ignored that clause. Cost savings, no doubt—the guiding principle of AIP's boss, Sam Arkoff. This meant hanging around, sometimes for hours, waiting for Vinnie to finish. One of those little indignities that spells out for you, in case you hadn't noticed, that you're no longer a big star.

I'd ordered a new Mercedes from the Stuttgart factory earlier that year. When I learned it was ready, I had it shipped to London. Soon as it arrived, I called the Pinewood driver and said I'd get myself to the lot. The next morning, around eight thirty, I called the studio:

"Where the heck is Pinewood?" I asked.

"Where are you?" the producer panted. "We'll send a car."

"Oh, that won't be necessary," I told her. "I'll be there shortly." I hung up.

I had juice and coffee at a wonderful little spot near the river. Watched ducks swim for a while. Most pleasant. I called the studio again, from one of those charming red phone booths.

"Things are starting to look familiar," I told the now-hyperventilating producer. "I'm not lost. I know I'll find it soon." *Click.*

It was a beautiful day to enjoy the magnificent English countryside, especially in a brand-new Mercedes.

I got to Pinewood sometime after lunch. The producer stormed up ranting, distinctly un-British. I politely explained that she should have read my contract more closely. She became a raving bitch, screaming about the budget, blah, blah, blah.

"No problem," I told her. "If money's an issue, I'll just drive my own car."

"No! All right, all right!" she hollered. "You'll get your own car and driver!"

Other than that, everything went well on the film. It reunited me with my *Ride the Wild Surf* costar Susan Hart, the fiancée of Jim Nicholson, Arkoff's partner in AIP. And I note, for what it's worth, that once again I was working with a great director on his last legs. Jacques Tourneur had made memorable movies like *The Flame and the Arrow, Stars in My Crown,* and *Out of the Past,* but this film—called *City under the Sea* everywhere but the United States (a reference to the Poe poem on which it's based)—would be Tourneur's last.

I was on the set for the last roars of so many old lions—Walsh, Wellman, Heisler, Tourneur—as well as for the first forays of young turks who'd inspire a whole new style of filmmaking: Frankenheimer, Lumet, Penn. My career fell smack in the middle of the changing of the guard.

Luchino arrived in London to direct his acclaimed production of *Il Trovatore* at Covent Garden. He called and invited me to be his guest at the opening gala. Vinnie was my date that night. We shared Luchino's box with another of his seemingly endless list of intriguing friends: Rudolf Nureyev, king of modern ballet, one of the most passionate artists in the world. His performances in the 1950s with the Kirov Ballet, when he was still a teenager, had made him a legend. At the age of twenty-three, he'd defected from the Soviet Union. Now he was dancing with the Royal Ballet. His later collaborations with Margot Fonteyn would knock the dance establishment on its collective ear.

High-toned company, to say the least.

As the queen mother arrived, the pomp of "God Save the Queen" filled the concert hall. Rudy acted like it was a hootenanny, loudly and merrily humming and clapping along. The royals were seated only a few boxes away. Fearful the queen might hear him, I jabbed Rudy in the ribs and told him to shut up.

Nureyev was, in many ways, a little kid. And this festive evening wouldn't be our last adventure.

When *War Gods* wrapped, I immediately agreed to another picture, a low-budget potboiler called *Troubled Waters,* with a fine actress named Zena Walker. I didn't do it for the art, let's face it. I did it to stay in England and enjoy a life I'd never have otherwise experienced.

Troubled Waters has fallen through the cracks, both in public consciousness and my own memory. What I more readily recall of England, besides a freak summer heat wave that had people dropping like flies, was spending every free moment in the country with the horses, and in the fall, foxhunting. I thrived on English rural life. I rode regularly with Anneli Drummond-Hay, one of the world's finest equestrians. Her aunt introduced me to whippets, which I've owned ever since. Weekends were spent either at Syersham Priory, with the accomplished dressage rider Delia Cunningham, or with Tim Rootes, scion of the Rootes Motor Car Company, at his magnificent Barn House in Banbury. Whether out foxhunting or breezing Tim's steeplechasers, life couldn't get any better.

To hell with the movie business.

"Hey, Shit Face! You better get over here before going back to the States." It was Terry Marsteller. He'd heard that I'd run out of work and was thinking about returning to California. Terry was living in Menton, in the south of France, at Serre de la Madone, an impressive villa with world-renowned gardens. The former bus-station ticket taker from Torrance, my "pajama party" cohort, was living the high life, splitting time between London and the Riviera. We'd stayed in touch over the years. Terry always made me smile.

"You were the one who talked me into buying a place in Jamaica," he reminded me over the wire. "And then you never once came to visit. You have to come visit now!"

I figured I'd spend a couple of weeks in France. I ended up spending the summer.

The life of leisure sneaked up on me. Before I knew it, it was Christmas, 1964. I'd overstayed my welcome. Even though I was having the time of my life, part of me was slipping away. I needed work, to get back to my "real world," the world of acting. Only one problem: you need to be *invited* back.

Fortunately, another Tennessee Williams play, *Period of Adjustment,* was offered, one year after the *Milk Train* debacle. I bid adieu to Terry and Serre de la Madone and set sail on January 13, 1965, from Cherbourg to New York. I wouldn't be long in Manhattan, since this wasn't a Broadway show. I kept rolling right past the big cities, all the way to the Pheasant Run Playhouse in St. Charles, Illinois.

One of our first nights, a drunk in the audience kept disrupting the show with obnoxious comments. During a tender moment between the two actresses, he called out, "Just like home!"

I peered into the darkness. "Hey, loudmouth!" I hollered. "Why don't you shut up!"

Thus began my glorious run as a full-time stage actor.

Period of Adjustment lasted about a month. A Chicago actress, Mary Frann, costarred. She'd soon head for Hollywood and regular TV work on *Days of Our Lives* and *The Bob Newhart Show*. For me, something as good, if not better, came out of the play: a lasting friendship with the prop master, Katie Lindsay. Outside the theater, she was master of hounds for the Wayne-DuPage Hunt, as was her father before her. We rode or hunted daily throughout the run and stayed close friends.

That April, I was stunned by the news of Linda Darnell's death. I learned it from the newspaper, while on the road. She was staying in a Chicago suburb with her former secretary and had fallen asleep watching one of her first movies, *Star Dust,* on the late show. The house caught fire—apparently from a cigarette she'd been smoking—and Linda died the next day, from severe burns to 90 percent of her body.

It was especially gruesome because everyone who knew her knew Linda was deathly afraid of fire. Almost perversely, she'd been "burned to death" in two of her movies, *Hangover Square* and *Anna and the King of Siam,* and she barely survived the Great Fire of London in *Forever Amber.*

I couldn't get my mind around it. This was the woman who had ushered me into the movies with my first screen kiss, thrown me a party on my twentieth birthday, given me that gorgeous scrapbook—now in storage—commemorating my entry into a magical new realm. She'd been a huge star but in recent years had struggled to find work. Producers thought she was "old."

Linda was forty-one when she died.

All I could think of was work, any kind of work, anywhere. I'd seen *Mr. Roberts* on Broadway, with Henry Fonda in the title role. I offered my version of the character in small playhouses in Illinois and Pennsylvania. After that I went straight to the Starlight Theatre in Kansas City for a week of *Here's Love,* a mediocre musical with Gretchen Wyler, who always seemed to be replacing Gwen Verdon in something or other. We knew the show was no good and renamed it *Here's Dreck.*

Letters from Walt caught up with me on the road. He'd just arrived in Vietnam, two days before his thirty-fifth birthday. Even though he was in the war zone, Walt was upbeat, confident there was a mission to be accomplished and he'd get it done. That was my brother, never doubting himself or his duties for a minute.

One of my earliest memories of Walt was him leading me around by the hand, exploring the ship that took us from the misery of New York to our new life in California. We were dressed in the brand-new clothes Opa had bought us for the trip. Walt was only three, but he was already my "big" brother. As we passed the swimming pool, I broke away. I wanted to touch the water. I slipped and fell in, my suddenly saturated clothes pulling me under. Walt knew to run and get a steward, who jumped in and rescued me.

I always got a laugh out of recalling the time Mother walked us down Market Street in San Francisco, all dressed up in our short pants, navy blazers, and caps. Passersby gawked: "What beautifully mannered children you have." Mother glowed. Suddenly, loud enough for the whole street to hear, Walt yelled at me: "You son of a bitch!" A little something he picked up back in New York. Mother dragged us straight home and washed *both* our mouths out with soap, just for good measure. After all, I did everything Walt did.

I grew up wanting to emulate his courage, his cavalier style. When he joined the band at St. John's, so did I. When he went out for football, I tried it and made it, just to prove I could. Walt could do anything, and I wanted to be just like him.

"You have to learn to be on your own," my brother told me one day. "You've got to learn to take care of yourself. And most important—you've got to learn to be responsible." Walt planted the seeds of confidence in me. He was a born leader. He taught me, "People can help, but in the long run, it's all up to you."

After reading his latest letter, I went to church and prayed for him. And for Pat and their seven kids. I prayed for all the soldiers serving our country. When I saw on television the growing hordes of young people protesting the war in the streets, burning our flag, my blood boiled. If they didn't like this country, they could all get the hell out.

JUST WHEN IT SEEMED I might never make another movie, Tony Richardson came to the rescue. He'd been hired to adapt Evelyn Waugh's black comedy about the mortuary business, *The Loved One*. He stocked the cast with stars in cameo roles. Mine was only two days' work, playing a cemetery tour guide.

How oddly fitting, considering that my movie career was dead.

I ran off to a horse show that November, at the Cow Palace in San Francisco. The arena had gotten its name during the Depression, when some local columnist wrote, "People are starving and here they build a palace for cows."

I was poised on my horse Nob Hill at the in gate, waiting to be called to the ring. From the corner of my eye, I noticed a soldier moving through the crowd of horses, trainers, and grooms.

"Are you Arthur Gelien?" the soldier asked, blank faced.

I nodded. My concentration was on the ride at hand.

"I'd appreciate a word with you."

"Not right now," I said. "They're about to call my number."

As I turned away, the soldier said: "I regret to inform you that your brother has been killed in Vietnam."

The loudspeaker blared, "Entry one twenty-six, Nob Hill, ridden by blah blah blah!" The gate opened and we entered the arena. Nothing made sense. The buzzer sounded. I closed my eyes and said a silent prayer, ending with, *Walt, I offer this class for you.*

We started the course. Nobby sensed something in me. Horses know. Nobby jumped his heart out. We won the class.

Afterward, in the quiet of Nobby's stall, with no one around, I broke down and wept uncontrollably. There was comfort in being surrounded by horses, the constant consolation in my life. Something else for which I had my brother to thank.

Walt died on October 28, 1965, two months after arriving in Vietnam. It happened in Da Nang, at the Marble Mountain Air Facility, where Walt's hospital corps was receiving incoming wounded on medevac helicopters. Everyone was killed in the ambush.

Why? Dear God, why? I asked. Why couldn't it have been me? Walt has a family. It's not fair. Why wasn't it me instead of him?

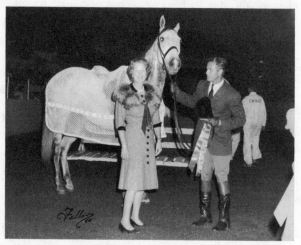

Nob Hill and me winning a class, on the worst day of my life.

Limbo

OR WAS IT PURGATORY?

There was no work in Hollywood, not even TV guest shots. To get a job I had to go cross-country, to the "other" Hollywood, in Florida. That's where we shot *Birds Do It,* with Soupy Sales and Judy the Chimp, a viable contender for Worst Film Ever Made. Filming at Ivan Tors Studio did have one advantage, however: I was able to get a photo for Walt's kids of me swimming with TV's slickest new star. They took turns bringing the picture to school, proudly telling their friends: "Look—my uncle Art knows Flipper!"

The government's payout to Pat Gelien was ten thousand dollars. I desperately wanted to contribute more to the care of the seven kids, but it was getting harder all the time. My mother's monthly expenses, which I'd vowed to pay in full for the rest of her life, steadily increased. Her guardian devil, Bernice, then died of a heart attack, and Mother decided that she wanted to live by herself in Monterey, California. She refused to live with Pat and the grandchildren, despite the common sense of such an arrangement. Gertrude Gelien insisted on maintaining her "freedom," and as long as she did, her surviving son insisted on paying for it.

I bounced back to the West Coast for a stint in the national touring company of Neil Simon's *Barefoot in the Park,* bumping from the lead a wonderful young actor named Joel Crothers. The producers thought I still had some marquee value. Poor Joel must have resented a fading star taking over his role for two weeks in San Francisco, four in Los Angeles.

Returning to L.A., I looked forward to spending more time with Joan, but she was busy spending it with Larry Harvey, building him a new home on Cabrillo Drive or flying out with him on weekends, in a private Learjet, to her second home in Palm Springs. A bit showy, since you could make the drive in an hour and a half. I still got weeknight invitations for dinner, movies, and card games at the Beverly Hills spread, occasions from which Larry was often noticeably absent.

With jobs few and far between, I figured I should invest what I'd managed to save in something stable, something that I understood and enjoyed. I became partners with Jack and Kay Conner, Dodgers pitchers Don Drysdale and Bob Miller, and a couple of other game souls in a horse breeding operation on the Oregon coast.

The 128-acre Seaside Stock Farm was based around a string of ninety brood mares, show horses, hunters, and jumpers, anchored by a thoroughbred stud named War Flirt, who was supposed to rake in the breeding fees. We never made a dime.

I moved to Oregon to be around Jack and Kay and the horses but never really settled in. Probably a good thing, considering that Clatsop County had the highest suicide rate in the nation. I lived in a small apartment above Sea Meadows Antiques and spent a lot of time riding long stretches of the coast, collecting Japanese glass floats that washed ashore from across the Pacific. For a while, these days were tranquil and memorable. Before long, the memory of it was enough.

"Why don't you spend more time in Hollywood?" people asked me incessantly.

"Why sit around a pool reading scripts, waiting for the phone to ring?" was my stock answer. "You'll wake up one morning and find you've turned into a brown Mercedes." That's what everyone in Hollywood was driving back then.

In truth, I was incredibly relieved when A. C. Lyles, an old-school publicist-producer at Paramount, tracked me down and put me in a low-budget 1967 western, *Hostile Guns,* with George Montgomery, Yvonne de Carlo, and Brian Donlevy. The studio let Lyles have free rein with his low-budget B productions, and he loved to cast old-time stars struggling to find work in the aftermath of the studio system's collapse.

I couldn't handle the Hollywood cocktail-party circuit, however, hoping to run into a producer with work to offer. Better to hit the road with a touring company, doing summer stock, or even dinner theater, where people in the audience noisily wolf down prime rib and ambrosia while watching you perform.

At thirty-five, I finally got my chance to play Tony in *West Side Story*—at the Meadowbrook Dinner Theatre in New Jersey. One night, after I had been killed in act 3, my farsighted Maria, Joanna Lester, ran screaming to my side. As she fell to her knees, one of her hands hit the floor, and the other went right into my balls, instantly raising Tony from the dead.

After that it was *Barefoot in the Park* again, at the Little Theatre on the Square in Sullivan, Illinois, one of the best stock theaters in the country. Offstage, I'd

have died of boredom if not for Katie Lindsay, who hauled a horse down to keep me occupied. I agreed to go right into a road show of *Bye Bye Birdie* as soon as *Barefoot* closed. Without the work, I was afraid I might disappear.

We rolled *Barefoot* on through Ohio and Massachusetts and up through New England, with the fabulous Thelma Ritter and her daughter, Monica Moran, joining the show along the way. We closed in Ogunquit, Maine, on July 15. I then drove nonstop to Charlotte, North Carolina, to start rehearsals of *Bye Bye Birdie*.

When the summer season ended, so did my prospects. Dick Clayton suggested I return to Italy, where American actors like Clint Eastwood and Lee Van Cleef were becoming big stars. The western may have been on its last legs in Hollywood, but the spaghetti western was keeping the genre alive. Dick helped fix me up with a new agent in Rome. With no solid offers to keep me stateside, I once again set sail for Europe.

THIS TIME, HOWEVER, there was a difference: I wasn't traveling alone. I'd met Neal Noorlag the previous February at a horse show in Indio, California. During a Jumpers Class, a slim, sensitive-looking guy came up to me at the back gate and sheepishly struck up a conversation. His family, he said, fled their home in the rain-soaked Pacific Northwest each winter for the arid California desert. He'd come to the show because he'd grown up around horses and had always wanted to learn how to ride jumpers. The kid—he was twenty-three—seemed sincere, so I invited him out to Clyde's for lessons.

My crowd at the barn—Venetia, Stephanie Zimbalist, J. J. Smith—all found Neal charming and likable. He was a pretty good horseman but was tense with them—as he was with himself. I was rough on him at times, trying to encourage him to be more assertive. I could be a slave driver when it came to teaching someone the proper way to work with horses. Neal seemed willing to learn, and we started seeing each other regularly.

Neal was a bit of a lost soul. He worked in the mail room at KABC-TV in Los Angeles, and although he was drawn to show business, he wasn't at all sure of where he might fit in. His parents were devoutly religious, Dutch Christian Reformed, and they instilled in him a strong sense of values that I appreciated. But those values also caused him great conflict in terms of his sexuality. That didn't stop him, however, from taking the first steps toward a relationship, even though he knew my life was in constant flux.

Neal often joined me on the road. Suitcase living can be extremely lonely, so I was grateful that he wanted to come along. Neal wrote regularly to his mother: "Tab talks about you and Dad to everyone. I'm beginning to think he's adopted us as his family."

I wish I could have. I idealized the Noorlag family because they were everything I'd never had: a close-knit clan built on rock-solid values, who exuded faith and love. I started writing to Mrs. Noorlag more often than I did my own mother: "Your prayers have been doing us both good. Things have been going so very well. I'll see that Neal and I both don't forget our obligations in that department. Thanks for the cookies."

If they thought Neal and I were "living in sin," they kept it to themselves.

My own conflicts were resolved by this time. I knew who I was, but I remained guarded about what I showed to the world. I appreciated that Neal never flaunted that he was gay and never pushed any agenda in our friendship. He was comfortable letting things develop in due course, and he never acted like I was a movie star or like he was *with* a movie star. We took it slowly, which allows you the pleasure of discovering, as you go along, what makes a person tick. This was essential, considering that my nomadic life—and my obsession with work—wasn't exactly conducive to a "relationship."

WHEN NEAL AND I arrived in Rome, my next new agent, Guiseppi Perrone, sent me straight to Spain for a western called *The Christmas Kid*. Arriving in Madrid, I ran into my old waterskiing pal from Lake Arrowhead,

En route to Europe with Neal Noorlag.

Jeffrey Hunter. We swapped stories of Watson Webb, with whom we'd both kept in touch. Jeff was there to make a thriller, *The Cup of St. Sebastian*. Over dinner and drinks that evening, we hatched a plan.

"What the hell?" we agreed. "The producers won't know Jeffrey Hunter from Tab Hunter. Let's switch movies!"

And we did. Jeff did the western, I did the thriller. No one was the wiser. Nobody was really paying much attention anyway during the production of *The Cup of St. Sebastian*, including the director, a young American named Richard Rush, who seemed to focus less on the film than on getting laid. To "protect" myself, I rewrote a lot of the screenplay, basically turning it from a lackluster thriller into a lackluster comedy, full of slapstick chases and cases of mistaken identity. When it was released in the United States, *The Cup of St. Sebastian* was retitled *The Fickle Finger of Fate*.

It was about this time that I learned a valuable tax tip: if you were out of the country for eighteen months, you didn't have to pay income tax for the previous year. My accumulating expenses—caring for my mother and the horses, giving whatever I could to Walt's family, and maintaining my shaky investment in the horse farm—were barely covered by my sporadic paychecks. I didn't want the government to take what little I had left over.

Neal was game to continue the European adventure. I loved seeing his subtle reactions to all the new people, places, and things. I enjoyed playing the role of worldy tour guide and helping Neal emerge from his straitlaced shell.

LA VENDETTA È IL MIO PERDONO (*Shotgun* in North America) was a spaghetti western short on meat sauce. We worked long, hard hours at a tiny studio in Rome, and Neal even had a small role, whetting his appetite for acting. Fellini was shooting next door, parading carnival freaks and gypsies through the soundstages all day long.

I became friends with Marina Cicogna, whom I'd met years earlier at Visconti's villa. She was a successful film producer now, who'd learned moviemaking in Hollywood as a protégé of David O. Selznick. She was in preproduction on *I Giovani Tigri*, starring the handsome Austrian actor Helmut Berger. Not to put too fine a point on it, but Berger was a Continental version of Tab Hunter, a young, unschooled actor exploited for his handsome features, still learning his craft as he was thrust into the limelight.

Marina had a breathtakingly beautiful Brazilian girlfriend by the name of

Florinda Bolkan. Over dinner one evening, Marina asked if I'd appear with Florinda in her screen test, to be directed by her good friend . . . Luchino Visconti. I leaped at the chance.

After spending the day shooting a disjointed western, I'd be picked up by Visconti's chauffeur, who'd whisk me to another soundstage across town, where I'd put in a few more hours working with Florinda and the Master. After that, I'd join Florinda, Helmut, and another Brazilian actor, Carlos de Castro, roaring through Rome in a Cadillac convertible that belonged to Carlos's boyfriend, Arndt Krupp, scion of the German industrialist family that had supplied the Nazis all their munitions. Even in Rome, a city as wide open and sultry as an elegant whore, this group could stop traffic, anytime, anywhere.

Europe in the sixties was a heady place, sexy and decadent, which is as good a description as any, I guess, of the brief indulgence Helmut and I shared. I rarely resisted such temptations, even though I was with Neal. I'd developed the ability to compartmentalize the sexual aspect of my character, a trait I shared with a lot of Catholics. I may not have denied myself much, but I could always later deny, at least in my own mind, what I'd done.

Afterward, I'd send a note to Neal's parents, something like: "Found a nice restaurant for Thanksgiving dinner. Also read Psalm 103, as you had suggested. We think of you and speak of you both all the time."

3 1

The Idle Rich

EUROPEAN FILMS EARNED ME a good salary, but since there weren't many of them, life on the Continent was either feast or famine. One day Neal and I would be living like movie stars, but just as quickly it could become a hand-to-mouth existence.

My Rome agent, Guiseppi "Peppino" Perrone, was short, slim, and excitable, a male Carmen Miranda without the fruit on his head. Not only did Peppino make a commission as an agent, he also got kickbacks from actors. He had one dirty hand in everything—a crook, but a charming crook.

Peppino got me the lead in a James Bond ripoff called *International Checkmate,* aka *The Last Chance,* costarring an actual Bond girl, *From Russia with Love*'s Daniela Bianchi. He then landed me a job in Spain, starring in a war film called *Bridge Over Elba.* No one was going to confuse it with the *River Kwai.*

My contract for that one stipulated that I be paid in cash every Monday, but when production fell behind, so did the payment schedule. After two weeks on the cuff, I called Peppino in Rome.

"If I don't have all the money I'm due in my hands by this weekend, I'm taking a walk."

Peppino ranted and raved, which he was especially good at. "I can't just drop everything I'm doing here in Rome for you," he sputtered. I hung up.

The next day, the tiny agent minced into my hotel room in Spain with a suitcase full of cash. I made coffee while we chatted for a few immensely insincere moments. I told him what a great agent he was, how I was sure it was all an oversight, how I knew this would never happen again. We smiled, we hugged, he caught the next plane back to Rome.

I never saw Peppino again and never did another film for that company.

As the holidays approached, Neal got homesick. He always spent Christmas with his family, but this yule season would be spent in Rome, at the top of the Spanish Steps, in the Hotel de la Ville.

Across town, the Piazza Navona was bright and festive, filled with strolling musicians and shepherds from Abruzzi selling their wares. We bought ornaments and Christmas lights and strung them all around the hotel room, trying to fill the place with holiday spirit. We attended Mass at St. Peter's and went to hear Christmas carols at an Anglican church. That's when my own homesickness kicked in—an especially lonely feeling when you don't know where "home" is.

I picked up the telephone and called Terry Marsteller, the closest thing I had to family.

"Get your asses up here," came the familiar shout. "We're spending Christmas together." Terry could always be counted on when the hand-to-mouth phase kicked in.

Serre de la Madone was ablaze when we arrived a few days later. Mr. Baring had flown in from London. He had a full-time driver who lived at the villa, above the garage, but whenever I stayed there I offered to take over those duties. He jokingly offered to buy me a uniform, since he loved the thought of a liveried movie star at the wheel of his Jaguar, chauffeuring him through the Alpes Maritimes.

Neal and I went to midnight Mass in Monte Carlo at the palace cathedral, and the next day, Terry prepared a Mexican Christmas dinner for a few select friends, including the elderly Princess Margrethe of Denmark, who'd just returned from a cleansing at the thermal baths of Montecatini. Terry was an artist when it came to surrounding himself with interesting people from all walks of life, all well mannered, well read, well traveled. For King Michael and Queen Anne of Romania, Terry cooked a sumptuous leg of lamb dinner, after which we all sat around looking at the latest issue of *Playboy*. Earlier that day we'd lunched with the Baron and Baroness de Rothschild.

The New Year, 1968, started badly when Dick called from Hollywood to report that a couple of movie deals had fallen through. The bridge back to Hollywood seemed to be burning, but I pushed those thoughts out of my mind. Instead, I decided that Neal needed to meet Peter Bull, who was now staying at his place on Paxos, a little island in Greece.

Peter was an actor, writer, and all-around eccentric with whom I'd become good friends. He had been in movies since the midthirties, most recently in Stanley Kubrick's *Dr. Strangelove*. He'd also written the definitive book on teddy bears.

Peter would stage impromptu shows for the three boats that arrived daily from Corfu and Gaios. With a broom in one hand, an open parasol in the other, and a pink plastic washbasin on his head, he'd take up position on the cliff overlooking the harbor. A snorkel and mask covering his face, he waved and carried on with great delight. The few tourists that traveled to Lakka thought he was nuts, but the locals loved him.

Then it was on to Ipsos to visit Albert Finney and his zany group of friends. Albert loved Greece—and Peter—and vacationed on the island as often as he could. We referred to his entourage as the Hammock People because all they wanted to do was take turns lying in the hammock, letting the world drift by.

In the blink of an eye, Neal and I were at a party on Capri, overlooking Piccolo Marina, high above the moored yachts of the world's millionnaires. One particular 135-foot beauty caught my eye.

"That's the one I'd like to go aboard," I said to Neal. Overhearing me, Jack Kleiser, the ship's owner, turned around and introduced himself. His family owned Foster-Kleiser Outdoor Advertising, the biggest billboard company in America. Jack invited us to lunch the next afternoon onboard the *San Luis*.

I'd embarked on an unusually rich and possibly dangerous phase of my life—the dessert course that never ends.

WHEN WE RETURNED to Serre de la Madone, Rudolf Nureyev had arrived at his villa in La Turbie, on a hilltop overlooking the Mediterranean. He was taking some R & R from his hectic dance schedule. Some mornings he'd materialize on the quay, his bone white body with blue veins clad only in a silver lamé swimsuit. Rudy looked like a finely chiseled corpse freshly risen from an ancient crypt, and he walked as if the world was far beneath him.

Underneath that haughty demeanor, however, he was utterly guileless. We started playing around together almost daily, which I'm sure piqued the curiosity of even the most jaded Riviera revelers. We traded constant come-ons, which started out as simple teasing but before long took on bona fide heat. Something was in the air.

Summer storms struck unexpectedly in the Alpes Maritimes. During one dinner party a bolt of lightning hit scarily close, sending me diving to the floor—politeness be damned. I figured Rudy, vampirelike, would be in his element. The next day on the beach I told him, "I had visions of you leaping bare-assed through the trees in the midst of it all."

"Oh, no, Tab." He laughed. "I was so scared I ran and jumped into bed with my maid." So much for my visions.

It seemed inevitable that something was going to happen between Rudy and me, but then—just like that—he vanished back into the ballet circuit. But not before offering the use of his home in England, should I find myself back there, either for work or riding.

Dick Clayton, still trying desperately to line something up for me, put me in touch with the British theatrical agents Fraser and Dunlop Ltd. John Fraser was a good agent, and to call him flamboyant would be a gross understatement. He invited me to come to England, and from our first meeting, it became his mission to make me "more hip, more with it." He had me decked out in the latest Carnaby Street fashions until I looked like the original Austin Powers. Nothing came of it except some incredibly embarrassing photographs.

While in London, Neal and I stayed at 6 Fife Road in Richmond Park—Nureyev's exquisitely stylish home. Rudy would be on the road during our stay, but he ended up returning home a day early from his travels. Neal was out getting in some last-minute shopping before our return to Rome the next day. Timing is everything, and this turned out to be the right time for Rudy and me to drop the coy routine and culminate our long-running flirtation.

I never mentioned it to Neal, but I didn't feel guilty, either. I'd made it clear that I needed to maintain my freedom, that I could be with someone only if I didn't feel smothered. Neal knew that it took two to tango—and I loved to dance.

WITH NO WORK in England, Neal and I flew back to the Côte d'Azur. We spent days lounging around verandas or at luncheons or on yachts. We attended galas in Monte Carlo and elegant parties at magnificent villas up and down the Riviera. Artists, aristocrats, models, tycoons, trust-fund babies, genuine kings and queens—they all swirled around Terry at Serre de le Madone.

The bunch of us would meet daily on a private terrace overlooking the sea at the old Monte Carlo Beach Hotel. We'd roast in the sun and swim and fill ourselves with caviar and champagne. Once a week, Terry's group of international beauties, male and female, would congregate at the open air cinema to watch *Bonnie and Clyde, Barbarella,* or *Candy.*

Terry Southern's send-up of *Candide* had been shot in Rome, and Neal had a small role in it. He'd been bitten by the acting bug after getting that bit part in *Bridge Over Elba*. *Candy*'s director actually used Neal to help audition all the girls vying for the title role. Neal couldn't resist writing to his dad about his big movie break—he had a scene with Richard Burton in the film—but he cringed when his father wrote back that he'd seen the film at Radio City Music Hall and had to sit through "sex garbage" in order to see his son on the big screen.

In the midst of this endless summer, I came across an item in the *International Herald-Tribune:* LAURENCE HARVEY MARRIES WIDOW OF HOLLYWOOD MOGUL. I wished Joan well and sincerely hoped she'd be happy.

At a gala thrown by the owners of the *Daily Mail*, we met Princess Grace and Prince Rainier. As we were introduced, I knocked over a bottle of champagne, spilling it on the princess. She couldn't have been nicer, but all she wanted to talk about was Hollywood, which by then was the furthest thing from my mind. Or so I told myself.

Terry, Neal, and I all danced with the princess, after which she excused herself to use the loo. The lock on the door was broken, so she asked the three of us to stand guard while she ascended the throne.

A beauty by the name of Odette Gilbert was Princess Grace's personal secretary. She set heads spinning whenever we danced the night away at a local disco. Neal was particularly fond of Odette, as they were both from Washington State. They'd dance and talk deep into the night, sharing stories of growing up in Oak Harbor and Walla Walla. She confided to Neal that she was terribly homesick. The young shah of Iran was relentlessly pursuing Odette, lavishing her with jewels, trying to woo her into becoming his mistress. Neal told her to return to Spokane and marry her childhood sweetheart—which is exactly what she ended up doing. That was impressive to me, because once people are immersed in the glittering jet-set lifestyle, not many can give it up. I was starting to wonder if I could.

Terry's pals King Michael and Queen Anne offered to rent Neal and me a charming guesthouse nestled beside theirs on a glorious Riviera hillside. It would be the perfect place to work on the screenplay I'd decided to write, a comedy called *The Idle Rich*. The central character would be based on my dear friend Peter Bull. I'd draw on his marvelous sense of humor and his wide array of eccentric friends to spin a little piece of fluff.

The temptation to abandon the United States forever was surprisingly strong. Neal and I had long, soul-searching discussions about whether we belonged here. He'd grown restless and was eager to go back home, to reclaim the career he'd short-circuited by following me to Europe. Deep inside I knew that writing a script was only a ruse, something to distract me from my dimming prospects as a performer.

I passed on the king and queen's offer and made plans to return home. My love affair with the south of France was over. Playing the role of a sun-bronzed, waterskiing jet-setter was fun, but the fit just wasn't right.

I was an actor. That's what fulfilled me. I wanted work, any way I could get it—in my *own* voice, not dubbed in Italian.

La dolce vita—(left to right) Odette Gilbert, Neal, me, Katya Losser, and my old friend Terry Marsteller.

3 2

Panhandling

A COUPLE OF YEARS EARLIER, Bette Davis, past her prime, had taken out an ad in the trades, looking for work. If she had done it, I figured it had to be a good idea.

I bought space in *Variety* and the *Hollywood Reporter*, full-page head shots of the "new me," mature and determined, under the heading "One Serious Actor." It listed my credits—including a spurious Emmy nomination—and ended with the understated tagline "Any Suggestions?"

By the calendar, I'd only been away from Hollywood three years. But "industry" years, like dog years, are a whole other way of marking time. Thirty-six months out of circulation? I might as well have been a relic from the silent era.

It wasn't only acting jobs I was after; I needed a new agent. Dick Clayton, who by the end of the 1960s had built up a select talent roster at Famous Artists, had suffered a heart attack. Once recovered, he left FAA to become a personal manager, trimming his client list but assuming more responsibility for the careers of his best prospects: Jane Fonda, Burt Reynolds, Angie Dickinson, Jan-Michael Vincent, and many others.

Dick was a major player, and he genuinely regretted that there was no longer a place for me in his stable. I couldn't hold it against him, since he was more responsible than anyone for my having a career in the first place.

As I was interviewing, and dismissing, a sorry handful of glib hustlers spouting lines like "It's gonna happen for you, baby!" I got another nasty slap in the face from the so-called fourth estate: a rotten little tabloid, *The National Tattler*, reprinted my *Variety* ad but pasted over it the caption "Has Been No. 1."

At least I wasn't singled out—I shared the ridicule with my showbiz doppelgänger: "Troy and Tab Panhandling in Hollywood," shouted the article's headline. "Give Us a Job, Castoffs Plead," the kicker said. Troy Donahue's picture carried the tag "Has Been No. 2."

> Just six weeks ago Troy, now 33, appeared on the Johnny Carson Show. It was like seeing a man who has so completely dropped from public view that one would think him dead!
>
> Troy's voice was breaking as he revealed that he hadn't had a movie or TV offer in more than two years, other than bit parts.
>
> Almost at the same time, Tab Hunter was running a pathetic ad in *Daily Variety* —pathetic because only a half-dozen years ago it would have been unthinkable for him to panhandle in print . . .
> Then there was the final line: "Any suggestions?" The more cynical may be tempted to answer: "Yeah, get lost."

This was just a sample of the sarcasm and mockery slung my way. In this culture, the only thing the media and public enjoy more than manufacturing celebrities is ripping them apart.

Fortunately, a five-man start-up agency called November Ninth Management showed enthusiasm for reviving my career, especially two young go-getters, Joel Stevens and Darryl Marshak. They obviously didn't see me as over-the-hill: when I flew in to meet them, they'd rented me a Trans Am, car of choice for young macho studs. I got a laugh out of that.

I set up base in Beverly Hills in one of the twenty-eight homes my jet-setting pal Jack Kleiser had owned. He and his companion, Brad Fuller, were still off sailing the *San Luis* around the Greek islands. He lent Neal and me his place indefinitely while we house-hunted. Eventually we found a small place out in Burbank, up against the hills of Griffith Park, perfect for legging up the show horses.

On my own, I pursued director John Schlesinger, trying to convince him that I'd be perfect—*perfect!*—for the role of Joe Buck in *Midnight Cowboy*. Schlesinger agreed—if only I were ten years younger. To add insult to injury, Jon Voight, who ended up with the career-making part, told an interviewer: "They'll never make a Tab Hunter out of me."

Joel and Darryl worked diligently to resuscitate my dying career, which wasn't easy. *Hacksaw*, a TV movie I did in early 1970 for *The Wonderful World of Disney*, only came about because the producer, Larry Lansburgh, and his wife, Liz, were horse friends of mine from way back. Joel Stevens managed to get me another TV movie, *San Francisco International,* in which I played a heavy opposite Van Johnson and David Hartman.

Although I got good reviews, it was hard to be taken seriously by producers and casting agents when the only feature write-ups I'd get were titled "Whatever Happened to Tab Hunter?" or "Remembering Tab Hunter." Some enterprising guy even came out with a button: "What's a Tab Hunter?"

IN THE SPRING of 1971, I attended a dedication ceremony at the naval air station in Alameda, California, Admiral Elmo R. Zumwalt, U.S. Navy, presiding. It was to officially open a new seventy-five-unit building that offered temporary lodging for naval personnel. It was christened the Gelien Navy Lodge in honor of my brother.

Walt had flown over twenty missions with the Marines in Vietnam and had been decorated with the Air Medal, the Purple Heart, the Good Conduct Medal, three Bronze Stars, and the Gallantry Cross with Palm.

Pat and all the children were there, standing tall and proud throughout the ceremony. It was especially moving when Admiral Zumwalt presented my mother with the folded American flag. If I was expecting her to shed a tear, I'd have kept waiting till hell froze over.

If anything, my mother had become even more stoic following Walt's death, to the point of seeming disconnected from her own life. There was virtually nothing left of the mother I knew growing up. She was incapable of displaying any emotion other than a vague condescension. "Wretched creatures" is how she referred to vast segments of humanity. By this time, unbelievable as it seemed, my mother had assumed responsibility for the care of her own mother, Oma. The two of them lived together in Pacific Grove, just south of Monterey, in an apartment I maintained.

I dutifully drove up to visit them as often as I could—my eternal optimism (or naïveté) making me believe that maybe this time we'd *enjoy* each other's company. I wouldn't be with her five minutes before she'd start in, picking away at me, getting under my skin.

After one particularly unpleasant visit, I wrote "Gertrude Gelien" on a piece of paper and ceremoniously burned it, like a voodoo ritual.

"You're dead to me," I declared.

I continued paying the bills, of course. A promise is a promise, after all.

MY FRIEND JOHN FOREMAN offered me a featured role in *The Life and Times of Judge Roy Bean,* a movie he was producing that represented the intersection of old and new Hollywood. The script was by John Milius, a brash young turk determined to make a mark in the business. It was directed by the legendary John Huston, who forty years earlier had been a brash young turk himself. Huston had left a *major* mark on Hollywood history, but now, like so many of the old guard, he was working picture-to-picture, wondering if each assignment might be the last.

Tony Perkins was also cast, but our paths crossed only briefly on the Tucson location. We hadn't seen each other in almost ten years. Tony's life, like mine, had taken many turns in the interim. Unlike me, he'd found that elusive defining role. The downside of Tony's memorable performance as Norman Bates in *Psycho* was that it typecast him forever. The public never again enjoyed his charm and vulnerability without the suspicion that something very wrong lurked beneath the surface.

What I didn't know at the time of our brief reunion was that Tony's long-running battle with his personal demons had reached a breaking point. He was ending a long relationship with dancer Grover Dale and had started therapy with Mildred Newman, author of a best-selling book called *How to Be Your Own Best Friend,* which had become the bible for him. Newman convinced Tony that his personal problems stemmed in large measure from his being gay, and she prescribed a course of action—including electroshock therapy—to turn him straight. Part of his "recovery" had included an affair with Victoria Principal, the young ingenue in *Roy Bean*.

Neal Noorlag was also in *The Life and Times of Judge Roy Bean,* a bit of casting I had nothing to do with. We weren't even in Tucson at the same time. John Foreman liked Neal and offered him a bit part in a scene with Ava Gardner, who portrayed Lilly Langtry. By this time Neal had pretty much given up the notion of becoming an actor, and the scene with Ava was his movie swan song.

Our relationship had pretty much waned by this time, as well. Neal lived with me in Burbank about a year too long. We both knew it. He'd matured considerably in the seven years we'd been together, becoming a self-sufficient and gregarious guy who didn't need to live in my shadow, or put up with my constant hunt for work. Thanks to his upbringing, which I envied tremendously, Neal was destined to live a much more grounded life than me.

Not long after he returned from Arizona, Neal made the decision to move out, which I encouraged. He needed his own life, his own identity. He wanted to carry his own weight, which I respected. Dick Clayton, who had great insight into the unsettled lives of actors, always preached about ending relationships by "releasing with love." And that's how it was with me and Neal.

Truthfully, it wasn't hard. My life had been so unsettled and rootless from its earliest days, I easily accepted that nothing was permanent and that no relationship should be expected to last.

THE BEST PROJECT November Ninth Management sent my way was a script called *A Kiss from Eddie*, by a twenty-six-year-old writer-director named Curtis Hanson. It was a character study of a guy compelled by a childhood trauma to kill women—sort of a seventies spin on *Psycho*. Once in production, the title was changed to *Sweet Kill*. There was no budget to speak of, but the role was challenging, and Curtis really knew what he was doing. The producer, Tamara Asseyev, was smart and assertive, and my costar, Nadyne Turney, was a wonderfully accomplished member of the Actors Studio. It was also a totally new look for Tab Hunter: a jeans-wearing Venice Beach bohemian, with longer, unkempt hair and something nervous and unbalanced in the eyes.

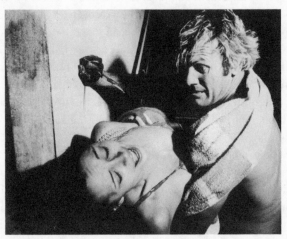

No longer the boy next door, playing a psycho killer in Curtis Hanson's first film, Sweet Kill.

It was an interesting, somber little film, distributed by Roger Corman, who'd established a reputation for kick-starting the careers of many talented people: Jack Nicholson, Peter Bogdanovich, Francis Ford Coppola, and Martin Scorsese among them. Unfortunately, Corman felt the movie had to be spiced up to make money, so Curtis was obliged to shoot nude inserts of the actresses and splash some more blood around. Corman then changed the title to *The Arousers* and created a poster showing half-naked women in suggestive poses under the caption, "What's your arousal quotient? Take the sexual stimulation test and see! Free at this theater!" I felt embarrassed for Curtis and Tamara. I didn't need to, of course. Tamara went on to produce the Oscar-winning *Norma Rae,* and Curtis would become one of the top directors in Hollywood.

I stopped by Venetia Stevenson's garage apartment one day to pick her up for dinner. We were heading out to the Del Mar Horse Show in the morning. The door was answered by a young man I'd never seen before.

What a cute little ass, I thought, watching him go up the stairs.

His name was John Donalson, and he joined Venetia and me for dinner that night. I was surprised to learn that he'd lived in New York and run with Andy Warhol's crowd, where he was known as John Boy. Now a couple of years older and a little wiser, he seemed to have his head screwed on straight. After dinner I drove him home, to a tiny garage apartment behind a Hollywood bungalow. He'd pruned his life back to an almost-monastic existence, surrounded only with his library of books, a cat, and a little garden he loved to maintain.

John was ecstatic when I called later that week to invite him to the theater. We started spending more time together, and before long, he moved into my place in Burbank, happily overseeing the house, the horses, and the dogs. I wasn't entirely sure if I was in another relationship or if I'd hired a personal assistant.

John didn't complain; he was a homebody and I was giving him a nest to tend. But I'm a perfectionist, and everything had to run according to my agenda and my schedule. I must have been a major pain in the ass with all that uptight energy I had, always hustling to find work, to pay all the bills I'd accumulated. What I really wanted was to chuck the whole rat race and move to Virginia's horse country, just like Danny Wills had suggested almost twenty years earlier. John said he was ready to go whenever I was.

Instead I opted for a stopgap measure, selling the Burbank house and moving to the El Capitan Ranch, north of Santa Barbara. The horse facilities were excellent, but the living space was tight for John and me and his cat, my whippet, Rat, her nine pups, and the endless stream of mice that came with the place.

On Labor Day weekend in 1972, I went to a party at 1000 North Crescent, a gathering of industry players assembled by Joan Harvey. It took a little getting used to, calling her Joan Harvey—even though she'd emblazoned her new name on everything, from towels and soap in the bathrooms to matchbooks in the ashtrays to the linens in the guest rooms to the phone by her bed (did she need to be reminded when she woke up?). Her insistence at using her husband's name proved how deeply Joan took her calling as a wife.

What made it bittersweet was that Larry wasn't around much anymore. Joan kept up a brave facade, but rumors were rampant: While in England a couple of years earlier, Larry had fallen in love with another woman, Pauline Stone, and she'd had his baby. Worse than that, he was now taking secret trips to Mexico, the suspicion being that he was taking treatments for inoperable cancer.

Joan, with the best of intentions, had staged the Labor Day entertainment for my benefit. Postcocktails, she herded everyone into her private screening room—with the deep, overstuffed club chairs—for a preview of *The Arousers*, the final Corman-sanctioned title of Curtis Hanson's movie. Joan's efforts to boost my career made me incredibly uncomfortable. I didn't want people thinking our friendship was based on what she could do for me.

3 3

Joanie Pony

JOAN AND I WERE seeing each other almost every day. She presented herself to the world as Mrs. Laurence Harvey, but she rarely spoke of him. More than ever, she needed an escape from the castle she'd built for herself; she needed an alternative to always having to be Queen Joan. Luckily, she had the ability to fit in anywhere if she chose to make the effort.

We were leaving a party at Jules Stein's home one night when the parking attendant recognized her. "Evening, Mrs. Harvey," he said, then barked to another valet: "Move that Rolls! Get the Bentley out of the way! Get Mr. Hunter's El Camino up here!"

Pieces of hay were always blowing around the bed of my truck, and the floor mats were always muddy. Joan consented to stepping out of my dirt-encrusted heap at glittery events, looking like a million bucks.

Our friendship took a significant turn, thanks to Katie Lindsay. She called from Illinois, all excited about a fantastic horse that belonged to our friend Carol Plass. She'd been jumped off Collector's Item one too many times and had decided to sell him. I immediately hopped a flight to Chicago, arrived in the middle of the night, tried the horse, bought him on the spot, and flew home.

Happy (his nonshow name) was everything Katie had said and more. At his first jumping competition, a number of top trainers, including Jimmy Williams and Barbara Oakford, fell over each other trying to buy him from me.

But I thought he'd be perfect for Joan. "You can have him for what I paid," I told her, "*if* you keep him with me—and I want first right of refusal if you ever decide to sell him." She agreed.

Happy put Joan on the horse-show circuit, and she enjoyed the radical diversion from her opulent lifestyle. Big money was still required to get in the game, of course, but among horse people you didn't find the kind of phonies who filled Hollywood parties. My relationship with Joan flourished in this world, and I loved presenting her with all the ribbons and trophies Collector's Item won with me in the saddle. She loved being around the horses and pretty soon picked up a new nickname, Joanie Pony.

She started spending more time in Santa Barbara, often as a houseguest of my friends Bill Wilcox and Jerry Porsche, who owned Sea Meadows Antiques in Gearhart, Oregon, where I lived while at the Seaside Stock Farm.

Bill owned the old Morton Salt mansion in Montecito, a palatial estate straight out of *Architectural Digest*. We'd picnic by their private man-made lake, from which a geyser shot sixty feet into the air against the majestic mountain backdrop. Jerry would spread out a huge Oriental rug and we'd feast on the potluck provisions we'd all brought. Everyone had whippets, which I'd given them from Rat's litters. Our dogs had the run of the place. Basking in the good life at Bill and Jerry's was as close as I got to recapturing what I'd left behind in the south of France.

Regular guests included Joan's loyal secretary and confidante, Marge Barzey, the backbone of Joan's household from her earliest days with Harry Cohn; horse trainer and riding competitor J. J. Smith; John Huston; and Colonel and Liz Tippett, who ran Llangollen Farms West and East, a huge horse-breeding operation in California and Virginia.

At Liz Tippett's beach house in Del Mar, Joan Harvey proudly wears a ribbon won by Happy.

Neal Noorlag often joined us, too. Now a videotape editor for one of the major networks, he attended church regularly, played the organ for the choir, and had bought his first home in Pasadena. Joan had a real fondness for Neal.

The same couldn't be said for John Donalson, who was rarely invited to the Gathering of the Whippets. Joan tolerated John—like the time the three of us went to see his idol, Joni Mitchell, in concert—but she had little use for him. John may simply have rubbed her the wrong way, but more likely—with Larry now a phantom in her life—Joan didn't like anything, or anyone, coming between us.

The time seemed right for Joan to get out of Beverly Hills. She'd lived at 1000 North Crescent Drive since the 1940s, when Harry Cohn bought it for her as a wedding present. I encouraged her to move up the coast permanently. For months I diligently scouted properties, and I finally found the perfect place: a beautiful, unbastardized George Washington Smith home on nine acres in Montecito, with an asking price of $190,000. It was located right across from Lotusland, the estate owned by opera diva Madame Ganna Walska, who created a world-famous botanical garden on the grounds.

I raced into Beverly Hills to tell Joan about it and found her holding court with the usual ass-kissing assortment of jesters and hangers-on, mostly the fawning fags who clung to her as a way of keeping their love of old Hollywood alive. They badgered me with snotty questions while Joan finished her bridge game. Finally, Joan emerged from her clique, and I eagerly explained about the treasure I'd uncovered in Montecito.

"Oh, Tab, it's all so boring," Joan sighed, as if giving a performance to impress her court. The haughty queen had reascended her throne. Humiliating me in front of her entourage was one thing, but discounting the work I'd done on her behalf didn't set well.

"Well, Joan, if you think it's *all* so boring, you can take all this"—my gesture encompassed every square inch of her castle—"and shove it up your ass."

AFTER THAT, I FLEW straight to Alaska for a terrible film called *Timber Tramps*. The scenery was spectacular, the fishing excellent, the movie abysmal. Joseph Cotten, Rosie Grier, and Cesar Romero were trapped in it with me. Tay Garnett, maker of memorable Golden Age classics like *Trade Winds, Bataan,* and *The Postman Always Rings Twice,* was now scraping the bottom of the for-hire barrel, working for a fat little starstruck lumberjack who wrote, produced, and financed this piece of junk himself. If Garnett was there, he must have blended into the scenery, because I have no recollection of working for him.

While I was away, Mr. and Mrs. Laurence Harvey were divorced.

For most of their time together, Larry was great for Joan. He made her happy and helped her escape the Widow Cohn persona. She certainly was good to him, having no qualms about keeping him in the style to which he'd become accustomed. Sadly, once they'd tied the knot, things went downhill fast. Joan's need to *keep* a husband, like the crown jewel in her personal kingdom, obviously clashed with Larry's need to live his own life, his own way. They probably should have just stayed friends.

When I returned to Santa Barbara, Joan was ready to patch things up. Not only did she buy the George Washington Smith house, but she planned to remodel it, as well as a fabulous old barn and separate guesthouse on the property—which she offered to me for my next home. We never got to the part about whether or not John would live there with me, since I declined the offer as politely as possible.

For better or worse, I was still Gertrude Gelien's son, determined to live as a "self-sufficient machine," no strings attached to any place or anyone.

TAB HUNTER'S IN LOVE WITH JOAN COHN, LAURENCE HARVEY'S EX-WIFE

It was only a matter of time before the gossip magazines got ahold of us. Joan took the offensive, giving straight talk to the *National Enquirer*: "Tab and I had been friends for years before I married Larry," she told the reporter. "But after our wedding . . . Larry cut Tab out of my life. He was extremely jealous . . . But as soon as I split with Larry, Tab and I started going out again . . . Personally, I hope our relationship continues for a long, long time."

I told the press the God's honest truth: "She is a marvelous, wonderful lady and I dig being with her," I said. "We're just enjoying life and each other. No problems. No hang-ups."

Unfortunately, other rags started embellishing: TAB HUNTER AFTER BRIDE, 58, BUT WANTS MALE FRIEND ALONG read the headline of one piece. I had no intention of marrying Joan, but the columnists wouldn't leave it alone, insinuating that with Larry out of the picture I was angling for Joan's millions.

There was about as much truth to that as there was to another headline that appeared around the same time: TAB HUNTER HOSPITALIZED AFTER FREAK-ING OUT ON LSD. "Tab Hunter is reported recovering in a Chicago hospital after a mind-shattering experience with LSD," read the item. "Friends say Tab thought he'd turned into a woman and went stark raving mad."

Who makes up this crap?

JOAN STAYED WITH Bill Wilcox and Jerry Porsche on weekends while the new palace was being readied. She could have stayed in any one of their spacious guest rooms, but Joan loved the grand powder room, which they'd filled with antiques, including a gorgeous French daybed. She referred to it as "her womb." After dinner and drinks, we'd retire there, talking away the night like we had in her kitchen, ten years earlier. Some mornings I'd bring her fresh orange juice and climb into bed to talk about what we'd been up to lately. It was beautifully uncomplicated.

It was in the "womb" that Joan proposed. I was shocked. Not because I was gay—Joan knew it, even if we never addressed the fact head-on. I was more surprised by how desperately Joan needed to be a man's wife and how she needed to be absolutely in control while enacting the role of dedicated spouse.

Hadn't she learned anything from the last three years with Larry? Or like me, maybe Joan simply pushed out of her mind the things she didn't want to face.

I loved Joan as much as I did anyone in my life—but I had no intention of marrying her. Why spoil a perfectly good relationship?

Not long after that, Joan took Happy out of training and moved him over to her Montecito property. That was a blow. Happy was one of the best horses I'd ever ridden, but Joan owned him, so she could do what she wanted. It came as no surprise to me when I heard that one of Harry Cohn Jr.'s spaced-out girlfriends was found one night galloping bareback on Happy down posh East Valley Road, naked under a flowing black cape. I was pissed off.

I told Joan that if she didn't know how to properly care for a horse of that caliber, I'd buy him back. Her response was to unload Happy for one dollar, to one of my main competitors on the show circuit.

All those dinner-theater offers back east suddenly looked good, especially since Liz Tippett had issued me a standing offer to rent one of the houses on Llangollen Farm in Upperville, Virginia.

John and I had long discussed our mutual desire to live on a farm, far from prying eyes. It didn't take us long to talk each other into it. We didn't have a lot, besides the animals. John managed the entire move himself while I went back on the road.

It was now 1973. I was forty-two years old and starting to worry that my earning days were numbered. A voice kept telling me, *Tab, you've been a good ol' wagon, but you done broke down.* I had to prove that voice wrong, even if it meant becoming a full-blown workaholic.

3 4

Locomotion

Liz Tippett rented us a wonderful old tenant house, with stalls for the horses at a nearby barn. John moved out ahead to get the place in shape. He said the house was a real pigsty, but by the time I arrived, he'd transformed it into a warm and inviting home. He'd made wonderful friends, whom he was eager to introduce me to. We shared fantastic days of riding, hunting, and showing the horses on the circuit. I relished it all—but those days turned out to be few and far between.

My life in the seventies was like being on a runaway train. Endless dinner-theater engagements, television guest shots—I never turned down a thing. I careered around the United States crazily, doggedly performing, onstage and off, like I was still twenty years old. I ended up spending barely any time at the dream farm all this hard work was paying for.

Ben Pierson, my theatrical agent, was crucial to the solvency of Tab Hunter. He was a genius at finding work in places I'd never have known existed, were it not for productions of *Bye Bye Birdie, Under the Yum Yum Tree, The Tender Trap, Here Lies Jeremy Troy,* and other staples of summer stock and dinner theater.

The audiences for these shows were married middle-aged women with grumpy husbands in tow, hoping to relive their youth by seeing their onetime matinee idol in person. The fame I'd achieved thanks to the old Hollywood system was what now made a lucrative career in dinner theater possible. Such was the lasting allure of being a movie star—the closest thing to royalty in this country. Celebrity, nostalgia, a craving for lost innocence—all of that is what brought people to these shows and kept me fiscally afloat.

A return to Broadway was a longshot, but Michael Hartig, my New York agent (I had lots of agents beating the bushes), arranged an audition for me to replace Ken Howard, who was leaving the hit show *Seesaw* to do a TV series. I was introduced to the director and choreographer Michael Bennett, darling of New York theater thanks to *A Chorus Line.* He'd written the book for *Seesaw,* as well as being its director and choreographer. His assistant was Grover Dale, Tony's former companion. Straightaway, Bennett asked me if I could dance.

"Bob Fosse made it look like I could in *Damn Yankees,"* I said, trying to make light of it. "But then, Bobby was a genius."

I guess it didn't come out right, because Bennett, Cy Coleman, the show's composer, and a whole gaggle of co-producers sat as rigid as cardboard cutouts in the dark theater. I could feel their eyes on me, staring down their snooty Broadway noses at the washed-up Hollywood star.

Bennett then snapped off some flashy steps, which he expected me to repeat. I failed miserably. It was bad enough, without attitude being flung my way, and the jaded faces out there sneering.

It was the worst audition I ever endured. In my book, Michael Bennett was no Bob Fosse.

INSTEAD, IT WAS *Bye Bye Birdie* again, February through March '74, Warwick, Rhode Island, the Château de Ville dinner-theater chain.

One actress in the company was a persistent pain in the ass, always telling me what to do and how to do it. I didn't need some other actor giving me direction. During one rehearsal, I finally reached my limit. I grabbed her by the arm, led her outside, and pointed to my name up on the marquee.

"When it says STELLA LONGO IN *BYE BYE BIRDIE,"* I snapped, "we'll do it your way."

We traveled all over the South that spring, and by mid-June I was back working for Château de Ville, in Cohasset, outside of Boston. This time "Tab Hunter" wasn't on the marquee. Neither was the name of the show. Instead, it read SPECIAL TONITE: LOBSTER $9.95.

"What's going on?" I asked the manager. "Fugedaboudit," he said. "You just do your play thing. We got a hot load of lobster that's gotta be dumped."

They put me up in a tiny apartment perched over the water, across the inlet from a Catholic retreat. Nuns in black habits sat on a big rock, dangling their tootsies in the water while reading their prayer books. They made me smile.

When the curtain came down, the cast would often head into Boston's North End, to a restaurant called Felicia's, where the owner would cook up a storm and regale us with stories of Bob Hope flying her out to the coast to cater his parties. Hollywood was everybody's big-ticket destination.

I'd still fly out to the coast every so often, whenever Joel Stevens got me a couple of days' work guesting on a TV series: *Ghost Story, The Six Million Dollar Man, Ellery Queen, McMillan and Wife, The Love Boat*. It was all a sorry substitute and didn't really feel much like acting. *Stand here. Move there. Say this. Turn that way. Say it faster*. A bunch of traffic-cop directors.

It wasn't like we were producing anything of substance; it was more like we were grinding out sausages.

I had become aware of the three stages of stardom. First is "Get me Tab Hunter," followed by, "Get me a Tab Hunter type," followed by, "Who the hell is Tab Hunter?"

REYNOLDSBURG, OHIO, early 1975: *Here Lies Jeremy Troy*. A blue-ribbon cast turned a mediocre play into a rollicking evening. I looked forward to every performance. How ironic: I finally felt that I could walk onto any stage, any night, any town, and give an honest, fearless, and affecting performance — but the chance to prove it, on the grand scale I'd once had, had passed me by.

The only film offer that year was from an unexpected source: Andy Warhol sent me a script, *Bad*, explaining that he wanted me to costar with one of his "superstars," Geri Miller, the groupie girl with the silicone tits. It didn't pan out.

To keep myself occupied, I began writing a script of my own, a lighthearted western called *The Reverend and Rosie*. I'd noodle around with it during the day, before shows, or late at night if I couldn't sleep.

Millburn, New Jersey, early 1976: *6 RMS RIV VU*, at the Papermill Playhouse, with Monica Moran and Christine Baranski. Then on to Charlotte, North Carolina. Closing there, I returned to Virginia — for one night — then headed straight to Maryland for more *Jeremy Troy*. We jumped all over the map that spring and summer and finally closed in Austin.

"Tab Hunter — son of a bitch!" a big Texan bellowed after our last show, slapping me on the back. "I always thought you was a real asshole, but you done real good!"

On matinee days, which I affectionately referred to as "double-barreled ballbreakers," the audience was a sea of blue hair. One afternoon between performances, John called from Virginia, practically in tears. Things between him and Big Liz had taken a turn for the worse. They had a huge argument over a fence in a pasture or some equally stupid thing, and she wanted him off Llangollen Farm. I knew Liz—she'd throw John right out on the highway and not think about it twice.

I tried to play peacemaker long-distance, to no avail. Instead, I made arrangements for us to move as soon as I returned from bouncing around the country.

Back "home," at a party of Virginia horse folk, I happened to strike up a conversation with Sydney Anne Willson, who invited me to hunt over in Clarke County at her farm, Bellfield, 135 idyllic acres overlooking the Shenandoah River. It had a charming stone home, barn, and tenant house. Sydney Anne and her husband, George, lived in Maryland and kept Bellfield as a second farm. Coincidentally, twenty years earlier, Danny Wills owned the adjoining property, and he'd wanted me to buy Bellfield back then. I should have listened.

We had an excellent day out with the Blue Ridge Hunt, and by evening, even before the horses had been bedded down, I knew Bellfield would be my next home.

John and I became good friends with Betty Meade Stuart, who lived down the road a piece in White Post, which is, literally, a white post in the middle of the road, erected by Lord Fairfax back when anything beyond it was Indian territory. Betty wasn't born with a silver spoon in her mouth, even though her ancestors went way back in that part of Virginia. She was an eccentric, as far from the glitterati as a person could get, a terrific, hardheaded broad without a mean bone in her body.

Journalist Sally Quinn came to do a story on me for the *Washington Post*. She brought a video crew, since she was also working for a TV show on one of the networks. Sally was one of the few media people I genuinely liked and respected. She documented my life for what it was: subsistence on a working farm, with a live-in male "assistant." Only the dullest tool in the shed could not have figured out what was going on. It was interesting to realize that after everything I'd been through, the years of hiding the truth and playing it straight—for what?—I didn't pretend anything with Sally. She presented the facts respectfully, without being patronizing or judgmental. Others in the media could learn a few things from her.

• • •

MILWAUKEE, WISCONSIN, summer 1976: *Bells Are Ringing*
Melody Top Theater with Rita Moreno. I'd seen *Bells* on Broadway, starring
Judy Holliday, and always wanted to do it. Rita and I never got close, but we
had great chemistry onstage.

Next, Cincinnati, where I bought a horse off the track. I knew he had problems, but he had a good eye, and there was something about him I liked. Since
we were in Ohio, I named him Holy Toledo. John came over and hauled him
back to the farm while I went on to Albuquerque for another run of *Here Lies
Jeremy Troy*. John had become a pretty good rider by now, and he did well on
the new horse.

How about that? There was John Donalson, living the life of a gentleman
farmer—by himself—while I was ricocheting all over America, working at
least forty-five weeks out of the year to pay for it. He had the life I'd always
wanted.

SALT LAKE CITY, December '76: More *Jeremy Troy*, at the Tiffany
Dinner Theatre.

Evenings were spent on the boards, and so were the days—on skis. I became obsessed with skiing. I struck a deal with Barbara Wicks, a local writer
for *Ski* magazine, who also owned horses. "Help me with my skiing," I said,
"and I'll help you with your horses." It was a great trade-off. I'd be on the
mountain as soon as the lifts opened, ski all morning, work with Barbara's
horses all afternoon, then rush to the theater a half hour before curtain. It was
hectic as hell.

We closed February 5, and I went straight to Albuquerque to give a riding
clinic, dashed to Aspen for more skiing, then flew to Los Angeles to see about
some television work.

I had a meeting with my friend Howard Koch at Paramount to pitch *The
Reverend and Rosie* as a feature, but it went nowhere. Whenever I saw Howard,
he'd say: "Tab, you oughta write a book."

"I don't have the guts," I replied.

The trip west was a waste of a plane ticket. I returned to Bellfield for a couple of weeks, then was off to Texas for another run of *Jeremy Troy*. We played
and stayed at the Theatre, a massive Texas-size aluminum-sided building right
off the highway, smack-dab between Midland and Odessa. There was nothing else for miles around. I got the "star's quarters," at the top of a grand stair-
case overhanging the lobby.

One of the hundreds of performances of Here Lies Jeremy Troy, here with costar Ann Willis.

The apartment was a cavernous space, decorated by the local furniture store. It had no windows, which drove me nuts. I went straight to the hardware store, bought an aluminum window frame, nailed it over my bed, and put a poster in it of grazing cows. Years later, on a return visit, I noticed they'd installed the window frame, providing an endless view of tumbleweed and sand. Bleak, but better than a bare wall.

Some nights after a show, my fellow actors Mort Sertner, Nick Malekos, and I would venture into Odessa's only gay bar. A few butch cowgirls and a few not-so-butch cowboys loitered in the dim blue light, shooting pool, drinking longnecks, dancing to the jukebox. I spotted a cute little cowboy across the room and asked if he wanted to dance. "Gordon" said his wife and kids were visiting family in San Angelo. Under a mirrored ball that threw refracted light around the room, we slow-danced to "Misty Blue."

I was still circumspect about going out in public. The bar scene wasn't a part of my routine. But by 1977, even an old-schooler like me could tell that things had changed considerably since the fifties.

I barreled through America as a dinner-theater pioneer, working constantly and making a damned good living. *Jeremy Troy* rolled on, like one of those montages in an old Hollywood film, the train racing through the night while the names of cities flash past . . . Pittsburgh . . . Louisville . . . Charlotte . . . Little Rock . . . Dallas . . . Jacksonville . . . Albuquerque . . . Sacramento . . .

This train didn't have any brakes. Not that I wanted it to stop. When you're afraid you might not get another job, you'll agree to anything . . .

• • •

HEALTH TALK WAS the brainchild of Dr. Lawrence E. Lamb. He'd seen an item in the newspaper about me and wondered if I was hard up enough to cohost a TV show that "provided a broad spectrum of health and medical information to the public."

Hey, why not try my hand at infotainment?

Dr. Lamb came from southeast Kansas, where he had grown up in the poorest of families. He had pulled himself up by the bootstraps to graduate from medical school at the University of Kansas. Working for Aerospace Medicine in Houston, he was entrusted with deciding which NASA astronauts qualified for space missions. He became Lyndon Johnson's personal heart physician, a respected author of medical texts, and a syndicated columnist for the Hearst Newspapers.

We filmed *Health Talk* at Trinity University in San Antonio, near Larry's home. Let's just say that my new colleague was "cost conscious"—while filming the show, he insisted I stay at his house, in the middle of a nice upper-middle class neighborhood.

First thing I noticed when I arrived at his plain, fifties-style brick ranch house was that all the windows were boarded over with sheets of plywood.

"I save money on air-conditioning," Larry quickly explained.

Uh . . . right.

Larry lived alone, but for two yappy dogs. The living room was sparse—a threadbare monkey-shit brown sofa sat on a chintzy yellow shag rug.

Huh . . . eccentric.

Larry was a self-made man and never stopped letting you know it. He was brilliant, keenly sensitive, generous to a fault, and so anal-retentive you wanted to kill him. From the start, it was obvious there was only one way to do something—Larry's way. *What the hell.* It was his show. He conceived it, wrote it, produced it, distributed it, bought the furniture for the set, decorated it, supplied the props. I just played straight man.

Little did I realize that Dr. Larry Lamb would end up being one of the most influential people in my life.

We did dozens of *Health Talk* shows, spanning three years. During that time, Larry and I became great friends—he even got close to Gertrude Gelien. Dr. Lamb encouraged me, for health reasons, to resolve the lingering issues I had with my mother. She loved Larry, perhaps recognizing in him a kindred control freak.

"Larry, be good to yourself," she'd lecture. "You only come down this road one time." The two of them were experts at dispensing advice, without always heeding it themselves. "Success can only be measured by your own personal happiness," she'd tell him. "It has nothing to do with how much you have in the bank. There are no Brink's trucks where we're going."

Larry would laugh and give her a big hug, which, remarkably, she'd accept. "I love you, *mamacita!*" he'd say.

SUDDENLY, FROM OUT of nowhere, Norman Lear wanted me for his television series *Forever Fernwood,* a spin-off from his hugely popular soap-opera satire, *Mary Hartman, Mary Hartman.* When contractual problems arose with Philip Bruns, the actor who played Mary's father, George Shumway, Norman came up with a novel solution: George would fall into a vat of Rust-Oleum and *voilà*—he'd emerge looking like 1950s screen heartthrob Tab Hunter. My TV wife, played by Dody Goodman, wanted her old husband back, but my daughter developed a hot-and-heavy crush on her new daddy.

We did nineteen episodes. I loved doing the show but hated being back in Hollywood. The exposure landed me some more work: *Police Woman* with Angie Dickinson and Earl Holliman, a *Challenge of the Stars* show where I rode in a friendly jumping competition with Linda Blair, and a return to Oahu for a *Hawaii Five-0* episode with Samantha Eggar. Jack Lord was The Man, and you'd better not forget it. When anybody on the set gave him static, he'd glare at them, point out to sea, and say, "Get off my island."

It was while I was guesting on an early episode of Bob Wagner's TV show *Hart to Hart* that he suddenly turned to me and said, "When was the last time you talked to Natalie?"

"I can't even remember," I told him. "Maybe twenty-five years."

R. J. pulled out his portable phone and dialed home. This was his second marriage to Natalie; the first union lasted from 1957 to 1962. They'd married again in 1972, after realizing that they were meant for each other all along.

"Hey, Nat," R. J. said, "I'm sitting here with someone who wants to say hello—an old boyfriend of yours."

Hearing Natalie's voice again was like traveling through time. We only had a chance for some rushed small talk before it was time for the cameras to roll. "I look forward to getting together soon," I told her. "My dance card's free. I send you love, Nat."

And with that I handed the phone back to R. J., who had a big smile on his face. It was the last time I ever spoke to Natalie. Not long after that, I was shocked to learn of her death—an accidental drowning off Catalina Island. Nat had always been afraid of water (like Linda Darnell was afraid of fire), and it was hard to comprehend that *drowning*, of all things, would be her fate. My heart went out to R. J., who was completely devoted to her. I couldn't imagine the pain he must have endured, being that close to someone, loving them so much, and losing them so young.

Natalie only lived to be forty-two years old.

THINGS FINALLY FELL apart between me and John Donalson. Life in Clarke County had become incredibly lonely for him. He began to resent that I was always on the road and that I couldn't share more time with him.

He became more and more annoyed with my gallivanting between dinner theaters all over the country. He wanted me at home. It never seemed to dawn on him that it was my constant freelance work that paid for everything.

John became a shrewish, neglected housewife. That didn't sit well with me, and we finally had it out. John may not have realized that he was dealing with someone who was a master at cutting ties quickly and moving on, especially when, in the wake of *Fernwood,* my agent demanded I move back to California so he could try to rekindle my career.

I decided one night to dump it all and return to the coast. John elected to stay on in Virginia. He kept the Mercedes; I kept my freedom.

Frankly, I'm amazed that John stuck it out as long as he did. I wondered if he felt like I did about "releasing with love."

I'd find out soon enough.

THE YEARS ON THE road were wearing thin. By now, plenty of Golden Age stars filled dinner theaters across America: Dorothy Lamour, Van Johnson, Ann Sothern, Martha Raye, Maureen O'Sullivan — I started calling it the Elephant's Graveyard.

In Pineville, North Carolina, following a performance of *Jeremy Troy* (how many hundreds had I done?), a guy in a leisure suit came up out of the crowd, dragging his wife behind him. Wearing a wide shit-eating grin, he proudly said: "My wife came to see Tab Hunter; I came for the roast beef!"

That summer ended at the Limestone Valley Dinner Theatre in Timonium, Maryland. The cast had been together, in one form or another, almost two years. They were as close to family as any I ever had. But I wanted to get off the road for a while, stop living out of a suitcase.

After we closed, I spent a few days at the American Jumping Derby in Newport, Rhode Island, before heading back to Santa Barbara, where I kept writing and pitching *The Reverend and Rosie*. Interviews in L.A. for acting jobs were scarce. In Montecito I did the cocktail-party circuit. That's where I met Michael Corr.

I was leaving the next day to do a play in Dallas. Michael batted his sad-puppy-dog eyes and announced that he had no place to stay.

"You can stay at my place," I told him, playing Mr. Magnanimous to the hilt. "Just take good care of the dogs and keep an eye on things till I get back."

"I'd love to," he said.

The son of a bitch robbed me blind. I could sometimes be incredibly stupid when it came to one-night stands.

He sold off virtually all of the cherished antiques I'd amassed over the years, including rugs, art, and silver, to a Bay Area dealer and skipped town with the money. I was back to square one. Out of desperation, I turned to my mother, who was now on her own following Oma's death. She came to my rescue, moving in to care for the whippets and look after things while I left for yet another theater engagement.

As I was heading out the door, Mother asked: "How can a man soil his hands like that?"

I wondered if she meant Michael Corr—or me.

Occasionally, the thieving bastard would send me postcards, mailed from various exotic locales, advising me of what a wonderful time he was having. Until he ventured into Saudi Arabia, where he crossed a few people and wound up in jail. Last I heard, he'd gotten his just reward.

After the robbery, I never again felt comfortable in that house. So I headed south, poking around Laguna Beach for another place to live.

Arriving at a friend's home for dinner one night, I heard a familiar voice boom from the terrace.

"What the hell are you doing here?"

I looked up to see John Raven, my old landlord from Shoreham Drive.

"Ever see Ma Perkins anymore?" he asked. I shook my head and told him I was in the market for a house.

"Where?"

"Dana Point."

"*I've* got a place in Dana Point," he said, incredulous. "Find anything you like yet?"

"Yeah, but the place is being leased to an attorney."

"I'm leasing *my* place to an attorney," John said. A big smile broke across his face.

"Let's talk business," I said.

I bought Raven's house in Dana Point on my birthday, July 11, 1979, and moved into it on my brother's birthday, August 18. I loved that place and felt that I'd found a spot where I might settle down for a while, but I promptly left for Seattle and stayed through November . . . yep, more *Jeremy Troy.*

When I got home, I found messages piled up from John Donalson, so I called him in the Bay Area, where he was now living. I could tell things were rough for him. I paid his way to Dana Point, where he earned some money helping me fix up the house. He still had the whippet I'd given him.

John had almost finished painting the place when one afternoon he casually mentioned that he'd kept all the letters and postcards I'd sent him over the years.

"Would you like to see them?" he asked.

"Not really," I said.

"I'll bet the *National Enquirer* would."

I couldn't believe that John had gotten desperate enough to pull a stunt like this. He'd lived well in Virginia and had apparently gotten used to it. Despite everything I'd done for him, John felt justified in trying to extort money from me. It was tragic, really. But blackmail is still blackmail, and my sympathy only went so far. When I cut somebody off, it's blunt and final.

I rang up my attorney friend, Martha Anderson, and told her that I was being squeezed in a most unpleasant way by a former friend. We concluded that the best course of action was simply to pay John off and be done with it: in exchange for ten thousand dollars, John promised never to make the letters public. He pleaded to keep them—because they meant so much to him.

"Just get out of my life," I said.

Martha drove John, and his whippet, to the airport. I never saw him again.

BEN PIERSON CALLED.

"Want to do a play in Canada?" he inquired. "The money's excellent."

It had to be, to get *anybody* to play Regina, Saskatchewan, followed by Edmonton, Alberta, in the dead of winter. Everybody in the company bought a fur coat. In my raccoon, I looked like Rudy Vallee, sans megaphone.

When the play closed, I was out of there like I'd been shot from a cannon:

I skied Vail, judged a horse show in Virginia, ran around with my friend Rose Driver, buying antiques for her shop in Dallas, and did another play. Busy, busy, busy. Push, push, push.

Then, "John Kenley wants you to do *Chapter Two* at his theaters in Ohio," Pierson told me. "But Joyce DeWitt has to approve her leading man. When can you meet with her?" This was something new—having to be approved by someone I'd never heard of. I didn't watch TV, so I hadn't seen *Three's Company*. I drove to Malibu to meet with Joyce. We got along famously while doing the Neil Simon play in June 1980.

Maybe the road was taking its toll on me, because Joyce had to save my ass more than once during a show. She was a marvelous, underrated actress. When she returned to California for another season of *Three's Company*, I took the show to Dallas and Indianapolis with a whole new cast.

There was no way off the fucking treadmill.

Then one day in my hotel room in Indianapolis, the phone rang.

"Is this Tab Hunter?"

"Yes, it is."

"I just want you to know, right off, that I bought 'Young Love' when it first came out."

Another goofy fan, I thought.

"That's nice. Thank you." I started to hang up.

"And I want you to know—I have never confused you with Troy Donahue. I am a *big* fan of yours."

"Well, I appreciate that. Thanks very much."

"My name's John Waters. I make movies. Not big Hollywood movies like you've made, but, well, *quirky* little movies. And I was wondering if you'd like to be in one."

3 5

Divine Intervention

"I KNOW YOUR WORK," I SAID.

"Oh, my God, you haven't seen *Pink Flamingos,* have you? *Don't.*"

"Too late. I already have."

I'd seen *Multiple Maniacs, Mondo Trasho,* and *The Diane Linkletter Story.* When it comes to movies, I'm no elitist.

"And you're still willing to talk to me?" he said, laughing.

"Do you have a script?" I inquired.

"You'd play Todd Tomorrow, the love interest of a suburban housewife, Francine Fishpaw. And I want you to know, you're my first and only choice. But before we get into the character or how much I can *almost* pay you, I think we'd better make sure we're, you know, on the same page: are you going to have any problem kissing a three-hundred-pound drag queen?"

I'd kissed a lot worse, I thought. I knew he was talking about Divine, whom I'd already met, briefly, at the opening of a David Hockney exhibition. He was surprisingly introverted, not at all like the campy diva he was so notorious for playing on-screen.

"How long would you need me for?"

I could hear the sharp intake of breath on the other end of the line. "Maybe a week," John said. "We can work around your schedule. I can send you the script today if you're interested."

Over the phone, John exuded charm, wit, humility, and enthusiasm. He sheepishly told me how much he could afford to pay, which was a pittance by Hollywood standards but a huge chunk of his total budget, judging by the look of his previous films.

"I have to tell you something else," he went on. "This is the biggest film I've done, in terms of the budget and everything, and I'd be insanely happy to have you in it—but it's not SAG. I'm telling you that up front, in case you think that doing this will cause you problems with the union."

The Screen Actors Guild prohibited its members from working on films that employed nonunion talent.

"Look, why don't you send me the script, and if I like it, I'll have my agent call your agent."

John laughed. "Tab, I don't have an agent." He'd raised the development money, fifty thousand dollars, from five friends, and New Line Cinema was putting up the rest. It was nothing for a feature film.

I called Joel Stevens in Hollywood to get his advice.

"Are you crazy?" he fumed. "Kiss a drag queen? You have no idea what that guy's had in his mouth!"

"Joel, I've seen *Pink Flamingos*. I know."

"As your agent, I'm telling you that making a picture with a transvestite is career suicide. And the money is shit. Do you want to completely kill your career? I'm telling you—don't do it."

THE SCREENPLAY FOR *Polyester* made me laugh out loud. I couldn't say the same for *Timber Tramps* or *Won Ton Ton, the Dog Who Saved Holly-wood,* the last two feature films I'd made, ages ago. How bad could it be, shooting a little movie in Baltimore for a week? It's not like the whole world was lining up to watch John Waters's latest picture, *Desperate Living*. John was strictly underground, like Andy Warhol. You had to go digging to find their films playing anywhere other than midnight shows in college towns. If *Polyester* stunk, nobody'd ever see it, providing it even got released. But if the finished film turned out as funny as the script—then I'd look pretty smart for having taken the chance.

John told me later that he ran through the streets of his neighborhood screaming, "Tab Hunter's going to do my movie!" after I called to accept the part. To him, I was still "Tab Hunter: Matinee Idol."

I was a little nervous the first day of filming, not knowing what to expect from this bunch of misfits. The first scene we shot was Cuddles's debutante party, where I come out of the men's room having just snorted a line of coke and boogie into a little bump-and-grind with Divine, who was shaking like a schoolgirl.

"I can't believe I'm dancing with Tab Hunter," he'd whispered to John between takes.

John Waters is always John Waters. What you see is what you get. He doesn't *play* John Waters; that's who he is. But Harris Glenn Milstead, aka Divine, was a different person, reserved and quiet when he wasn't in drag. The moment he put on his "work clothes," sparks would come out his ass. Turn a camera on him and he was a natural performer with tremendous charisma.

Divine brought an underlying sweetness and commitment to the absurd scenes of us running hand in hand through the fields, cavorting in the hay in a barn—all those corny scenes John was sending up. Divine had a great work ethic and always brought something extra to a scene; he fed me as an actor, which you can't say for many of Hollywood's seasoned pros. I looked forward to every scene we had together.

Although John had a definite vision, he was a collaborative creator, always open to suggestions. When Divine and I first meet, at the site of a car wreck, John staged it so a severed head rolled into the scene at our feet. "Pick up the head, Tab!" John said during the run-through. Once it was in my hands, I couldn't figure out what to do with the damn thing, so I said: "How about if I toss it over my shoulder into the bushes?"

On the set of Polyester *with my friend, the Sultan of Sleaze, John Waters. (Photo courtesy of Bob Adams.)*

"Oh, that's *good*."

He was an inspired, and inspiring, director. He was always coming up with great ideas, and he knew how to infect others with his enthusiasm. That's why his "family" was so loyal, why Divine, Edith Massey, Mink Stole, David Lochary, Mary Vivian Pearce, cameraman David Insley, art director Vince Peranio, and all the rest shared such affection and dedication. He made movies the way the Italians made movies—with love and excitement. Only a little less organized, if that was possible.

When it came time to shoot the big love scene with Divine, John knew exactly what he wanted, so there wasn't any awkwardness.

"Be gentle," Divine moans. "Please be gentle," she says as I take her in my arms and we sink out of frame while kissing, camera holding on the logs in the fire. John crowed that it was the high point of his career. I'd played the same scene in dozens of films, only this time my leading lady was a man.

My agent actually thought this would destroy my career. It's a joke, for crying out loud. What was the big deal?

The week of filming ended too soon, and by the time we were done, Divine had joined the top rank of "female" costars I'd worked with. He was right up there with Sophia and Natalie and Rita and Lana. And you might say John was his George Cukor.

Divine got such a huge charge out of working with a Hollywood star. But I got something even more valuable from our collaboration: a whole new take on my treatment of *The Reverend and Rosie*—what if Divine played Rosie? The comedic possibilities multiplied in my mind.

The week spent making *Polyester* was a hoot, and I learned an important lesson. John said it beautifully: "If you've got an image you want to change, baby—come play with me!" He doesn't take anything too seriously, except his commitment to making movies and his loyalty to his friends.

Before I headed back to the coast, John got me in a recording studio for the first time in almost twenty years, to sing the title song for his movie. Deborah Harry, the lead singer of Blondie—the hottest band in pop music at the time—sang backup, along with Chris Stein, her Blondie partner. Old Wave meets New Wave.

John was a carnival ringmaster, mixing and matching all sorts of people from different backgrounds, different generations, different genders, to create a bubbling pop-culture stew.

I returned to California on cloud nine, only to have the Screen Actors

Guild immediately call me on the carpet for working in a nonunion film. Many of the board members on that "tribunal" were old friends I'd worked with over the years.

"How many hours a day were you forced to work?" "Were you given proper meal breaks?" "Did you witness any egregiously exploitive practices during the making of the film?"

I reflected on that whirlwind week in Baltimore before answering: I had visions of being crushed into the backseat of John's tiny little car every morning on the way to

With Deborah Harry at the recording session for the Polyester theme song.

work, about the twenty-hour workdays, about the limp, cold pizza we had at 2:00 a.m. for "dinner," about having no place to sit or rest or sleep except the floor of the cameraman's house, which doubled as a set.

Smiling, I told the SAG inquisitors, "It was probably the best experience I ever had making a movie."

John eventually testified, agreed to pay a small fine, and the whole thing blew over. He's dealt up front with the guild ever since.

I figured that *Polyester* might never reach the screen. Nobody ever saw *The Arousers,* where I'd previously risked my "image" by savagely stabbing a succession of women. If that film couldn't find an audience, with Roger Corman promoting it, what chance did John's offbeat little comedy from Baltimore have of reaching the mainstream?

Leafing through *Variety* one day, I was startled to see a photo of myself, clutching Divine in a passionate embrace. "Principal Photography Completed," the ad trumpeted, in grand Hollywood style. So much for no one ever knowing about my trashy little "underground" movie.

"Nobody can believe it!" John said when we next talked. "'Tab Hunter in a movie with Divine?' Thank you so much for agreeing to do it—it's going to be my breakthrough movie. I just know it."

I'D BEEN PUSHING myself pretty hard all year, so I decided to spend Christmas skiing in Taos, New Mexico. Taos feeds the soul, and mine needed nourishment. Those cold, starry December nights with the smell of piñon burning in kiva fireplaces were magical, intoxicating.

Eager to make tracks on the morning of December 23, I stopped at Michael's Kitchen for a quick bowl of oats before heading up the mountain. I'd skied hard with one of the locals the day before and was tired. My body told me to go easy, but I didn't pay attention, ignoring Gertrude Gelien Platitude 137: "Listen to your inner."

On the mountain I felt dizzy, so I decided to head down for an early lunch. Suddenly I was overcome with exhaustion and fell to my knees right in the middle of the run. My body became weaker and weaker, like the life was draining out of me. I pitched over face-first into the snow. My arms wouldn't move, and I started throwing up.

A girl noticed me lying in my vomit and skied over.

"Are you all right?"

I couldn't answer.

"I'll get the ski patrol," she said, anxiously heading off.

I was incoherent when help finally arrived. They hoisted me on a stretcher and hauled it down the mountain. I'd suffered a heart attack. In the first-aid hut I could utter only two words: "Larry Lamb." They found his number in my wallet.

A nurse got hold of him in San Antonio and described my condition. Larry told them to give me an injection of atropine and to repeat it if necessary, because my pulse was below thirty beats a minute. He was afraid that if my heart rate didn't pick up immediately, I'd go into shock and die.

---

3 6

Lust

NEWS OF MY HEART ATTACK hit the papers, and flowers from well-wishers all over the world began filling my tiny room at Taos's Holy Cross Hospital. My room looked like a well-adorned grave site. I told the nurses to spread the flowers around between all the patients, to offer a little holiday cheer. Larry immediately flew in to consult with the staff specialist, Dr. Hawley. What scared me about the very real prospect of dying, at forty-nine, was never again seeing all the friends I'd made, never again riding a horse. I'd thought I was as strong as an ox, and now I was bedridden, praying constantly, asking, *How could this have happened to me?*

The early part of the New Year was spent at Larry's house in San Antonio. Recuperating was worse than having the heart attack. The sedentary recovery process was agony for someone who'd spent virtually every day on the move. Larry took total control of my daily life, dictating everything I could and couldn't do, which didn't amount to much more than watching the sun come up, cast some shadows on the wall, then go back down.

This is the point in the story where I'm supposed to say that I learned my lesson and developed a new perspective, and that I cherished each and every one of those sunrises and sunsets that had been granted by my stay of execution.

Frankly, I was bored out of my mind. Whenever life had overwhelmed me in the past, I just packed up and took off. Now there was nowhere to run.

Larry Lamb was a godsend, but I couldn't wait to get the hell out of there. By the end of January, I was champing at the bit to return to Dana Point, see the dogs, feed the koi in the pond, and sleep in my own bed. I promised Dr. Hawley that I'd take seriously his admonition to "stop and smell the roses." But as soon as I was strong enough, I traveled back to Virginia so I could ride out in the Piedmont countryside. Getting back in the saddle, literally, was essential to my recovery.

JOHN WATERS'S MOVIE debuted that spring. And it *did* stink. That's because as an added bonus, John released *Polyester* in Odorama, with specially made scratch-and-sniff cards distributed to audiences so they could actually smell what they were seeing on-screen. The movie caused a sensation at the Cannes Film Festival, where it was promoted with a huge banner hovering over the terrace of the Carlton Hotel: Divine and me in our passionate clinch.

I didn't attend the U.S. premiere that followed, in John's hometown of Baltimore—a decision I regret to this day. Joel Stevens, my manager, argued that after all his hard work, he wasn't going to let me flush it down the drain by getting lumped in with Divine and Waters and their crazy crowd.

Joel was flat-out wrong. Everybody got the joke. Reviews for *Polyester* were among the best I'd ever received, and the film became a bona fide hit. It introduced me to a whole new generation of moviegoers who'd never heard of Tab Hunter. For both John and me, our collaboration paid huge dividends: I'd helped "legitimize" his brand of movie, and he made me "hip" overnight.

The *Polyester* buzz caught the ear of diminutive dynamo Allan Carr, a hot property who'd recently made *Grease* and *Can't Stop the Music*. Before becoming a producer, he was a personal manager for many movie and musical stars, including Ann-Margret, Peter Sellers, Marvin Hamlisch, Tony Curtis, and Paul Anka. He'd gotten his start as a Hollywood party planner—as good a euphemism as any, I guess.

Allan offered me a plum role in his newest, *Grease 2*. The original had become the highest-grossing musical in history, so this seemed like a surefire step to a full-fledged comeback. I also figured it'd be a good opportunity to pitch Carr on *The Reverend and Rosie*.

In *Grease 2,* I played the sex-education teacher, Mr. Stuart, who leads his students in a musical number called "Reproduction." I was in good company, with talented performers like Lorna Luft, old pros Eve Arden, Connie Stevens, and my *Fernwood* costar, Dody Goodman, and magnetic newcomers Maxwell Caulfield and Michelle Pfeiffer. You knew stardom was inevitable for Michelle.

Paramount pulled out all the stops to promote *Grease 2;* the ingredients were in place for a box-office bonanza. Ten out of ten industry execs would have picked it to hit way bigger than *Polyester*. But it tanked, while John's modest little movie put New Line Cinema on the map. That's show business in a nutshell—no one can ever predict a hit.

Although Allan Carr passed on getting involved in *The Reverend and Rosie,* he did suggest I change the title to *Lust in the Dust,* the name Gregory Peck had jokingly given his overheated 1947 western melodrama, *Duel in the Sun.* I loved it.

Comedies were suddenly all the rage, and I was cast in a low-budget horror spoof from United Artists called *Pandemonium,* with Carol Kane and Tommy Smothers. It's not even worth mentioning, except for the fact that I played a cross-dressing, cheerleading serial killer.

Then I let myself get roped into a project called *And They're Off,* a horse-racing story shot in Lexington, Kentucky. I'd have had better luck at the track. The producer, director, and writer was a triple threat: inept at all three. He paid me handsomely, gave me a nice wardrobe, and I enjoyed working in the Bluegrass State, but the film was so bad it never found a distributor. For every unstoppable visionary like John Waters, there are hundreds, if not thousands, of delusional egomaniacs who think they have what it takes to make a movie. In fact, delusion is what drives the movie business.

Even though the films were bad, my return to the screen allowed me to finally abandon, once and for all, life on the road. I gave my last performance of *Here Lies Jeremy Troy* on October 17, 1982, in Anaheim, California. I was now fifty-two years old; it was time to stop living like a nomad and settle into some sort of home life. Luckily, I'd been able to squirrel away some money for my old age, which was coming on fast. Larry Lamb's expertise wasn't limited to medicine—his counsel in money matters helped me achieve a level of financial stability I'd never enjoyed before.

I'd survived a heart attack, revived my film career, and had reason to believe that 1983 would be a fresh start. On page one of the brand-new appointment book I'd given myself for Christmas, I wrote:

New Year's Resolutions
Watch diet
Try to be more patient and live with less tension
Get *Lust in the Dust* done as a film

Driving onto the lot at 20th Century Fox later that month to shoot a guest appearance on *The Fall Guy* (its star, Lee Majors, was a Dick Clayton client), I noticed a young, good-looking kid driving through the other side of the guard's gate. He had a Fox employee sticker affixed to the windshield. The kid didn't seem old enough to be *driving*, let alone working for a major studio. I figured this was one of the new Hollywood breed I'd been hearing about: Baby Moguls, barely out of school, barely old enough to shave.

A few months later I returned to the Fox lot to shoot another spot on *The Fall Guy*. I'd figured I'd kill two birds with one stone, so I'd made an appointment to pitch *Lust in the Dust* to a new guy in the studio's Creative Development department.

When I walked into the office, I recognized the kid from the guard's gate. The Baby Mogul. His name was Allan Glaser. He'd worked in the studio's television division, on shows like *M*A*S*H* and *Trapper John, M.D.*, but had graduated, through kismet, into Creative Development.

I confess that pitching is not my strong suit, but Glaser showed an immediate enthusiasm for the idea of me and Divine reuniting in a spoof of old Hollywood westerns. He impressed me by knowing my body of work, although I suspected that, at his age, he'd really only seen *Polyester*. He wasn't even born when I was at the peak of my popularity. As we talked, something definitely clicked . . . an instant attraction. Allan was definitely my type. I invited him to lunch and left him with a copy of *Lust*.

So impressed was I with this kid, that the next day in a stationery shop I bought a card for him. It showed a pair of hands holding a crystal ball, with an Oscar inside. I sent it to him, with the inscription "I see great things in your future."

I started calling Allan regularly, discussing the fractured state of moviemaking and how different it was from when I was in my prime, when studios were all-powerful. Allan astounded me with his knowledge of Hollywood and its history. Other appealing things about him were his razor-sharp sense of humor and an eclectic nature. His friends included Maxene Andrews, of the famed Andrews Sisters, and former child actress Peggy Ann Garner. He listened to Chet Baker and Blossom Dearie. He even knew who Steve Trilling was. Not your average twenty-three-year-old, inside or outside Hollywood.

Allan had left his home in Norfolk, Virginia, at eighteen to attend the University of Southern California. Unlike so many young people with stars in their eyes, he didn't want to direct, and he didn't want to be in front on the camera, which I found refreshing. He wanted to produce movies. As a junior executive at Fox, he was on the Hollywood fast track. I immediately nicknamed him

Irving, joking that he was the reincarnation of legendary wunderkind producer Irving Thalberg. Allan had all the qualifications to be a successful producer—tenacity, drive, common sense—and he was Jewish!

"Tab, the timing could be perfect for *Lust in the Dust*," Allan said. He explained that many of the studios, Fox included, were now creating "classics" divisions, to produce lower-budget films for smaller, more film-savvy markets.

We had numerous meetings with Fox execs regarding the project, all lip service, which is the specialty of the house in Hollywood, served hot and cold, day in and day out. Fox eventually passed, but Allan wasn't deterred.

"The script needs work, but I think we can set it up as an independent feature." I had to laugh at his bravado, thinking to myself: *It ain't that easy, kid.* But over the coming weeks, I learned never to underestimate Allan Glaser. Professionally, and personally, I had a hunch that I should take this kid seriously.

Sparked by Allan's enthusiasm, I moved back to Los Angeles from Dana Point. Watson Webb even lent me the Happy Hut, where I'd lived before making *Battle Cry*, thirty years earlier. It was like starting all over again, only this time trying to make it as a producer. Over the months that followed, Allan and I proved to be very compatible partners, and not just when it came to movies.

We worked out of his office, trying to put together the *Lust* "package," first attaching talent to it, then going after investors. We hired a writer, Philip John Taylor, who delivered a wonderfully bizarre, eccentric finished screenplay, juicing up what I'd written.

Allan found $150,000 in seed money from eastern sources and, to avoid any conflicts of interest with his employers, hired an executive producer to pitch the film outside Fox, hoping to find more funding and a distributor. After agreeing to pay this guy a salary for his "best efforts," Allan caught him with his hand in the till.

"Get in the car," Allan yelled as soon as he uncovered the truth. "I'm putting a stop to this." We drove straight to the hotshot's house, where Allan fired him on the spot. I was mightily impressed. This Baby Mogul had balls to spare. The more I was around him, the more I came to respect Allan—which wasn't always the case with previous partners.

Jim Katz, former president of Universal Pictures Classics and a genius at film marketing, replaced the fired executive producer and kept the ship sailing.

Allan and I ended up flying all over the country, meeting all sorts of wealthy people we hoped could be convinced that moviemaking was a glamorous, sexy investment. All of a sudden I wasn't tired of the road anymore! Fueled by the exuberance of youth, we were unstoppable. At investor meetings, Allan kept referring to *Lust* as "Divine's breakout film." His pitch was "We've got no competition—who else is producing a western musical starring a three-hundred-pound transvestite?"

Finally the funding came through.

Divine called us constantly. He desperately wanted to do this movie, to prove he could thrive in a Hollywood film, alongside real Hollywood stars. The first star I wanted to play his half sister was Shirley MacLaine. Once that proved impossible, I went after my old friend Chita Rivera. Perfect: they would have looked like Mutt and Jeff. Chita loved the idea but was tied up on Broadway, doing *The Rink* with Liza.

"What about Shelley Winters?" Allan asked.

I'd met Shelley in the fifties in London, during the filming of *Island of Desire,* when she was there with Farley Granger. Shelley and Divine—together? As John Waters would say: "Oh, that's *good.*" Shelley read the script, thought it was funny, but was hesitant about having a man play her half sister. Next case.

Allan then thought of Lainie Kazan. We took her to lunch, went over the particulars, and gave her a copy of the script. Lainie *got it.* She was in. We were certain she and Divine would be magic on-screen. Not since Vera-Ellen and Rosemary Clooney played sisters in *White Christmas* had there been such perfect casting of siblings.

We quickly lined up a roster of veteran character actors, like Woody Strode, Pedro Gonzalez-Gonzalez, Henry Silva, and Cesar Romero, whom Divine was over-the-moon about working with. It was also the first screen appearance for thirteen-year-old Noah Wyle, Jim Katz's stepson, who'd become a big TV star years later thanks to *ER.*

Once the whole deal was in place, Allan left Fox to dedicate himself fully to our project. But this, of course, is show business. The deal fell through, leaving us with no money. Allan was now unemployed, but this kid had no quit in him. We took an office off the Sunset Strip, on Holloway Drive, and went into business as Fox Run Productions. In February 1984, Allan arranged a cocktail party at the Happy Hut for a group of East Coast investors. Everything clicked. They committed financing and we had the green light. Allan had single-handedly raised $4 million.

With Allan Glaser at his 20th Century Fox going-away party.

Things rapidly fell into place. We flew to New Mexico and negotiated with the Film Commission, since the advantages of filming there suited our tight budget. A dilapidated Mexican village on the Eaves Ranch just south of Santa Fe became the town of Chili Verde, the central location of our story. Venetia Stevenson's sister, Caroline, who now lived in New Mexico, supplied all the horses for us at a great price.

We were still searching for the perfect actor to play the deranged villain, Hardcase Williams.

Allan suggested Anthony Perkins.

He knew nothing of my past with Tony. Allan reasoned that it would help lure distributors if we cast the star of a current hit film. Tony had just achieved something of a comeback, reprising his most famous role in *Psycho 2.* "I might as well face it," he said in one interview, "I *am* Norman Bates."

I visited Tony in his new home, high off Mulholland Drive. Since I'd last seen him, that one day making *Judge Roy Bean,* Tony had drastically changed his life. He was married to photographer Berry Berenson, whom he'd met when she did a piece on him for *Interview* magazine in the early 1970s. They had two beautiful sons, Osgood and Elvis. He and Berry seemed to be a happily married couple. Tony seemed genuinely comfortable in his new role as husband and father. I didn't really dwell on how he'd gotten to this new place or if he really was or wasn't gay anymore. Berry was a warm and delightful woman. Tony was who he was, or maybe who he wanted to be, and that was good enough for me. I had no right—no one does—to be judgmental or to second-guess his pursuit of happiness.

I tried to convince Tony to come to New Mexico and make *Lust in the Dust* with me, but he declined. I choose not to think about his reasons for turning down what would have been a wonderful role. When Tony and I said good-bye that afternoon, I was sincerely happy for him. He'd achieved the kind of family life I'd never had and never would.

It would be the last time we ever saw each other.

ALLAN AND I FLEW BACK east to beg John Waters to direct our movie. Begging is essential when you're making an independent film. But John explained that he only directed pictures he'd written himself. When Andy Warhol learned from John that Divine and I were doing a western, he invited Allan and me to The Factory, where he offered to create a one-sheet poster for five thousand dollars. Our budget was too tight; we couldn't afford the "luxury." Today, you could probably sell *one* of those posters for five thousand dollars.

Style. A rare and vital ingredient in everything. Our comedy had to have it, and we got it in spades from two primary sources. Dona Granata, a newcomer, did wonders with the costumes, and George Masters agreed to do hair and makeup. George was a friend from the old days, who'd glamorized some of Hollywood's finest: Jennifer Jones, Rita Hayworth, Marilyn Monroe, and many more. The most chic women in the country had clamored to have George work his magic on them, but if he didn't like you . . . forget it. He turned down one rich matron because she wore plastic shoes.

George Masters had been ridden hard and put away wet. Drugs and alcohol had left him on the skids. But I wanted him, despite the risk that he'd go off the deep end during production. I always had a soft spot for people down on their luck. George held it together beautifully, his makeup artistry greatly adding to Lainie and Divine being believable as sisters.

Our director of photography, Paul Lohmann, had the distinction of shooting the last film ever made in the three-strip Technicolor process, something we all thought would accentuate *Lust*'s lurid, saturated visuals, designed to parody fifties-era Hollywood westerns.

Only one problem remained: no director.

Jim Katz suggested Paul Bartel, fresh off *Eating Raoul*, a pretty successful art-house comedy. Allan and I screened the film, liked it, and met with Paul. He didn't bowl you over with his personality, but he did agree with our vision for the film. Talent tends to do that when they want a job. An agreement was quickly struck, since our start date was rapidly approaching.

After the deal was signed, Paul invited us to a screening of his work in progress, a film called *Not for Publication*. The movie was not for public consumption. Allan and I were stunned. "This might be the worst movie ever made," Allan whispered to me. We convinced ourselves it was the story, not the director, that was to blame.

Filming began in New Mexico in late April 1984. We had worked so closely with Philip Taylor, honing the screenplay, and had assembled such a first-rate cast (Geoffrey Lewis played Hardcase Williams and was perfect) that we felt the production was foolproof. We handed the whole package to Paul Bartel and said, "Here it is. Don't screw it up." We had endlessly discussed with him our essential concept: "Imagine Divine in a Sam Peckinpah film."

On location for Lust *with "Mr. Producer" and Divine.*

Paul had a rather effete, languid way of doing things, far from the take-no-prisoners approach the picture needed. Based on my moviemaking experience, I'd come to believe that if you have good actors performing a good script, most times you're going to end up with a decent film. A quality director, however, is what kicks "decent" up to the level of "superior," and in those rare cases, "classic." Too bad we couldn't get Peckinpah.

I wanted a director who could take what we had and make it better. Paul didn't do much with the material; if anything, he toned down things that should have been balls-out outrageous. He directed like a den mother, reining in our enthusiasm when he should have been inspiring it. There's nothing you can do when a director belongs to the guild, since it has the power to fight anyone who questions a director's ultimate control of a film. I'll be damned if the finished picture was "A Film by Paul Bartel."

Not to say making it wasn't fun. It was probably the most pleasurable experience I'd ever had doing a movie. Divine had a delightful way of mocking his own diva persona, always calling Allan "Mr. Producer" and needling Lainie in a competitive, but totally affectionate, way. Lainie was a riot warbling, "Let me take you south of my border just north of my garter." Divine topped that with "These Lips Are Made for Kissing." The cast and crew packed in to view the rushes every day, everyone howling at the outrageousness.

I wanted to fully exploit the fantastic vistas of New Mexico, but production manager John Smith fretted that we didn't have enough time or money for pickup shots. "Just set up the camera and let me gallop through as various characters," I told him. In one sequence, filmed in long shots, I rode through as Abel Wood, the Clint Eastwood–style hero, then changed wardrobe and horse to chase myself across a spectacular sunset.

I loved making movies!

Everything was going fine until Divine's collapse. Remember, this was a three-hundred-pound man—running, falling, singing, dancing—in the thin air of the high desert, six thousand feet up. When he toppled over one day during filming, we actually thought he'd died—a producer's worst nightmare. Divine was all right, thank God, but he had to finish the film with an oxygen tank at hand, which he relied on between every take. Divine also suffered from narcolepsy—he'd regularly fall into a deep sleep on the set and have to be shaken awake. He'd go right into character, nail the take, then fall asleep again as soon as Paul yelled, "Cut!"

Everyone loved Divine and knew how desperately he wanted to be taken seriously as an actor. I'll never forget how emotional he got trying, and failing, to execute the fall from a donkey that introduces him in the film. The stunt was simply too difficult and dangerous, but he insisted on trying. When I told him that we'd use a female stunt double, he tried to hide his tears.

Together, Allan and I had assembled the family I always wanted, so we could shoot my own project in a place I loved. It was a special feeling of camaraderie, even more so than with my dinner-theater "families" because I was the patriarch of this group, the one responsible for all of them being there. I'd become the father I never had.

We wrapped at the end of May, after surviving a knock-down, drag-out creative battle with Paul over the ending of the film. He had devised his own climax, which I thought was total bullshit. After much arguing, we'd agreed to shoot two endings: his and ours. Once we wrapped, we returned to Hollywood and immediately went into postproduction. We used our ending, fortified with an additional day of reshoots, Soledad Canyon doubling for the original New Mexico locations.

Once we started screening a rough cut for distributors, all the studios that had turned us down began lining up. We eventually settled on New World Pictures. *Lust in the Dust* was shown at the United States Film Festival in Park City, Utah (pre-Sundance), and it opened nationally in March 1985, enjoying great success, including extended engagements in New York and San Francisco, where it set a box-office record at the Castro Theatre. It even opened the Berlin Film Festival, alongside Robert Benton's *Places in the Heart*.

We knew *Lust* wasn't the kind of film to garner critical acclaim, but the reviews were surprisingly good: *Variety* called it "a saucy, irreverant, quite funny send-up." *Us* magazine said it was "a wicked must," and more than one media wag labeled it "a Divine comedy."

Glenn Milstead's dream had come true. The picture broke Divine completely into the mainstream; in smaller markets, some audience members weren't even aware She was a He. But we were caught totally off-guard when he refused to promote the film in drag. Instead, he loved to show up in one of his extensive collection of hand-sewn Tommy Nutter suits. Divine flatly refused to be labeled a transvestite, insisting that he was a legitimate actor who specialized in portraying women.

New World Pictures erected a collosal *Lust in the Dust* billboard, photographed by Greg Gorman, showing me sandwiched between Lainie and Divine. For months it stood beside the Chateau Marmont, looming over all the deal makers driving back and forth along the Sunset Strip.

The phones at Fox Run Productions started ringing and wouldn't stop. Doors that had previously been slammed in my face began flying open. My partnership with Allan Glaser was off and running.

The New Hollywood

OPPORTUNITIES CAME FAST and furious. Allan and I took meetings all over town, getting the royal treatment from a new generation of high-powered executives like Sherry Lansing, Dawn Steel, and Alan Ladd Jr. Overnight, we'd gotten a passport to the executive office towers. My name opened the doors, and Allan went in talking a blue streak.

Fox Run Productions, rechristened Glaser/Hunter Productions, immediately developed *James Blond*, in which I'd parody a 1960s secret agent and Divine would play seven different female roles. Another feature project, *Sorority Sluts,* written by Pat (*9 to 5*) Resnick was slated at Allan's former studio, 20th Century Fox. Philip John Taylor was putting the finishing touches on a horror comedy, *Pitch Black*, which we had high hopes for. I worked every day on the screenplay for *Ski Vacation,* a comedy to star John Candy. We went in on a deal with R. J. Wagner's production company for a remake of Margaret O'Brien's classic *Lost Angel.* There were more: for every project that went to preproduction, there were four or five others that expended just as much energy, without ever getting out of development.

Allan had found his calling. He assured me that my role in the business end of the partnership was essential, stressing that my rejuvenated celebrity was a major reason we were getting all these meetings. But he also asked that I show up at the office every day and work regular hours. All the frantic deal making was exciting, but it wasn't *all* I was interested in. I liked to ski; Allan liked to work. I liked to putter in the garden; Allan liked to work. I liked to ride horses; Allan liked to work.

While in New Orleans for the National Association of Television Program

Executives' annual conference, Allan sold—through a chance meeting—
Hollywood on Horses, a dream project of mine, as a twenty-six-episode television series. I was the co–executive producer and host, interviewing and riding with fellow actor-equestrians—Ursula Andress, Bo Derek, Ben Johnson,
Patrick Swayze, Linda Blair, and James Woods among them—who shared my
passion for horses.

With everything popping in Los Angeles, I rarely made it home to Dana
Point. I'd worn out my welcome at Watson's Happy Hut, so Allan found us a
house close to the action, at 9460 Beverlycrest Drive.

Right after we'd moved in, the phone rang.

"Welcome to the neighborhood," said Rock Hudson. We'd snapped up
these Beverly Hills digs without realizing Rock lived right up the street. We
hadn't seen each other since a *McMillan and Wife* episode about ten years earlier. The last we'd talked on the phone was a memorable occasion: February 6,
1971—6:02 a.m. to be exact. A major earthquake, 6.5 on the Richter scale,
rocked Southern California, the worst shaker since 1933.

I had leaped from bed, things falling all around me. Through the window
I saw electrical bursts erupting from power lines in the distance, lighting up
the sky. The phone rang.

"Did you feel that?" It was Rock, scared out of his wits. Why in the world
would he be calling me?

"Because you're the only person I know who'd be awake at this hour," he said.

That was a laugh. *Everybody* in Southern California was awake. We chatted through a few scary aftershocks before saying good-bye.

Now, more than a decade later, we expected to be seeing a lot more of each
other. Rock was eager to see the improvements we were making to the house.
The next time I saw Rock, however, was in a hospital room. George Maharis
and I had gotten permission to visit after we'd learned he was seriously ill. I
was horrified by how haggard and emaciated he was. This was my first real exposure to the effects of AIDS. I felt damn lucky that my extracurricular ac-
tivities hadn't resulted in my being infected with the virus, and relieved that
all that was behind me, now that I'd settled down.

Beverlycrest Drive was cordoned off when Elizabeth Taylor hosted a memorial service at Rock's house, "A Gathering of Friends." Rock was the first
major celebrity to succumb to AIDS, and his death was a lightning rod for the
public. Unfortunately, the disease was "reported" by tabloids like the *Enquirer*
and the *Star*—as well as many respectable publications—in an ignorant and

sensationalized way that made the epidemic seem like God's vengeance on homosexuals. Virtually every star in town attended the "Gathering of Friends," but the press was noticeably absent. Extra security had been hired to keep them out.

REMODELING THE BEVERLY HILLS house allowed me to ease off on the office routine. Allan doggedly rode the Hollywood merry-go-round every day, chasing the brass ring. "Call me when you've got good news," I'd yell to him as I helped workers tear off the roof and toss it into a Dumpster below.

We'd bought the place before finding a buyer for my house in Dana Point, which was a little scary. Somebody told me that sticking a statue of St. Joseph upside down in the dirt helps a sale, so I rushed out, bought a plastic one, drove to Dana Point, said a prayer, and shoved St. Joseph headfirst into the dirt. It did the trick.

Too bad there was no superstitious gimmick for getting a movie made. As the years passed, *Sorority Sluts,* now called *Sorority Confidential,* was put on life support at Fox: not dead, but barely breathing. It'd eventually go into "turnaround," industryspeak for "dump it." We never got a script for *Pitch Black* that we were confident about, so it never got out of development. *Lost Angel* got stuck in limbo at Columbia. Allan eventually got financing for *Ski Vacation;* it was ready to shoot in Yugoslavia, where we'd just returned from scouting locations, when John Candy died. The project died with him.

Now, Glaser/Hunter's most promising project was one that started through a bizarre coincidence. Perry Bullington worked in casting at Canon Films. One night while he was lying in bed, a book fell off the shelf above and conked him: it was Evelyn Keyes's novel, *I Am a Billboard.* Perry knew a good thing when it hit him in the head. He raved to us about the story, and once Allan and I read the thinly veiled memoir about a young Georgia girl's coming-of-age in the 1930s and her journey to Hollywood, we agreed—it would make a terrific movie.

I'd always loved Evelyn Keyes, not just in *Gone with the Wind,* where she played Scarlett O'Hara's sister, but in pictures like *Here Comes Mr. Jordan, The Jolson Story,* and *The Prowler.* By the time we met, she was in her seventies and writing a regular column for the *Los Angeles Times,* "Keyes to the Town." She was excited about our plan to turn *I Am a Billboard* into a film, and she sold us the rights. Evelyn was still so sharp, so opinionated, so full of piss and vinegar, and so brilliant a writer, that when she insisted on taking a crack at the screenplay, we eagerly agreed.

Evelyn practically lived in our Beverly Hills house, working with me every day on that script. She had a volatile personality—extremely engaging, but relentlessly combative. It was easy to see how major talents like Charles Vidor, John Huston, Mike Todd, and Artie Shaw had all been beguiled by her—and how eventually they'd all had enough.

"Don't let the door hit you in the ass on your way out!" I yelled after one of our countless battles. Evelyn stormed out, drove around the block, and came back to finish the scene we were working on. Over the course of a year, that incident repeated itself innumerable times, but out of it all came a terrific script, titled *Georgia Peach*.

We weren't the only ones who thought highly of it. Allan sold it the first

Allan and me with Evelyn Keyes at an Academy of Motion Picture Arts and Sciences event. She is determined to win an Oscar for her screenplay.

place he pitched it, to Scotti Brothers Pictures, a newly formed offshoot of Scotti Brothers Records, which had scored with several hit records in the eighties, *Eye of the Tiger* being the biggest of the bunch.

Georgia Peach quickly went into preproduction—where it languished for two years. Finally we got a start date and were scouting locations when Scotti Brothers decided to quit the movies and return to record making exclusively.

Such is the treacherous nature of independent filmmaking.

Hollywood changes its mind like I change my socks. I don't recommend this business for the faint of heart. Good intentions aren't enough to hold together a house of cards. Actors, directors, and writers can be heralded as heroes one day and branded bums the next. It's all about luck, but no one who makes it wants to believe that. They'd rather believe it's their undeniable talent or incredible business acumen. In some cases, that's true. But mostly, it's pure luck. Coupled with the kind of relentlessness that Allan Glaser has in endless supply.

He gave me a copy of Gene Tierney's autobiography, *Self Portrait,* the amazing saga of this movie star's traumatic life. Allan wanted to acquire the rights but had heard that the actress was reticent. "My friend Margaret Harris knows Gene Tierney," I told him. Margaret arranged the connection, and over the course of several months we exchanged phone calls with Gene until she was comfortable enough to invite us to her elegant home in Houston.

She'd gained a few years and several pounds, but the catlike eyes and fetching overbite, so memorable in films like *The Ghost and Mrs. Muir* and *Leave Her to Heaven,* were still enchanting. Genuine movie stars could still throw a spark into me. Gene was extremely modest, poised on a grand sofa beneath a portrait that looked eerily like the one of her in *Laura.* The room was filled with silver-framed photos of her husbands, couturier Oleg Cassini and oil magnate Howard Lee, and her two daughters, one of whom, Daria, was born brain-damaged at the height of Tierney's fame, only one example of the many tragic turns in the woman's life.

"Many have wanted to do my story," she said. "But I wasn't comfortable about it at the time." Out of the blue, she gave us permission to pursue a film project. We'd have to pay for the rights only if the project sold.

"Biopics" had become hot properties—*Mommie Dearest, Coal Miner's Daughter,* and *two* films about the troubled actress Frances Farmer. Allan and I could barely contain ourselves on the flight back to L.A. As soon as we were home, Allan set up a pitch meeting at Columbia. Brimming with enthusiasm, we blew into the office of another fresh-faced executive. Small talk was shelved when he saw how excited we were.

"Sooooo, whatd'ya got for me?" he said, practically licking his lips.

"Rights to the Gene Tierney story," Allan proudly beamed.

The executive pondered it for a moment.

"Gene Tierney," he mused. "He was a boxer, right?"

I shot Allan a look of disgust: "Come on, let's go."

Allan was aghast—more at my rudeness than at his fellow Baby Mogul's ignorance. I gave Sammy Glick a weak handshake and bolted.

I couldn't bring myself to suck up to these kids any longer. Any connection that I'd retained to the Hollywood I once knew had evaporated. Not that it mattered anyway, because Allan didn't want me at pitch meetings anymore. I'd invariably ruin things, he said, by blurting out caustic comments to the arrogant assholes who stupidly believed they had some sort of pipeline to the Hit Factory.

By 1988, Divine had reached the pinnacle of his fame with the release of another John Waters film, *Hairspray,* a bigger hit than *Polyester* and *Lust* combined. He seemed incredibly happy when he came for dinner to discuss the prospects of getting financing for *James Blond.* He raved about his *Hairspray* costar Ricki Lake and was thrilled at landing a nondrag part in the TV series *Married . . . with Children.*

A week later, Divine was found dead of a heart attack in a Hollywood hotel room. Various maladies, compounded by his excessive weight, had finally caught up with him. Thank God he died peacefully, in his sleep. To this day, I never fail to cite Divine as one of my favorite "leading ladies."

My mother was now living alone up in Pacific Grove. I invited her to Beverly Hills for an extended visit. She got along great with Allan, who attributed it to my mother's newfound obsession with comparative religions.

"I'm lucky she's going through her Jewish period," he said.

It was seeing my mother from someone else's perspective that finally allowed me to accept Gertrude Gelien as a complex woman who'd suffered her own demons for a long time. Before, I'd only related to her as my mother, font of all willpower and wisdom. She *couldn't* be a troubled soul. If your *mother* isn't normal—then who is?

Much of the friction between us had stemmed from the pressure she must have felt trying to live up to her own standards and wanting so much for her two sons. I'd drawn so much strength from her that I refused to see the pain she was in—and that she needed sustained medical attention.

Late one night during her visit in Beverly Hills, there was a gentle knocking on my bedroom door.

"Arthur," my mother's voice wheezed faintly. "Arthur—I am having a heart attack."

Allan and I bundled her into the car and rushed to Cedars-Sinai. She survived and made a surprisingly rapid recovery. But the idea that she could have died alone in Pacific Grove, if she'd had the heart attack there, preyed on my conscience.

People were dying all around me; did I have the time, or the energy, to repeat all over again the quest for some Hollywood triumph? Maybe I had simpler, more profound things to do with the days I had left, however many there might be.

Allan was still young; he had a fire in his belly for the Hollywood life. Mine was slowly burning out.

SOME FRESHLY MINTED industry hotshot knocked on the front door of our Beverly Hills home and offered an outrageous sum to buy the place out from under us. Literally, it was a deal we couldn't refuse.

The sale of the house sent Allan and me in opposite directions: He refused to move to the San Fernando Valley, where I could at least be near the horses. Instead, Allan took an apartment in a classic old Hollywood building on Sunset Plaza Drive, right in the thick of it. He was in his element, living between two Golden Age actresses, Phyllis (*House of Wax*) Kirk and Andrea (*Beast with Five Fingers*) King.

My element turned out to be hundreds of miles away, in New Mexico. With the proceeds from the house sale burning a hole in my pocket, I scouted for another ranch, someplace where I could finally settle into a southwest version of the gentleman-farmer life that I'd always wanted. I found ten terrific acres outside Santa Fe, perfect for me and the horses.

Not so perfect, however, for Allan, who'd fly in, *Variety* under one arm, the *Hollywood Reporter* under the other, about as relaxed as spit on a griddle. To him, Santa Fe was nothing but rocks and dirt and endless empty space—great backdrop for a movie, not his first choice for daily life. Or his second or third. He couldn't zip back to the Sunset Strip fast enough. After much debate— and a slew of huge phone bills—we agreed to a "dual homestead" that would keep our professional, and personal, partnership intact.

I moved my mother to Santa Fe as well. Her iron will had weakened considerably after the heart attack, even though she keep insisting that "My special angels are taking care of me."

"That's lovely, Mother," said Special Angel Number One, "but let's be practical." She'd been prescribed various medications, some for her heart, some for her head. Even though she was still fiesty and independent, someone needed to be near her most of the time. Perhaps she realized that at this point in her life, I was all she had. There were no other family or friends left — the result of a life lived in self-constructed isolation.

Fortunately she loved Santa Fe, believing, like me, that it was a very spiritual place. She happily agreed to the move.

I had a renewed peace of mind, with horses in my backyard, and skiing only minutes away. At a local flea market one Sunday, a man sheepishly approached me. "You're Tab Hunter, aren't you?" he asked.

I nodded.

"I ended up with your dog Fritz."

My jaw dropped. As far as coincidences go, this one was off the charts. This fellow had owned a pet store in West Hollywood, and he'd gotten Fritz from Dick Clayton.

"I had him for almost ten years before he died," the guy said. "It was too bad about all the trouble you went through with him, but I want you to know — he had a really happy life. He was a great dog."

THOSE TEN ACRES in New Mexico proved to be anything but the basis of a tranquil retirement. I toiled over them every day, sunrise to sundown, planting trees, improving irrigation, reshaping landscape, and redoing the house and barn. Years as a nomad had conditioned me for constant activity. To me, it was heaven.

The only thing missing was Allan. We made the phone company a fortune, but the daily calls weren't enough. Something in me had changed over the years, and as my sixtieth birthday approached, I couldn't shake the feeling that the "self-sufficient machine" needed another person — one person, specifically — to keep its batteries charged.

ON A LOVELY MARCH NIGHT, beneath a vast canopy of stars, I went to the barn to check on the horses, my nightly ritual. Suddenly, the stars started swimming in the sky. I staggered around, pitching into the stall of Mark, my thoroughbred jumper, where I got violently ill. It wasn't another heart attack, I knew that. I dragged myself back to the house, where I collapsed on the bed and suffered through an excruciating night. When dawn finally broke, I called Larry Lamb in Texas.

"Tab, what's wrong?" he asked. "You're slurring your words." His voice rattled around in my head. I couldn't focus.

"I think it's food poisoning," I told him.

Larry was smart enough to dismiss my diagnosis. He called my friend Chery Finley and had her check on me. I was like a tightly wound watch that had come unsprung. Nothing worked right anymore. When Chery saw my slow-motion state, she immediately called 911.

It was déjà vu all over again. An ambulance rushed me to the hospital. Allan promptly flew in from the coast. He said nothing to my mother, for fear of upsetting her. Larry arrived. He consulted with a neurologist. X-rays and CAT scans were taken, revealing a suspicious mass in my brain.

The doctor in charge boldly announced, "Tab Hunter needs to be sent to a special center that treats AIDS."

"That's ridiculous!" Larry declared. "Tab has already been tested—the results were negative."

My doctor in Los Angeles immediately sent copies of all my recent blood work. At that time, any public figure rumored to be gay could only be in a hospital for one reason. Even doctors weren't immune to the rumormongering that was the press's specialty.

What I'd actually suffered was a stroke. I'd done a shitty job of learning to live with less stress, and since I hadn't gotten the message, life had hit me over the head with a sledgehammer—shutting me down completely. Allan filled the hospital room with flash cards and children's puzzles, preparing for the possibility that I'd emerge from this catastrophe with the mental and motor skills of a two-year-old.

I was spared that horror but still had to endure a prolonged rehabilitation at Larry Lamb's ranch in Boerne, Texas. I needed a walker just to put one foot in front of the other. Shaving became a bloody adventure. Cleaning my teeth— when I could land the brush on them—was an arduous, exhausting task. For the first time in my life, I knew *depression*.

Slowly, I progressed from tentative treks across the living room, to forays around the yard, to mile hikes down the road. I finally sucked up the stamina for the endless journey to a nearby dam, where I'd struggle to take off all my clothes and throw myself into the lake. It was a baptism of sorts, a cleansing. Sometimes I'd go there to fish, or just to be alone with my thoughts. What would happen to my mother if I wound up incapacitated?

Larry declared Allan off-limits, thinking his presence would be disruptive to my recovery. The weeks dragged by.

"I'm going stir-crazy," I told Allan long-distance.

"Well, you just got something in the mail that might snap you out of it," he said. "It's an invitation to the rededication of Warner Brothers." In 1973, the Warners lot had its name changed to the Burbank Studios, when Columbia rented a huge chunk of the place. Despite my turbulent history with Jack Warner, the change of names was as sacrilegious as tearing down the Brown Derby.

"It's going to be some party," Allan said. "This invitation is spectacular."

Though I usually ran from this kind of event, it sounded awfully appealing after two months in solitary confinement. "I'll go anywhere," I said. "Just come and get me out of here."

Allan arrived in Texas at the end of April. We rented a car and drove to Santa Fe so my mother could see for herself that I was all right.

Then it was on to California. Zooming out of the desert into Las Vegas, I felt as if my eyeballs were being tossed into a Waring blender. I didn't mind at all. I was happy to be alive.

The Warner Bros. shindig, called "A Celebration of Traditions," was a monumental conjoining of old and new Hollywood, studded with stars from every era: Ruby Keeler, Demi Moore, Tony Curtis, Kevin Costner, Claire Trevor, Meryl Streep, Ernest Borgnine, Harrison Ford, Rhonda Fleming, Goldie Hawn, Ronald Reagan, Sylvester Stallone, Loretta Young, Liza Minnelli, Charlton Heston, Jack Nicholson, Virginia Mayo, Faye Dunaway, Robert Stack, Robert De Niro—the list seemed endless.

Evelyn Keyes was my date that night. Both she and I had traveled around the world, lived overseas, and at various times sworn off this insane industry. Yet here we were, years later, back in the fold. Once in your blood, show business, it seems, is there forever.

All the guests boarded little trolleys that chugged around the lot, weaving through hundreds of performers reenacting scenes from classic Warner Bros. movies. Evelyn acted completely blasé about this kind of industry function, but the whole thing hit me that night like a ton of bricks, perhaps because my stroke had left me hypersensitive, susceptible to intense swings of emotion.

As the trolley turned a corner, I recognized the area where my spacious old dressing room had been. As we drew nearer, I noticed that it had been converted into offices—it was the headquarters of Clint Eastwood's production company, Malpaso. Clint, a bit player in *Lafayette Escadrille*, was now one of the most powerful producer-directors in the industry.

Thirty years had passed since I'd set foot inside these walls, and the memories came flooding back: the soundstage where Henry Willson introduced me to Rock, during the making of *Fighter Squadron*; the set where Dorothy Malone and I had the *Battle Cry* affair that catapulted me to stardom; the house where Joe Hardy made his pact with the Devil in *Damn Yankees*. Evelyn squeezed my hand when she saw tears welling up in my eyes.

During dinner, scenes from Warners movies were projected on a massive screen erected on a soundstage that had been remodeled into a grand movie theater. A snippet of me from *Battle Cry* appeared between clips of Humphrey Bogart and Bette Davis.

It was hard to believe that the kid who'd ridden horses in the hills above Burbank, who'd lived with his mother right outside these walls, who'd earned a steady paycheck within the studio and become one of its biggest box-office draws—was now being remembered as part of Warners' illustrious legacy, along with cultural icons like Bogart and Davis.

I felt honored, certainly, but doubly determined to bounce back from the stroke. I wasn't ready to become "history" just yet.

A Horse of a Different Color

I WAS READY to make another movie.

Some years earlier, during the filming of an episode of *Hollywood on Horses,* I'd seen a spirited Arabian that had been used as a double for *The Black Stallion.* He had broken his leg and ordinarily would have been put down. But his owner, trainer Glenn Randall, couldn't bring himself to do it. Instead the horse spent an entire year recuperating in a sling, after which it never again walked properly. When this horse was turned loose, however, it miraculously ran like the wind.

Inspired, I came up with a story about a girl and her horse, both crippled in the same accident. The wheelchair-bound girl learns to overcome her handicap through the indomitable spirit of her horse, who beats the odds to run again. I called it *Dark Horse.*

If Allan could sell a TV show about horses, maybe he'd have equal luck with a feature. He got Disney all lathered up, and in turn they hired Janet Maclean to adapt my story into a screenplay. When Disney fell by the wayside, Allan found a fresh backer in a distribution outfit called Live Entertainment, previously owned by Jose Enrique Menendez, whose career as a Hollywood executive had been cut short the night his sons, Erik and Lyle, returned to their Beverly Hills mansion toting a shotgun.

The domestic distribution deal with Live Entertainment supplied only half the budget, however. Allan was out searching for the rest of the money when I mentioned, in one of our daily phone conversations, a benefit dinner I'd be attending for the local Greer Garson Theatre at the College of Sante Fe. Before I could finish my sentence, Allan interrupted.

"Tab, the Sugars will be at that dinner," he said. "Arrange it so you sit with Larry Sugar and his wife, Bonnie."

"Who are the Sugars?"

"Just trust me on this one."

Allan had been doing his homework—which meant microscopic inspection of *Daily Variety,* which contained an item about the event. The Sugars, he later explained, could get things done: Larry was the founder of Sugar Entertainment, as well as the president of Republic Pictures International. His wife, Bonnie, was the vice president. They might be the piece of the puzzle we needed to complete financing.

Over dinner I just happened to mention our *Dark Horse* project and that Allan was diligently searching for the second half of the budget. I knew right off that Allan and Bonnie would be an ideal match; they shared the same kind of energy and were equally enthusiastic about making movies.

"I'm heading back to Hollywood this week," Bonnie said. "Have Allan call me."

I think Allan was sitting in her office before the plane landed at LAX. Before the week was out, he had closed the deal, and the Sugars had lined up enough foreign presales on *Dark Horse* to make it become a reality.

We were back in business.

Luck, timing, and perseverance—that's how it happens, every time.

I was happy to keep making movies, as long as I didn't have to suffer the roller-coaster ride of putting the deal together. I'd come to depend on Allan to solely handle that part of the process. *Dark Horse* was my baby, and despite not being back to full strength in the wake of my stroke, I was determined to be involved in the film's evolution.

The first order of business was hiring a director who was the opposite of Paul Bartel. We sought someone dynamic, passionate, professional—and affordable. David Hemmings, who'd soared to international acclaim in 1966 as the modish star of Michelangelo Antonioni's *Blow-Up,* was by 1991 working more as a director than an actor, mostly in episodic television. He'd directed a couple of well-regarded features in the early 1970s, *Running Scared* and *The Wild Little Bunch.* How *Dark Horse* found its way into David's hands, I have no idea, but when he read the screenplay, he pursued us relentlessly, eager to once again direct a feature film.

Hemmings was a complex man with an amazing résumé. He'd been an opera singer as a boy, a marvelous actor, and a founding partner of the film-financing company Hemdale, which bankrolled a number of major movies, including *The Last Emperor, Platoon,* and *The Terminator.* Allan and I were suitably impressed. He said all the right things to get the job, and I felt his instincts as an actor would be a big bonus to our production. Allan especially appreciated David's thorough knowledge of the business.

Preproduction meetings were held at David's home in Sun Valley, Idaho. I'd envisioned New Mexico as the setting for the story, but David insisted we relocate to Sun Valley, giving all kinds of cinematic and practical reasons for the change. It certainly allowed him to load the crew with "his people," including his wife, Pru, whom he wanted as his production designer. More alarm bells went off when David locked himself in his upstairs office and didn't emerge for three days—until he'd finished rewriting our script to his specifications.

It was *better.*

Clearly, there were going to be power struggles with David, but Allan and I sensed that it could be worth it. David had a strong personality, a persuasive manner, and obvious talent—just what you need in a director.

We chose Ari Meyers, a gifted young actress, for the lead role of Allison. She'd be in virtually every scene, so the picture rested squarely on her capable shoulders. Ed Begley Jr., a delightful pro, was cast as her widower father. As the horse trainer, we cast Mimi Rogers. She was our "name," having just come off starring roles in *Someone to Watch Over Me* and *The Rapture*, as well as a highly publicized divorce from Tom Cruise.

Casting a "name" was essential to securing financing. Whether that "name" is actually right for the role is frequently a secondary consideration in the new Hollywood. Long gone are the days of screen tests, in which the chemistry between performers was carefully considered before making a commitment. Back then, more film stock was used shooting *tests* for *Battle Cry* than we now had to shoot our entire feature.

My old stage colleague Ann Sothern lived in Sun Valley, and I went after her for one of the supporting roles. She was too frail, but we did cast her daughter, Tisha Sterling, in a featured role. We lucked out when one of my favorites, Samantha Eggar, suddenly became available. She already knew David, having acted with him in two previous films.

I considered myself retired as an actor, since I'd appeared in only a couple of forgettable movies since *Lust in the Dust*. As far as I was concerned, acting was my "past life." But Allan prevailed on me to play the mean horse trainer, mainly as a way of saving money. We could only afford an actor who'd work for SAG minimum, since Mimi's salary had eaten up a sizable chunk of our budget.

Ross Brown, our casting director, excitedly called us from Hollywood about an actress he'd just auditioned for the role of Allison's best friend, Martha. She was wonderful, he said, but completely inexperienced. We trusted Ross's instincts and told him to send her photo along for our approval.

"My God," I exclaimed when I saw the photo, "it's Natalie!"

I wasn't far off. Natasha Gregson Wagner was Natalie Wood's twenty-year-old daughter, born during her mother's marriage to British agent Richard Gregson. We met Natasha for dinner upon her arrival in Sun Valley. The moment I heard her laugh, it sent shivers through me. "You sound just like your mother," I told her.

Natasha had no idea how close I'd been to her mom—and no interest in riding those coattails. I'm sure Natalie would never have imagined that it would be her "boyfriend" from a bygone era who'd give her daughter her initial film role.

As it turned out, it was essential for David to shoot the film on his home turf because that's where he had an entourage to support him. And

Like mother . . . (Natalie on her eighteenth birthday, on the set of The Girl He Left Behind.*)*

. . . like daughter. (Natasha on her twenty-first birthday, on the set of Dark Horse.*)*

"support" was critical, considering that he drank constantly, to the point where he was barely functional by the end of each day.

David's drinking drove Allan, and executive producer Bonnie Sugar, to the verge of homicide. Allan had slaved for four years to get this film into production, even agreeing to defer his own salary, and now David was taking us all hostage with his Jekyll-and-Hyde persona: charming and creative when sober, a boorish lout when drunk. He even barred me from the set after we clashed over his unrealistic depiction of a bit of horse handling.

But we tolerated David's self-destruction because he delivered the goods. The rushes proved it. If Paul Bartel had behaved like David Hemmings, we'd have fired his ass in a heartbeat. In this business, however, you cut talent miles of slack—and hoped they didn't kill themselves before the movie was in the can.

Allan wasn't a big fan of Mimi Rogers, either. She treated him, and the whole production, as strictly second class. She was shooting a studio movie simultaneously, the bigger-budgeted *White Sands,* with Mickey Rourke and Willem Dafoe. Bouncing between Sun Valley and New Mexico locations didn't do much for her disposition—or her phoned-in performance.

For *Lust in the Dust,* Allan had managed to secure independent financing, with no strings attached. That's like winning the lottery. Well, what are the odds of winning the lottery twice? The *Dark Horse* budget came from various—and precarious—industry sources, on top of which we had to convince our bond company, Film Finance, to let us treat the 10 percent typically held in a contingency fund as part of our production budget. That's how close to the bone we were cutting things.

What that meant, in a practical sense, was that the moneymen were always lurking over our shoulders. This resulted in some bitterly ironic situations— like Film Finance agents taking an all-expenses-paid vacation to Sun Valley to "oversee" production. Before scooting off for several days of tax-deductible fly-fishing, they stopped by to police the set: we couldn't shoot too many takes, couldn't spend too much on authentic props, couldn't travel too far for a good shot. And God forbid we fall behind schedule—they'd just rip unshot pages out of the script. Larry and Bonnie Sugar were wonderful buffers between the accountants and the creatives.

Lust in the Dust had been a thoroughly enjoyable experience for everyone involved. *Dark Horse,* by comparison, felt like a death march. The countdown to the end of production was suspenseful: would we get everything we needed before David went down in flames?

Ah, but remember, this is Hollywood—you can never predict anything.

The finished film was *excellent.* It garnered great reviews and wound up on plenty of Top Ten lists. *Dark Horse* turned out to be a better film than *Lust in the Dust,* largely due to Ari Meyers's performance and the director's talent as a storyteller. It's a tragedy that so much of David's immense energy and creativity was washed away by booze. It would eventually kill him, at only sixty-two years of age—in the middle of directing a film.

DARK HORSE PUT Glaser/Hunter Productions back in play, and Allan once again was taking meetings and making deals left and right. His motto was "A project isn't dead until the producer gives up." He proved it hooking up with Four Seasons Entertainment to produce Evelyn's *Georgia Peach* screenplay, which we had retitled *Blues in the Night* to avoid confusion with a film being made about ballplayer Ty Cobb, who was nicknamed the Georgia Peach.

After finishing *Dark Horse,* I couldn't wait to get back to Santa Fe. Whiling away the days with two- and four-legged friends would be a welcome relief

David Hemmings and Allan on the set of Dark Horse.

from the aggravation of that particular production. I was also eager to start work on a screenplay called *Provenance,* based on a best-selling thriller I'd optioned. Santa Fe, I figured, was where I'd be spending the rest of my life.

Until Allan called one summer day in 1994.

"Tab, I've got three movie deals set up out here, and I'll be damned if I'm going to bust my ass making these projects happen while you ride horses and eat chiles rellenos. Either you come back to California and work with me," he declared, "or we're going to dissolve our partnership right now."

I was stunned. No one had ever given me an ultimatum or dared suggest how I should live.

"Well?" he persisted. "Will you move back to Los Angeles?"

Allan had become ingrained in my life, something I'd never let happen with anyone before. Even though he thrived on the frantic pace of moviemaking, underneath that show-business veneer, Allan was a rock-solid character. My mother had pegged him right off as "an old soul." He'd become the stabilizing influence in my life.

Having already suffered a heart attack and a stroke, I couldn't kid myself anymore. Being a loner was a far more promising prospect at twenty-nine than it was at fifty-nine.

"No, I won't move back to Los Angeles," I told Allan flatly. "But I might consider Santa Barbara."

Happy to Be Forgotten

JOAN COHN, NOW ENSCONCED in another classic George Washington Smith estate, invited me and Allan to live with her while we looked for a home in Santa Barbara. Both Joan and I had brushed up against mortality, so we now had the perspective needed to put aside any petty squabbles we once had.

Now in her eighties, Joan still lived a regal life, although most of it was spent in a wheelchair with a full-time staff of private nurses tending to her every whim. She couldn't keep them sorted out, so she christened them all Maria. Joan had finally quit smoking—too late. An oxygen tank was always at hand. She could still enjoy the occasional glass of wine, which never failed to put a twinkle in her eye and loosen her tongue. Fortunately, it also quickened her wit.

A lot of people treated Joan, especially at this stage in her life, as a Hollywood relic, the real-life reincarnation of Norma Desmond. To me, she was a friend. We'd always enjoyed a special kinship, and I was happy to be reunited with her. Not many of the old guard were left, but the ones who remained were loyal: Luis Estevez, Sydney Guilaroff, Jean Louis and his wife, Maggie, and Sam Spiegel's widow, Betty. Marge Barzey, who'd been the bedrock of the Cohn household for years, had returned to England during the eighties, but she'd recently resettled in Vista, California. When she was summoned, usually if Joan was particularly fragile, Marge was at her side in a heartbeat.

Joan took an instant shine to Allan, which was no surprise, given his enthusiasm for classic Hollywood, of which Joan still saw herself as gatekeeper and standard-bearer. She still displayed her late husband's Best Picture Oscar for *From Here to Eternity* in the foyer, where no guest could miss it. Whenever she and I drifted into discussions about things other than Hollywood, Allan would excuse himself—to pore over Harry Cohn's personal files down in the basement. Joan had kept them intact all those years, as if she was waiting for someone who could appreciate them.

We lived with her for only a month before Allan and I found our own home in Montecito, a gorgeous little gem just around the corner. As we settled in, I got the feeling that I wouldn't be uprooting myself again. Santa Barbara had pretty much everything I needed within a five-minute drive. As for being horse country—it was no Middleburg, Virginia, but it would have to do. And Allan was close enough to Hollywood to still make a meeting on an hour's notice.

Joan invited me over virtually every day. She was never an early riser, so it was usually midafternoon before she was ready to receive guests at poolside, where luncheon would be served. If Allan or I came over in the evening, Joan would invariably hold court in her bedroom, eager to hear the latest news and gossip. Often you'd have to wait in the library while one of the nurses prepared the lady of the house for her audience.

"It's good to keep a man waiting," Joan would always say.

Allan and I often joined her for dinner, served in the bedroom on an antique card table. Joan parked her wheelchair at the table, the telephone always by her side, keeping her connected to what was left of her coterie. Several whippets related to mine, and a greyhound she got from Animal Rescue, would curl up on the sofa by the fireplace.

Time did nothing to change our relationship. We picked up right where we had left off, and got on brilliantly—as long as no one mentioned the film project we had brewing with Evelyn Keyes. Joan and Evelyn hated each other. The animosity stemmed from Evelyn's autobiography *Scarlett O'Hara's Younger Sister,* in which she claimed that Harry Cohn had a decade-long infatuation with her.

"That's complete bullshit," Joan declared. "Harry had better things to do than obsess over a second-rate actress."

By this time, Allan and Evelyn had become thicker than thieves, and whenever he'd mention Joan in conversation, Evelyn would hiss, "What line of bullshit is Queen Cohn telling you now?"

Around dinnertime, Joan's fifty-year-old son, John, would amble into her bedroom and give his mother a perfunctory peck on the cheek. He'd flop down, eat till his belly was full, then fall asleep at the foot of his mother's bed, having barely spoken a word to her. Eventually, the noise from the television would rouse him, and he'd shuffle off to his room downstairs. What made this scene especially odd was that John lived in his own multi-million-dollar house a mile away, which his mother had bought for him. Yet he still came "home" every night to eat dinner with his mother and then fall asleep.

DRIVING THROUGH BEVERLY HILLS one day, Allan and I spotted a sign for a garage sale and decided to stop. Imagine my surprise when the "proprietor" turned out to be Tony Perkins's old pal Gwen Davis. Since we'd last seen each other, in the fifties, Gwen had stopped writing songs and had reinvented herself as a successful romance novelist.

We reminisced about Tony. I hadn't spoken of him since Dick Clayton told me he'd run into Tony at Project Angel Food, an organization that delivered food to AIDS patients in Los Angeles. Like Dick, Tony worked there as a volunteer, delivering food.

Tony had learned he was HIV-positive while standing in a checkout line at his local supermarket; he read it in a *National Enquirer* headline. A nurse who'd taken Tony's blood when he was undergoing treatments for facial palsy had leaked the test results to the press. It was never revealed how he had contracted the disease.

"There are many who believe this disease is God's vengeance," Tony said in a prepared statement, read upon his death in 1992. "But I believe that it was sent to teach people how to love and understand and have compassion for each other. I have learned more about love, selflessness and human understanding from people I have met in this great adventure in the world of AIDS, than I ever did in the cutthroat, competitive world in which I spent my life."

I believe Tony found an inner peace and acceptance with himself before he died.

That day at Gwen's garage sale, as I absentmindedly sifted through some things on a fifty-cent table, I came across a snapshot hidden amongst the clutter. I had taken it, more than thirty years earlier, in my Shoreham Drive apartment.

There was Tony, my companion in the Hollywood fishbowl, with his coy, mischievous smile frozen in time. His career, his future, his stardom, all his turmoil and happiness, were there waiting to be played out.

"I WOULD VERY MUCH like to spend my last days in Santa Barbara," my mother once told me. "It is a little bit of heaven." I decided to grant her wish. Joan loved the idea. She and my mother had always liked each other and

had corresponded over the years. Joan sent her German-speaking nurse to accompany my mother on the trip out from New Mexico.

I arranged for her to live at the lovely Cliff View Terrace, one of the nicest
retirement homes in Santa Barbara.

Over lunch at Fresco, one of her favorite restaurants, Mother suddenly
asked, apropos of nothing, "Was I really that difficult when you were growing
up?"

I almost gagged. After a few thoughtful moments, I said, "Let's put it this
way—if you'd been on the drugs forty years ago that you're on today, we'd have
had a great relationship."

Her laughter was like music to my ears.

I visited my mom every day for the five years she lived in Santa Barbara,
first at Cliff View Terrace, then at the Beverly La Cumbre elder-care facility.
I'd bring her little gifts, do her laundry, dote on her—all a drop in the bucket
compared to the effort she'd expended on me and Walt.

Then one day, for no reason, she said to me, "I love you." That was perhaps
the sweetest day of my life. It was a long time coming, and it may have been
partially drug-induced, but it felt *good*. She even started enjoying hugs, when
once she couldn't stand to be touched. She'd place her arms around me and
give a little squeeze, and I'd smile and say, "Mom, that's just not good enough."

She'd smile and squeeze harder.

"Still not good enough," I'd tease. "You can do better than that."

She'd giggle and beam like a little girl.

"C'mon, Mom—gimme a kiss."

As she approached ninety years of age, my mother was finally coming out
of her shell.

"Tab, it's not right for a woman to be without a man," Joan said to
me over dinner one night. "We need to get married."

Despite all my polite demurrals, Joan proposed two more times over the
subsequent months. The grande dame still wouldn't take no for an answer and
wanted to throw Allan in as part of the package deal.

Joan took to her bed late one afternoon in September 1996, and by nightfall she was ready for a graceful exit. I knelt beside her, held her hand, and told
her how much I loved her. I whispered to her the prayer that an "angel" on a
transcontinental flight years earlier had told me:

With my mom in Santa Barbara, 2000.

> I am a place where God shines through;
> God and I are one, not two.
> If I relax and just be free,
> He will reveal himself through me.

It brought the last smile I saw on her face.

There were two funeral services for Joan. A private family gathering in Montecito, at Our Lady of Mount Carmel, and the more lavish "Hollywood" ceremony, at St. Ambrose in West Hollywood. One for the woman who was Betty Miller; one for Joan Cohn Harvey.

Allan and I served as pallbearers. Neal Noorlag was there to pay his respects—a touching gesture from a compassionate, considerate man. It was sad that our reunion was under such circumstances.

Joan was buried next to Harry Cohn at the Hollywood Memorial Cemetery, where her new neighbors were Douglas Fairbanks, Cecil B. DeMille, Tyrone Power, and Rudolph Valentino.

SINCE SETTLING DOWN in Santa Barbara, Allan and I have kept busy. Not frantic, just busy. Four Seasons Entertainment never got *Blues in the Night* on track, and Allan ended up selling it twice more, to Avenue Entertainment and Republic Pictures. He developed a "neo-noir" called *The Big Hurt*, got Drew Barrymore attached, and hunted down financing . . . Oh, you know the story.

We scouted locations in Ireland for *The Road Rise Up*, a historical drama we still have in the works, about the life of Irish folk hero Turlough O'Carolan.

Troy Donahue tracked me down, asking if I'd work with him on a book about Henry Willson. Over the years, Troy and I had morphed into a single person in the minds of many people, and I'd heard he could be pretty snide about it, snapping, "I'm the straight one," to people who made the mistake.

That didn't really bother me, and it's not why I declined to participate. I'd discovered a new life, a calmer, more peaceful life, and I always referred to my movie-star status—much to Allan's chagrin—as "my past life." He felt there was still some mileage in the old wagon yet, some leverage to be gained with the name Tab Hunter, but I was ready to let the old warhorse take a rest.

After a recent trip back to Virginia, Allan dragged me to Washington, D.C., for a visit to the Census Bureau, which keeps records on every citizen. While he researched his family's lineage, I couldn't resist looking up Charles Kelm, the biological father who'd vanished from my life almost seventy years earlier.

I found him, at least on paper. I learned more in five minutes than I had in a lifetime from my mother. My father was much older than my mother, he had worked in a Brooklyn slaughterhouse most of his life, and he'd been mar-

A once-in-a-lifetime sighting—Troy Donahue and me, together in Hollywood, 1997.

ried to someone before my mother, a woman with whom he'd had two daughters; somewhere I had a pair of half sisters, Rebecca and Sarah. Perhaps one of them was the woman who'd answered the door that day I went looking for my father in a New York blizzard. I also learned that Charles Kelm was Jewish, making me half-Jewish, as well—a development that certainly amused Allan.

I immediately called my mother to relate all of this.

"Oh, Arthur," she said, sighing. "Why do you want to know such things? What difference does it all make now?"

She was right. It didn't mean anything, and since that day I've never had any interest in tracking down my missing "siblings." Like my mother, I've spent most of my life being insatiably curious about the world in which I live—but far less curious about the facts of my own background and the inner workings of my own psyche.

Evelyn Keyes used to argue with me all the time about psychoanalysis. She'd been through it back in the fifties and found it essential to understanding herself. By contrast, I've never spent one minute of my life in any kind of analysis.

When I was young, things happened so fast, for so long, that I rarely took the time to examine my life, which, I must admit, sometimes led to my taking good fortune—and good people—for granted. That doesn't happen anymore.

Every Sunday morning I head down the hill to attend eight o'clock mass at my local church. Why would I remain dedicated to a religion that considers "my kind" sinners? Simple: I believe in God, and I owe Him all my gratitude and humility for blessing me, and everyone, with two precious gifts—life and free will.

Let the person without sin cast the first stone.

For a good stretch of time, my life was like a kaleidoscope in which I moved relentlessly through a swirling mix of people, places, and events. Later on, I moved just as fast, but down a pretty desolate, lonesome road.

Finally, the running stopped. I found myself, and I found a permanent home.

My new writing partner is Betty Marvin, Lee's first wife. She's a terrific writer and artist and always serves up a fabulous home-cooked dinner after a day of work. Allan and I were returning the favor one March night in 2001 when the phone rang.

It was Dr. Diaz. I knew instantly. I don't know how, but I knew.

"Mr. Hunter, we're sorry to tell you this, but your mother has passed away."

I had very little reaction. A certain emptiness, but no welling of emotion, no wave of grief. I reacted to the tragic news exactly as my mother had always reacted—stoically.

She and I had already discussed the particulars of where she wanted to be buried, and I focused on arranging all the details. She'd picked out a plot overlooking the ocean and the mountains, next to a beautiful oak tree. There was no elaborate funeral. Allan and I were the only ones present, besides Father O'Mahony, who quietly recited prayers.

A car suddenly pulled up to the side of the road, and out stepped two of my brother's now-grown kids, Susie and Mike. They'd arrived unannounced to pay their respects to Grandma Gertie. That's when my formidable reserve finally broke; I lost it. It wasn't death that made the tears flow, it was the realization that perhaps I actually did have the one thing that had always eluded me: a family.

TODAY, I AM HAPPY to be "forgotten." I can go anywhere and for the first time in my adult life be unrecognized. On occasion, someone might still rush up and excitedly exclaim, "I loved you in *A Summer Place!*"

These days, I might even agree to be Troy Donahue for that moment, just for the hell of it.

Proving his dictum, "A project isn't dead until the producer gives up," Allan recently arranged a "power" dinner in a restaurant on the Sunset Strip, which is a frenzied, congested zoo compared to the glory days at Ciro's, La Rue, and Mocambo.

We were joined by an interesting trio of guests. First, there was Neil Koenigsberg, a powerful Hollywood player—as well as one of the town's genuinely trustworthy people. He was one of the founders of PMK, the industry's premier public-relations firm. In addition to being the personal manager of major talents like Jeff Bridges and Ed Harris, Neil's got a knack for packaging high-quality movies. He'd recently read Evelyn's *Blues in the Night* screenplay, loved it, and wanted to help us get it made.

To that end, he orchestrated this dinner meeting with a potential director. Peter Bogdanovich's reverence for old Hollywood made him the ideal choice for our story. Peter, of course—whose knowledge of movie history surpasses even Allan's—was eager to meet the screenplay's author.

Evelyn Keyes rounded out our dinner party. More than twenty years had flowed past since she and I had first met. Her razor-sharp brain was by this time being inexorably dulled by the early stages of Alzheimer's.

"John Huston was certainly an amazing man," Peter said to her. "What was it like being married to him?"

"John who?" Evelyn responded, bewildered. "Who's he? Oh, that's right, I *was* married to him."

Although the odds have greatly improved that *Blues in the Night* might finally be produced, Evelyn won't be able to savor the satisfaction of seeing her story on the silver screen. She lived it, she wrote it, but she doesn't even recognize her own script when it's in her hands.

Allan and I still see Evelyn regularly. She lives just down the road, at a retirement home that looks, appropriately enough, like a set from *Gone with the Wind*. Allan, now her conservator, moved her when she became too forgetful. All things considered, she has it pretty good. She gets treated like royalty, has gained thirty pounds from all the home cooking, and remembers mostly the good things — but it's heartbreaking to see her losing pieces from the incredible canvas of her life.

Perhaps that's one of the things that inspired me to put *my* life down on paper.

Well, that and Allan walking into my room a while back and saying, "Tab, somebody is planning an unauthorized biography of you. It'll end up being nothing but *National Enquirer* stories. You have to do your own book — are you going to let somebody else, some stranger, write your epitaph?"

"Who wants to read a book about Tab Hunter?" I said.

"A lot of people," he answered.

Better to get it from the horse's mouth, I decided, and not from some horse's ass.

I NO LONGER CRAM my days full of furious activity in order to get the most out of my life. The endless search for some pot of gold at the end of the rainbow — who needs it? Great friends are more important.

Mine were always there to lend a helping hand when the road got dark or treacherous. Dick Clayton, now in his nineties, is still my closest friend in the world. I often rely on the sage counsel of Larry Lamb, and I talk with Betty Meade, back in Virginia, at least three times a week. I'm working on another script with Betty Marvin. "You're lucky if you have five good friends in this life," my mother always said. I'm lucky to have many more than that. You can't wish for anything of greater value.

As I head into the home stretch, it has been nothing short of a revelation to know and love Allan Glaser. He is the best.

There may still be another movie in our future. It doesn't really matter. Either way, I'll go on playing with the dogs, riding the horses, and enjoying, with absolutely no regrets, every minute I have left.

And if you happen to spot me, in the middle of some seemingly insignificant chore, lifting my face to the sky and mumbling something—don't worry. I'm only saying, "Thank You."

That's what life is all about.

ACKNOWLEDGMENTS

IN MY TWO LIVES, reel and real, I've covered a lot of ground. Many of the people dear to me have been mentioned already. I'll do my best to acknowledge others who have gone out of their way to extend a hand and offer encouragement and love, but if someone has been overlooked, please attribute it to my getting on in years.

Many thanks to my skating colleagues, Armando "Pancho" Rodriguez, Hans Johnson, Frank Carroll, Tenley Albright, Joyce Lockwood, Catherine Machado, and everyone at the Polar Palace and in the *Ice Capades* at that time of my life.

In my beautiful world of horses I'll never forget Rudy Smithers and his one-eyed paint jumper, Rex; Victor Hugo Vidal; George Morris, Mousie and Jimmy Williams; Diane Grod; Dody Vehr; Eve Fout; Jimmy Hatcher; Mairead Carr; Beverly Petal; Delia Cunningham; Barbara, Paul and Allison Wicks—and that list of horse lovers goes on and on.

My gratitude also extends to Signe Hasso, Bullah Bondi, Gretchen Wyler, Rowena Rollins, Cisse Cameron, Paul Ferrante, Tommy and Gracie Raynor, Reba "Woozie" Turner, Kerwin Matthews and Tommy Nichols, Dr. Harvey Ross, Arthur Feldman, Ann England, Chery Fenley, Anna Huserik, Mel Fillini, Gay Speirbhain, Allene and Jerry Lapides, Bill Sibley, Edward Z. Epstein, Maxine Filippin, Norma Frederick, Paula DiSante, and Ellie Farrell, for managing Tabhunter.com.

"A picture is worth a thousand words," and for the many we have used, a special thanks to Leith Adams, Marlene Eastman and Judith Singer at Warners; Noelle Carter and Randi Hockett and everyone at the USC Warner Bros. Archives; Margarita Harder at Columbia TriStar; Larry McCallister at Paramount; New Line Cinema; Dick DeNeut and Henry McGee at Globe Photos.

And during the process: Betty Marvin, Mary Jo England, Dan Blackwelder, and my agents, Jed Mattes and Fred Morris.

How lucky to have an editor like Chuck Adams, who wanted this book and believed in it from the start.

Alison Pinsler deserves a huge thanks for suggesting to me Eddie Muller, who is unequivocally the *best* writer/collaborator anyone could ever hope for. I cannot praise him enough.

And finally, my biggest thank you to the one who made it all happen . . . Allan Glaser. My partner for life.

I am indebted to you all.

INDEX